DECONSTRUCTION

Omnibus Volume

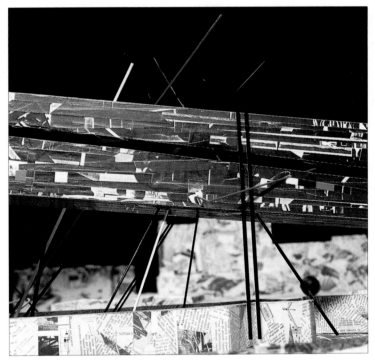

DANIEL LIBESKIND, BERLIN CITY EDGE, 1987, MODEL ALPHA DETAIL

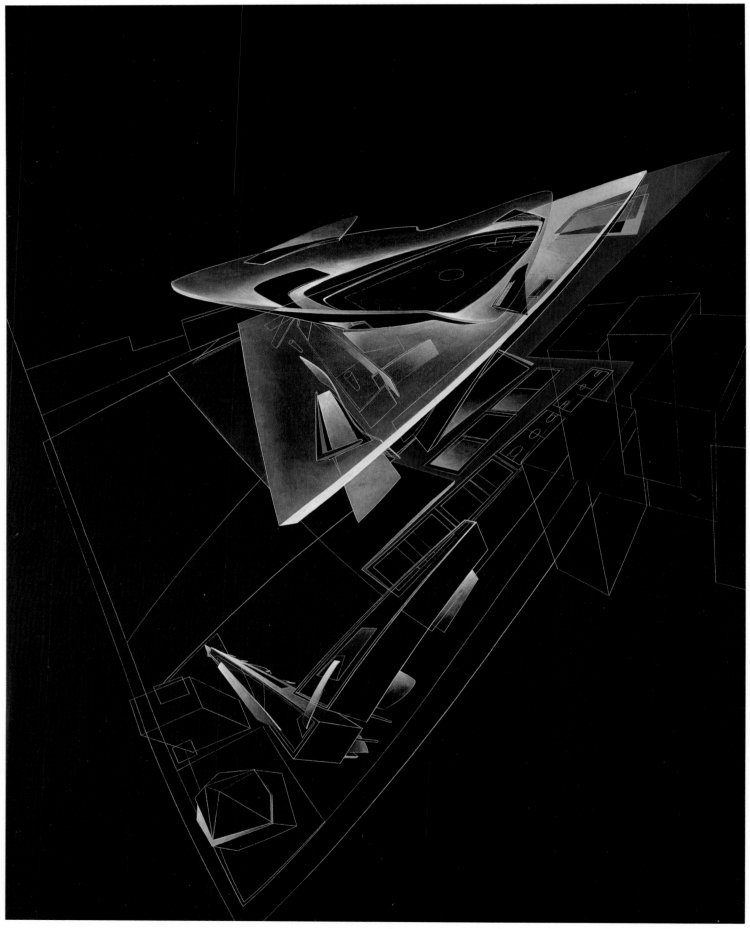

ZAHA HADID, AL WAHDA SPORTS CENTRE, 1988, AERIAL VIEW

DECONSTRUCTION

Omnibus Volume

Edited by

Andreas Papadakis

Catherine Cooke & Andrew Benjamin

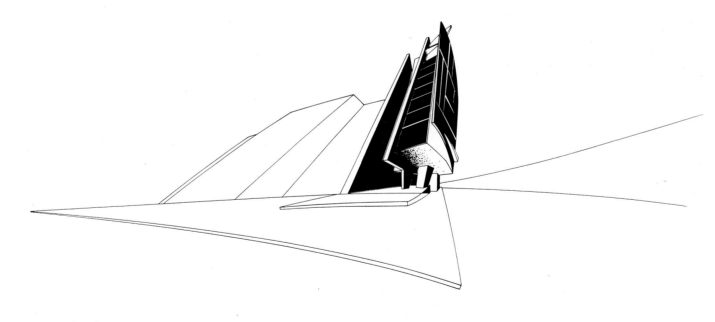

ZAHA HADID, OFFICE BUILDING, BERLIN, 1986

ACADEMY EDITIONS LONDON

EDITORIAL NOTE

In assembling this publication we have received assistance, often enthusiastic, from a wide variety of sources. We are grateful to the numerous authors, artists and architects who have collaborated on this project. We are especially indebted to Jacques Derrida for his inspiration and positive collaboration. In particular we acknowledge the help of Peter Eisenman, Zaha Hadid, Daniel Libeskind and Bernard Tschumi. We also wish to thank the Trustees and Director of the Tate Gallery for encouraging the exploration of the theme of Deconstruction within the Academy Forum. An extensive list of credits and information on individual and institutional sources will be found in the acknowledgements at the end of the book.

Published in Great Britain in 1989 by
ACADEMY EDITIONS
an imprint of the Academy Group Ltd, 7 Holland Street, London W8 4NA

ISBN 0-85670-996-4 (hb)
ISBN 0-85670-967-0 (pb)

Printed and bound in Singapore

CONTENTS

OMA, *EGG OF COLUMBUS CENTER*, 1973, DETAIL, PAINTING BY ZOE ZENGHELIS

Foreword

BERNARD TSCHUMI, NEW NATIONAL THEATRE OF JAPAN, TOKYO, PERSPECTIVE

Few ideas in architecture have created such a stir as Deconstruction in the relatively short time since it gained currency and public prominence. Even Jacques Derrida, the main definer of Deconstruction, was surprised at the alacrity and enthusiasm with which Deconstructive thinking, previously the private reserve of philosophy and literary criticism, has been applied in these fields. Thanks to the efforts of theoretically-minded architects such as Bernard Tschumi and Peter Eisenman, a direct connection with architectural theory has been made.

Deconstruction addresses notions in thinking to show how these rest on deeply-entrenched binary oppositions and it operates by suspending the correspondence between the two. According to Peter Eisenman, architecture 'must move away from the rigidity and value structure of the dialectic oppositions. For example the traditional opposition between structure and decoration, abstraction and figuration, figure and ground. Architecture could begin an exploration of the "between" within these categories.'

In so doing, Deconstruction creates a disturbance at the signifier's level, employing the strategy of *différance* (the term being a word-play upon the verbs 'to differ' and 'to defer') whereby meaning differs and is deferred from an expected definition. It might appear that Deconstruction defers and even evades a definition of itself, never wishing to show what it is. It will not set down strict parameters but constantly questions and expands through a *critique*, operating by dislocating meaning. Architects have thus appropriated the methods of Deconstruction in order to call into question the notions of housing. Bernard Tschumi thinks that Deconstruction is 'not only the analysis of concepts in their most rigorous and internalised manner, but also their analysis from without, to question what these concepts and their history hide, as repression or dissimulation.'

At the beginning of the century a conscious theoretical development within architecture took place in Russia, and Deconstructivist theories owe a debt to the Constructivists of that time. Indeed, much of the present work stems from earlier, often intuitive, moves in this direction. But 1988 was a milestone year in its acceptance in architecture, beginning with the Academy Forum at London's Tate Gallery with the publication of an issue of *Architectural Design* devoted to it, to be followed by the *Deconstructivist Architecture* exhibition at New York's Museum of Modern Art, which gave rise to much controversy and debate over the selection of work and even the term 'Deconstructivist'.

The application of Deconstruction in the visual arts leads to a further reassessment of value structures. In Valerio Adami's work, for example, the *critique* lies in a highly conscious juxtaposition of visual and textual elements. Deconstructionist art stimulates the viewer to take part in the analysis of the 'between' and explores – as does the work of Anselm Kiefer – the possibilities of the frame. Jacques Derrida, in his book *The Truth in Painting*, has commented on the importance of this concept: 'One space needs to be broached in order to give place to the truth in painting. Neither inside nor outside, it spaces itself without letting itself be framed but it does not stand outside the frame. It works the frame, makes it work, gives it work to do . . .'

Deconstruction, both in architecture and the visual arts, may still be in its early stages but it does exist, and the imagery it uses is fresh and appeals to a new generation. However, as Derrida pointed out regarding architecture in his discussion with Christopher Norris: 'you can't (or you shouldn't) simply dismiss those values of dwelling, functionality, beauty and so on. You have to construct, so to speak, a new space and a new form, to shape a new way of building in which these motifs or values are reinscribed, having meanwhile lost their external hegemony.'

Deconstruction does not strictly demarcate a framework. Its critique is continual and it would be useful to remember that Deconstruction is above all an activity, an open-ended practice, rather than a method convinced of its own correct reasoning.   *AP*

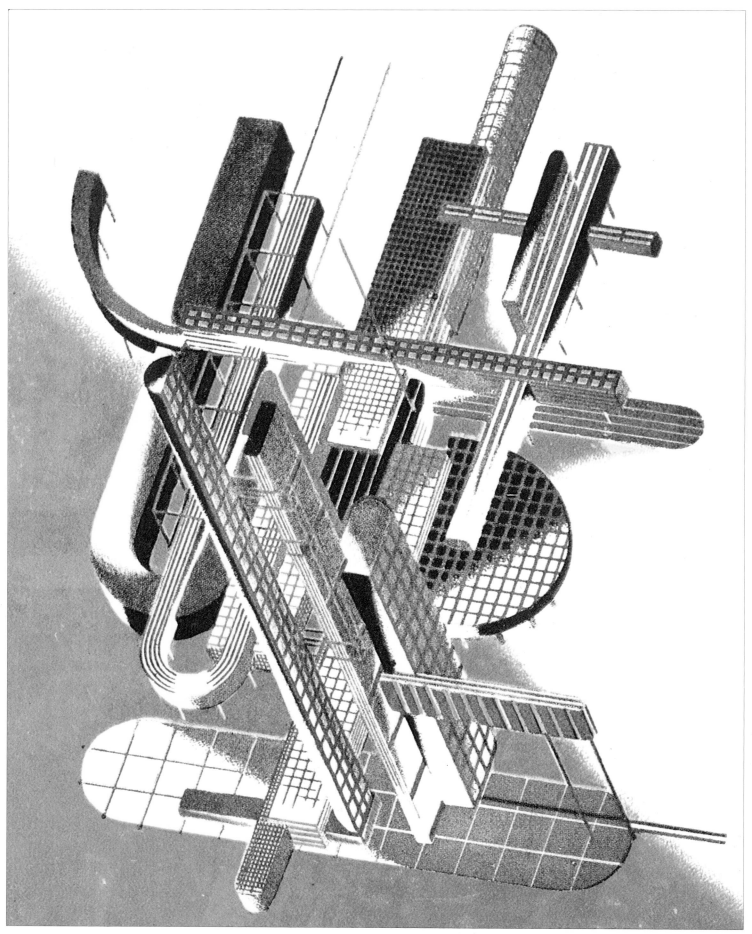

IAKOV CHERNIKHOV, AXONOMETRIC OF AN INTEGRATED INDUSTRIAL COMPLEX, FANTASY NO 91 FROM *ARCHITECTURAL FANTASIES*, 1933

PART I

CONSTRUCTIVIST ORIGINS
Catherine Cooke

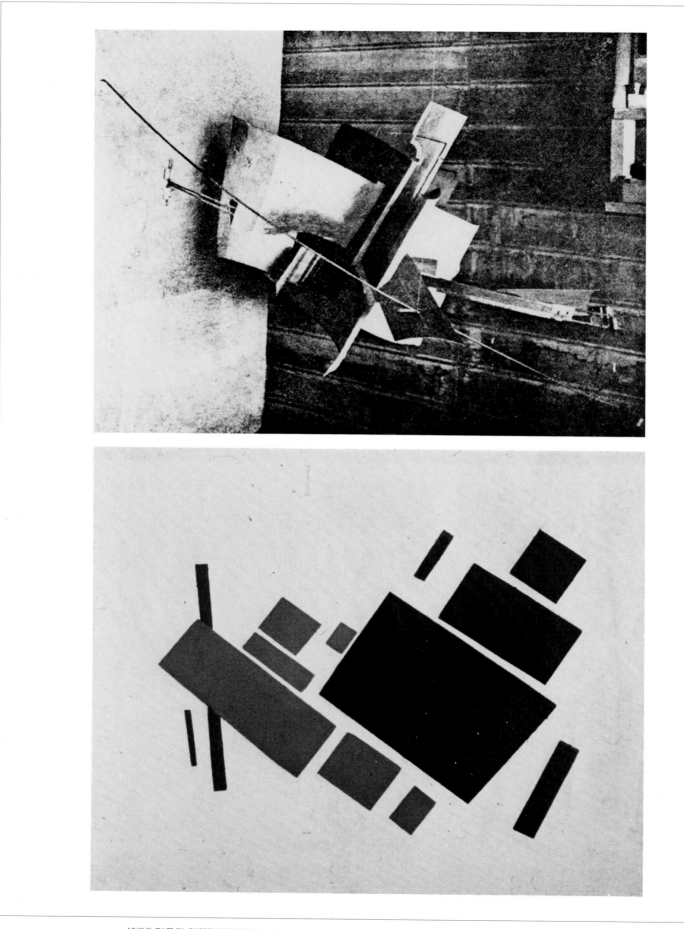

ABOVE: TATLIN, SUSPENDED CORNER RELIEF: SELECTION OF MATERIALS, 1915; *BELOW*: MALEVICH, AEROPLANE FLYING, 1915

CATHERINE COOKE
Russian Precursors

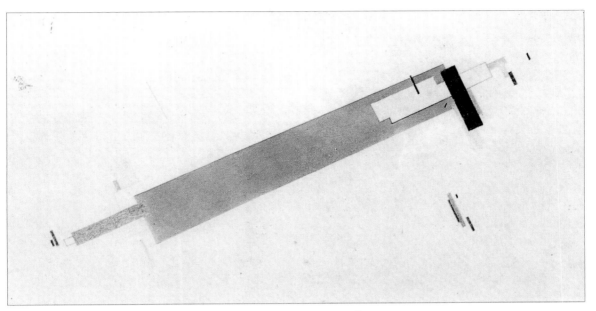

NIKOLAI SUETIN, *SUPREMATISM*, 1931

The development of physics this century has revolutionised communications, and information systems and technology. Former Cartesian divisions have had to be rejected to make way for a new thinking. Here the experiments and achievements of the Russian avant-garde are surveyed, showing their endeavours to come to terms with not only the physical, but the metaphysical and philosophical implications of a world that is subject to continuous change.

So we arrive at the conception that a great deal of biological and human behaviour is beyond the principles of utility, homeostasis and stimulous-response, and that it is precisely this which is characteristic of human and cultural activities. Such a new look opens new perspectives not only in theory but in practical applications.'
Ludwig von Bertalanffy, *General System Theory*, 1968.[1]

My function here, as I see it, is to lay a ghost. The ghost is that of the Russian avant-garde. Peter Eisenman has shown us a scheme by Iakov Chernikhov. From Zaha Hadid we have seen images from two people of quite different philosophies – Malevich, a Suprematist, and Leonidov, a rather dissenting and non-typical Constructivist – and she has given us some sense of the role these people's work has played in inspiring and informing her own.

There are two things that I want to do. One is to deal with the question of why some of these images might be being used today at all, not only by Hadid but by other people in the present movement, and whether such a use of this work is legitimate. The other is a rather more fundamental question relating to the nature of Constructivism itself, which in this context has too often been used as a general term to include much that properly belongs to the very different movement of Suprematism.

I shall deal with this second issue first, as it relates to something Peter Eisenman said earlier this morning about deficiencies of the English language.

Eisenman observed that we have a problem in looking at Deconstruction because we do not know when we are talking about construction as building, and when we are talking about construction in a linguistic sense. As a result Deconstruction, which is essentially about the way that information is understood or exchanged in the late 20th-century society, tends to be identified with buildings that look massively 'constructed' or 'deconstructed' in a physical respect.

Here we touch the very essence of Constructivism and, consciously or unconsciously, the reason for the present attention to this Russian work. As I have stressed in my own writings about the Constructivists, one of the most interesting aspects of their thought is the clarity with which they posited a number of issues, theoretical as well as formal, which still concern architecture today.[2] In respect of the particular confusion to which Peter has referred, the Russian language gave them an immediate advantage over us. They themselves took advantage of the fact they had two words for 'construction', and they made absolutely clear what the difference was between them. In fact, Russian has a lot of other words that can also only be translated into English as 'construction', some being further nouns, some being verbs, but these introduce nuances that are not relevant here.

The Russians have one word for construction in the building sense which is *stroitel 'stvo*, from *stroit'*, to build: this is what you do in muddy boots on a building site. It demands that you understand about materials; that you are, in their period in particular, concerned with the material reality of the physical world. Then there is quite another word, the one from which the term Constructivism comes, which is *konstruktsia*. This is construction in the sense of structural organisation, and finds its most literal use in the grammatical sense. *Konstruktsia* has to do with the structure of ideas, with the construction of arguments through assembling sequences of ideas. It is, as the Constructivists said, an intellectual category. It is through attention to this distinction,

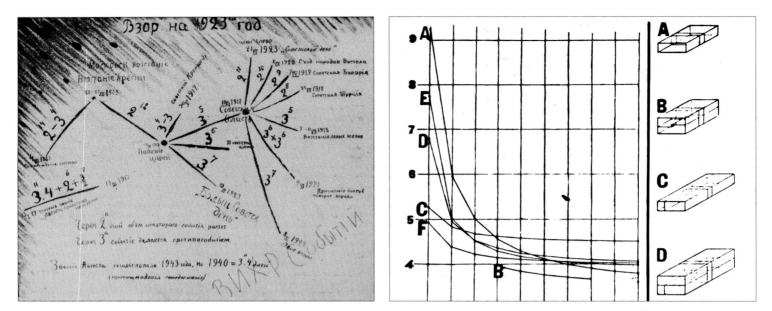

L TO R: KHLEBNIKOV, *VESTNIK* (HERALD), NO. 2, 1922: 'A LOOK AT 1923'; EVALUATING PROPERTIES OF FOUR VOLUMETRIC OPTIONS IN HOUSING DESIGN, GINZBURG AND OTHERS, 1928

I think, that we can most usefully address and illuminate the relationship between historical Constructivism, and Deconstruction.

Konstruktsiia denotes a mode of thinking, a certain ordering of the processes of thought. And in considering this aspect of it, we are brought up against the very important fact which we tend to forget when these images are so powerful, and in a sense timeless: the fact that this Russian material we are looking at derives from sixty, and in some cases seventy, years ago. That is to say, it belongs in a world – and we think here of the issues Bernard Tschumi was talking about earlier – which was not at all today's information-based world, but one where mechanical engineering was the basic logical paradigm of thinking. As Reyner Banham taught us to think of it, this was the 'First Machine Age'. We are now in the Second, the age of information technology, where space, as Tschumi said, is measured by time, and these two concepts have an entirely different kind of relationship. What is interesting, as I shall briefly show, is that at the end of the twenties the Constructivists already understood that this shift was coming, and talked about its implications in precisely the same language.

In this situation, therefore, the kind of linear, deterministic logic which the Constructivists saw as the very essence of their approach to building design, is certainly not any longer an appropriate paradigm for thinking about how we design buildings – or think of their functional operation in society. We no longer see a building as necessarily having a one-to-one relationship, and a deterministic relationship, to a particular function. Our greater understanding of how buildings are used over time and perceived, quite apart from any larger shifts in philosophical position deriving from outside architecture itself, have been enough to indicate that a building has a much more probabilistic relationship both to what causes it to happen, and to the way it will be used and as a result, to the way it is understood in space. So the Constructivist notion of what *konstruktsiia* meant helps us to understand why Deconstruction is a natural phenomenon, I would almost say, of an information-based society which uses systems analysis to redefine the boundaries of almost every territory it examines, and where science already has quite different concepts of how matter, if it can still be called that, is actually structured.

It is part of the poverty of our cultural experience today that these shifts at the frontiers of knowledge are not mediated conceptually to the intelligentsia at large in any general or systematic way, across the artificial boundaries of 'disciplines' that we inherited from the pre-relativity age when everything could be broken down into mechanis-

L TO R: EL LISSITZKY, *PROUN 1E 'THE CITY'*, 1921, LITHOGRAPH; TSCHUMI, PARC DE LA VILLETTE, LANDSCAPE SUPERIMPOSITION, 1984

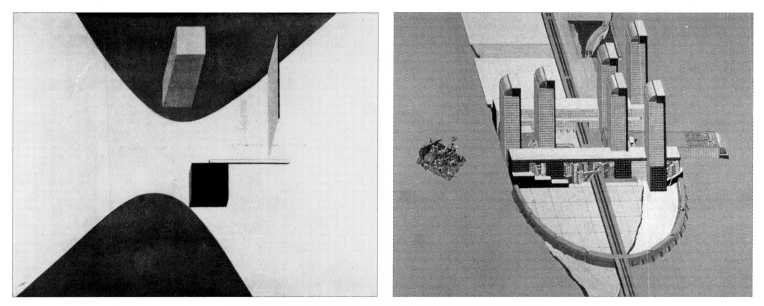

L TO R: EL LISSITZKY, *PROUN 23, NO. 6*, 1919; OMA, WELFARE PALACE HOTEL, 1976-7

tically connected or unconnected 'entities'. Through the impact of microelectronics, in particular, and the information and communications revolutions it has brought, as well as deeper questionings of the nature of cognition and intelligence, the world at large is directly exposed to the consequences of these structural shifts. Without understanding, however, it is at their mercy. As could be predicted, it resists the 'adventure into the unknown' of which it is already an actual, but involuntary and non-cogniscent participant.

Perhaps no-one has recently better described the nature of the shift here than the theoretical physicist Fritjof Capra, in particular in his book *The Turning Point*, in 1982. His lucid account of the drastic modifications to classical concepts of space and time introduced by Einstein's General Theory, and of the complete disintegration of classical atomic physics produced by the works of Niels Bohr, Max Planck and their generation, makes very clear the essential parallels between this metaphysic and that of Derridean Deconstruction. Capra quotes thus Werner Heisenberg:

I remember discussions with Bohr which went on through many hours till very late at night and ended almost in despair; and when at the end of the discussion I went alone for a walk in the neighbouring park I repeated to myself again and again the question: Can nature possibly be so absurd as it seemed to us in these atomic experiments?[3]

Capra's own comment is à propos here:

It took these physicists a long time to accept the fact that the paradoxes they encountered are an essential aspect of atomic physics, and to realise that they arise whenever one tries to describe atomic phenomena in terms of classical concepts.

There is a direct parallel here with the Deconstructive programme, whether in architecture or elsewhere, of locating the inherent dilemmas within the conventional institution of a 'building', and with the view of structure which follows, in which the flaws are the intrinsic indicators of its ordering at another and deeper level of structure, rather than flaws. In both cases there are problems of accepting the conceptual framework.

The new physics [of quantum theory] necessitated profound changes in concepts of space, time, matter, object, and cause and effect; and because these concepts are so fundamental to our way of experiencing the world, their transformation came as a great shock.

In this connection Capra quotes Heisenberg again:

The violent reaction to the recent developments of modern

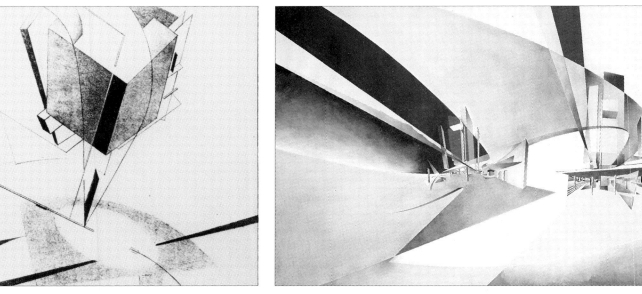

L TO R: EL LISSITZKY, *PROUN 5A*, LITHOGRAPH FROM THE PROUN FOLIO, 1921; HADID, TRAFALGAR SQUARE GRAND BUILDINGS PROJECT, 1985, LOBBIES OF TOWERS

L TO R: STENBERG, CONSTRUCTION IN METAL, 1921; TSCHUMI, PARC DE LA VILLETTE STUDY, 1984

physics can only be understood when one realises that here the foundations of modern physics have started moving; and that this motion has caused the feeling that the ground would be cut from science.

Even Einstein admitted the same:

All my attempts to adapt the theoretical foundations of physics to this [new type of] knowledge failed completely. It was as if the ground had been pulled out from under one, with no firm foundation to be seen anywhere, upon which one could have built.

Capra's own very straightforward description of the essentials of the new view can hardly be bettered in this context.

In contrast to the mechanistic, Cartesian view of the world, the world view emerging from modern physics can be characterised by words like organic, holistic, and ecological. It might also be called a systems view, in the sense of general systems theory. The universe is no longer seen as a machine, made up of a multitude of objects, but has to be pictured as one indivisible, dynamic whole whose parts are essentially inter-related and can be understood only as patterns of a cosmic process . . .

In quantum theory you never end up with 'things'; you always deal with interconnections . . . It shows that we cannot decompose the world into independently existing smallest units. As we penetrate into matter, nature does not show us any isolated building blocks, but rather appears as a complicated web of relations between various parts of a unified whole.[4]

In Heisenberg's description, which he quotes: 'The world thus appears as a complicated tissue of events, in which connections of different kinds alternate or overlap or combine and thereby determine the texture of the whole.' And in the words of the physicist Henry Stapp, 'an elementary particle is not an independently existing unanalysable entity. It is, in essence, a set of relationships that reach outward to other things'.[5]

This matter of connections leads to the significance of the concept of probability, and Capra is also particularly good in his description of the different applications of the concept of probability in classical and quantum physics. Thus in classical physics probability is used as a predictive tool 'whenever the mechanical details involved in an event are unknown' at the level of local mechanisms. In quantum physics, on the other hand, the concept is used to handle uncertainties in mechanisms that are non-local. Here the mechanisms concerned are those 'instantaneous connections to the universe as a whole' which at

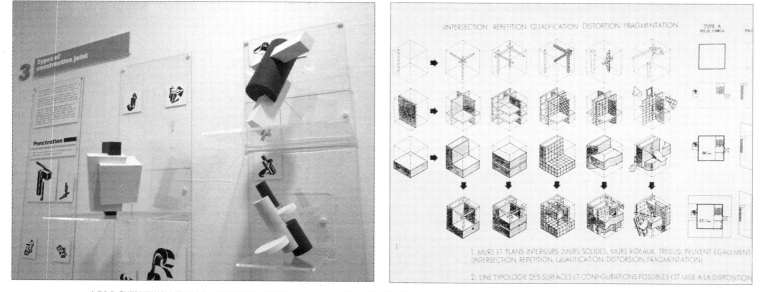

L TO R: CHERNIKHOV, TYPES OF CONSTRUCTIVE JOINT, NO. 1: PENETRATION; TSCHUMI, PARC DE LA VILLETTE, PRINCIPLES OF FORMAL CONSTRUCTION

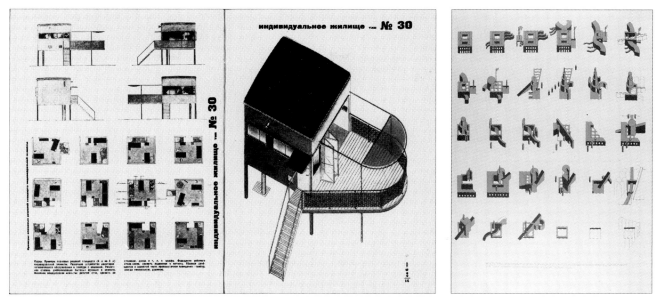

L TO R: CONSTRUCTIVIST ARCHITECTS' DISURBANIST PROPOSAL, 1929-30; TSCHUMI, PARC DE LA VILLETTE, PROCESS OF TRANSFORMATION OF THE FOLIES FROM THE BOURSE

the level of everyday experience have no direct impact on a given case. In decision-theoretic terms these would be called the 'state' variables. But as we move in either direction away from the macroscopic terrestrial world of our everyday sensual perception, 'the influence of non-local conditions becomes stronger; the laws of physics can be formulated only in terms of probabilities, and it becomes more and more difficult to separate any part of the universe from the whole.' Indeed more than that: 'Whereas in classical mechanics the properties and behaviour of the parts determine those of the whole, the situation is reversed in quantum mechanics: it is the whole that determines the behaviour of its parts.'[6] What Deconstruction is trying to do, it seems to me, with all the enormous difficulties of thought that are involved, is to come to grips with the philosophical and metaphysical implications of that shift in the realms of our own cultural activity.

The necessity for a General System Theory arose over the same period, in the words of one of its pioneers, biologist Ludwig von Bertalanffy, 'as a useful tool providing models that can be used in, and transferred to, different fields' in a process such as this. Where there is a danger of merely aggregating numerous 'vague analogies' between the particular behavioural patterns observed in different fields (a tendency to which architecture, having a weak theoretical basis itself, is very prone), systems thinking seeks to provide a rigorous meta-theory for the understanding of what hitherto appeared 'unorganised' complexities.[7] In its ruthless pursuit of the 'real realities' beneath conventional accounts of the connectivities between 'events' in the situations its addresses; in its identification of the boundary areas, the peripheries, as the territory of real and defining revelations; in its breaking open of conventional surfaces to redefine the terms and parameters, to relocate the axes of a situation in relation to the human cultural intentions explicitly or covertly present, Deconstruction is an essentially similar tactic to systems analysis and has similar aspirations. Both equally insist on that same relativity in relation to the presence or otherwise of a given human intelligence which is essential to modern physics. In this conception, in Capra's words,

> The electron does not *have* objective properties independent of my mind. In atomic physics the sharp Cartesian division between mind and matter, between the observer and the observed, can no longer be maintained. We can never speak about nature without, at the same time, speaking about ourselves.'[8]

The Constructivist architects were already of course exposed to the beginning of this cognitive and intellectual revolution. Already in 1930, for example, James Jeans was able to make his celebrated

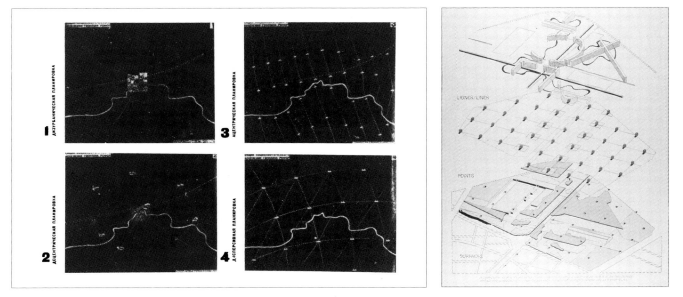

L TO R: CONSTRUCTIVIST ARCHITECTS, 1929-30: EVOLUTION OF SETTLEMENT TYPES; TSCHUMI, PARC DE LA VILLETTE, SUPERIMPOSITION OF THE 3 SYSTEMS (POINTS/LINES/SURFACES), 1982

CONSTRUCTIVIST ARCHITECTS' DISURBANIST PROPOSAL, 1929-30

statement that 'Today there is a wide measure of agreement. . .that the stream of knowledge is heading towards a non-mechanical reality; the universe begins to look more like a great thought than a great machine.'[9] This was the same year in which the Constructivists gave architectural form to the perception already voiced in the previous year by their sociologist colleague Mikhail Okhitovich when he wrote in their journal on 'the problem of the city' in the age of 'electrical transmission at a distance', and explored the implications for urban form of 'the revolution in transportation' brought about by 'universal automobilisation'.

'Distance is now measured by time' wrote Okhitovich, and 'the age of industrial revolutions is not yet ended.' Therefore

it is necessary to reassess the nature of the possible in accordance with the conditions of the epoch. Under present conditions, with utilities overheads proportional to the frontage of the plot etc, buildings have had to be built upwards and backwards, and must be constructed of strong and durable materials on solid foundations. . .

Does it emerge however, that the dense city is the inevitable result of the technical and economic possibilities, that all other solutions are impossible?

Certainly not:

The rapid growth in the means of communication and mechanical transport is every day diminishing the extent to which a man's life is rooted and centred in a fixed dwelling. Simultaneously, the unit of habitation itself is becoming ever more and more shaped by the nature and forms of communal production and transport. Transport may even call for the total collapse of the dwelling as we know it. Although we may not notice it happening, this will take place simultaneously with the collapse of the city, for existing building forms . . . only have any inevitability inside the city whilst it continues to exist in its present form.

That would not be for long, since

The exceptional growth in the strength, quality, quantity and speed of the means of mechanical transportation now permits separation from centres: space is now measured by time. And that time is itself constantly being shortened.

'The city', wrote Okhitovich, 'is not some kind of sum of people living in "one" place. The city is a socially, not territorially, determined human entity. . . It is an economic and cultural complex.' Moreover:

The question to be elucidated now is, must the different func-

Conceptual diagram

TSCHUMI, PARC DE LA VILLETTE, MUSICAL NOTATION, 1987

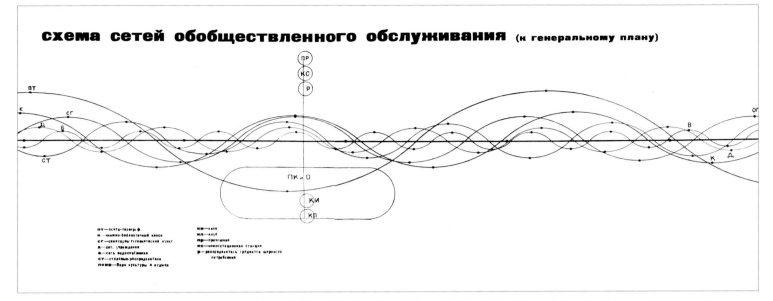

CONSTRUCTIVIST ARCHITECTS' DISURBANIST PROPOSAL, 1929-30: RHYTHMIC DISTRIBUTION OF SERIES ALONG THE CONTINUOUS, NATIONWIDE 'RIBBONS OF SETTLEMENT'

tions of the 'city' exist in one physical body; will they become estranged by separation, as the parts of a biological organism would be? In other words, is the ever increasing crowding of people, buildings etc on one spot inevitable or not? Let us examine by what means are people fastened to one place; from what does this attraction to one another derive, this mighty centripetal force?

What happens when 'In place of territorial contiguity comes the question of transportation and communications possibilities'? These factors 'reverse all the usual arguments about the inevitability of congestion and the crowding together of buildings.' The 'organism' becomes a set of 'linked functions making up a single organisational complex.' 'But' as he continues, 'the city was also a complex. If you like an argument over terminology, let the new complex also be called a city.' Prefiguring Marshal McLuhan's conception of the 'Global Village' he says: 'Let us call it, shall we say, The Red City of the Planet of Communism.' And with similar appositeness to the present context he continues:

If one talks about the essence, then this new complex will be called not a point, not a place nor a city, but a process, and this process will be called Disurbanisation. Disurbanisation is the

process of centrifugal force and repulsion. It is based on just such a centrifugal tendency in technology. . . which reverses all the former assumptions. Proximity is henceforth a function of distance, and community a function of separateness.

'Machine technology', as Okhitovich already foresees it, can readily organise dispersed services for food, laundries, shops, libraries, and can replace 'family concerns' and 'the needs of meeting which tie us together in shared accommodations.' In this future,

The whole world is at our service, and first and foremost, transportation and communications. . . We ask ourselves, how shall we resettle all the urban populations and economic activities? Answer: not according to the principle of crowding, but according to the principle of maximum freedom, ease and speed of communication.[10]

Certainly here was already a perfect understanding of the essence of the Second Machine Age as a spatial system. Okhitovich's Constructivist architectural colleagues used several planning competitions of that year to explore the possible physical nature of such an a-nodal, 'disurbanised' settlement form.[11] The result was a 'ribbon' of parallel 'functional zones' which combined permutationally different pavilions of standard elements, and 'rhythmically' spaced servicing

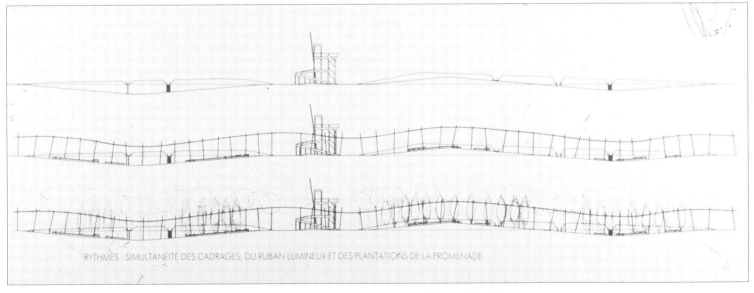

TSCHUMI, PARC DE LA VILLETTE, CINEMATIC SEQUENCES, 1986

events, in a manner immediately redolent of forms we find in Tschumi's work. Even the Party authorities who saw the proposal as subversive of the state's effort to build a new social consciousness recognised that 'Comrade Okhitovich may well be right about the future.' [12]

Also interesting in relation to the spatial characteristics of today's Deconstructive architectural work are Okhitovich's comments in a paper of early 1930, on how 'the revolutionary dispersal will free building construction for a technical revolution for which it is already beginning to prepare.' In the historic city of the age of 'fuel', he said, 'the external forms of buildings were generated not by internal requirements, not even by materials, but by external spatial requirements and the geometrical possibilities of maximum density.' Hence the rectangular, box-like forms, durable building materials, and artisan technologies needed to fit every new structure into the confined space available for it. When 'fuel', ie material lumps of power, has been replaced by 'energy', ie dematerialised, transmissible power.

its [geographically] universal availability will destroy urban land values. The technical revolution will come to the assistance of the social revolution, and the result will be the end of heavy, static long-lived forms of building. The new patterns of location will release construction spatially, making possible both the technical revolution in building construction, and that flexibility which our rapid social changes demand. Only prefabricated, demountable, changeable buildings will answer the needs of developed man. [13]

Earlier in the twenties, before Okhitovich's persuasive observations had lead Ginzburg and other mainstream Constructivists to examine a future of spatial discontiguities, only one of the group had stood out against their conviction that spatial compactness was, as Barshch put it in 1927, 'mercilessly dictated to us by today's technologies'. [14]

This exception was Ivan Leonidov. It is significant that of the Constructivist work which has been generally well known (and the Disurbanist theory, as opposed to the projects, has not been well known), Leonidov's was that which offered the most potent and useful formal paradigms for Deconstructionist architectural work. In particular, it has been a central and acknowledged source for OMA and such former pupils of Rem Koolhaas as Zaha Hadid.

At the same time when Leonidov produced his seminal Lenin Institute in 1927, its technological 'unreality' in relation to the possibilities of the Soviet building industry forced Ginzburg to defend his young colleague in face of growing public attack, and a wave of student projects aping his exciting forms. (A familiar story. . .) Ginzburg's defence of Leonidov's project focused precisely upon its spatial aspects. 'It is most of all valuable for us' he declared to his colleagues at their Conference in 1927,

as a categorical break with that system of volumes and elements which is inevitably becoming general amongst us. At its best, [this common spatial language] is the result of a unity of working method; at its worst, it is being used as a stylistic cliché.

Leonidov has moved towards a purely spatial solution, which is wholly different from the traditional approach, and must lead to a reorganisation of the actual arrangement of the sites in a town into which such a design might be put. [15]

This work of Leonidov's is of particular interest in connection with the discussion of sources with which I began, for the origins of that 'purely spatial' vocabulary lay in Suprematism. Leonidov is one of three figures – the other two, both more distant from the Constructivist architectural group proper, being El Lissitzky and Iakov Chernikhov – who pursued a synthesis of these two aesthetic languages and philosophies.

The interest and power of the attempts at synthesis derive from the fact that the concerns of these two movements were actually entirely opposed. The nature of the difference is clear if we compare two exactly contemporary works by their founders, from the pre-revolutionary period. Vladimir Tatlin's constructions are absolutely con-

crete explorations of 'real materials in real space'. The 'supreme abstraction' of Kazimir Malevich's Suprematism, on the other hand, is concerned with a four-dimensional space in which the spiritual dimension of perception, meaning and time is integral. It is a space without real dimensional measure, and programmatically eliminates 'real material' in favour of pure form. Here the fourth dimension of an experiential time serves as the dematerialiser, as the dimension which explodes the material into the spiritual.

The Suprematist 'field' is thus a space of collisions and 'events' rather than of objects with precise measure. Any Suprematist work is manifestly scaleless and measureless. Its very otherness, in relation to the tactile solidity and mechanically interconnected 'objects' of Modernism, provides a paradigm of a space-time universe which is logically appropriate to the new perceptions of how the cognitive and phenomenal world of the late 20th century is operating.

The work of these three 'synthesisers', El Lissitzky, Iakov Chernikhov and Ivan Leonidov, recognised the positive differences between the two movements and philosophies as a positive set of polarities against which to establish the appropriate position in any given artistic or design situation. As I see it, the problem addressed by those architects whom we loosely class as 'deconstructionst' is the cognitive and experiential conflict between 'building' as a physical entity, and 'time' as a demolisher of entity, 'memory' being part of the broad category of time. In this context it is hardly surprising that some formal resonances should be observable between their work and that of precursors in the same aesthetic and iconographic culture who pursued these two separate propositions of 'building' and 'time' with unique rigour.

Given the complex, non-linear manner in which form is generated in design, and the numerous ways in which formal parallels may arise, I would be the last to assert the existence of 'borrowings' where none are explicitly acknowledged by the work's authors themselves. In these cases, a juxtaposition of images read against the background I have drawn is as far as one may legitimately go. The illustrations here are selected on that principle.

There are of course cases where the influence has been a matter of open homage and pilgrimage. Thus Rem Koolhaas, for example, travelled to the Soviet Union to see the drawn and painted projects of Ivan Leonidov, in the flesh and in quantity, when very little of his work had previously been exposed to public view. Indeed I recall first seeing some works now published in our new study of Leonidov[16] when Koolhaas returned to London taken in Leonidov's son's flat in Moscow. Likewise Zaha Hadid, as Koolhaas' pupil, acknowledges a direct and powerful debt. In her symposium presentation here, she has also acknowledged the seminal role of student exercises on Malevich's three-dimensional *arkhitektoniki.*

Another oeuvre undoubtedly reflected in the work of Koolhaas and OMA is that of Lissitzky. He too explicitly posited the notion of interchange between scales, and between the material and spiritual universes in his notion of the *proun.* This 'project affirming the new' was conceived as 'a half-way station between painting and architecture'. Here the language is Suprematist: pure and primary geometrical figures of the circle, rectangle, line and plane, scaleless in a Suprematist space but interrelating in a manner that could be a model for real spatial relationships.

Where Lissitzky occupied a middle position in his personal role between Constructivists and Suprematists, working at different times with both, as he did between East and West, there is similar work by more direct followers of Malevich, such as Nikolai Suetin and Ilya Chashnik, which finds frequent echoes in the painterly representations of architecture which are another feature of today's Deconstructionist scene. Perhaps the best examples here are the paintings of Zoe Zenghelis, who has worked closely with the architects of OMA.

In some of Bernard Tschumi's work, too, we find a language akin to that of Lissitzky. Again the way of ordering space which was explored in the scale-less *proun* has found useful application in real work of broadly similar philosophical aspirations. Elsewhere in Tschumi's work the closer parallel is with the Leningrad teacher and theorist Chernikhov, whose most important book on the formal language of Modernism posited the formal logic of the First Machine Age in the very juxtaposition of architecture to the mechanical principle in its title, *The Construction of Architectural and Machine Forms*.[17] A hyper-constructive language, absolutely articulate in the relationships between its parts, is used by Tschumi not to make statements about mechanistic relationships in three-dimensional space but as the most powerful language for making negative, dissociative or probabilistic statements, for demonstrating non-structure and questioning conventional connectivities. Also paralleling the logic of Chernikhov's approach is the sort of clear combinatorial and permutational principle which Tschumi uses, for example at Parc de la Villette, to generate sets or sequences of forms, and likewise the very clear distinctions between 'point, line and plane' which he uses as the structuring principle of different dimensions of the Parc scheme.

Here we have parallels with the Disurbanist planning projects done by the Constructivist architectural group proper, in Moscow, as explorations of Okhitovich's theory that 'distance is now measured by time'.

In the ribbon of settlement, with its horizontal banding of functional zones, there is a parallel with the planning principle developed so clearly by Tschumi in his project for the Tokyo National Theatre. The user is offered bands of certain types of activity, and the path taken between them is not deterministically prescribed. On a democratic and pluralist principle each user combines the options and orders them according to his tastes and intentions. Likewise in the Constructivists' 'network system of servicing' each network of a given facility-type would be 'spatially and organisationally independent, and for that reason free to find its own optimal form, the most favourable sizes of its elements, and their most appropriate spacing amongst the consumers'[18] without constraint from the needs of other types of facility. Once any given sequence of facilities is located in real space it acquires a characteristic 'rhythm', and that experiential concept of it is another common dimension shared by Tschumi's work, in the Parc de la Villette, and the Disurbanist planning schemes, as both of them embrace the dimension of time in their handling of space.

Many of these parallels unquestionably result from independent responses to the inner logic of similar interests and intentions, pursued quite separately in different decades. Common forms result from shared origins within the same broad cultural tradition and the same perception of a three-dimensional space. Other parallels, on the other hand, result from direct use of the earlier work as inspiration and learning source, producing a continuity of thought across the fifty year divide between a first perception of certain imminent cultural shifts, and their becoming the reality of mass cultural experience. The latter case raises the issue of the legitimacy of such 'borrowings'. Here the attitude of the 'originators' would have been unequivocal.

It was an explicit and central principle of formal research throughout the Russian avant-garde that it had a role as what the Constructivist architects called 'laboratory work', or what their designer colleague Alexander Rodchenko referred to as a 'spatial inventory'.[19] It was a body of researched material available for future use in relevant design problems. On one level it represented stored experience for each designer himself, as he moved on from training exercises in a teaching programme like Chernikhov's to a lifetime of real design tasks; or pursued the logic of Lissitzky's *proun* principle as an interface between non-functional and functional areas of the aesthetic territory. On another level, it formed a collective resource and certainly one (though their time horizons were not then so broad) for use by future generations. Without doubt they would have been gratified to see how elements of their thinking have subsequently been used, for they saw it precisely as a setting up of systems, of a set of consistent languages, to be available when a problem of similar structure presented itself to the designer.

In one crucial way, perhaps, the passage of cultural change has left its mark. This is in the attitude to materials. Tschumi has said here that he doesn't care whether one of his 'constructivist' objects is built out of concrete or out of steel. To those for whom form was generated by the nature of the material such a statement would have been heretical. But that statement of Tschumi's speaks perhaps more clearly than any other of the extent to which a new synthesis has been created in work such as his, between the philosophical underpinnings of Constructivism on the one hand, and Suprematism on the other. To me that is perhaps the best way of understanding what Deconstruction actually means in architecture. In such a model we can see it as a reworking of the Newtonian concepts of space we inherited, to reflect the new relationships of space and time thrust upon us by the technologies of late 20th-century communications, and with them, the new awareness of those locational factors which we carry with us as we move, in the form of memory.

Notes

1 L von Bertalanffy, *General System Theory*. First published New York 1968, reference is made here to the London edition, 1971, p 115

2 See for example, C Cooke, 'Nikolai Krasilnikov's quantified approach to architectural design: an early example', *Environment & Planning B*, 1975, vol 2, pp 3-20; 'Form is a function, x: the development of the Constructivist architects' design method', *Architectural Design*, 1983, no 5/6, pp 34-49, of which a version appears in the present volume as 'The Development of the Constructivist Architects' Design Method'. also: C Cooke, *Fantasy and Construction: Iakov Chernikhov's Approach to Architectural Design*, AD Profile no 55, London 1984

3 Fritjof Capra, *The Turning Point*, New York 1982; reference is made here to the London edition, 1983. This and subsequent quotations from pp 64-66

4 Capra, *Turning Point*, pp 66, 70

5 This and subsequent quotations from *ibid*, pp 70-71

8 *ibid* p 76

7 Von Bertalanffy, *General System Theory*, p 33

8 Capra, *Turning Point*, p 77

9 *ibid*, p 76, quoting from James Jeans, *The Mysterious Universe*, New York & London, 1930

10 M Okhitovich, '*K probleme goroda*' (On the problem of the city), *Sovremennaia Arkhitektura* (*SA*), 1929, no 4, pp 130-134

11 The most important examples were the entries of Barshch and Ginzburg for the Green City competition, published in *SA*, 1930, no 1-2, pp 17-37, and of Barshch, Vladimirov, Okhitovich et al for Magnitogorsk, published *ibid*, pp 38-53

12 I Chernya, '*Na zemliu!*' (Onto the land!), *Revoliutsiia i kultura*, 1930, VII, pp 35-45

13 M Okhitovich, '*Zametki po teorii rasseleniia*' (Notes on the theory of settlement), *SA*, 1930, no 1-2, pp 7-16

14 M Barshch, '*Ekstensivnaia ili intensivnaia zastroika?*' (Extensive or intensive development?), *SA*, 1927, no 3, pp 90-95

15 M Ginzburg, '*Itogi i perspectivy*' (Achievements and prospects), *SA*, 1927, no 4-5, pp 112-118

16 *Ivan Leonidov: The Complete Works*, by Andrei Gozak and Andrei Leonidov, edited by Catherine Cooke, Academy Editions, London, 1988

17 Iakov Chernikhov, *Konstruktsiia arkhitekturnykh i mashinykh form*, Leningrad 1931. The full text of this book appears in English in Cooke, *Fantasy and Construction*, pp 41-88

18 M Ginzburg, '*Sotsialisticheskaia rekonstruktsiia sushchestvuiushchikh gorodov*' (The socialist reconstruction of existing cities), *Revoliutsiia i kultura*, 1930, no 1, pp 50-53

19 See Cooke, 'The Development of the Constructivist Architects' Design Method' in the present volume

KRASIL'NIKOV, VKHUTEMAS FINAL PROJECT: TRADES UNION HEADQUARTERS BUILDING IN A NEW CITY, FROM THE JOURNAL *SA* 1928

CATHERINE COOKE
The Development of the Constructivist Architects' Design Method

ПЕРВАЯ
КОНФЕРЕНЦИЯ ОБЩЕСТВА СОВРЕМЕННЫХ
АРХИТЕКТОРОВ. ERSTE KONFERENZ DER OSA

OCA

ГРУППА УЧАСТНИКОВ КОНФЕРЕНЦИИ ОСА

THE CONSTRUCTIVIST ARCHITECTS AT THEIR FIRST CONFERENCE, 1927

Constructivism in architecture has been subject to many varied interpretations. By admirers and denigrators alike, it has been presented as a philosophy predominantly concerned with the function of architecture as a social catalyst, with what Soviet terminology calls literally 'social construction'. It has been presented as an obsession with the space-forming role of structural technologies, with 'building construction' and with 'constructing possible shapes', that is as an overwhelm-

ing concern for formal construction: at worst, as formalism. No wonder the literature, and admirers of the resulting architecture, are confused. How can a small corpus of work have acquired dogmatic labels of such diversity?

The answer is simple. Like any serious professional architect, the Constructivist group were obsessively concerned with all these dimensions of the architectural problem. They were practitioners *par excellence*, crippled though they were by poverty of resources. Leading members of the group were unquestionably amongst the finest practising architects of their period anywhere. Not for nothing did every one of them remain, through changing times, at the centre of Soviet architectural practice and education right through till his death or old age. Unlike most others however, they were not prepared to leave questions of the interrelationships between these different dimensions of the architectural problem to chance, or to 'intuition'.

In the words of Lenin quoted in their journal, they believed that 'In order really to know an object, it is necessary to comprehend, to study, all aspects of it: all its internal and external connectivities.[1] Their's was what today would be called a 'systems' approach, or in the older and more general Russian term, a *kompleksnyi* approach. It addressed the design problem as an integrated complex; it was concerned with solving the problem as a whole. 'Form is a function, x,' said their leader Moisei Ginzburg, 'which has always to be evaluated afresh by the architect in response to the changing preconditions of the form-making.'[2] In modern jargon, which is not so far from their own at times, they aspired to model the entire decision space surrounding that form.

There is a direct generic relationship to much modern thinking here,

but also a crucial difference from most of what has passed for systems thinking about environmental problems thereafter. The Constructivists were not nihilist in the face of architecture's traditional concerns with the delineation and organisation of real space, or with the necessity for expression in architecture through well-understood languages of form. Compared to the aesthetic concerns of the 1930s, or of recent years, their's was distinctly a poetry of the concrete rather than the rhetorical, but men of Ginzburg's sophistication were too deeply rooted in what Russians call 'architectural culture' to deny that their objective must be poetry.

A recent Soviet theorist M R Savchenko has described 'architectural research' as having properly 'a duel orientation, towards both spatial and societal aspects of architecture', that 'dual orientation' being 'repeated in a distinction between a building's *parameters* and its *properties*'.[3]

Systematic Soviet analysis of these two dimensions of the design problem, and their infinite interrelationships, stretches back directly to Constructivist thinking in the 1920s. '*Parameters*' says Savchenko 'are direct measurements of a building and its spaces, of the consumers involved and of the activities it accommodates. *Properties* are measurements of consumers' reactions to that same building . . . They are therefore measurements through an "intermediary", measurements of decisions made, of symbolic situations overlaid, as the user "enters into" the actual building . . . Properties, like parameters reflect the object as a whole, but they do so through the prism of social attitudes to the architecture in the context of some corpus of architectural values.'[4] In a textbook for students, another recent Soviet commentator has accurately described Moisei Ginzburg as the principal Soviet pioneer of 'systematic attempts to develop a theoretical basis for design as a field of human activity'.[5] Whether wittingly or not, she speaks correctly of Soviet pioneers, not Russian; although before the Revolution, as I have described elsewhere,[6] there had already been significant thinking in this field. However these were the areas – the characteristics of the object and the manner of its interaction with people – in which the Constructivists believed there must be principle. They saw it as their professional obligation to their Marxist-materialist society to develop organised bodies of testable knowledge in these fields – what Russian calls *nauki*: literally 'sciences' – out of which solutions could in the broadest sense be 'constructed'.

Some issues of vocabulary have to be elaborated here, in as far as English allows it. Whether we speak of 'designing', 'creating', 'building' or 'construction', the Russian language has numerous words available, and each has a distinct meaning which only context can attach to their synonyms in English.

If we return to the forms of 'construction' I mentioned earlier, we already encounter the distinction which is crucial to understanding the aims of Constructivism. In 'social construction' and 'building construction' the Russian noun is *stroitel' stvo*. *Stroitel' stvo* takes place in real space and time: the *stroitel* is the builder on a real site with muddy

the formation of a Soviet Union of Designers, has the Russian word *dizainer* acquired the same neutrality of meaning it has internationally. Hitherto, the engineer in particular would have considered the description *dizainer* to imply, insultingly, that he was a mere stylist. Already 19th-century Rationalists in Russia used the adjective *konstruktivnyi* as high praise, for a manifestly 'built' piece of architecture. Smirnitsky represents the active verb *konstruirovat* very precisely with the alternative translations 'to construct; to design; to form; to organise', and Constructivists were *Konstruktivisty* They were concerned with how an architect organises or structures his thinking; how he organises the actual work of designing, and how he 'constructs' a set of appropriate forms.

They were also very interested in *stroitel' stvo* in all its dimensions. As loyal Soviets, social construction, and particularly 'the building of socialism' were the unquestioned *raison d'être* of their work. Material construction is the physical means whereby architecture exists at all: the materialist, in particular, must have the constraints and possibilities of all its media at his finger tips. In problems of *konstruktsiia* however, the choices are rooted in philosophic or aesthetic principle rather than physics. Aesthetic principle defines choices amongst possible systems of formal construction. The overall approach to the

L TO R: RODCHENKO'S 'SPATIAL CONSTRUCTIONS'; ADVERTISEMENT, *SA* 927 NO. 1, URGING READERS TO 'DEMAND' THEIR 'CATALOGUE OF SCIENTIFIC JOURNALS'

boots. 'Social construction' in this sense may be a strange concept to us, but this understanding of the phrase illuminates the way Soviet thinking envisages possibilities in this area. In the phrase 'formal construction', by contrast, we are using the word *konstruktsiia*. Its meaning is indicated by the fact that a major Russian dictionary like Smirnitsky will indicate that this word often has linguistic connotations. A grammatical construction is a *konstruktsiia*. It should not be forgotten here that the Constructivist movement had some roots amongst those precursors of linguistic Structuralism, the Russian Formalists, and also amongst the literary circles around Osip Brik, Vladimir Mayakovsky and the journal LEF.[7] Thus in the final analysis *stroitel' stvo* is a material process where *konstruktsiia* is an intellectual one.

When the early Constructivist artists like Alexei Gan and Alexandr Rodchenko formulated the profile of that 'artist-constructor' whom they aspired to produce through their curricula in the VKhUTEMAS, he was not a *khudozhnik-stroitel* – an artist-*builder*, some legatee of the Arts-and-Crafts tradition. He was a *khudozhnik-konstruktor* – an artist-*designer*. And here are further innuendos. The *konstruktor* is a specialist, highly qualified designer in industry: in engineering, for example, or today in electronics. Only in the last couple of years, with

task of designing; the ordering of data and prioritising of objectives; the methods of synthesis; and the criteria of evaluation; these are the philosophic problems of *konstruktsiia*

Moisei Ginzburg, leader of the Constructivist architects, insisted 'There can be no question of any sort of artist losing creativity just because he knows clearly what he wants, what he is aiming for, and in what consists the meaning of his work. But subconscious, impulsive creativity must be replaced by a clear and distinctly organised method, which is economical of the architect's energy and transfers the freed surplus of it into inventiveness and the force of the creative impulse'.[8] In the words of another, younger, founder-member of the group Nikolai Krassil'nikov: 'Intuition is not eliminated thereby; it merely comes to occupy its proper place.'[9] Constructivism was distinguished by its refusal to leave these *methodological* problems to the mercy of 'intuition'.

In the light of this, what follows is perhaps less unexpected.

The pursuit of a monistic method

Constructivists believed that the Soviet architect's mode of working must exhibit the same holism as the material and cognitive worlds in which he was 'constructing'. Precisely in order to 'guarantee' that a monistic integration of the material and the cognitive aspects of the world was preserved in design work, they formalised their 'method of functional creativity', or in later shorthand, their 'functional method'.[10] This was a set of procedures whereby the totality of factors they saw impinging upon a design would be taken into account objectively, 'moving from the first priority to the second', in generating a 'basic spatial organism' and in its technical and formal refinement. Bodies of background knowledge were the subject of 'laboratory work'. As Ginzburg explained in 1927: 'Methodologically, in order to subject the whole productive process of the architect to evaluation, Constructivism has recourse to many other scientific disciplines, and uses the laboratory method, of separating out one reaction, that is of taking one integral process' – in today's jargon, one subsystem – 'into temporary isolation from the others, in order to get the most favourable conditions for analysing it.'[11] Considerable work was done by these Constructivist architects in generating new 'classes of spatial organism', or building types and in exact analysis of what Savchenko would call their 'parameters' (as well as some of their 'properties', though this field generally belonged to the Rationalists under Ladovsky, Krinsky and others). Given the very short period – hardly four years – over which they were working as an organised group, their œuvre

'new', Soviet, generation in its own terms.

The central focus of Constructivist architectural theory was its machine-inspired, essentially linear 'working method' for design. The fullest exposition of this was published at the peak of their activity, in late 1927, as a paper by Ginzburg in their journal *Contemporary Architecture (SA)*. Entitled 'Constructivism as a method of laboratory and teaching work', the article was 'a schematic plan of the course in the theory of architecture being given by the author in the architectural departments of VKhUTEMAS and MVTU [Moscow Higher Technical School]'.[13]

This functional method was how Constructivists taught design. It was how they themselves operated in designing, and it was the framework whereby different 'laboratory investigations' by themselves and others – in building science, in social aspects of their briefs, in visual psychology, in development of formal languages and the rest – were organised into the process of designing new buildings to catalyse the process of 'building the new way of life'.

That five-part 'schematic plan' has been further edited into Diagram 2. Diagram 1 traces the development of the ideas in that schema through Ginzburg's earlier writings. These stretch back over the two preceding years of *SA*'s publication, 1927 and 1926, beyond the

Тектоника

Фактура

и Конструкция

L TO R: MOSCOW STREET SCENE, BY GOLTS, 1925; 'TEKTONIKA, FAKTURA AND KONSTRUKTSIIA', FROM GAN

was impressive as a demonstration of the standards they believed necessary. Some examples are illustrated here.

How does all this relate to the familiar roots of Constructivism: to Tatlin's Tower of 1919-20; to the geometrical 'structures' of Rodchenko and the First Working Group of Constructivists around 1920; to the ideas of Alexei Gan, revered as a founder theorist of Constructivism but known to us professionally only as a graphic- and exhibition-designer?

If we examine what these artists said, in the texts with which they illuminated their intentions, we find a development of ideas that is directly continued into the thinking of Ginzburg and the other Constructivist architects through the middle and later twenties. There is also a distinct continuity within architecture itself, between 19th and early 20th-century-theorist and Constructivist architectural theory.[12] These roots are undoubtedly real: amongst leading members of the profession there is a continuity of personal biographies across the divide of the Revolution – as there is of building technologies and much else – which conventional readings of this period wholly ignore. But given the political obligations to 'forget the old ways', these continuites were not part of the logical argument which the 'new men' were trying to construct. I shall therefore examine the thinking of the

formation of the Constructivist architectural group OSA in late 1925, to Ginzburg's seminal 'manifesto' of a constructive architecture, the book *Style and Epoch* of 1924, and earlier articles.

This consecutive enrichment and increasing detail of his thinking is a feature of Ginzburg's work in this period: through the writings one grows in understanding of the group's aspirations as they are further articulated. As a man of broad, largely European education, of wide reading and already significant professional experience, the sources of his thinking are complex. In respect of the three main ideas concerning us here, namely: the catalytic role of architecture and the built environment in effecting social change; the need for an organised method of working whereby the designer can respond logically, and the proper range of factors to be embraced by that 'method', there are also direct sources within the thinking of Constructivist artists in the three years following the Revolution, when Ginzburg himself was far away from the Moscow-Petrograd avant-garde axis, working and writing down in the Crimea.

Tatlin and Gan: the essential programme
Much later, in 1928, Ginzburg was to dismiss Tatlin's Tower to his colleagues as 'idealistic symbolism'; as manifesting only 'the acute

wish of a talented man to communicate emotionally.'[14] In its time, however, that grand and original scheme had been seminal to their own thinking.

Many putative 'sources' and 'meanings' have been attributed to this monument to the Third International. A typically rich array can be found in John Milners monograph on Tatlin.[15] Art historians may find satisfaction in such vague speculation; for architects it is more fruitful to examine the designers' own explanatory statements. Russians of this period do not use words pointlessly: even paper, as Lubetkin has reminded us, was an extraordinarily precious commodity. In his nice phrase, this 'was a wonderful time for poetry':[16] texts were concise and closely wrought. They deserve equally careful reading.

When Tatlin took his dismantled model Tower from Petrograd to Moscow in December 1920 to re-erect it for the Eigth Congress of Soviets, he and his three assistants published a brief newspaper statement entitled 'The work that faces us', often translated, more passively, as 'The work ahead of us.' An English translation is available in several sources.[17]

Here they explained the role which Tatlin's 'reliefs and contre-reliefs' had played, since 1914, as 'laboratory scale' preparation for the Tower project, and indicated how such explorations of 'materials, volume and the way these come together (konstruktsiia)' could be the starting point for new disciplines. These disciplines would be 'comparable in their severity' to those of Classicism, but where the Classical language had been constrained by the structural limitations of marble, these new languages would be liberated by the potential of 'modern' materials 'like iron and glass'. 'In this way' they declared, 'an opportunity emerges of uniting purely artistic forms with utilitarian intentions . . . The results are models which stimulate us to inventions in our work of creating a new world' and which 'call upon [us] to exercise control over the forms encountered in our new everyday life.' Ridiculing Fedor Shekhtel's moderne-style Iaroslavl Station in Moscow with its 'applied art' from Abramtsevo, they postulated this new path to a 'synthesis of painting, sculpture and architecture'. Non-functional 'art', be it two- or three-dimensional, in modern technological materials, must now serve as 'laboratory work' for the formal aspects of functional tasks. They saw this as the proper parallel in 'art' to 'what happened from the social point of view in 1917'.

During that same year of 1920 another group of artists, based permanently in Moscow, had started talking in very similar terms. The debates of early 1921 in which they juxtaposed the old artistic principle of kompozitsiia to their new concern with konstruktsiia were meticulously recorded at the time in shorthand. The typed records which resulted, the stenograficheskye otchety, have been published in extenso in Selim Khan-Magomedov's recent monograph on Rodchenko. The same study documents the formal emergence of a 'First Working Group of Constructivists', in the spring of 1921, within their discussion society, the Institute of Artistic Culture or InKhuK.[18] The seven artists who came together as the Group to pursue the implications of this new concept of konstruktsiia were Alexander Rodchenko, his wife Varvara Stepanova, the brothers Georgii and Vladimir Stenberg, Kazimir Medunetsky, Karl Iogansen and Alexei Gan.

In this working group's declaration the vocabulary is already more explicitly politicised. 'The group's sole premise' they declared, 'is scientific communism, based on the theory of historical materialism.'[19] These phrases were the common currency of the period: what matters is their interpretation of the underlying philosophical concepts. Important for its continuity with Tatlin's statement was their affirmation of 'the necessity of synthesising the ideological and formal parts [of their task] so as to direct the laboratory work onto the tracks of practical activity'. Yet more important, they started to frame some concepts which could help effect this synthesis operationally. Those 'elements of the group's work' which would make an 'organic link' here were three synthetic concepts which they termed 'tektonika, konstruktsiia and faktura'. The definitions are brief but already they demand mastery of enormous and diverse fields. Through principles

of 'organisation' embraced by a 'science' of konstruktsiia, Constructivists will effect 'an organic link between political values, industrial techniques and the specific possibilities of manipulated materials. Tektonika is a synthesis of the first two; faktura is the latter. 'Konstruktsiia is formulating activity taken to the extreme.'

Alexei Gan was soon to develop these themes more fully in his book Constructivism of 1922, and with them the First Working group's radical views on the past and future of 'art'.[20] He opened the book with punchy restatements of the Group's view that the traditional concept of 'art' must die naturally with the old culture, but here as throughout he builds a yet more explicitly Marxist-materialist rationale around their thoughts.

'The present publication' he declared, 'is an agitational book with which the Constructivists begin the fight against supporters of traditional art.' The enemy are those unable to grasp the 'fact', which their own Marxist rationale makes logically inevitable, that there cannot be a peaceful evolutionary transition in Russia's concept of art if there has been a violent Revolution in her politics.

Portions of this book have been translated into English, but editing has distorted the emphasis.[21] Much of its explicit politicality has been drained by omitting long quotations from the Communist Manifesto. More significant here is omission of the climactic sections that direct Constructivist energies towards architecture and the whole urban environment, and of the full definitions of their three new 'disciplines'.

Artists who work 'on this side of October 1917' says Gan, 'should not be reflecting, depicting and interpreting reality. They should build practically and express the planned objectives of the new and actively working class . . . which is building the foundation of the future society . . . as an organised force in possession of a plan.' The master of colour and line, the combiner of spatio-volumetric solids . . . must all become Constructivists.[22] But that too means organisation. 'In order to produce practitioners and theoreticians of Constructivism who are qualified, in a Marxist sense' he warned, 'It is essential to channel [our] work into a definite system; to create disciplines through which all the Constructivists' experimental work would be directed.'[23] They all had teaching jobs, in the new VKhUTEMAS particularly, and 'the production of qualified Constructivists' – of 'artist-constructors' – became the objective of their curricula.

Here in Gan's 'definite system' is our first hint of a 'method'. Its components would be those new synthetic 'disciplines' of tektonika, faktura and konstruktsiia, but now, from Gan, we get fuller definitions.

With tektonika as their first discipline, Constructivists are trying to chop away the ignorance and tyranny exercised by architects and builders under capitalism. Tektonika, or tectonic style organically emerges and is formed on the one hand out of the characteristics of Communism itself, and on the other from the appropriate utilisation of industrial material. The word tectonic is taken from geology, where it signifies violent restructurings coming out of the Earth's core.

Tektonika is a synonym of organicness, of an eruption from the inner essence.

Tektonika as a discipline must lead the Constructivist in practice towards a synthesis of the new content with new forms. He must be a person educated in a Marxist way, who has eliminated from his life all vestiges of "art" and has started advancing his knowledge of industrial material. Tektonika is his guiding star, the very cerebrum of his experimental and practical activity.

Constructivism without tektonika is like painting without colour.'[24]

Of the three concepts, this is perhaps the most obscure; the final sentence, which seems to compound the obscurity, in fact offers a key. Every professional act of the Constructivist must be coloured, or informed, by the understanding that a violent restructuring of underlying relationships has profoundly changed the way industry should shape and distribute material in space.

Faktura is simpler. This word emphatically 'must not be understood from the painter's point of view', 'as just the handling of a surface'. On the example of cast iron, it implies 'the character of the whole processing', the melting, casting and turning, say, 'whereby it becomes an object'. As 'the appropriate use of material' *faktura* 'means the selection and processing from the raw material'. Also, 'more specifically, *faktura* is the organic condition of processed material or the new condition of its organism.' 'It is material consciously chosen and appropriately used in a manner that does not limit the *tektonika* or obstruct the *konstruktsiia*.'[25]

In the light of much that has been said earlier, the meaning of *konstruktsiia* should be clear. In Gan's words:

Konstruktsiia must be understood as the assembling and ordering function within Constructivism.

While *tektonika* comprises an interconnection of the ideological and the formal and as a result gives a unity of conception, and *faktura* takes account of the state of the material, *konstruktsiia* reveals the actual process of putting together.

Thus the third discipline involves giving form to the concept through the use of processed material.[26]

Konstruktsiia, in short, was design, but these expansive new synthetic disciplines still omitted the sciences of real space.

In challenging 'the combiner of spatio-volumetric solids' and 'the master of colour and line' to become Constructivists, Gan was not suggesting that they leave those skills behind them. On the contrary, 'A system must also be worked out in the field of producing forms', and he explained how that system would be developed by quoting his colleague 'the Constructivist Rodchenko', 'elucidating one of his experiments in spatial constructivism.' The works concerned would be items from his 'spatial inventory' or studies of similar geometrical forms from the period around 1920-21, which are well known.

Rodchenko had written: 'I have devised these latest spatial constructions as experiments, specifically to make the designer (*konstruktor*) bound by the law of appropriateness of applied forms, to constrain him to assemble the forms according to laws, and also to show their universalism, how from identical forms he may assemble (*konstruirovat*) all possible constructions, of diverse systems, kinds and applications.'[27] Here was 'art' already consciously executed as lab work for design. Contemporaneous photographs indicate that such exercises were already central to Rodchenko and Stepanova's teaching.[28]

Rodchenko and his immediate colleagues did not pursue these ideas into architecture. Others were to carry the baton forward in that direction, and Gan thrust it at them unequivocally.

'The planned working out of the whole area of the urban territory, of its individual districts and also its proper solution in the vertical dimension, in the *tektonika* of its masses and volumes, in the faktura of its materials and the *konstruktsiia* of its structures – these' he declared 'are the basic task of our Constructivism, which arose in the fresh cornfields of the proletarian revolution and is actively and consciously fighting for communism.'[29] In developing their 'definite system', their 'primary objective' must be 'to establish a scientific foundation for the approach to constructing buildings and services that would fulfil the demands of Communist culture in its transient state, through all stages of its future development out of this period of ruin'.[30]

Already here, if vaguely, is the idea later central to architectural Constructivism, that form must accommodate or respond to social evolution. Yet more importantly, however, Gan introduces the notion that architecture, by its spatial organisation, itself actively influences that evolution.

He raises the question negatively:

As the material, technological 'organs' of society, the capitalist towns that we inherited are staunch allies of counter-revolution. Soviet communism has already discovered that the capitalist

town not only cannot accommodate even the most timid measures of Revolutionary reorganisation, but more than that! *It stubbornly obstructs the path of that reorganisation.* Its small and awkward buildings have been totally unable to accommodate the operational requirements of the various new Soviet organisations. They are too cramped, just as the streets and squares which we inherited have not afforded the spatial conditions that we need for mass parades and vast assemblies.[31]

'We must get human consciousness organised' he declares. 'We must force the active revolutionary groups and the working masses to see this disformity, this misfit, to see it just as clearly as they see a misfit when some reorganisation brings disorder into their own home.'[32] The logical implication is present here, though Gan does not develop it: if a 'misfitting' environment can obstruct social change, a 'fitting' one can foster it. If spatial organisation can be a negative catalyst, it can also be a positive one. Over the next few years, that view of architecture was to become the central motivation of the Constructivist architects, as they pursued in greater detail the implications of Gan's other injunction, 'to develop a system of forming objects in general'.[33]

Moisei Ginzburg: toward architectural Constructivism

Gan's book *Constructivism* came off the presses in 1922. During the previous year there had returned to Moscow a young architect who previously spent three wartime years there, from 1914-17, at the Polytechnical Institute. Son of an architect in Minsk, this twenty-nine year old Moisei Ginzburg had had a head-start to early professional maturity. He had been amongst the last young Russians to complete a university education abroad before the First World War. Three years at the Milan Academy had left him experienced in both the beneficial disciplines and the inhibiting limitations of the classical architectural education.[34] His stay had coincided with Marinetti's most active and noisy years, but behind the verity and appeal of that vision he plainly perceived all too clearly the lack of any practical signposts for the professional. Returning to Russia in 1914, he balanced his education with the engineering-oriented courses at the Moscow Polytechnical School. After four years down in the Crimea during the Revolution and Civil War, in practice and studying the regional vernacular, he was an exceptionally travelled young architect amongst the generation to which he returned in the decimated and isolated Moscow of 1921.

Ginzburg's student years in Moscow, during the War, had been the period of Tatlin's first experiments into three dimensional 'constructions' and the 'culture of materials'. His four years absence had seen those beginnings evolve into politically committed programmes and educational curricula. Architect friends of Tatlin like the Vesnin brothers, all a decade older than Ginzburg, were already engrossed in exploring the consequences of this committment for architecture; but at a time when words attracted more attention than designs for which there were no materials, they were more at home at the drawing board than the typewriter. Ginzburg, like Alexandr Vesnin, was attracted by ideas being expressed by Mayakovsky, Osip Brik and others in the journal LEF, and during 1922 the two became the nucleus of a small architectural group amongst these literary Constructivists. Already having several articles to his name in the journal *Amongst the Collectors*[35] Ginzburg also moved quickly to the centre of reviving professional circles in the old-established Moscow Architectural Society, MAO, and a year later became chief editor of its new journal *Architecture*.[36] During the next few years, talking, writing and teaching were the active architect's most rewarding media, and Ginzburg used them all.

MAO was the main forum for progressives of the pre-Revolutionary generation. Ginzburg's two editorial colleagues on *Architecture* were Leonid Vesnin, eldest brother of the successful pre-War trio, and Edgar Norvert, an established expert on building rationalisation. Amongst their larger editorial committee were two leading pioneers of new building techniques Ivan Rerberg and Alexander Kuznetsov, and two leading architects-turned-planners Aleksei Shchusev and Vladimir Semionov. The new position in which the whole profession found itself was expressed by the latter in the first issue of *Architecture*, under the title 'Priority tasks', in terms which show the young avantgarde was far from alone in its concerns. 'It will soon be ten years since any of us built anything' began Semionov. 'Our very approach to work has to change. Where previously we converted reliably proven technical knowledge into concrete facts, we now have to blaze entirely new trails not just in architecture, in the narrow sense of that word, but also in the broadest sense of architecture, as creative construction (*stroitel'stvo*), where logic, the way of life, community attitudes and every side of civil life all make their demands equally. Before the Revolution we knew neither this complexity, nor this responsibility.' Professionally, it will be 'the task of the future public architecture to understand these new conditions, these new requirements of the present time, and to find forms answering the real situation'. But 'The battle requires organisation, and the changed circumstances call for new methods.'[37]

As editorial writer for this issue, Ginzburg took the opportunity to offer some pointers from other circles. 'Contemporary researches in the field of artistic form' he wrote, 'are speaking of a new phase of

Style and Epoch: theory meets history

Style and Epoch was seminal to the whole development of Constructivist thinking about architecture. It also provides an important point of comparison with Western thinking, in particular that of Le Corbusier, who to Soviets always occupied the foreground of it.

With its further illustrations of Buffalo grain silos, and now also of aeroplanes, the book looks sufficiently like *Vers une architecture* for Corbusier to have felt no doubt immensely flattered when his inscribed copy arrived in the mail.[41] (It is still held in the Fondation Corbusier.) One can only speculate as to how it might have influenced his approach if he had been able to read the text. Precisely how and when the message of *L'Esprit Nouveau* arrived in the Soviet Union remains to be discovered, but as far as Irina Kokkinaki has ascertained, the first copies to arrive were those which 'Le Corbusier sent to the Commissar of Enlightenment A V Lunacharsky... in 1922, long before the establishment of diplomatic relations between the Soviet State and France.'[42] In early 1923 MAO's *Architecture* referred in its 'Survey of journals' to there being 'a few copies in Moscow in private hands' with more expected by the 'university and neo-philological libraries soon'.[43] The strength and authority of Ginzburg's ideas already derived, however, from the very wide range of stimuli on which he drew. The

L TO R: GEORGII GOLTS, UNKNOWN, ANDREI BUROV, LE CORBUSIER AND GINZBURG, LATE 20S; MOISEI GINZBURG

creative activity' which must take account of 'that new element of our lives ... psychology and ... aesthetics: the machine.' 'Architecture today must find sources of inspiration in the best achievements of engineers and of industrial architecture' he declared, and in a four-page article, all six illustrations were 'Grain elevators in Buffalo, New York.' With 'the descent of artists from Olympia' to become 'master-craftsmen ... in the real world' said Ginzburg, they have brought a 'healthy ... coarsening of our concept of the creative process'.[38]

The other Moscow forum where Ginzburg was active was one fully sensitive to the traditional refinements he invoked in that remark. RAKhN, the Russian Academy of Artistic Sciences, was formed in 1921 as a talking shop on a modernised model of eighteenth-century European academies. It was dedicated 'to discovering the inner, positive laws on whose basis aesthetic works are produced in each branch of art, and to deriving from that the principles of synthetic artistic expression'.[39] Ginzburg read numerous papers in the architectural section lead by Ivan Zholtovsky. In February 1924 he presented the argument of a book he had already completed entitled *Style and Epoch*. It was typical of the approach observed by one recent Soviet writer to be characteristic of RAKhN, that 'theory and history are bound together as a single topic of investigation'.[40]

architectural philosophy expounded here can be seen as a natural, indeed logical synthesis of the various influences in his training, his early professional life, and the Moscow circles around him. The essay with which Anatole Senkevitch has introduced his translation of this book provides a rich commentary on these sources.[44]

While *L'Esprit Nouveau* was not the only influence behind Ginzburg's book, the end product was plainly modelled closely upon it. *Style and Epoch* shows us that this material which the West has always found to be an indigestible lump had already been critically digested in the Soviet Union. Yet more significantly, it had already been used as the first stepping stone to an operational method that would bring to architecture the qualities so lauded in engineering, rather than just the forms.

Out of those initial observations about the honesty of form in grain silos, cars and aeroplanes, Ginzburg had built a consistent little Marxist-theoretical work (though he did not call it that), which makes *Vers une architecture* look more than ever like a loose piece of journalism. Although then, and later, Corbusier made many comments upon historical architecture, he never attempted to pull them together into any theory of the general development of architectures. Gan had insisted that 'The theory of historical materialism through which the

Constructivists are assimilating history in general and the basic laws . . . of society must serve them equally as a method of studying the history of art' to develop 'a science of the history of its formal development.'[45] Here Ginzburg produced a first such analysis of architecture.

For all Corbusier's eulogies on the logical and precise methods whereby engineers create forms, nowhere did he attempt to build a bridge into the practice of architecture. All too clearly he had no aptitude for the sort of calculations involved. Ginzburg by contrast, with the engineering emphasis of his polytechnic degree, was a prototype of his own vision of the architect. His mentor Alexander Kuznetsov had addressed the last pre-War Congress of Russian Architects a decade before on the theme that 'The architect, according to the definition of the London congress, "*is an artist with a scientific education*"'.[46] Insisting as Ginzburg did that architectural creation is a monistic process and a distinct activity (though elements from many others are synthesised into it), he saw however that only those whose central concern was architecture could build a bridge from engineering that was useful to it. While circumstances made Corbusier's fundamentally romantic book a major inspiration to architectural thinking world-wide, there is no doubt that Ginzburg's is the more

never fitted Corbusier's formal predilections.

Ginzburg called the first phase of a typical architectural cycle *konstruktivnyi*: 'constructive'. Neatly he spans the gap here between the limited 19th-century architect's understanding of that term, and the broader meaning already established amongst Soviet artists. In a constructive phase, says Ginzburg, unprejudiced responses are being made to the mass of what are, axiomatically, new social and technical problems. In these periods, the chief task in every field of design is that of 'devising the characteristic plastic types for the epoch', and the present coincidence of social and technical revolutions made their own period unquestionably one of them.[50] In these periods, 'the new style will always be aesthetically strong and organically logical'.[51] In Viollet-le-Duc's terms, the '*principes*' will be pure, for 'the architect is facing the very basic problem of the delimiting of space with material forms, and this requires the creation of elements working constructively'.[52]

In their own, early-Soviet period however, Ginzburg perceived factors making it 'doubly constructive'. Exceptional economic stringency required the maximum possible economy of material in that 'delimiting' and therefore a maximising of the constructive work done by the building elements. But it also happened that the principles on

L TO R: TATLIN'S TOWER AND BUFFALO GRAIN ELEVATORS IN *STYLE AND EPOCH*, CHAP 5; 'THE FORM OF THE AEROPLANE AND THE METHODS OF DESIGNING IT' *SA* 1926 NO 3

useful and thoughtful work, which would have served the practice of architecture better in that role. To those exploring Constructivism's implications for architecture, it provided both historical legitimacy, and an operational starting point for their approach to building design.

To Corbusier, 'style' was never much more than an attribute of artefacts. To Ginzburg it was 'some kind of regularity, a similarity through conformity to the same laws (*zakonomernoe edinstvo*)'[47] which relentlessly characterises every branch and product of the life of a human, historical period. It can only be identified through as intimate an understanding of the period's 'social, economic, climatic and national particularities' as of its 'artistic environment'.[48] Wolflin's *Renaissance and Baroque* had influenced him here, and he quotes it widely. Crudely summarised, it was Ginzburg's observation from extensive historical study that what one might call the 'health' of architecture follows that of culture and their respective *Weltanschauungs*, as they pass through phases of fresh, creative 'flowering', 'organic' maturity and decline into 'decorative' rhetoric.[49] It was to illustrate this theory of a cyclical process that he used the historical examples which Corbusier would have found familiar. With his concern for historical objectivity, as well as dynamic processes, Ginzburg also paid considerable attention to the Gothic, which had

which every branch of their contemporary life was organised, or more accurately aspired to be organised, were precisely those embodied *par excellence* in the machine: the principles of honesty, structural simplicity, objectivity, precise organisation and thus economy of all the means. Returning to themes we have already observed in his writings he declared: 'The essence of this machine, which is beginning to play such an exceptional psychological role in our lives, consists in the naked constructiveness of its component organisms.'[53] 'The machine is creativity at its most organised, the greatest clarity and power in the formulation of the creative idea.'[54] 'In the machine there can be nothing superfluous, accidental, "decorative"', and never forgetting architectural history: 'In essence we find in the machine, before all, the clearest expression of that ideal of harmonious creativity long ago formulated by the first Italian theoretician, Alberti.'[55] It was in this sense that the machine was the symbol of their present epoch, and these characteristics of the style of every 'constructive' period thus happened, in this one, to be also the characteristics of its own particular *Weltanschauung*. How then could the correct architectural style of the young Soviet Union be anything but 'constructive'?

This argument was to be the primary source of the Constructivist architects' strong self-confidence. It gave them a conviction that their

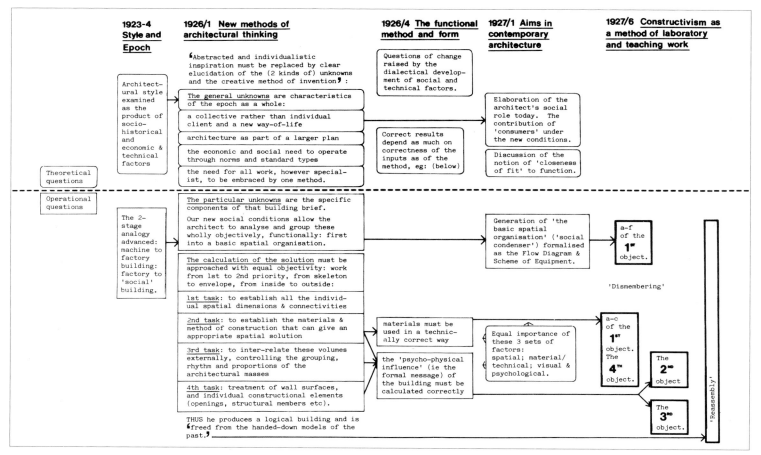

1923-4 **Style and Epoch**	1926/1 **New methods of architectural thinking**	1926/4 **The functional method and form**	1927/1 **Aims in contemporary architecture**	1927/6 **Constructivism as a method of laboratory and teaching work**

DIAGRAM 1: DEVELOPMENT OF IDEAS IN THE FUNCTIONAL METHOD THROUGH GINZBURG'S WRITINGS FROM 1924

stance was historically 'correct': a conviction quite as strong as that which motivated their political leaders. The particular characteristics and protypes of modern 'organisedness' gave them the starting point for their method of design.

As forms said Ginzburg in *Style and Epoch*, 'neither the engineering structure nor the machine gives us an expressive *spatial* solution, which is what constitutes the distinguishing mark of architecture'.[56] 'How' he asked, 'are we to build a bridge between these contemporary ensembles and the architectural monuments, once we realise that this is possible only through the principles of creativity and not through the actual forms? We will try to continue our analysis.'[57] His 'continued analysis' showed the machine to be potentially an appropriate model for the organisation of any functionally interconnected agglomeration of specialised and diverse activities, dynamic and static. Here was already a quite sophisticated methodological concept that left Corbusier's mere image of the house as a 'machine à habiter' in the realm of aphorisms.

From this general idea of the machine as an organisational prototype, Ginzburg developed a two-stage analogy. The first stage was an analogy between the machine and the factory, which

> is a collective of machines; . . . all linked together by desirable necessity just as the parts of an individual machine are, . . . and at the same time it is also a 'dwelling', not for people primarily but for machines, but [in a way that makes it] an architectural object none the less, with all the spatial connotations of that.[58]

'Industrial architecture' therefore 'serves as the connecting link, . . . but factories and silos cannot be the sole contents of modern architecture.'[59] So, secondly,

> Precisely as we established the analogy between the machine and the industrial building, an analogy may be established between the industrial building and the architecture of the dwelling or the community building. Just precisely as the industrial building is not the conscious imitation of a machine, but

comprises forms that have been generated organically and quite independently, while reflecting the same contemporaneity through whatever are their own unique characteristics, so here in precisely the same way is it a question of building an analogy.[60]

Style and Epoch did not pass unappreciated by the architectural profession. 'In the excellent book of M la Ginzburg' said the established Leningrad architect and planner Professor Karpovich, reviewing it for the city's main environment journal *Questions of the Communal Economy*, 'the reader will find not only theoretical discussions on style in architecture, but also absolutely practical approaches to the creative problems of contemporary architecture.' The book demonstrates, said Karpovich, that 'the study of the machine can give a new stimulus to the creation of new architectural forms', though 'it shows us how far today's Constructivists are from the creation of such new forms'.[61] Karpovich was a relevant commentator on the book's originality, when nothing else emerging in Moscow, from such fora as RAKhN or INKhUK, was comparable. Its main competitor in sophistication at this date, in the pursuit of an approach to the whole architectural problem, was the work of his younger Leningrad colleague A E Rozenburg, a hospital design specialist before the Revolution, whose book of the previous year, *A Philosophy of Architecture*, was more synoptic, but less pregnant.[62]

Generating the new plastic types

From the basic analogy established in *Style and Epoch*, Ginzburg and his colleagues developed the central concepts and procedures of their design 'method'. First however they formed themselves into a group, and started a journal.

The Moscow Architectural Society, MAO, had proved itself inadequate as a platform for advancing genuinely new aesthetic ideas. Anathema to the young and engagés was the passive 'professionalism' of Edgar Norvert's view that 'the posing of general social questions and questions about the new way of life is outside the domain of the

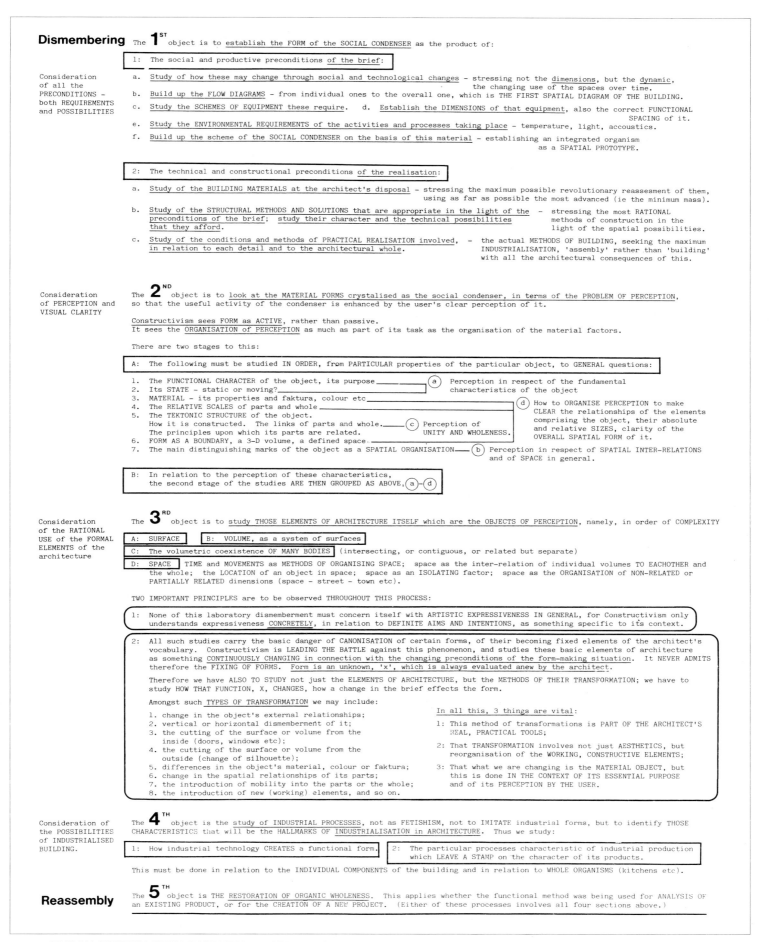

Dismembering   The **1**ST object is to establish the FORM of the SOCIAL CONDENSER as the product of:

> 1: The social and productive preconditions of the brief:

Consideration of all the PRECONDITIONS — both REQUIREMENTS and POSSIBILITIES

a. Study of how these may change through social and technological changes – stressing not the dimensions, but the dynamic, the changing use of the spaces over time.

b. Build up the FLOW DIAGRAMS – from individual ones to the overall one, which is THE FIRST SPATIAL DIAGRAM OF THE BUILDING.

c. Study the SCHEMES OF EQUIPMENT these require.   d. Establish the DIMENSIONS of that equipment, also the correct FUNCTIONAL SPACING of it.

e. Study the ENVIRONMENTAL REQUIREMENTS of the activities and processes taking place – temperature, light, accoustics.

f. Build up the scheme of the SOCIAL CONDENSER on the basis of this material – establishing an integrated organism as a SPATIAL PROTOTYPE.

> 2: The technical and constructional preconditions of the realisation:

a. Study of the BUILDING MATERIALS at the architect's disposal – stressing the maximum possible revolutionary reassesment of them, using as far as possible the most advanced (ie the minimum mass).

b. Study of the STRUCTURAL METHODS AND SOLUTIONS that are appropriate in the light of the preconditions of the brief; study their character and the technical possibilities that they afford. – stressing the most RATIONAL methods of construction in the light of the spatial possibilities.

c. Study of the conditions and methods of PRACTICAL REALISATION involved, in relation to each detail and to the architectural whole. – the actual METHODS OF BUILDING, seeking the maximum INDUSTRIALISATION, 'assembly' rather than 'building' with all the architectural consequences of this.

Consideration of PERCEPTION and VISUAL CLARITY

The **2**ND object is to look at the MATERIAL FORMS crystalised as the social condenser, in terms of the PROBLEM OF PERCEPTION, so that the useful activity of the condenser is enhanced by the user's clear perception of it.

Constructivism sees FORM as ACTIVE, rather than passive.
It sees the ORGANISATION of PERCEPTION as much as part of its task as the organisation of the material factors.

There are two stages to this:

> A: The following must be studied IN ORDER, from PARTICULAR properties of the particular object, to GENERAL questions:

1. The FUNCTIONAL CHARACTER of the object, its purpose _____ (a) Perception in respect of the fundamental characteristics of the object
2. Its STATE – static or moving?_____
3. MATERIAL – its properties and faktura, colour etc_____
4. The RELATIVE SCALES of parts and whole _____ (d) How to ORGANISE PERCEPTION to make CLEAR the relationships of the elements comprising the object, their absolute and relative SIZES, clarity of the OVERALL SPATIAL FORM of it.
5. The TEKTONIC STRUCTURE of the object. How it is constructed. The links of parts and whole._____ (c) Perception of UNITY AND WHOLENESS. The principles upon which its parts are related. _____
6. FORM AS A BOUNDARY, a 3-D volume, a defined space._____
7. The main distinguishing marks of the object as a SPATIAL ORGANISATION_____ (b) Perception in respect of SPATIAL INTER-RELATIONS and of SPACE in general.

> B: In relation to the perception of these characteristics, the second stage of the studies ARE THEN GROUPED AS ABOVE, (a)-(d)

Consideration of the RATIONAL USE of the FORMAL ELEMENTS of the architecture

The **3**RD object is to study THOSE ELEMENTS OF ARCHITECTURE ITSELF which are the OBJECTS OF PERCEPTION, namely, in order of COMPLEXITY

> A: SURFACE   B: VOLUME, as a system of surfaces

> C: The volumetric coexistence OF MANY BODIES (intersecting, or contiguous, or related but separate)

> D: SPACE   TIME and MOVEMENTS as METHODS OF ORGANISING SPACE; space as the inter-relation of individual volumes TO EACHOTHER and the whole; the LOCATION of an object in space; space as an ISOLATING factor; space as the ORGANISATION of NON-RELATED or PARTIALLY RELATED dimensions (space – street – town etc).

TWO IMPORTANT PRINCIPLES are to be observed THROUGHOUT THIS PROCESS:

> 1: None of this laboratory dismemberment must concern itself with ARTISTIC EXPRESSIVENESS IN GENERAL, for Constructivism only understands expressiveness CONCRETELY, in relation to DEFINITE AIMS AND INTENTIONS, as something specific to its context.

> 2: All such studies carry the basic danger of CANONISATION of certain forms, of their becoming fixed elements of the architect's vocabulary. Constructivism is LEADING THE BATTLE against this phenomenon, and studies these basic elements of architecture as something CONTINUOUSLY CHANGING in connection with the changing preconditions of the form-making situation. It NEVER ADMITS therefore the FIXING OF FORMS. Form is an unknown, 'x', which is always evaluated anew by the architect.
>
> Therefore we have ALSO TO STUDY not just the ELEMENTS OF ARCHITECTURE, but the METHODS OF THEIR TRANSFORMATION; we have to study HOW THAT FUNCTION, X, CHANGES, how a change in the brief effects the form.
>
> Amongst such TYPES OF TRANSFORMATION we may include:
>
> 1. change in the object's external relationships;
> 2. vertical or horizontal dismemberment of it;
> 3. the cutting of the surface or volume from the inside (doors, windows etc);
> 4. the cutting of the surface or volume from the outside (change of silhouette);
> 5. differences in the object's material, colour or faktura;
> 6. change in the spatial relationships of its parts;
> 7. the introduction of mobility into the parts or the whole;
> 8. the introduction of new (working) elements, and so on.
>
> In all this, 3 things are vital:
>
> 1: This method of transformations is PART OF THE ARCHITECT'S REAL, PRACTICAL TOOLS;
>
> 2: That TRANSFORMATION involves not just AESTHETICS, but reorganisation of the WORKING, CONSTRUCTIVE ELEMENTS;
>
> 3: That what we are changing is the MATERIAL OBJECT, but this is done IN THE CONTEXT OF ITS ESSENTIAL PURPOSE and of its PERCEPTION BY THE USER.

Consideration of the POSSIBILITIES of INDUSTRIALISED BUILDING.

The **4**TH object is the study of INDUSTRIAL PROCESSES, not as FETISHISM, not to IMITATE industrial forms, but to identify THOSE CHARACTERISTICS that will be the HALLMARKS OF INDUSTRIALISATION in ARCHITECTURE. Thus we study:

> 1: How industrial technology CREATES a functional form.   2: The particular processes characteristic of industrial production which LEAVE A STAMP on the character of its products.

This must be done in relation to the INDIVIDUAL COMPONENTS of the building and in relation to WHOLE ORGANISMS (kitchens etc).

Reassembly   The **5**TH object is THE RESTORATION OF ORGANIC WHOLENESS. This applies whether the functional method was being used for ANALYSIS OF an EXISTING PRODUCT, or for the CREATION OF A NEW PROJECT. (Either of these processes involves all four sections above.)

DIAGRAM 2: FUNCTIONAL METHOD PROCEDURES SUMMARISED FROM GINZBURG, 'CONSTRUCTIVISM AS A METHOD OF LABORATORY AND TEACHING WORK', *SA* 1927 NO. 6

architect'. Too dominant was his opinion, expressed in *Architecture* in 1923, that architecture could not serve society until distinct social forms had crystallised out of the present transitional period.[63]

The first new, post-Revolutionary architectural society, the Association of New Architects or ASNOVA, had been formed in 1923 under the leadership of Nikolai Ladovsky and Vladimir Krinsky. To the Constructivists, however, the psycho-formal work of these so-called Rationalists 'could only acquire a genuinely scientific materialistic basis if it was always made clear what real problems the theoretical work was directed at', and 'if the methods being applied in solution of these tasks were fundamentally those of the architect, so that they could be put to real and practical use in the present-day architect's work as an organiser of building.[64] In late 1925, Ginzburg and the Vesnin brothers formed a Constructivist architectural group to fill the gap, and called it OSA: the Union of Contemporary Architects.[65]

Ginzburg and the three Vesnins, Leonid, Viktor and Alexander, represented a bridge between progressives of the older generation and the younger avant-garde. Alexei Gan was a central participant from the first, in launching their journal during the next year; in staging their exhibition, and in developing theory. He and Alexander Vesnin brought a direct link to the aesthetic debates of the First Working Group and the attitude to materials of Tatlin, whom Vesnin knew well. The Vesnins, with their Palace of Labour competition project of 1923, had provided what Ginzburg would later call 'a landmark for Constructivism in its first concrete architectural action'. In the context of discussions over Deconstruction, that paper of Ginzburg's from 1927 is interesting for its emphasis on this project as the model of a new approach to building design 'for our historical epoch', rather than a model for 'a new style'.[66] Both Ginzburg and Leonid Vesnin also brought to this new Constructivist group the experience of pre-Revolutionary Russian pioneers of a technologically and aesthetically 'modern' architecture, particularly through their connections with Norvert, Artur Loleit and Alexander Kuznetsov, who had founded the architectural department where they taught at MVTU. Much of the group's authority derived from the fact it was a synthesis of this broad thinking and experience. Their method sought to formalise 'correct' relationships between these very diverse components.

After the demise of other new magazines, OSA's journal *SA* (*Contemporary Architecture*) was Russia's only purely architectural journal during the four pre-Five-Year-Plan years 1926-30. On page 1 of number 1, it was launched with an article by Ginzburg entitled 'New Methods of Architectural Thinking'.[67] Here as in his next two major articles on this theme (see Diagram 1),[68] as already in *Style and Epoch*, he addressed both theoretical and operational questions. These now became two distinct categories of 'variables': the 'general unknowns' and the 'particular' ones.

'General unknowns' were those identifying 'characteristics of the epoch as a whole' whose influence must permeate the entire design and construction process. In *Style and Epoch* he had discussed these 'social, economic and national peculiarities' of a culture as inevitably influencing building form.[69] From further analysis of their own emerging culture Ginzburg now identified four such 'peculiarities' of the Soviet situation. These were the fact of a collective, rather than an individual, client, which was trying to build 'a new way of life'; the concomitant shift in architecture's position, to become one part of a larger social and economic plan; the conjunction of these factors to produce a new, ideological and technical status for norms and standard types, and the overriding, methodological obligation under the new ideology, to 'solve the architectural task, like any other, only through precise evaluation of its "unknowns" and the pursuit of a correct method of solution'.[70] The deductions were not all novel, but the codified statement was new.

In *Style and Epoch* Ginzburg illustrated Tatlin's Tower as an example of the new approach. So complex and unrealisable in the decimated state of Russia, it had been reduced to a piece of technologi-cal symbolism in the public mind. Here therefore he condemned as 'merely naive . . . any attempt to replace the complexities of the art of architecture by forms, however sparkling' derived as 'symbolism . . . from other aspects of technology' Architecture was 'invention like any other', a task of 'organising and giving form to (*skonstruirovat'*) a concrete practical problem not only for the dictates of today, but to fit the needs of tomorrow'. 'From the inventor the contemporary architect must take only his creative method.[71] A later issue of *SA* drove home the difference from Corbusier here, with a feature on calculations underlying the design of those seductive biplanes.[72]

The conditions that had produced the architect's 'new social consumer' had also 'freed the architect from being a peacemaker in irreconcilable conflicts of interest', operating (if only in self-defence) behind closed doors. By the 'method of functional creativity' the Constructivists aspired to make design 'a unified organic process'. Having a 'single clear aim', the task could be 'hammered out logically . . . from first priorities to second . . . from skeleton to envelope, from inside to out, as a conscious process from beginning to end'.[73] Such a process would be open to scrutiny of its data and decisionmaking, and thus publicly accountable. It would be a collective act of 'construction' as the public and specialists contributed their components, and much of *SA*'s campaigning was directed at stimulating that participation. The architect's specialism however, was the synthesis: the *konstruktsiia*.

The main rules for that process of *konstruktsiia* had already been worked out. They are only outlined at this stage of Ginzburg's writing but the Constructivists' view of what should be primary in design, and what secondary, is clearly indicated by the ordering of stages within their 'logical process'. In this second paper of 1926, Ginzburg insisted that 'spatial parameters, their dimensions and interconnections are the first function of the brief'; and 'the spatial organisation is the starting point of the design and the place to which the main thrust must be directed'. Then secondly, the architect must establish the appropriate building materials and method of construction 'as functions of the basic spatial solution'. Thirdly, he must order the 'external interrelationships of spatial elements'. 'The grouping of the architectural masses, their rhythms and proportions will derive naturally from the first half of his activity: they are a function of the material envelopes and inner volumes he had "constructed".' Finally, he will give form to individual components and elements: to apertures, overhangs etc 'all on the basis of calculations or other types of consideration within the brief'. In this linear process, 'one task leads logically from another'. The architect 'is freed from the handed-down models of the past' and is 'forced to seek artistic expressiveness in that which is most important and necessary'. If the resulting architecture is currently 'ascetic', that is not the result of the process, merely of 'youth' in both the builders and the new life they are building. New systems of compositional principles will develop from the typical spatial patterns of the new problems themselves.[74]

Ginzburg's categories of 'general' and 'particular unknowns' correspond to today's 'state' and 'decision variables'. Gan and the First Working Group had established a role for the former category within the design process, but the mapping of Ginzburg's classification onto their concepts of *tektonika, faktura* and *konstruktsiia* is not exact. The notion of *konstruktsiia* had been absorbed as the premise of their whole approach; that is clear. The concept of *faktura* lay beneath all references to materials and 'appropriate' building methods in Ginzburg's 'second stage', and in his fourth, but more as an assumed rigour of analysis than as an explicit operation. Notions of an 'expressive' relationship between materials and their spatial possibilities stretched back to Tatlin. The complex 'geological' concept of *tektonika* as a synthesis of deep political and technological 'restructurings', is largely subsumed within Ginzburg's category of 'general unknowns', but technological elements of the concept, in particular, also permeate the rest. Gan's 'three new disciplines' had constituted a first redefinition of the 'whole' design problem in their expanded, Marxist-materialist context, but it was crude. In moving from Gan's 'general system' towards a 'method', the architects had articulated the intuitive categories into something approaching real tools.

In his next two papers Ginzburg elaborated certain ideas and introduced others. In 'The functional method and form', published later in 1926, he established a role within his four-stage process for those issues of visual psychology and of 'economy of perceptual energy' being explored by ASNOVA under Ladovsky and Krinsky.[75] From within earlier Constructivist thinking he took up the question of how form should relate to an evolving content. Gan had spoken in general terms; Ginzburg was now explicit. The Constructivist must 'calculate correctly' the complex overlapping relations between old and new within 'the dialectical development of life' at any given time. Then 'the functional method of thinking must always take as the precondition of its material forms not the areas of backwardness, but the landmarks of the new way of life and advanced technology'.[76] How he should take the new way-of-life as his starting point, and why, were the most important topics of his next paper, 'Aims in contemporary architecture', published early the following year.

Here two of the most powerful ideas in earlier Constructivist writing come together. Developing his own 'two-stage analogy' with the machine, and harnessing it to Gan's vision of spatial organisation as a catalytic force in social change, Ginzburg formulated the concept which henceforth became central to all his colleagues' propagandising and design work, the concept of 'the social condenser'.

Out of the basic analogy he identified in *Style and Epoch*, Ginzburg develops the two concepts of the 'scheme of equipment' and the 'flow diagram', which will be the tools for establishing the 'first spatial diagram of the building' in the first stage of the method. Here we see the first signs of that focus upon the form-generating role of movement which would lead to their arguments for compactness, in the middle twenties, and then conversely for a complete dispersion of settlement, at the end of the decade.[77] The 'scheme of equipment' is conceived as a description of the hardware involved in each of the myriad specialised and identifiable events within a building. In machine terms, these are the components of its specialised sub-assemblies. The 'flow diagram' describes the multiple human movements between them, which correspond to the conveyor belts of the factory or the drives of a complex machine. Henry Ford in his autobiography had described achieving great spatial economies in his production lines through rationalisations of this kind: plainly, he reasons, such economies must be equally accessible to the architects of a building. 'For Palladio in the Villa Rotunda' or the pre-Revolutionary palace 'accommodating only the mazurka or the polonaise', functions were not distinguishable said Ginzburg, always enjoying the historical example. 'With building in a socialist country' however, 'the difference is basic, and one of principle.'[78]

The influence of Russia's Taylorist movement for the 'Scientific Organisation of Work' (NOT) is certainly also strong here. It is not clear when the Constructivists first learnt of the Germans' use of such ideas in building design; probably not by 1925-6 when they started formalising their method, but in 1927 they used material from Bruno Taut and others as illustrations to their articles.[79] They also noted that Frank Lloyd Wright's houses were models of economic movement.[80] Eclectic or not in its origins, the status and role which OSA accorded to the resulting 'basic spatial diagram' was uniquely defined by Ginzburg's conception of their period as 'doubly constructive'. It constituted an empirical solution of a socially and technically new brief, in the fresh, creative 'flowering' stage of a new era. Within Ginzburg's historical schema such a 'spatial diagram' already outlined one of the 'characteristic plastic types for the epoch'. With the materialist's view of the power of organised matter, these embodiments of advanced 'landmarks' in social evolution were the architect's most important contribution to Soviet revolutionary objectives. Low-voltage activity and a weak consciousness would be focused through the circuits of these 'social condensers' into high-voltage catalysts of

change, in the habits and attitudes of the mass population. This contribution to the act of 'social construction' was OSA's mission as architects; it was their methodological objective that identified them as Constructivists.

Constructivism as a method of laboratory and teaching work
The last column of Diagram 1 shows how directly these arguments developed into the fuller procedures of the Constructivists' 'method of laboratory and teaching work', described in Ginzburg's paper of 1927 and detailed in Diagram 2.

In its logic the process is unchanged; under new numbering, a '4th object' reasserts the *faktura* concept in a concern with industrial production processes.

Most importantly, though, it has finally re-embraced that first category of 'laboratory work' pioneered and developed in teaching by Rodchenko to be, in Gan's words, 'a system for producing forms'. Rodchenko believed that the designer must be 'constrained to assemble forms according to laws'; must be able to make 'all possible combinations, of diverse systems, kinds and applications' through understanding the fundamentals of formal 'construction'.[81] In Ginzburg's new '3rd object' Rodchenko's 'rules' have been aggregated into 'types of transformations', whose logic will ensure that the clarity, consistency and flexibility of response to be achieved through the rest of the method, are matched in the logic of an architect's formal vocabulary.

These grammars and disciplines of formal construction were the essential prerequisite if the architect was to respond with perfect fluency to new social briefs, to handle the logical evolution of his own design solutions, and to refine those solutions to the point of perfect formal and stylistic coherence. 'Constructivism never admits the fixing of forms' writes Ginzburg, in a remark that reminds us of the continuity represented by Deconstruction.[82]

> Form is an unknown, 'x', which has always to be evaluated anew by the architect. We have therefore to study not just the elements of architecture, but the methods of transformation of those elements, to understand how changes in the brief must affect the form.

'Three points are vital here', he stresses:

> that this method of formal transformations be understood as an essential component of the architect's working tools; that this transformation process is never just an aesthetic one but involves reorganisation of the working, constructive elements of the building; and that what we are changing is the material object itself, but that this is done in the context of its essential purpose and of its perception by the building user.[83]

This is the point at which the particular concerns of the Leningrad architect Iakov Chernikhov engage with the larger programme of the Moscow-based Constructivist architects' group, OSA. OSA had its own local branch in Leningrad, as it did in several other major Soviet cities. The Leningrad group was lead by Alexander Nikolsky, and contributed actively to the journal *SA* and to its exhibition in 1927, as well as executing some good buildings, but it was not particularly significant for theoretical contributions. Chernikhov had nothing to do with this group. Professionally he was a relative loner, though always surrounded by numerous passionately devoted students who were also his assistants in preparation and execution of his abstract and architectural 'constructions' on paper. His theory of the role of the machine as the proper inspiration and logical paradigm of contemporary architecture was independently derived. Influenced though it may have been by contemporaneous work, it is a self-sufficient argument, and whilst his numerous books generally presuppose some larger 'model' of the design process outside his own special topic, he does not refer to it very often or very explicitly. On the other hand, Chernikhov's whole training programme was premised upon the value of what the Moscovites called 'laboratory work', and he pursued this problem of 'the method of formal transformations' and the possible 'organisations of the building's working, constructive elements', at a level of detail, energy and rigour far greater than was achieved, amidst their other concerns, by the members of OSA.[84]

Synthesising formal and theoretical principles derived variously from Suprematism and from mechanical engineering, Chernikhov produced an analysis and programme aimed even more exclusively than the Moscovites' work, at architectural training. In this formal area, in particular, the two programmes match very closely. Ginzburg's list of the 'types of transformation' to be mastered is almost identical to Chernikhov's list of 'the fundamentals of constructivism' in the second part of *The Construction of Architectural and Machine Forms*, where he says:

> The fundamental elements of constructivism consist of all the various possible unions of elements which go to make up a structure. The following formal relationships of elements must therefore be recognised as the basic principles of constructivism: a) Insertion b) Clamping c) Twisting d) Embracing e) Mounting f) Bending g) Coupling h) Piercing, and so on. All these fundamental relationships are in essence simple, but they can create complex combinations which amaze us by the refinement and richness of the shapes they produce. As a supplement to these

the pursuit of a 'new' architecture inspired by the machine. As he wrote in *Fundamentals*, 'We must ask the general question as to which factors in contemporary technology and our modern way of life have the power to determine the character of the new architecture?' The answer lay in 'the multiple principles and properties of engineering.'[87] Though he does not deploy the mathematical vocabulary, his approach to achieving this aim is the same. 'The replacement of outdated forms in architecture can only be achieved' says Chernikhov, 'through a radical reconstruction of the basic architectural means and devices. The elements of that new architecture will emerge as a result of the limitless varying of the abstract (non-objective) forms which are at architecture's disposal.'[88] Though he does not use the phrase 'laboratory work', the function of abstraction in this process is perfectly clear, and again the concept is identical to that which emerges in the Moscow Constructivists' teaching via Rodchenko.

> With the help of so-called non-objective elements we have the possibility for creating a series of the most fantastic formal constructions which are not initially constrained by any direct practical application, but in return possess properties which make them available for real and direct application in the future. Having been trained through the development of multiple series

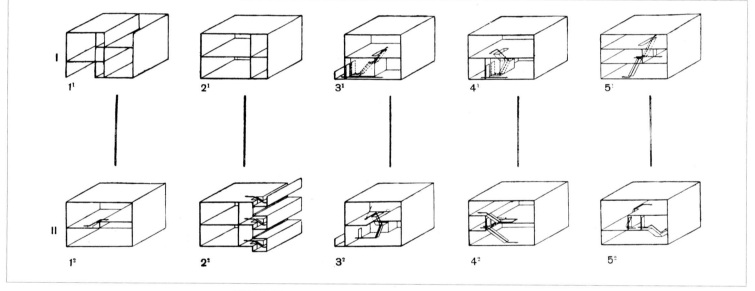

FURTHER DEVELOPMENTS OF THEIR NEW 'SPATIAL TYPES' AT STROIKOM

essentially static relationships there is the possibility of a dynamic element. Knowledge of these fundamentals of formal construction greatly helps in the elucidation of the essence of constructivism, but it is not enough to be familiar with the forms themselves. Complete familiarity with the principles underlying them is essential. One must study the insertion of one element into another with all the possible individual variations and combinations. Training, practice and innate flair play no small part in this, and exactly the same approach must be applied to study of all the other fundamental elements.[85]

The theory and programme which Chernikhov expounds in that book, and in the preceding *Fundamentals of Contemporary Architecture*, present this 'approach' in exhaustive detail, from its starting point in the simplest exercises of linear construction through to the fully developed fictional building complexes which form the 'fantasies'. 'This approach requires that there be specific, clearly defined tasks set as examples' he says, 'which clarify in detail the essence of the specific formal constructive problem we are studying thereby.'[86] The illustrations to all his books are just that: solutions to clearly defined tasks of formal construction or composition.

Chernikhov was as dedicated as the Constructivist group proper to

of constructive structures and through designing multiple diverse combinations, we shall be fully equipped for the moment when a completely new and original formal solution is required of us in the future.[89]

As he wrote here in *The Construction of Architectural and Machine Forms*, by this rigorous training in the generation of architectural 'fictions', or *fantazii*, 'our inventive capacities will be developed to their full potential.' Or as he put it in *Architectural Fantasies*, the aspiration is to develop 'the ability of the individual in question to imagine different forms in all their possible interrelations and combinations'.[90]

Herein of course lies the value of his analyses and his grammars in an age that can now generate 'all possible interrelations and combinations' of its selected formal vocabularies automatically, with new technology, and can exploit the ruthlessly clear logic of relations which he codified to make different, but equally lucid, relational statements.

For the sake of history, however, it should be recorded that this complementarity of Chernikhov's work to their own was not admitted (even if it was perceived), by the Constructivists. The work's reception manifestly suffered from the delay which separated the development of his ideas from their publication. By 1930 when his first major architectural treatise came out, the modernist groups in Soviet architecture were already embattled against the growing opposition. Moreover that first book, *Fundamentals of Contemporary Architecture*, being as much concerned with architectural expression as with pure formal construction, was not the best exemplar of the complementary relationship (not that these were years for vaunting the 'machine' inspiration of architecture either). Thus the review of Chernikhov's *Fundamentals* in *SA* was dismissive. 'Our architecture has long ago outlived the "symbolic" formalism of Iakov Chernikhov', wrote Khiger. 'If this book had appeared in 1921-1922, when symbolism was flowering here, and we were concerned with the 'dynamic' in all its forms and diversity . . . it might perhaps have played a certain role.'[91] In the historical perspective, however, Chernikhov's work on the formal principles of a Constructive architecture represents an important elaboration of the general theory in areas where the Constructivists themselves have not left us records of anything so exhaustive.

'The application of mathematical methods'
In the paper preceding his full exposition of 'Constructivism as a method', Ginzburg had recognised that 'the whole Soviet community

mulae. So too did the 'transrational' poet Khlebnikov, close colleague at one stage of Tatlin, who expounded the idea of a complex periodicity in Russian revolutionary events that was capable of precise mathematical formulation.[93] Most advanced for its time in the archiectural world, however, was the Constructivist group's work on optimising the parameters of their 'spatial prototypes' by quantitative methods.

All their design work involved minimising the lengths of flow diagrams. Underlying the well-known apartment types 'A-F', which Ginzburg and others developed for the Russian Building Committee, STROIKOM, lay very interesting work on the static parameters of spatial organisations produced when the apartment units are linked by circulation systems to form whole buildings. More complex interactions of 'flow' factors were the focus of their mathematical arguments with Garden City adherents, on the relative economic and human merits of 'extensive or intensive' residential development. However, as one young founder-member of OSA pointed out in his VKhUTEMAS final diploma thesis, while these limited and essentially technical studies gave 'undeniably useful results', they were still 'considering requirements too much in isolation'.[94] They did not tackle the problem of synthesis. Ginzburg's conspicuous silence on the nature of the

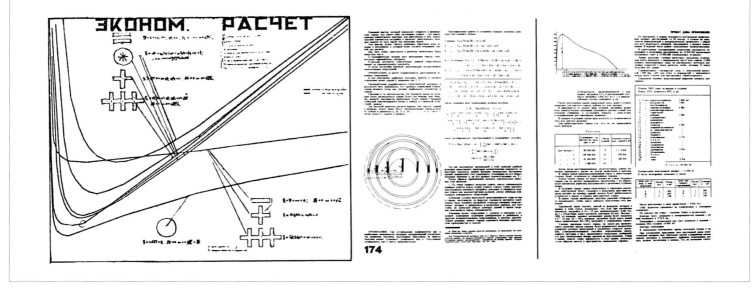

L TO R: KRASIL'NIKOV ANALYSES EVACUATION TIME AND BUILDING SURFACE FOR HIS PLAN FORMS; HIS CALCULATIONS TO MAXIMISE BUILT VOLUME ON A GIVEN CITY AREA

must be drawn into solving the task' which that 'functional method' outlined. The task which it defined was 'not within the powers of the single architect or even a collective of architects'.[92] The exhaustive precision to which they aspired also demanded bodies of data and research that were decades beyond the Soviet Union's horizon at that time. All the same, some remarkable work was done in broaching these topics, and in particular in mathematicising them.

Working with leading structural engineers, for example, they themselves explored the relative economics of various new structural systems. Using the latest foreign data and research they advanced building science aspects. On lighting issues, they made pioneering studies of the relationships between colour and working efficiency; between fenestration and illumination patterns. This work is published in their journal and elsewhere.

The passion for number has to be seen in the context of injunctions to quantified precision which rang through all the Soviet state campaigns of that time for rationalisation and efficiency, in social as well as economic and industrial fields. At the same time, however, there are interesting echoes here of early Constructivism's links with avant-garde literary circles. Formalist critics such as Shklovsky delighted to express semantic and structural relations in quasi-mathematical for-

'reassembly' process in the '5th object' of the functional method made it all too clear that this Nikolai Krasil'nikov was right. Here in the very heart of the architect's province, any question of 'a scientific . . . replacement for the habitual intuitive-graphic method of designing [had] hardly been broached'.[95] In his diploma and a joint paper with fellow-student Lidiia Komarova, Krasil'nikov 'tried to open up this question . . . to creep towards . . . a mathematical-graphic method' of solving it.[96]

Krasil'nikov believed that 'A scientific theory of the design of form is possible through the dialectical method of thinking by the application of mathematical methods of analysis; that is, by analysis which uses the infinitesimal concepts underlying analytical geometry and the differential and integral calculus, and the theories of probability and mathematical statistics.'[97] His thesis was devoted to demonstrating how these techniques could be used to optimise 'the actual form of the building' in terms of 'the material resources for constructing and running it'; 'amortisation and repairs'; 'the time spent by people in all kinds of movement'; 'amortisation of the health of the individual'; which was a function of 'sanitary-technical and psychological factors'; the extent to which 'conditions in particular parts of it favour the maximum "productivity" of mental or physical work, and of leisure'.

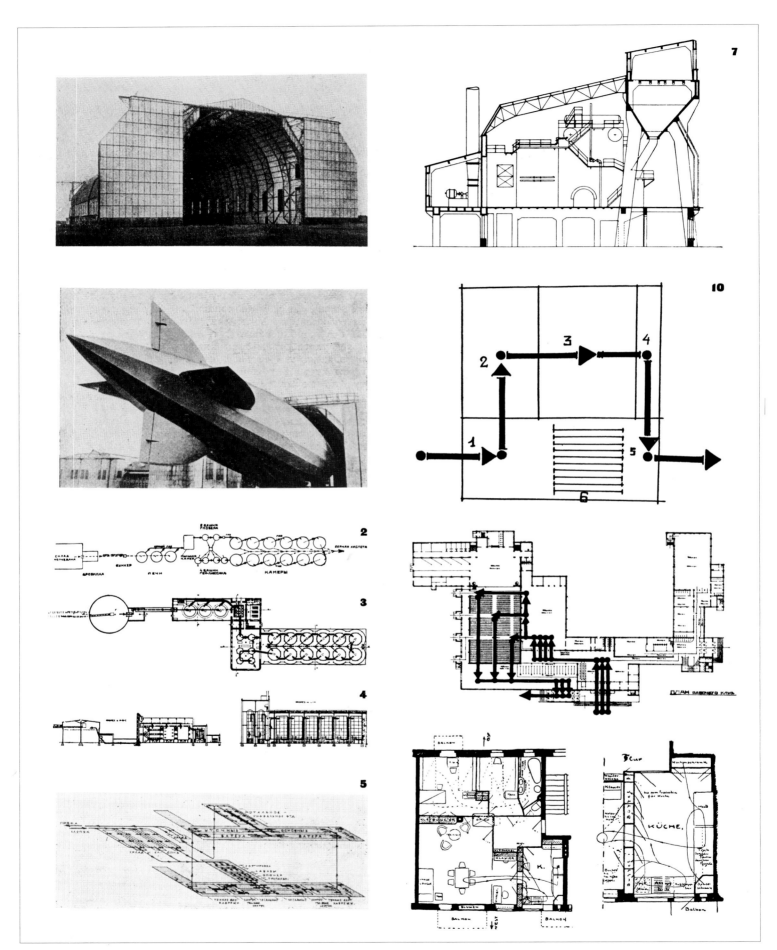

FLOW DIAGRAM AND SCHEME OF EQUIPMENT DERIVED FROM GINZBURG'S ANALOGY BETWEEN BUILDING FOR 'MACHINES' AND BUILDING FOR 'PEOPLE', FROM *SA* 1927 NO. 1

KRASIL'NIKOV AND KOMAROVA, THIRD AND FOURTH FROM L, WITH LEONIDOV, BELOW KOMAROVA AND OTHER STUDENTS

His particular objective was 'the building form which diverges least from the maxima or minima of each of these factors' whilst also achieving 'the maximum cubic volume of building on a given site area'. At the planning scale, he then optimised 'conditions of daylighting, exposure to wind, and ventilation of the whole administrative complex, and links between this building and other parts of the town'.[98] The detailed mathematics are inappropriate here: I have translated the whole paper elsewhere.[99] Some illustrations indicate the flavour. It is clear that the group as a whole were using their mathematics to the limit, as SA published one graph whose strange change of gradient immediately attracts the mathematical eye – and in fact results from a mistake when Krasil'nikov evaluated his quite complex formulae.

As architecture, his circular town of skyscraper office-blocks was somewhat traditionally conceived, but his concern was with method. His attempt to include factors which Savchenko would call 'properties', as well as 'parameters', was important. His procedure for optimising, however, remained linear. He established the best spatial configurations 'in relation to each of these factors individually'. He still started from the optimal flow diagram – albeit one now defined in greater detail, and probabilistically – and compared that to other optima by inspection, in a pre-established order of priorities. Thus far he had not moved beyond the linear *konstruktsiia* of the functional method under which he had been taught.

Krasil'nikov recognised that, as he did the primitiveness of his techniques by the standards of 'higher mathematics', even then. In the subsequent paper with Komarova he recognised that this was still essentially the age-old process whereby the architect examines a series of discreet, alternative forms 'and divines empirically . . . the most successful combinations of those variants he has put to the test'. Under the title 'A method of investigating the generation of building form' they declared 'Our aim must be to advance this process in order to make possible an objective scientific assessment of *all* the possible

variants available to the designer.'[100]

It was the conceptual step embodied in that '*all* ' which was historically important. Since Rodchenko first spoke of 'showing the designer how he may assemble all possible constructions', the idea had remained a chimera to them.

From the premise that 'the form of any body is a function of many variables', Krasil'nikov and Komarova argued that a dialectical process takes place in which even purely quantitative changes in the brief lead to a qualitatively different form, and the 'correct' form emerges from a resolution of competing or conflicting demands. 'A continuous sequence of variants therefore exists.' This concept is quite different from the series of discreet, alternative forms. With two examples, they outlined a mathematical procedure 'for finding the most advantageous possible dimensions' of a given spatial organisation in terms of 'cost, for a given form of construction'. It involved 'drawing up equations' describing 'costs of a specific form of any one part of the building in relation to all different forms of each other part. These equations would produce 'a series of cost curves. These we can build up into a surface, or system of curves in space, which will give us the position of minimum cost.'[101] In their list of 'all the requirements' for which they would establish were included all the organisational, material, environmental and social factors contained in Krasil'nikov's earlier list of building's five measures of 'cost-effectiveness, in the very broadest sense'. These in turn embraced the whole 'first object' of the functional method, from structural questions through to 'the flow diagrams and schemes of equipment, always remembering sanitary and hygiene factors such as daylighting'. This clear mathematical formulation of the concept of a multi-dimensional solution 'surface' seems to be unique in the architectural context for its time. It was to be about four decades before automated data-processing techniques emerged, and any architects started handling the enormous computational operations involved in an integrated, multi-variate optimisation of this kind.

With his realistic understanding of engineering, Ginzburg's 'functional method' was an almost literal response to the observation injunction in Bukharin and Preobrazhenskii's *ABC of communism*, of 1919, that 'Marx's chief instruction to his followers was that they should study life as it actually is... precisely after the manner in which we might study a machine.'[102] In its *konstruktsiia*, his whole, essentially linear process was also rooted in a mechanical analogy. With their grasp of mathematics, Krasil'nikov and Komarova sought to indicate the ultimate implications for architecture of a remark from Engels' *Dialectics and Natural Science*, and the almost identical one from Lenin which headed their papers, that 'In order to really know an object, it is necessary to comprehend, to study, all aspects of it: all its internal and external connectivities.' With this concept they brought the functional method several stages closer to later concepts of systems theory, and to later techniques for solving such multi-variate problems. The same two, canonical , ideas had lain behind the early Constructivists' redefinition of design as a function of '*tektonika, faktura* and *konstruktsiia*', but whilst the content and interrelationships of these three 'disciplines' remained ill-defined, their's was a very general model.

As a group, the Constructivist architects refuted charges of trying 'to eliminate the aesthetic emotion'. They were merely seeking to recognise that 'the character of it has changed under the influence of changed conditions of life, new economic priorities and new technology'.[103] Nor, Ginzburg insisted, did 'the functional method of thinking in any way eliminate the extremely complex tasks of architectural form-making'; 'it merely establishes a framework of procedures for that process.'[104]

Notes

1 *Sovremennaia arkhitektura (SA)*, 1828, no 6 p 170.
2 M Ginzburg, 'Konstruktivizm kak metod laboratornoi i pedagogicheskoi raboty', SA, 1927, no 6 pp 160-6.
3 M R Savchenko, 'The Nature and Methods of Applied Research in Architecture', *Environment and Planning B*, 1980, vol 7 no 1 pp 31-46.
4 *ibid*, p 39.
5 V S Naginskaia, *Avtomatizatsiia arkhitekturno-stroitel' nogo proektirovaniia*, Moscow, 1979, p 63.
6 C Cooke, 'Form is a function, "x" : the development of the Constructivist architects' design method', *Architectural Design*, 5/6, 1983, pp 34-49, especially pp 47-48.
7 These connections are further discussed in the second half of my article 'Images or Intelligence?' in this volume.
8 M Ginzburg, 'Tselevaia ustanovka v sovremennoi arkhitekture', *SA*, 1927, no 1 pp 4-10.
9 N Krasil'nikov, 'Problemy sovremennoi arkhitektury', *SA*, 1928, no 6 pp 170-6.
10 In *SA* 1926 no 1 he speaks of a 'metod funktsional' nogo tvorchestva', in no 4 he speaks of 'metod funktsional'nogo myshleniia' though the article is entitled 'Funktsional'nyi metod', and through 1927 onwards that phrase appears generally.
11 Ginzburg, 'Konstruktivizm kak metod', p 60.
12 As note 6.
13 As note 11.
14 M Ginzburg, 'Konstruktivizm v arkhitekture', *SA*, 1928, no 5 pp 143-5.
15 John Milner, *Vladimir Tatlin and the Russian Avant-Garde*, Yale, 1983, pp 151-80.
16 Lecture, 1 May 1969, Cambridge; a version published in: P Coe & M Reading *Lubetkin and Tecton*, London & Bristol, 1981, pp191-9
17 T Anderson, *Vladimir Tatlin*, Stockholm, 1968: S Bann, ed, *The Tradition of Constructivism*, London, 1974, pp11-14: J Bowlt, ed., *Russian Art of the Avant-Garde: Theory and Criticism 1902-1932*, New York, 1976, pp 205-6.
18 S O Khan-Magomedov, *Rodchenko*, London, 1986. On formation of the First Working Group of Constructivists, see pp 90-94. On debate about *kompozitsiia* and *konstruksiia*, see pp 83-89; accompanying visual material will be found in A Z Rudenstine, ed, *Russian Avant-Garde Art: The George Costakis Collection*, London, 1981, pp 110-127: 'The INKhUK Portfolio'.
19 There is confusion relative to archival sources here, but the essential text is that which appears as 'The programme of the Productivist Group' in Bann, The Tradition, pp18-20, also in N Gabo, *Gabo*, London 1957.
20 Aleksei Gan, *Konstrukivizm*, Tver, 1922.
21 Bann, The Tradition, pp 32-42; Bowlt, *Russian Art*, pp 214-225.
22 Gan, *Konstruktivizm*, pp 20; 53.
23 *ibid*, p 55.
24 *ibid*, p 61.
25 *ibid*, p 61-2.
26 *ibid*, p 62.
27 *ibid*, p 65.
28 cf D Elliot, ed, *Alexander Rodchenko*, Oxford 1979, p 46.
29 Gan, *Konstruktivizm*, p 64.
30 *ibid*, p 53.
31 *ibid*, p 63.
32 *ibid*, p 63.
33 *ibid*, p 64.
34 He discusses this in M Ginzburg, *Stil' i epokha*, Moscow 1924, pp 9, 10.
35 *Sredi kollektsionerov*, articles in 1921, nos 11-12; 1922, nos 1, 3, 7-8.
36 *Arkhitektura*, monthly of MAO; only 2 issues published: 1923, nos 1-2; 3-4.
37 VI Semionov, 'Ocherednye adachi', *Arkhitektura*, 1923 no 1-2 pp 28-30.
38 Ot Redaktsii, 'Estetika sovremennosti', *Arhitektura*, 1923, no 1-2, pp 3-6.
39 N T Savel'eva, 'Organizatsiia nauk ob arkhitekture v gosudarstvennoi akademii khudozhestvennykh nauk', in A A Strigalev, ed, *Problemy istorii sovetskoi arkhitetury: sbornik*, Moscow 1983, pp 48-56; also Bowlt, *Russian Art*, pp 196-8.
40 Savl'eva, 'Organizatsiia', p 53.
41 Ginzburg, *Stil' i epokha*.
42 I V Kokkinaki, 'K voprosu o vzaimosviazakh sovetskogo i zarubezhynkh arkhitektorov v 1920-1930-e gody', in *Voprosy sovetskogo izobrazitel'nogo iskusstva i arkhitektury*, Moscow 1976 pp 350-82. She also mentions that Lunarcharskii published a translation of 'Les yeux qui ne voient pas' in the journal he edited, *Khudozhestvennyi trud*, 1923, no 2, pp 25-8.
43 Edgar Norvert, 'Obzor zhurnalov', *Arkhitektura*, 1923 no 1-2 pp 42-44.
44 Moisei Ginzburg *Style and Epoch*, introduced and translated by Anotole Senkevitch, Jr, MIT, Cambridge, 1982.
45 Gan, *Konstruktivizm*, p 54.
46 A V Kuznetsov, 'Arkhitektura i zhelezobeton', *Zodchii*, 1915, no 19-20; version of a speech to the 5th Congress of Russian Architects, Moscow, 1913.
47 Ginzburg, *Stil' i epokha*, p 13.
48 *ibid*, pp 13-20.
49 *ibid*, pp 119-20; on the cultural dimension he refers to Russian editions of N Danilevsky's *Russia and Europe*, 1888, and O Spengler's *Der Untergang des Abendlandes*, 1923.
50 Ginzburg, *Stil' i epokha*, pp 78, 73-89, 121.
51 *ibid*, p 121.
52 *ibid*, p 111.
53 *ibid*, p 121.
54 *ibid*, p 94.
55 *ibid*, p 93.
56 *ibid*, p 131.
57 *ibid*, pp 128-9.
58 *ibid*, p 132.
59 *ibid*, p 133.
60 *ibid*, p 134.
61 Prof V K Karpovich, review of Ginzburg's *Stil' i epokha*, in *Kommunal'noe khoziaistvo*, 1925, no 2, pp 167-8.
62 A E Rozenburg, *Filosofia arkhitektury*, Leningrad, 1923.
63 Edgar Norvert, 'Priemy planirovki', in V N Semionov, ed, *Udeshevlenie stroitel'stva*, Moscow, 1925, pp 15-26.
64 'SA privetstvuet vykhod "ASNOVA", *SA*, 1926, no 2, p 59.
The best source on the Rationalists theories, ASNOVA's work and research is: Anatole Senkevitch Jr, 'Aspects of spatial form and perceptual psychology in Soviet architecture of the 1920s',
VIA-6, MIT, Cambridge, 1983, pp 79-115.
65 On the founding of OSA see: V E Khazanova, comp, *Iz istorii sovetskoi arkhitektury 1926-32: dokumenty i materialy*, Moscow 1970, pp 65-8.

66 M Ginzburg, 'Itogi i perspektivy', *SA*, 4-5, pp 112-118; this article appears in English translation in: T & CF Benton, eds, *Form and Function: A Source Book for the History of Modern Architecture and Design 1890-1930*, London, 1975, pp 156-160. On the Deconstruction discussion, see my article 'Images or Intelligence?' in the present volume.

67 M Ginzburg, 'Novye metody arkhitekturnogo myshleniia', *SA* 1926 no 1 pp 1-4.

68 M Ginzburg, 'Funktsional'nyi metod i forma', *SA*, 1926, no 4 p 89, and Ginzburg, 'Tselevaia ustanovka'.

69 Ginzburg, *Stil' i epokha*, later parts of Chapter 1.

70 Ginzburg, 'Novye metody', p 1.

71 *ibid*, p 2.

72 K Akashev, 'Forma samoleta i metody ego proektirovaniia', *SA*, 1926, no 3, pp 65-6.

73 Ginzburg, 'Novye metody', pp 1, 3.

74 *ibid*, pp 3-4.

75 Ginzburg, 'Funktsional'nyi metod', p 89.

76 *ibid*, p 89.

77 See latter part of my article 'The Russian precursors' in the present volume, and for more detail: C Cooke, 'A Russian Constructivism and the city', *UIA Journal of Architectural Theory and Criticism'* London, Vol 1, no 1 (19860, pp 16-25, or 'Russian responses to the Garden City Idea', *Architectural Review*, June 1978, pp 353-363.

78 Ginzburg, 'Tselevaia ustanovka', p 6.

79 *ibid*, p6.

80 *ibid*, p7.

81 Gan, *Konstruktivizm*, p 65.

82 See latter part of my article 'Images or Intelligence?' in the present volume.

83 Ginzburg, 'Konstruktivizm kak metod', p 165.

84 On Chernikhov and his work see: C Cooke, *Chernikhov: Fantasy and Construction. Iakov Chernikhov's Approach to Architectural Design*, Architectural Design Profile no 55, London, 1984, also selected material on Chernikhov's theories in the present volume.

85 Iakov Chernikhov, *Konstruktsiia arkhitekturnyka i mashinykh form*, Leningrad, 1931, pp 93-96.

86 Iakov Chernikhov, *Osnovy sovremennoi arkhitektury*, Leningrad 1931

(Second edition), p 49; this book was first published in 1930 in a slightly different format.

87 Chernikhov, *Osnovy* (1931 edition), pp 58-59.

88 *ibid*, p 51.

89 Chernikhov, *Konstruktsiia*, p 139.

90 Iakov Chernikhov, *Arkhitekturnye fantasii: 101 kompozitsii v kraskakh*, Leningrad, 1933, p 43.

91 R Khiger, review in *SA* 1930 no 3, inside back cover.

92 Ginzburg, 'Tselevaia ustanovka', p 10.

93 The critical usage derives from the observations in Shklovsky's seminal paper 'Art as a Device', of 1917, on the manner in which conventional language-use already operates through such simplification and abstraction. He discusses how 'habituation' in the use of language leads to 'the process of "algebrisation", the over automisation of an object [which] permits the greatest economy of perceptive effort' and how 'this characteristic of thought not only suggests the method of algebra but even prompts the choice of symbols ie, letters, especially initial letters'. The full paper appears in English under the title 'Art as Technique' in: L T Lemon & M J Reis, eds, *Russian Formalist Criticism: Four Essays*, Nebraska-London, 1965, pp 3-24. Khlebnikov's theories of the periodicity of events appeared in his two lithographed broadsheets *Vestnik Velimira Khlebnikova* (*Velimir Khlebnikov's Herald*), Moscow 1922, 1923.

94 Krasil'nikov, 'Problemy'.

95 *ibid*, p 170.

96 *ibid*, and N Krasil'nikov and L Komarova, 'Metod issledovaniia formobrazo-vaniia', *SA* 1929 no 55 pp 1834-4.

97 Krasil'nikov, 'Problemy', p 170.

98 *ibid*, pp 174-5.

99 Catherine Cooke, 'Nikolai Krasil'nikov's Quantitative Approach to Architectural Design: An Early Example', *Environment and Planning B*, 1975, vol 2 no 1 pp 3-20.

100 Krasil'nikov and Komarova, 'Metod', p 183.

101 *ibid*, pp 183-4.

102 N Bukharin and E Preobrazhenskii, *Azbuka kommunisma*, 1919; Penguin 1969, pp 66-7.

103 Ginzburg, *stil' i epokha*, p 122.

104 Ginzburg, 'Funktsional'nyi metod', p 89.

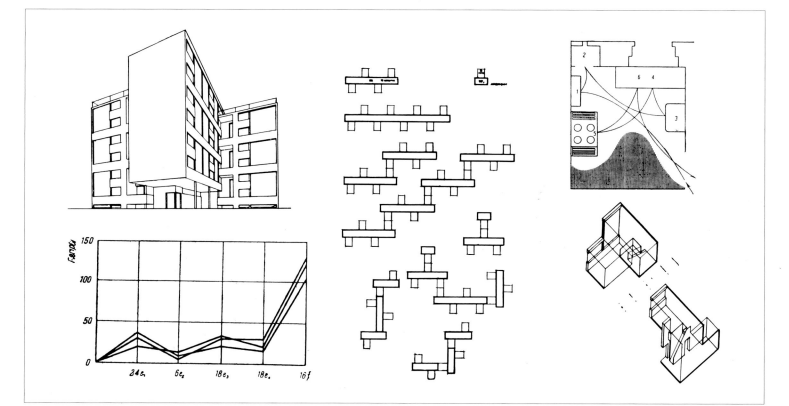

INTERLOCKING VOLUMES AND PLAN VARIANTS FROM VLADIMIROV'S SCHEME FOR OSA'S 'COMRADELY COMPETITION' FOR NEW HOUSING TYPES AND OSA WORKS

CONSTRUCTIVIST THEMES

Рис. 7. Центрофуга для отжимки белья.

THE MACHINE AS SYMBOL AND REALITY OF A TRANSFORMATION OF DAILY LIFE
BELOW: Poster from the Taylorist campaign of the Institute for Scientific Organisation of Work Processes: 'Let us take the storm of the Revolution in Russia and unite it to the pulse of life in America and do our work like a chronometer'.
LEFT: Visual feature from the Constructivist architecture journal *SA* showing, TOP: 'The pleasures of the individual household' compared with BOTTOM: 'The rationalised laundry in collective housing'.
ABOVE: 'Centrifuge for drying linen' to lighten the burdens of women workers in housing cooperatives etc, from the municipal affairs periodical *Stroitel' stvo Moskvy*, 1927.

The machine

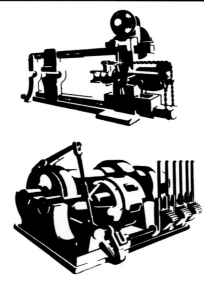

'THE MIND IS LIKE AN INTRICATE ENGINE'
ABOVE: Three studies of the assemblage of mechanisms in machines, and RIGHT: analysis of the principles demonstrated by various machine components, a 'complex form with inherently constructive characteristics' and 'example of the screw as a constructive principle', all by Iakov Chernikhov, mid-twenties, reproduced from *The Construction of Architectural and Machine Forms*.

CONSTRUCTIVE PRINCIPLES AS BASIS OF BUILDING DESIGN:
BELOW RIGHT: Abstract studies of the two 'constructive principles' of 'Embracing' and 'Mounting', with BELOW: design for 'a functional building' incorporating these principles (Chernikhov: *Construction of Architectural and Machine Forms*).

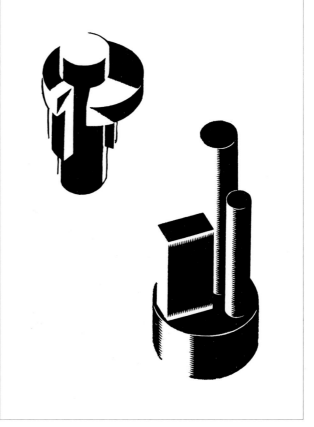

Art as laboratory work for design: 1

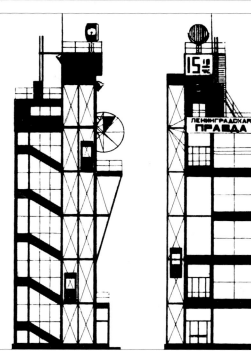

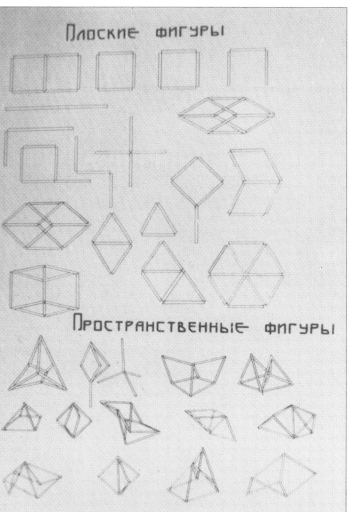

АРМАТУРА

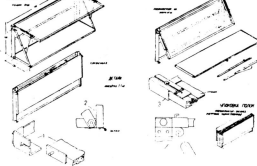

Складная полка для книг. Разложенная полка представляет из себя четырехугольную конструкцию со стеклом, которая вставляется в нишу. Каждая полка привинчивается по вертикали ниши и последняя может быть сплошь заполнена ими. Система построения видна из чертежей. Стекло при пользовании полкой вдвигается в желобки, расположенные в верхней части конструкции. Проект конструктив. Галактионова. Москва. Высшие Художествен. Государств. Мастерские. Металлический факультет.

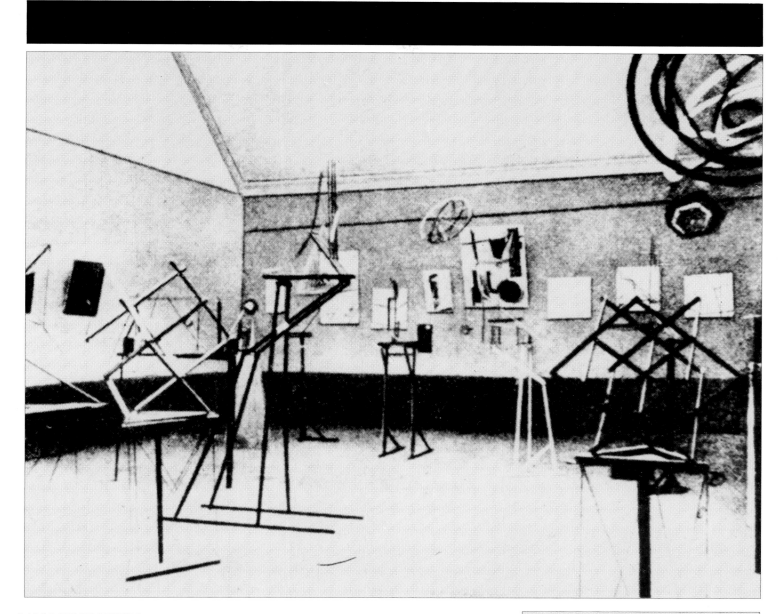

LABORATORY WORK 1

Vladimir Tatlin was the first to propound the idea that purely artistic 'investigations into the use of material itself and what this leads to in movement, tension and the relation between them' could serve as 'laboratory scale' research for 'creating a new world and . . . our new way of life' (Tatlin, 'The work ahead of us', 1919).

ABOVE CENTRE: Tatlin, Counter-relief: metal bars, sheet and timber, c1914, and LEFT: One of the first Constructivist building projects, by Tatlin's early colleagues the Vesnin brothers: steel-framed building for the paper *Leningrad Pravda*.

LABORATORY WORK 2: FRAME STRUCTURES

Artistic research 1:

FAR LEFT: Liubov Popova, 'formovariatory' ['form-variants'], 1921-1922. 'Planar figures' (top) and 'spatial figures' (below) from standard rods, used as 'devices for determining the capacities of students for work on spatial constructions'.

Artistic research 2:

ABOVE RIGHT: Early 'spatial constructions' by Rodchenko, Stenbergs and other members of the emerging Constructivist group, shown at an exhibition of the Young Artists group Obmokhu, Moscow, April 1921.

Technical studies:

LEFT: Self-assembly system of book shelving in glass and metal angle, 'by Constructivist Galaktionov, student [of Rodchenko] in the Metal-working Faculty of the Vkhutemas school' c1925.

Functional applications 1: Furniture

RIGHT: Stand for a street vendor of cigarettes and writing requisites designed for Mosselprom by Alexei Gan, 1922. Published in SA, with the comment that 'streets need functional equipment just as people's homes do. Constructivism must also devote its attention to identifying and fulfilling needs here.'

Арматура улицы. Складной станок с лотком для уличной торговли папиросами или бумагой и писчебумажными принадлежностями. Улица так же как и квартира требует рабочей обстановки. Конструктивизм и сюда должен направить свое внимание и наблюдать за бытом улицы. Станок сделал в 1922 году Алексей Ган, для Моссельпрома.

Art as laboratory work for design: 2

Functional applications 2: Rooms
ABOVE: Design for a complete room: workers' club interior by Rodchenko and students shown in Melnikov's Soviet Pavilion at the Paris International exhibition 1925; BELOW: chess table (reconstructions, Moscow 1980, photo Cooke).

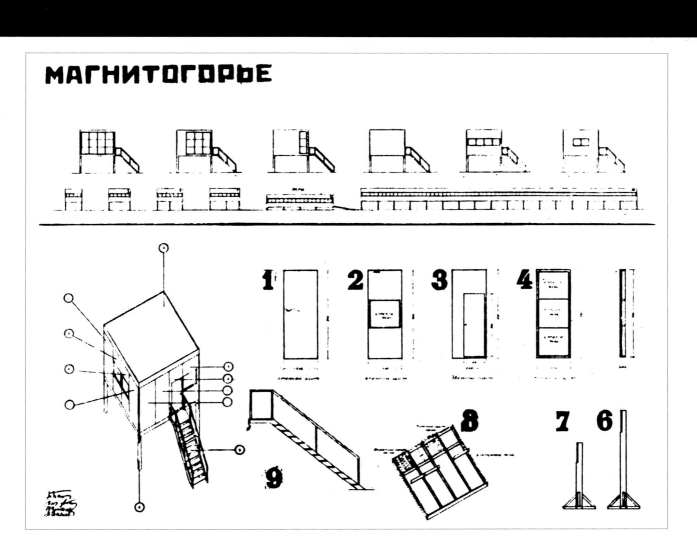

МАГНИТОГОРЬЕ

Functional applications 3: Buildings
Constructivist architects' designs for prefabricated housing building systems using locally available materials, 1929-30, TOP: for the new socialist industrial city of Magnitogorsk, by Barshch, Vladimirov and others, and BELOW: for Green City near Moscow, by Ginzburg and Barshch.

Art as laboratory work for design: 3

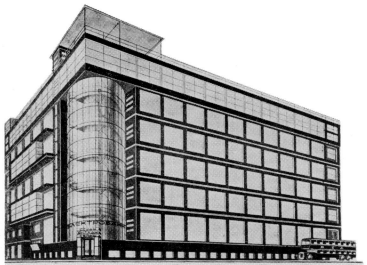

LABORATORY WORK 3: VOLUMES

ABOVE: Volumetric composition of circular and rectangular forms by a student of the Vkhutemas Basic Course under Babichev, early 20s, and ABOVE RIGHT: Design for a new type of school, by Leningrad Constructivist leader Alexander Nikolski.

RIGHT: demonstration of the principle of 'penetration of forms' with cylindrical and rectangular volumes, from Chernikhov (model Cooke, 1983), and CENTRE RIGHT: Ilia Golosov, design for the Electrobank building, Moscow, 1926.

BELOW: Student at work drawing the three-dimensional model of a 'construction' which he has made. From Chernikhov's *Ornament*.

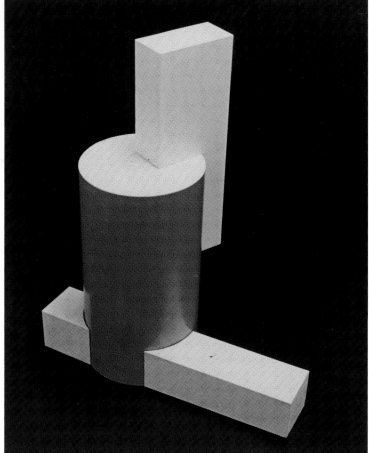

LABORATORY WORK 4: VOLUMES
ABOVE: Chernikhov: an exercise in 'penetration' with rectangular volumes (model
Cooke, 1983), and BELOW: G Vegman, 1927, design for a theatre in Samarkand:
axonometric view, from *SA*.

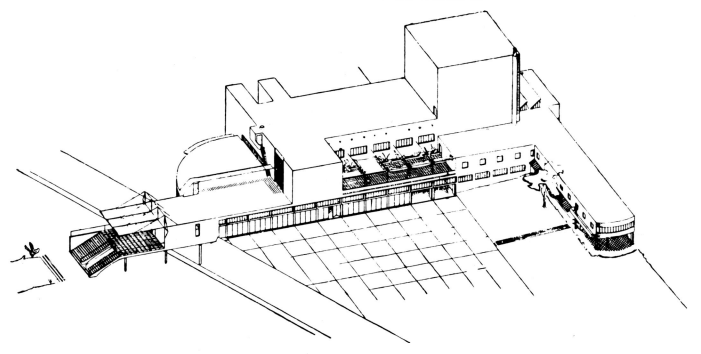

Art as laboratory work for design: 4

LABORATORY WORK 5: PLANES
ABOVE: Chernikhov: exercise in 'penetration' of rectangular planes (model Cooke, 1983), and BELOW: project for new 'transitional' (half-collectivised) housing by G Vegman: entry for the Constructivist group's internal competition, 1927, from *SA*.

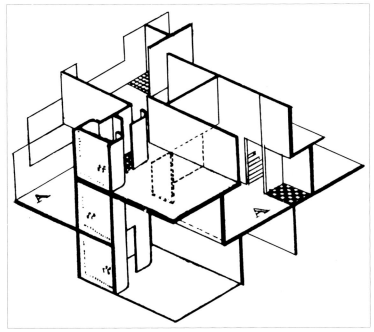

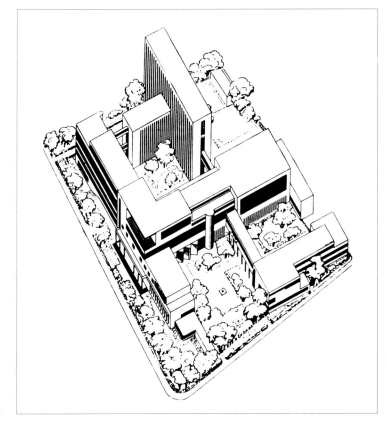

LABORATORY WORK 6: SIMILAR RECTILINEAR ELEMENTS

ABOVE: Rodchenko, 1924, 'spatial construction' demonstrating multiple use of the pinwheel principle: reconstruction by his grandson A Lavrentiev, Moscow 1980 (photo Cooke).

CENTRE LEFT: a selection of Rodchenko's 'spatial constructions', 1924, exploring the combinatorial possibilities of different kinds of joint between rectangular volumes of various proportions. Such constructions became a central part of his design teaching.

BELOW LEFT: a similar geometry used in the Vesnin brothers' competition design for the Lenin Library complex, Moscow, 1927; axonometric view.

TOP LEFT & BELOW: Moisei Ginzburg's entry for the Constructivists' housing competition, 1927.

The elements of form

CHERNIKHOV

The role of Iakov Chernikhov in developing formal aspects of Constructivism is described on pp. 35-37. The following pages present selected material on his teaching programme. A full exposition, from which this is adapted, may be found in my AD Profile Chernikhov: Fantasy & Construction. Presented here are the one- and two-dimensional sections of 'The elements of form'. Parts of the topic 'Types of constructive joint' appear in the exhibition photograph on page*. Further topics cover wider aspects of his thinking, and the use of colour. The rigour of these underlying formal disciplines is reflected in the strength and clarity of resultant building forms, and explains their continuing use as design reference points in work concerned with formal structure.   CC

The rhythm of masses, the rhythm of separate treatments of plane and surface, are comprehended by us and find their expression to the extent that we train our eyes to feel the realtionships of all these elements one to another.[1]

This question must be approached methodically and stated in a clearly formulated system.[2] ▬

Studying the fundamentals of architecture in sequential order of increasing complexity, we must so arrange all the material that the student of architecture can understand the real harmonies of a building as he gradually develops through the planar and spatial tasks.

This approach requires that there be specific, defined tasks which are problems and examples clarifying in detail the essence of each type in turn.[3] ▬▬

Before examining the principles of the organisation of space, we examine the elements which are necessary in non-objective structures.[4] Each of these basic, very simple elements require thorough study of their own characteristics, and if one wishes to unite them, one must also acquire appropriate knowledge of the essential methods of constructive design.[5] ▬

Elements on a plane
1 Linear elements

The line occupies the absolutely dominating position in all representation of form. It is therefore the starting point of all compositional work.
Lines may be classified in the following ways:

● according to the <u>movement characteristics</u> of the point generating the line, as:
  – straight
  – broken
  – curved
  – mixed

● according to <u>direction</u>, as:
  – vertical
  – horizontal
  – diagonal

● according to <u>position</u>, as:
  – lines on a plane
  – lines in space

● according to <u>degree of regularity</u>, as:
  – right
  – non-right

● according to <u>relationship</u> with other lines:
  – intersecting
  – non-intersecting
  – intertwining

They may also create <u>figures or part-figures</u> of 2 kinds: closed & non-closed

All these possible combinations of lines are available for expressing our ideas in a series of constructions.
Different technical devices, such a changes of thickness of the lines, are available for reinforcing a composition's constructiveness.

Constructive compositions of STRAIGHT lines are the first stage.
We may thus set exercises of the following kinds:

1 To assemble a harmonious combination of straight lines of different thicknesses in order to get a linear coloured ornament.

2 To compile a bunch of coloured straight lines with a dynamic slope.

3 From a series of vertical straight line lines to assemble an image which would produce the impression of a building.

4 The same, out of horizontal lines alone.

5 The same, out of vertical and horizontal lines.

BROKEN LINES are the next stage.
1 To compile from broken lines a bi-coloured ornament.
2 To compile from broken lines a bi-coloured figure drawing[6]

The third stage will be constructive compositions of CURVED LINES.

These have particular interest as a result of the abundance of compositional possibilities and the infinite diversity of possible curves, paying attention always to the smoothness of an elastic curve, which is the source of its dynamic properties. Their wide usefulness derives from the way these dynamic properties enhance the constructiveness of our constructions.

Curved lines may be classified into the following types:
– nodal
– spiral
– circular
– mixed with smooth transitions
– complex curves

Each has its own characteristics and its specific artistic value. The spiral, for example, is especially popular for its essential tension.

Through smoothly conjugated lines and complex curves we can construct the most intricate compositions which communicate our thoughts with intense visual conviction.[7]

Exercises might be:

1 To assemble from curved lines a dynamic ornament.

2 To assemble from curved lines a static drawing.

3 To build from curved lines a coloured spatial composition.

We may do the same with MIXED LINES.[8]

2 Planar elements

A composition is planar when all its elements are distributed on one plane surface. Planar compositions offer study material for many series of exercises. The simplest employ the so-called 'right' figures, the rectangle, square, triangle and circle.[9]

The non-right figures are infinitely numerous and potentially complex in construction. They may be classed by external configuration as follows:
- rectilinear figures containing right angles
- rectilinear figures with no right angles
- curvilinear figures
- figures of mixed outline

Rectilinear configurations have the greatest interest for us, since they have the widest range of practical applications, but those with acute and obtuse angles have less potential to make constructive combinations.
Curvilinear figures sometimes completely resist constructive combination. We cannot constructively link 2 circles, though curvilinear planes are sometimes capable of constructively embracing each other.

Figures of mixed outline can permit rich constructive combinations.[10]

Constructive combinations of PLANES ON A PLANE are the threshold of many practical tasks. The preliminary solution of a building plan requires constructions of this order. Planar figures, being diverse in their configurations, have equally diverse roles in design.[11]
Exercises may include:

1 A coloured harmonic combination of horizontal and vertical planes.

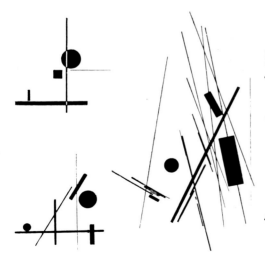

2 Composition of various transparent figures.

3 Treatment of the plane with an asymmetrical figure.

4 A complex coloured composition of a right-angled type with linear elements and a circle.

5 A bi-coloured composition from a series of elements.

STRAIGHT LINE figures.
BROKEN LINES.
CURVED LINES.

MIXED figures.

6 COMPLEX NON-RIGHT POLYGONAL figures with different colourations.

7 SYMMETRICAL COMPOSITION FROM A SERIES OF RECTANGLES producing an impression of a building.

THE SAME, but ASYMMETRICAL.

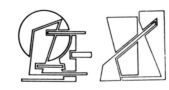

8 THE SAME, but NON-RECTANGULAR.

9 COMBINATIONS OF NON-RIGHT figures[12]

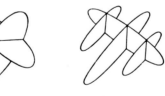

Elements in space
1 Planes

A BENT SINGLE PLANES ▬ are the first step towards a formal solution of the simplest spatial concepts. Artistic expressiveness depends on the designer's particular solution.

B SPATIAL COMBINATIONS OF SEVERAL PLANES ▬ are among the most valuable exercises for developing spatial thinking and familiarity with constructive principles. The basic principles of constructivism are encountered here. The intersection of one plane with another produces a constructive joint. Proportional relationships and relative angles determine the quality of overall constructive spatial combinations. The configuration of the component planes may be as follows:

1 Rightangled rectilinear planes are the most useful for building constructive combinations through the diversity of manipulation possible with these universal forms in the area of buildings and machines. The matching of one rectangular plane to another requires little force, and the compositions may have powerful dynamics of a horizontal, vertical, an inclined or mixed type.

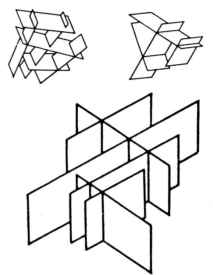

2 Polygonal rectilinear planes rarely offer useful constructive combinations.

3 Ovals and circles are more attractive, but their specific external configurations limit the constructive possibilities available.

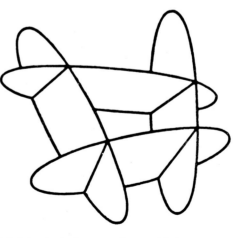

4 Indeterminate forms can be assembled constructively, but they have no interest for us, being very rarely encountered in practice.[13]

2 Surfaces

We are only considering here
SURFACES OF ROTATION ▆▆▆▆▆▆▆▆

These can be classified according to how they
are generated, into:
- cylindrical
- conical
- spherical
- complex

These surfaces may then acquire more complex
forms through the effects of external forces,
to become:
- spiral
- screw-threaded
- double-curved
- complexly curved

All these may be divided into right surfaces
of rotation which are those formed from
rotation around some single axis, and the
non-right, which are obtained without rotation
about any such axes.

Surfaces of rotation are important in
constructive compositions and especially
valuable when they help manifest dynamic
properties. Component parts of any complex
surface of rotation may be:
- of identical direction in both horizontal and
  vertical
- in an intersecting condition, in both a
  straightlined and acute angled combination
- of mixed combination
- of parallel direction
- of spiral form

When surfaces of rotation form constructive
combinations with planes, extremely distinctive
solutions of high artistic value may result.
Such intersections could be:
- at a right angle, at an obtuse angle, or in
  the direction of movement of the surface.

Constructions of this type can prove difficult
for beginners.[1]

Surfaces of rotation can be
closed or non-closed. We are
for the most part using
cylindrical surfaces, and to a
lesser degree spherical and
conical ones. Successfully
assembled cylindrical surfaces
in an overall composition give
in one case the impresion of
an imposing structure, in
another case that of profound
spatiality, and in a third,
that of beautiful perspective.

From the simplest compositions of surfaces of
rotation we can move by means of fragmentation
to a more complex one, where the combination of
elements is an expressive and harmonious
fantasy.[2]

3 Volumes

SIMPLE RECTILINEAR BODIES ▆▆▆▆▆▆

We generate the different classes of bodies in
this category through altering the relationship
of the three dimensions of a parallelipiped:
its height, width and depth. In changing these
relationships, we obtain all possible varieties,
starting from the cube, with the relationship

NOTES for page 26: 1. C-pp.169-172 2. F-p.36
3. C-pp.173-82, FIGURES of solids from a recent
Soviet textbook on drawing for architecture students, 1983. 4. F-pp.37,36, FIGURES from F-. 5.
C-pp.183-6, FIGURE from C-. ▆▆▆▆▆▆

1:1:1, through to the long plate, with a
relationship of say 1:5:25.

With constructive combinations of these bodies
we approach central questions of the field we
are examining. Whether the insertion of one
body into another, or the embracing of one body
by another, we have in all cases a directly
constructive combination, capable of serving as
a prototype of real and actual solutions.

We must examine the characteristic compositions
obtained by combining different classes of
these bodies as follows:
1 compositions of PLATES
2 compositions of BARS
3 compositions of CUBES
4 compositions of PARALLELIPIPEDS
   (4-edged prisms)
5 compositions of various RECTILINEAR
   NON-RIGHT BODIES & POLYGONAL PRISMS

1 PLATES

We shall define as a plate
that extended parallelipiped
in which the relationship of
its sides is larger than
1:8:12.

Plates may be combined constructively as
follows:
- in one vertical direction, with a mutual
  perpendicular cross-section
- in one horizontal direction with a common
  perpendicular cross-section
- in a vertical and horizontal combination
- in an inclined mutual intersection
- in a mixed combination

2 BARS

Bars can be classified
according to their cross-
section into two types:
square & rectangular

Compositions of bars tend to give us products
of a latticed and fragmented character, and
are conspicuous for their sharp delineation.

3 CUBES

The cube is one of the most
difficult bodies for forming
combinations. As the simplest
of all geometrical bodies it is
the most complete of forms, but
only dull to the non-inquisit-
ive. In its actual form reside
certain symbolic principles
operating on our psychology,
according to the cube's placing
and scale, but the cube must
always be executed with a
absolute precision and
accuracy to preserve its value.

4 FOUR-EDGED PRISM

The prism, in distinction from
the cube, possesses exceptional
characteristics combining
easily with other prismatic
bodies. Study of the
constructive fundamentals is
best solved through the building up of complexes of prisms.
Prismatic combinations are
found in vast multiplicity of
products of human creativity.
Their 'compatibility' makes
them central to constructive
education.

5 NON-RIGHT RECTILINEAR BODIES
AND POLYGONAL PRISMS

These do not have great
interst for study and design.
Only rarely do they produce an
interesting constructive form.[3]

THE STUDY OF VOLUMES MUST BEGIN ▆▆▆▆▆▆
with the combinations of these simplest forms in
order to gradually develop in the student a
feeling of mass and weight in volumes. He will
move on to combinations of 2 or 3 right bodies,
and then finally to static volumetric tasks in
constructive composition. ▆▆▆▆▆▆

COMPLEX RECTILINEAR BODIES ▆▆▆▆▆▆

These are of 2 kinds, right & non-right.
By a suitably scaled combination of the
selected parts and the development of rhythm
amongst them, we obtain the weight and
expressiveness we desire.

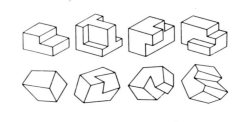

BODIES OF ROTATION ▆▆▆▆▆▆

The most widespread of these is the cylinder;
less common are the cone and the sphere. Such
forms may be complex to design in reality,
and their constructive combination requires
thorough knowledge of their own laws and rules.
All are most commonly encountered in machine
building, but widespread also in architecture,
where the most fantastic of our concepts can
find its answer in constructive combinations.

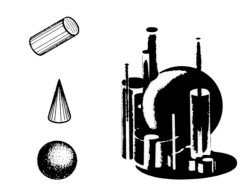

COMPLEX CURVILINEAR BODIES ▆▆▆▆▆▆

These too find their main application in machine
building at present. These strongly dynamic
bodies are difficult to classify because most
have multiple and diverse characteristics
depending upon the point of view.

Complex curved bodies have a special place in
the general system of constructive design,
because they make it possible to dispense with
penetration of one body by another. Embracing,
clamping and coupling by these curved bodies
can produce highly complex interconnections,
unifying constructive and dynamic principles.

Types of constructive joint

THE FUNDAMENTALS OF CONSTRUCTIVISM consist of all the various possible kinds of unions by which elements can be combined into a structure.

Each kind of union is in essence simple, but especially when supplemented by dynamics, they can create complex combinations which amaze us with the refinement and richness of their forms.[1]

COMPLETE FAMILIARITY WITH THESE PRINCIPLES is essential. One must study thoroughly the insertion of one element into another with ALL THE POSSIBLE INDIVIDUAL VARIATIONS. Exactly this approach must be applied to all the other fundamentals. Training, skill and flair play no small part in this.[2]

Penetration

This is the simplest way of combining bodies, where one is inserted into another.[3]

Non-right solids

Cylindrical forms

Right solids

Curvilinear forms

NOTES for page 27: 1. C-p.93 2. C-p.96 3. C-p. 42. FIGURES all from C-.

Embracing

This is more complicated, because there is a whole range of possible types of embrace, from that involving simple rectilinear forms to that with complex, curvilinear ones.[1]

Clamping

Clamping is when one body seems to be seized by another which grips it. The clamp is extremely characteristic of machines and mechanical engineering, and by its very nature comes in a variety of forms.[2]

Integration

This occurs when a single, integral body is given a shape which in itself demonstrates graphically constructive principles. This is a relatively rare phenomenon, and in all instances of an integral constructive form we are dealing with a dense mass weight is essential to its constructive properties.[4]

Mounting

This is where a series of volumes comes together with a single crowning body which unites all the rest. This mounting can be designed to take place from above, from below and even from the side of the group.[3]

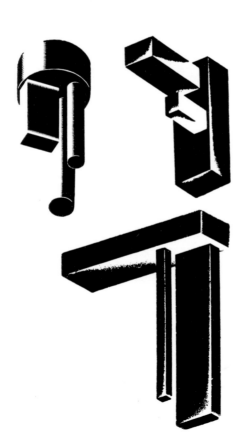

Interlacing

Interlacing is a synthesis of dynamic and constructive properties, and it has particularly strong visual and psychological effects. Interlaced forms divide into 2 categories, the first comprises uncomplicated bodies, where both constructive and dynamic properties are inherent in the very movement of the body's own masses.[5]

COMPLEX INTERLACING: the second category comprises those objects which represent a more complex system of many elements.[5]

INTERLACING
OF SOFT
MATERIALS

Coupling

Coupling differs from the other constructive joints in that it allows for free combinations without any tight or direct linking of parts, and each body remains a separate element whilst participating in the constructive unity. The example of coupling is the chain.

Another kind of coupling is found when two elements are more rigidly constrained into a constant relationship. This if often seen in machinery construction, when coupled parts are encompassed with a clamp or pierced with a bolt.

A third type occurs when elements create a cohesive whole possessing a specific functional rationality, as typically in a machine.[6]

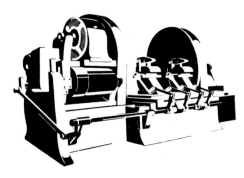

4 Force in constructions

The two concepts of **Force** and **Construction** are inseparably connected.

Construction is inconceivable without the presence of force. They complement each other functionally, but in various different ways.[7]

1 Force expended in the jointing process ▬

Certain forms of constructive joint cannot occur without the application of a specific level of force being applied. Thus, in the COUPLING of parts we exert the LOWEST level of force. The PENETRATION of one element into another requires a SECOND LEVEL of force to be applied. In EMBRACING and the CLAMPING of one part by another we see the THIRD LEVEL of force. ▬

2 Force as the action of weight ▬

Force is present in constructive compositions when we observe the action of weight or heaviness in a specific part of the whole assembled object. ▬

3 The force of influence ▬

This force is measured by the strength of the impression which the constructive product makes upon each of us. The longer that impression remains in our consciousness, the stronger the force of influence. ▬

4 The force of dynamics ▬

The dynamics manifested as movement in a constructive composition represent a subtle but powerful union of complex phenomena, operating in a coordinated way upon our psyche and giving us the possibility to feel a higher form of emotional sensation. ▬

NOTES for pages 28,29: 1.C-p.43 2. C-p.48 3. C-p.44 4. C-pp.44-45 5. C-pp.45-47 6. C-pp.49-51, all FIGURES here from C-. 7. This section from C- pp.133-134 ▬

Constructiveness as a high level of creative energy

Every person is endowed with the feeling for the CONSTRUCTIVE. But that feeling expresses itself in the most diverse ways and in different intensities. ▬▬▬▬▬

There are sudden moments of constructive inspiration, when new solutions and new ideas flow extremely rapidly in our creations. The force of the energy in these valuable moments can be measured only by the real results that follow.[1]

In contrast, there are depressive moments, when we lack any feeling for construction, and when the desire to resolve a problem constructively has atrophied. Then we desire to create more PEACEFUL compositions – compositions that are less demanding to formulate, than a constructive composition. In such cases we enter into the stream of as-it-were 'minimum consumption' of constructive principles, and we ignore the constructive possibilities.
This coincides with a LOWERING OF CREATIVE ENERGY but it can also be an appropriate creative response in certain situations.

It is necessary therefore to recognise the unarguable fact that the act of CONSTRUCTION must be regarded as a complex and powerful experience. ▬▬▬▬▬

On the basis of what has been said above, we can propose the following hierarchy of feelings for the constructive:

1 Higher moments of individual inspiration with its maximum tension.

2 Commonplace, everyday experiences, in accordance with the given requirements and solutions.

3 The depressive condition, as a result of which other approaches to designing ones object will be pursued.

4 An indifferent attitude to the questions of constructivism and as a result an atrophying of the feeling for constructiveness.

5 Absolute non-comprehension of the very nature of constructive principles and, as a result, a complete ignoring of this approach to design in all situations regardless of their characteristics.

Not every task can be solved constructively,▬▬ and we must never ARTIFICIALLY IMPOSE ▬▬▬▬ constructive forms in our creative work. ▬▬▬▬

KEY TO SOURCES IN CHERNIKHOV'S BOOKS: A-The Art of Graphic Representation (1927); F-Fundamentals of Comtemporary Architecture (1930 & 31); C-The Construction of Architectural and Machine Forms (1931); AF-Architectural Fantasies (1933).
SOURCES FOR PRECEDING PAGES: 1: F-p.49; 2. F-p.22; 3. F-p.49; 4. F-p.22; 5. C-p.98; 6.F-p.33; 7. C-pp.160-2; 8. F-p.33; 10. C-pp.163-5; 11. C-pp.162-3; 12. F-pp.33-4; all FIGURES in that section from F- or C-. 13. C-pp.165-9; FIGURES from C-. ▬▬

Classes of constructive solution

The wealth of forms in general and the diversity of possible combinations of different elements make the range of possible constructive solutions infinitely great. This does not at all ease the task of classifying constructions by types, given the lack of precision pervading this whole issue. However, we can classify constructive solutions according to their generally dominating properties. On this basis, we can distinguish the following general types:

1 Amalgamation ▬▬▬▬

ob"edinenie

Amalgamation of forms can occur by bringing together either identical elements, or different variants of the same element.

Amalgamation also includes the case when we receive the impression of a constructive solution simply by skillfully 'putting together' components without making any real constructive connections.

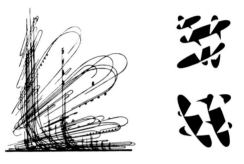

2 Combination ▬▬▬▬

soedinenie

A combination usually comprises elements which can come together without violating each other. In combining one body with another we study the particular characteristics of each, and if there are factors impeding their combination, these will represent a serious obstacle to executing the combination at all. The form and configuration of the elements themselves may provide obstacles. So too may their positions in relation to the surrounding space. In combining one element to another we are pursuing harmony. The very unity of the composition depends upon the fact that no antipathetic elements are present. 'Combination' often requires 'third parties', elements that serve to unify the rest.

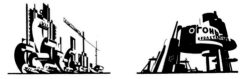

3 Assemblage ▬▬▬▬

sochlenenie

Assemblage can be characterised by the constructive look which finds particular reflection in the machine. The elements maintain their separate identities whilst being grouped into one whole. The principle of assemblage also implies that only a certain combination of specific parts is capable of creating the required solution; the absence of any one part may prevent the task being solved. As a result, the structure of the composition is often visually evident. Each component part in such an assemblage requires careful attention since only the absolute fit of parts is capable of producing the required effect. The designer has to give formal coherence to the parts of an assemblage as well as functional cohesion.

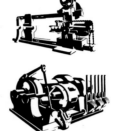

4 Conjugation ▬▬▬▬

sopriazhenie

Conjugation is the phenomenon which permits a transition from one condition of a form to another; or from one variant of a form into another. When the forms are lines, the task is fairly simple, though still interesting. When we conjugate complex objects, the task is both richer and more complicated. The integrity and constructive properties of the composition must be preserved in the transition.

Conjugation of elements is one of the most powerful tools the designer possesses, since it permits him to achieve those complex transformations which his inventive capacity dictates. By conjugation we can move freely from a configuration of one kind to a new configuration of quite another type, moving not only painlessly, but also rationally and meaningfully. The conjugation of elements occupies a large place in the life of every individual in his various forms of creativity, and we must pay it the maximum of attention.

A composition successfully derived by conjugation acquires dynamic properties from the fluency of the transitions.[2]

Functionality and legitimacy

The things that can be unified on the basis of constructive principles may be both material and non-material, but they are always subject to the recording action of our brain by means of SIGHT, HEARING and TOUCH.[1]

Every new construction is a result of a human being's INVESTIGATIONS, and of his requirement to be inventive and creative.[2]

Functionality
funktsional'nost'
means that every aspect of the real forms and their interconnections derives from the actions which have given birth to that form.[3]

Every constructive solution must have a MOTIVE on the basis of which the construction is made[4]

Every constructive composition must fulfill its IDEOLOGY and reflect the TOTALITY of the idea underlying it.[5]

Every construction is a construction ONLY when the unification of those elements in that way can be rationally JUSTIFIED.[6]

The greater the RATIONALITY in a construction, the more valuable it is; in other words, the significance of constructivism lies in its RATIONALITY.[7]

Legitimacy
opravdannost'
in all constructive structures depends upon our being simultaneously able to prove the TRUTH and CORRECTNESS of the chosen solution BY ANALYTICAL MEANS.
The form we have devised is LEGITIMATE to the extent that it is JUSTIFIABLE.[8]

In all design we face the necessity of giving foundations to, and thereby as it were legitimising the construction that we have finally adopted.
We must prove that the construction which we are proposing is correct and fits the case concerned.[9]

SOURCES FOR FACING PAGE: 1: This section from C-pp.128-132. 2: This section from C-pp.108-115. All FIGURES from C-.

SOURCES FOR THIS PAGE: 1: C-p.81; 2. C-p.83; 3. F-p.23; 4. C-p.84; 5. C-p.104; 6. C-p.81; 7. C-p.106; 8. C-p.85-86; 9. C-p.87; 10. F-p.80; 11. F-p.96; 12. F-p.76; 13. F-p.77; 14. Mainly from F-pp.38-39 with elements of AF-pp.58,61.
FIGURES: Lev Tolstoi; Karl Marx; Bolshoi Theatre, Moscow; Fantasy No.28 from AF-.

Harmony: new anti-classical principles

Lev Tolstoi regarded art as that activity through which one person consciously transmits, through certain eternal signs, the feelings he has experienced, and other people are infected by those feelings, which influence their lives. In this definition there is already a clear conception of the great social mission of art. Art socialises human feelings, unifies the vast multitude of consumers of it on the basis of a collaborative living experience, on the basis of the 'infectiousness' of the beautiful.

Equally important to a correct understanding of of the nature of art and the essence of the beautiful are the views developed by Marx, as the first to see art as part of the superstructure of the economic base, and those others who endorsed the materialist analysis of the history of art.[10]

The conception of beauty in our time is not determined by the cost of materials, not by their richness and variety, but by the compositional and constructive appropriateness, or by the expressiveness, level of resolution and formal consistency with which the final object manifests its function and social purpose.[11]

Even an industrial building must attempt to be beautiful, as well as pleasant, convenient, light and joyful.
Any worker can work better amidst the very best combination of surrounding walls and ceilings. Coming to the factory, or leaving it, the worker must perceive an interaction of exterior forms that helps raise his mood, and stimulate him to life, work and creativity.
The enjoyment of beauty will become an inalienable property and condition of existence of the individual.[12]

Thus the architect is required to create an object that answers aesthetic concerns and the requirements of convenience to an identical degree, and gives a clear visual answer to both.[13]

Classical aesthetics as historically developed were based upon:

1 enforced symmetry of structure

2 the rhythm of simple repetition

3 combination of different component elements on universally 'beautiful' principles

The first two of these compositional principles are too partial to serve as a basis for us. We have to look to other sources of formal harmony. Many such principles were present in classical work, but hidden. Their elucidation is amongst the most interesting of our present tasks, the main ones being:

1 free asymmetries in the assembly of the elements on functional principles

2 The minimum use of simple repetitive rhythms and their replacement by the rhythm of dynamic diversified combinations

3 the harmonic interrelationship of the component elements by the subtle proportions of their vertical and horizontal dimensions

4 adjustment of the tonal force of component elements in accordance with the impressions sought of the viewer

5 maximally expressive use of colour effects to manifest the constructive and other characteristics of the planes and surfaces being treated.

These are the rules which must be the basis of the new harmonies.

Through appropriate training in these compositional fundamentals we must nurture in ourselves the most precisely tuned feelings for combining all the component elements of a form.[14]

The harmony of colours

The colour impression produced by a given building may be influenced by:
1 the factural treatment of natural materials, whose diversity can be further enriched by skillful selection of surface treatments;
2 applied colours, such as paints, where an infinite diversity of colour combinations are possible for strengthening the architect's concept;
3 selected combinations of technologically produced materials such as concrete, glass, steel. These are giving the contemporary designer new tools for formal composition and expression and hence creating whole new types of rhythm and harmony.

Different colour combinations produce radically differing effects. Examples show that dark brown, dark red, dark grey and black will produce an impression of a building that is dirty and heavy. They give 'weight' and monumentality, where green, yellow, sky-blue, light grey and white all give a building a cheerful, light and invigorating look. By fragmentation of colours we approach that polychrome decorativeness characteristic of architecture in the East, the Ancient World and the Middle Ages.[1]

We shall not give any recipes for how to combine colour with colour, tone with tone, or different shades of colour with eachother. This would lead to cliched formulae and would devalue the work at its most interesting point.

Sometimes we shall go as far as to say, for example, that such-and-such a composition must be coloured with two hues, or that three should be applied in another. Sometimes we may indeed specify these colours exactly in order gradually to train the pupil in colour composition. When appropriate we may need to use one single paint, ie one single colour, in different strengths, and therefore shades, in order to compose our image. When we require colour to express a 'mood' which the image must convey to the viewer, we shall propose exercises composing the following:
1 a scale of gay tones, ie paint colours;
2 a scale of light colours;
3 a scale of sombre colours;
4 a range of playful colours;
5 a range of dull, greyish colours;
6 a range of pale colours;
7 a range of clear, 'screaming' colours;
8 a range of warm colours;
9 a range of cold colours, and so on.

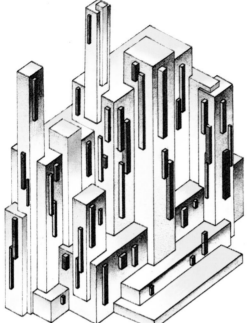

Coloured experimental composition from Chernikhov's series 'Principles of architecture': fantasy on the theme 'City of the East'.

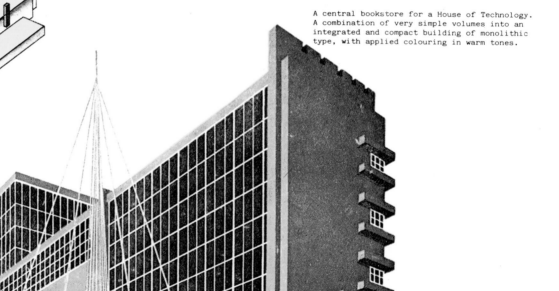

A central bookstore for a House of Technology. A combination of very simple volumes into an integrated and compact building of monolithic type, with applied colouring in warm tones.

Throughout this process we shall colour our
forms in different ways:
a. as overall colour;
b. shaded off from the corners;
c. shaded off from the edges;
d. as a transparent wash;
e. densely and dead;
f. lightly;
g. juicily, and so on.[2]

*SOURCES. 1: F-p.94; 2: A-p.18; Chernikhov's
coloured drawings: L-R: Collection A Chernikhov;
F-No.93; F-No.34; F-No.33. Next two pages, L-R:
top:AF-No.58;AF-No.26;AF-No.10; below:AF-No.13;A
F-No.99;AF-No.70.*

A rigorously constructive and compact combination
of architectural elements of the simplest
volumetric type, forming an industrial building.
Coloured plane by plane in two hues, using the
effect of 'shading off to nothing'.

A compactly constructive building of monolithic
character. A combination of diverse closed and
complete volumes with their main masses clearly
articulated.

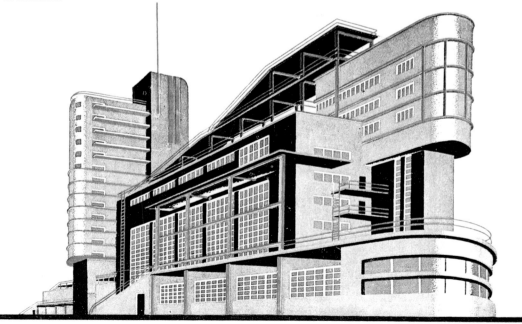

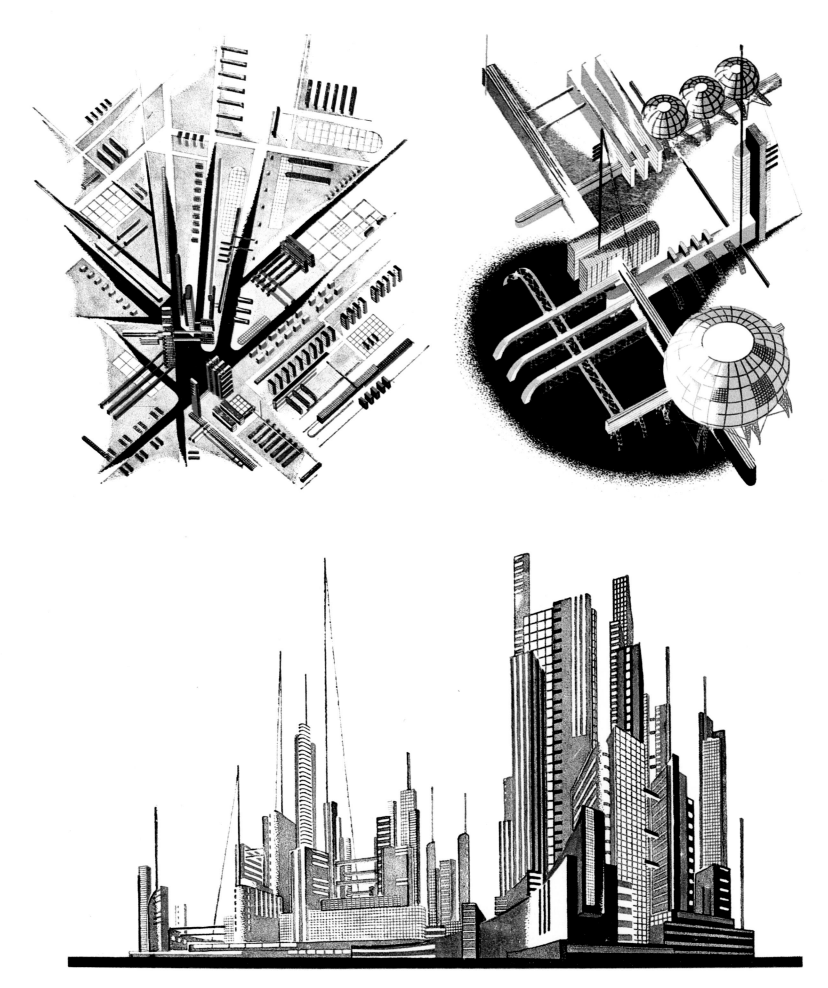

LEONIDOV

Ivan Leonidov's highly individual vision attracted much vitriol from Soviet architectural critics in his time, now documented in Gozak and Leonidov's *Ivan Leonidov: The Complete Works* (London, 1988). As described here on page 26 his fellow Constructivists were well aware of his 'categorical break with the system of volumes' common to the rest of them.

The cause of this difference, and one of the most significant aspects of Leonidov's work, was his perception of the effect which communications technologies would have on the spatial possibilities for human social organisation, and hence on the form and relative locations of buildings.

Five of his most important projects are shown here, exemplifying his use of Suprematist spatial devices to reflect that shift, with extracts from his own commentaries.   CC

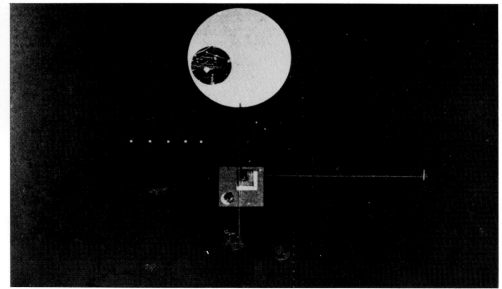

Lenin Institute, 1927

AIM: To answer the needs of contemporary life through maximal use of the possibilities of technology.

THEME: The Lenin Institute is to be a collective centre of knowledge for the USSR, located where the new city is developing, on the Lenin Hills of Moscow.

COMPONENTS: A library of 15 million volumes and 5 reading rooms of 500-1000 seat capacity; large auditoria, a planetarium, research institutes for individual academic work.

MECHANISATION: . . . The automated request from the catalogue room transfers the required book onto the conveyor system and into the appropriate reading room . . . The research institutes, links with the auditoria and reading rooms are provided with a whole series of devices: telephones, radios, and radio representational and reflecting equipment. By this the entire academic staff of the institute can work together simultaneously on a single project.

The connection with Moscow itself is made by an aerial tramway with a central aerodrome for the suspended roadway. The connection with the world is through a powerful radio station.

MATERIALS: Glass, steel, reinforced concrete.

Monument to Columbus, Santo Domingo, 1929

AIM: People of the nations in their millions must be told about the great man of action and his historic role in the development of modern culture.

The monument must act as a condenser of all the achievements of world progress. . . .

MEANS: This aim cannot be reduced to a 'monument' which is bounded by its means of logical impact and its small sphere of influence.

The present day, with its unlimited scientific and technological progress, makes it possible to expand both the aim and the means for realising it at a world scale.

Radio and radio-pictures transmitted at a distance, an air- and sea-port, become condensers of world culture. . . .

DESCRIPTION OF THE MONUMENT: The museum forms the centre of the monument, with memorabilia . . . and Columbus's body . . .

Construction: The large area of the museum is covered in armoured glass. Bearing in mind the conditions of the tropical climate, and the purpose of the museum, a powerful jet of air is released in place of walls, thereby providing the requisite insulation. On hot days, an artificial stream of air also passes over the roof. The chapel is covered by a glass dome surrounded by a spiral ramp which enables it to be seen from every angle.

Radio-base: The base is organised around two 300-metre masts. On the one facing the sea is a lighthouse with a high-voltage arc of one million candle-power. The lighthouse is operated from below, but it is connected to the ground by a lift.

There are a series of radio-laboratories and studios. The base has a two-way link with the world. In open squares and historical museums everywhere, special screens will be set up, onto which the story of Columbus will be transmitted by radio pictures. . . .

Columbus airport: Air links will connect the world. . . .Planes will take off from surfaces that rise up and descend, and there are mooring masts for dirigibles.

To handle the regular service of Columbus flights between Europe and America, a floating air base will be created in mid-Atlantic with all necessary facilities such as hangars, hotels, electricity generating stations, radio stations etc.

The Columbus meteorological station will be the barometer for the world's aerial and maritime communications systems. . . .

The brain of the monument will be the scientific laboratories where its operating plans will be worked out. It will comprise 1) radio, 2) film, 3) observatory, 4) Institute for Interplanetary Communications, whose task is to solve the problems of interplanetary communications by means of the latest achievements of science and technology. . . . 5) a hall for scientific and technological congresses organised by means of radio.

Overall plan: . . . The airport is located on the highest prominence of the site. Below it is the park and Government building [with] airport, museum and park linked by a suspended roadway. . . . In conclusion I consider that only a Columbus Monument system such as I have outlined here can be adequate as a cultural contribution to the history of mankind.

House of Industry, 1929

In our conditions every new building . . . must respond to the new conditions of life. An architect who disregards these conditions is a conservative.

Work is not a regrettable necessity but a sense of purpose in life. Work as a physical and psychological condition must be totally organised.

Features of the old way of organising buildings: confined courtyards, lack of visual escape, pokey rooms, lack of adequate ventilation and light, barrack-like corridors. Absence of any planned organisation. Nervousness, piles, lowered vitality, lowered productivity.

Features of the new way of organising buildings: Organised work, work and physical training exercises, light, air, organised rest and food, heightened vitality.

Organisation of the House of Industry: the departments are grouped according to the characteristics of their work. Each group occupies one floor. Connections are made by telephone and by conveyors. Each floor is divided into the relevant number of work spaces of five square metres each, excluding the passageways between them. There are no partitions. Between the work spaces is greenery. The floor surface is soft, to absorb sound, and so is the ceiling. On one side of the working areas is created a zone for rest and physical-culture exercises. With cabins for lying down; with library, places to get food, which is sent up from below; with showers, swimming pool, little walking areas and running tracks, and areas for receiving visitors. There is every opportunity for regular half-hour and ten-minute breaks, for exercise, a shower, to eat etc.

Light comes from both sides, and in the summer the walls open up. The open views and vistas all contribute to raising the individual's energy and vitality: a healthy leisure and healthy work. . . .

On the roof is a transformable swimming pool (a steel frame covered in resin-coated fabric), a gymnastics field, a running track for mass exercising before and after work. . . .

An intermediary floor is used for a restaurant and for walking in the fresh air. The roof is used for sporting games and leisure. Supplementary accommodation, garages, stores etc are located in the basement. As a result of this organisation we have:

1) raised labour productivity;
2) greater physical health;
3) greater energy and vitality for life;
4) a building of great economic . . . and spatial . . . efficiency.

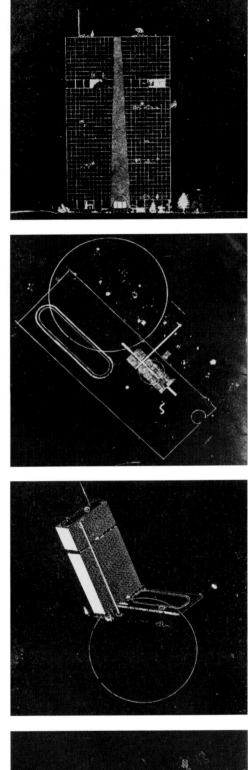

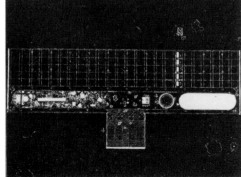

Workers' Club of New Social Type, 1928

Scheme of spatial organisation of cultural services
Interviewer: How is one to account for your use of identical forms for different functions, except by formalist aesthetic considerations?
Leonidov: . . . We are concerned with form as a product of the organisational and functional interdependence of workers' activities and structural factors. It is not the form one should consider and criticise, but the methods of cultural organisation.
Interviewer: If you are against music, what are they to listen to on the radio?
Leonidov: Life.

Commissariat of Heavy Industry, 1934

The foundations of the composition lie . . . in simplicity, severity, harmonious dynamism and a pithiness of content.

DANIEL LIBESKIND, 'NEVER IS THE CENTRE', (MIES VAN DER ROHE MEMORIAL), DETAIL

PART II

THEORY AND PHILOSOPHY

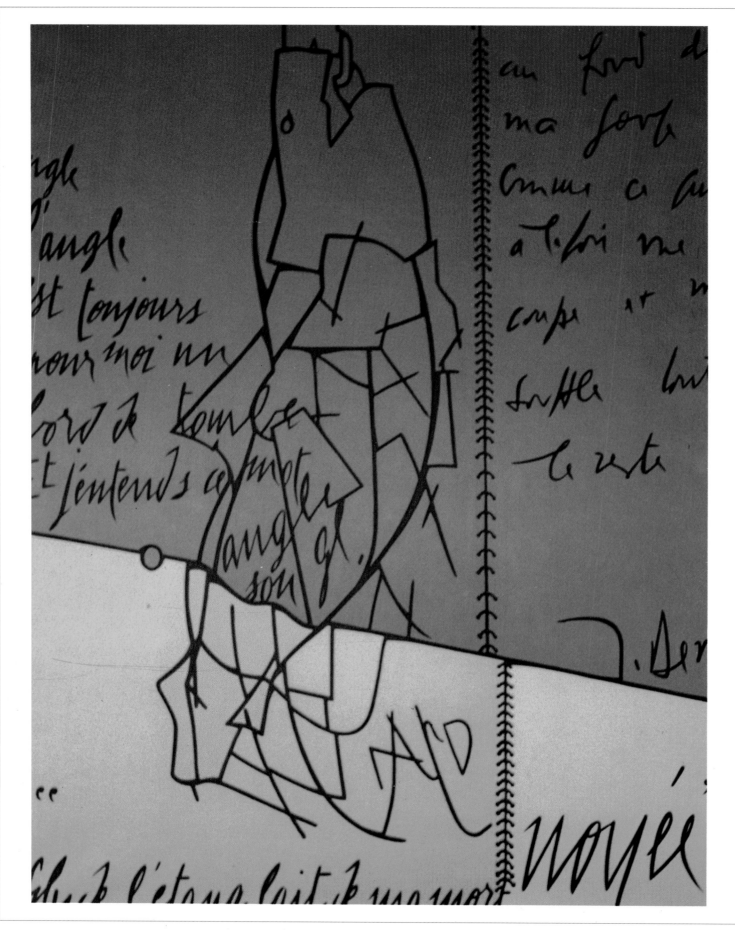

VALERIO ADAMI, *STUDY FOR A DRAWING AFTER* GLAS, 1975

JACQUES DERRIDA
Fifty-Two Aphorisms for a Foreword

1. The aphorism decides, but as much by its substance as by its form, it determines by word play. Even if it speaks of architecture it does not belong to it. That goes without saying and the aphorism which heightens discourse often gives to the trivially obvious the authority of a sentence.

2. One expects the aphorism to pronounce the truth. It prophesises, sometimes vaticinates, proffers that which will be, stops it in advance in a monumental form, certainly, but anarchitecturally: dissociated and a-systemic.

3. If there is a truth of architecture, it appears doubly allergic to the aphorism: essentially it is produced as such, outside of discourse. It concerns an articulated organisation, but a silent articulation.

4. Speaking here of aphorisms, and in an aphorism, one takes a position within the analogy between rhetoric and architecture. It is thus supposed that the problem is resolved and this is one of the problems in the face of which all the texts assembled here, each in their own way, expose themselves to a risk. The ana*logy* between *logos* (logy) and architecture is not an analogy amongst others. Moreover it is not reducible to a single figure of rhetoric. It might be said that the *problem* of analogy will define therefore the space of this book, the opening given to its *project*.

5. A *problem*, the subject of a discussion or the theme of a research project, always outlines, it sketches the outline of a construction. It is often a protective architecture. *Problema*: that which is anticipated or *proposed*, the obstacle, the clothing, the rampart, the ledge, the promontory, the barrier. One always stands both *before* and *behind* the problem.

6. What is a *project* in general? And what is the 'project' in architecture? How is its genealogy, its authority, its politics – in sum its philosophy at work, to be interpreted? If the texts collected in this volume often intersect around these questions, the question will be asked, what can this 'project' signify here, that which is exposed or assembled in a preface, the foreword, the initial outline [*l'avant-projet*] of a book on architecture and philosophy.

7. A text which is presented as the simulacrum of a foreword, a discontinuous series, an archipelago of aphorisms. That would be an intolerable composition in this place, a rhetorical and architectural monster. Demonstrate it. Then read this . . . You will begin perhaps to doubt it.

8. This is a word, a sentence, therefore this is not architecture. But prove it, show your axioms, definitions and postulates.

9. Here is architecture: an unreadable and future [*à venir*] project, a school still unknown, a style to be defined, an uninhabitable space, the invention of new paradigms.

10. *Paradeigma* means 'architectural plan', for example. But 'paradeigma' is also the example. It remains to be seen what happens when one speaks of an architectural paradigm for other spaces, other technologies, arts, and writings. The paradigm as paradigm for any paradigm. On the play on words in architecture – and if the *Witz* is possible there.

11. Architecture does not tolerate the aphorism, it is even said that architecture has always existed as such in the West. Perhaps the conclusion to be drawn from this would be that, being rigorous, an aphorism does not exist. It does not appear, it does not make itself visible in space, nor traverse nor inhabit it. It is not, even if some exist. How does it allow itself to be read? One never enters nor leaves it. It has therefore neither beginning nor end, neither foundation nor finality, neither base nor height, neither inside nor outside. These assertions only make sense on the condition of an analogy between discourse and all the so-called arts of space.

12. This is an aphorism, he says. People will be content simply to cite it.

13. Of the citation: even though it is engaged here according to a singular modality, even though it does not imitate in the manner of a painting or a sculpture which come to represent a model, the architecture of the 'tradition' belongs to the space of *mimesis*. It is traditional, it constitutes the tradition by itself. Despite appearances the 'presence' of an edifice does not refer only to itself. It also repeats, signifies, evokes, convokes, reproduces and cites. It *carries* towards the other and *refers* to itself, it divides even in its *reference*. Of the inverted commas in architecture.

14. There has never been an architecture without 'preface'. The quotation marks signal here the risk of the analogy. An architectural 'preface' includes, amongst other preliminaries, the project or its analogues, the methodology which defines the ways and the procedures, the principle or foundation, axiomatic preambles, the exposition of ends, then the models for the execution of the work, and finally, in the work itself, all the modes of access, the threshold, the door, the entrance hall. But the preface (without quotation marks this time, the preface of a book) must announce the 'architecture' of a work to which it is really difficult to say if, whether or not, it belongs.

15. It is expected of a preface that it describes and justifies the book's composition: why and how it was thus constructed. No preface/prefatory step [*pas de preface*] to a deconstruction. Unless it is an upside down [*à l'envers*] preface.

16. All prefaces are back to front [*à l'envers*]. It presents itself the right way round, as is required, but in its construction, it proceeds back to front. It is processed, as is said of photography and its negatives, from the point of the supposed end or finality: this is a certain conception of the architectural 'project'.

17. Analogy has always proceeded in these two senses, this book demonstrates it; one speaks of the architecture of a book but constructions in stone have often been compared to volumes to be deciphered.

18. The preface is not an institutional phenomenon amongst others. It presents itself as an institution through and through: the institution par excellence.

19. To ask for a preface is to rely on an idea in which the signature and architecture are conjoined: the law of the threshold, the law on the threshold or rather the law as the threshold itself, and the door (an immense tradition, the door 'before the law', the door in the place of the law, the door making the law what it is), the right of entry, the introductions, the titles, the legitimatisation which from the opening of the edifice gives the names, announces, anticipates, introduces, draws a perspective on the whole, sites, foundations, recalls the order of the beginning and the end, from the start to the end, from the *archè* with the *telos* in view.

20. A preface reassembles, links, articulates, anticipates the passages, denies the aphoristic discontinuities. There is a genre forbidden to the preface, it is the aphorism.

21. This is not an aphorism.

22. Le Collège International de Philosophie is duty-bound to give a place to an *encounter*, a thinking encounter, between philosophy and architecture. Not to put them face to face, but in order to think that which has always maintained them together in the most essential of cohabitations. They imply each other according to necessities which are not only attributed to or derived from metaphor or rhetoric in general. (Architectonic, system, foundation, project, etc)

23. Le Collège International de Philosophie is the true preface, the truth of the preface to this encounter and to this book. Its preface is on the right side since in a certain way it does not yet exist. This Collège has been working for the past four years on what it is, it searched for the form of its community, its political model, which perhaps will no longer be political, and therefore its architectural design, which perhaps will no longer be an architecture. But to do this, giving a place to this encounter and to this book, it is supported by the forces of a solid, open, friendly, institution: le Centre de Création Industrielle (CCI). This fact is a *problem*, ie the most generous of 'protection' (see aphorism 5): centre, creation, industry.

24. An authentic aphorism must never refer to another. It is sufficient unto itself, world or monad. But whether one wants it or not, whether one sees it or not, aphorisms interlink here *as* aphorisms, and in number, numbered. Their series yields to an *irreversible* order, in that it is without being architectural. Reader, visitor to work!

25. An aphorism never enjoins. It does not exclaim, it neither orders nor promises. On the contrary it proposes, stops and says what is. A full stop which is not an exclamation mark.

26. Le Collège International de Philosophie took on the task of thinking the institutionality of the institution. And from the start its own, notably in that which connects architecture, the signature and the preface (question of names, titles, project, legitimation, right of access, hierarchies etc). But the strange thing is that it has been able to *create a space for [donner lieu]* such encounters and to a book like this, it is perhaps insofar as it still does not have any space or architectural form of its own. That is due no doubt to the inherited limits of the old politico-institutional space, and to its most tenacious and least avoidable constraints.

27. From its initial outline the College International de Philosophie was obliged to think its own architecture, or at least its relation to architecture. It had to be prepared to invent, and not only for its own sake, a configuration of places which do not reproduce the philosophical topos [*topique*] which, quite rightly, was itself being interrogated or deconstructed. This topos reflects the models or reflects itself in them. The socio-academic structure, politico-pedagogical hierarchies, forms of community that preside over the organisation of places or in any case never let themselves be separated from them.

28. Deconstructing the *artefact* called architecture is perhaps to begin to think it as *artefact*, to rethink the artefacture from the starting point, and the technology, therefore, at the very point at which it remains uninhabitable.

29. To say that architecture must be withdrawn from the ends that are assigned to it and first of all from the value of habitation, is not to prescribe uninhabitable constructions, but to take an interest in the genealogy of an ageless contract between architecture and habitation. Is it possible to undertake a work without fitting it out to be habitable? Everything here must take into consideration those 'questions to Heidegger' on what he believed he could say about what we translate in Latin by 'inhabit' [*habiter*].

30. The architecture of an institution – for example, of a philosophical institution – is neither its essence, nor its attribute, nor its propriety, nor its accidence, nor its substance, nor its phenomenon, nor its inside, nor its outside. That which follows, which is not nothing, perhaps no longer depends [*relève*] on philosophical consequences: architecture will not exist.

31. In construction – de-constructing itself in this way, Le Collège International de Philosophie was obligated, from its initial outline, to open philosophy to other 'disciplines' (or rather to other questions on the possibility of 'discipline', on the space of teaching), to other theoretical and practical experiences. Not only in the name of a sacrosanct interdisciplinarity which supposes attested competences and already legitimate objects, but in view of new 'jects' (projects, objects, subjects) of new and still unqualified gestures. What is 'throwing' [*jeter*] for thought? And for architecture? What does 'laying the foundations' [*jeter des fondaments*] mean? What do 'starting', 'referring', 'soaring', 'erecting', 'instituting', mean here?

32. The deconstruction of the project in all its states. Architecture *is without being* in the project – in the technical sense or not of this term.

33. A question analogous to that of the *subjectile* (for example in painting, in the graphic or sculptural arts) must be posed to the architect. A question of the support or the substance, of the *subject* of what is *thrown [jeté] under*. But also of what is thrown in front or in advance in the *project* (projection, programme, prescription, promise, proposition) of everything that belongs, in the architectural process, to the movement of starting/launching [*lancer*] or of being started/launched [*l'être-lancé*], of throwing or being thrown [*l'être-jeté*] *jacere, jacio/jaceo*. Horizontally or vertically: from the foundation, for the erection of an edifice which soars towards the heavens. Where there is an apparent suspension of *mimesis*, there was nothing. A thesis poses something in the place of nothing or of lack. It is the project as prosthesis. Another value of the *pro*: not in front or in advance, neither the problem nor the protection, but what comes in the place of – on architectural supplementarity.

34. Le Collège International de Philosophie is obliged – and that was stated in the initial outline – to give a place to researches which for convenience's sake are called *performatives*. We understand by that these moments where knowledge becomes work, when the theoretical statement no longer allows itself to be dissociated from the event called 'creation', 'composition', 'construction'. It is not sufficient to say that architecture is one of its best paradigms. Even the word and the concept of paradigm have an exemplary architectural value.

35. Le Collège International de Philosophie announced in its initial outline that it would not neglect anything at stake in what is called teaching, and without limiting itself to the philosophical discipline. All didactics admit of a philosophy, a relation to philosophy, even if it was denied. What, in this country, is the philosophy practised or ignored by the pedagogy of architecture, the teaching of its history, its technology, its theory, its relations to the other 'arts', other texts, other institutions, the other politico-economic instances? In this country and in the others? The situation of France is, in this regard, very particular and this book, in attaching itself to certain philosophical premises, could contribute to a sort of general moving of boundaries and to another experience of internationalism. It is without doubt an urgent undertaking for architecture and in any case an essential project for a Collège International.

36. Taking account of what is taught of the architectural 'project' in this book, one hesitates to speak of Le Collège International de Philosophie having a 'project'. To say that it does not have a project does not amount to denouncing its empiricism or its adventurism. In the same way an architecture without a project is engaged perhaps in a more thoughtful, more inventive, more propitious work than ever came from the event.

37. To say of architecture that it is not is perhaps to understand that it happens. It gives place to itself without returning to it, there is the event.

38. There is no deconstructive project, no project/projective step [*pas de projet*] for deconstruction.

39. The project: it is and it is not the essence of architecture. Perhaps it will have been the history of architecture, its order in any case.

40. Leaving the aphorism on the threshold. There is no inhabitable place for the aphorism. The disjunctive force can only be put in the architectural work at the moment where, by some secret or denied synergy, it can be integrated into the order of a narrative [*récit*], whatever the dimension, in an uninterrupted history between the beginning and the end, the founding sub-foundation and the top of the house, the cellar and the roof, the ground and the point of the pyramid . . .

41. No habitat for the aphorism/inhabiting step for the aphorism [*pas d'habitat pour l'aphorisme*] but one does not inhabit an aphorism, neither man nor god. The aphorism is neither a house nor a temple, nor a school, nor a parliament, nor an *agora*, nor a tomb. Neither a pyramid nor above all a *stadium*. What else?

42. Whether we like it or not the aphorism is irremediably edifying.

43. There is nothing more architectural than a pure aphorism, says the other/so it is said [*dit l'autre*]. Architecture in the most philosophical form of its concept is neither a pure interruption, nor a dissociated fragment, but a totality which claims to be self-sufficient, the figure of a system (according to Kant the architectonic is the art of systems). It has its most authoritative, peremptory, dogmatic and complacently self-legitimatising eloquence when it does everything to leave out a structural demonstration.

44. The aphorism resumes, reassembles everything in itself, like absolute knowledge. It no longer poses any questions. No interrogation/point of interrogation [*point d'interrogation*]: it is thus impossible to punctuate a discourse which is or which produces its own method and includes within itself all its preambles and vestibules. If architecture is dominated by the *logos*, then the character of the aphorism which is at the same time prescriptive and entire allows this logocentric philosophy of architecture to triumph. The aphorism commands, it starts and finishes: architectonic, archi-eschatology and archi-teleology. It reassembles in itself, arranges the foreword, the project, the mastery of the work and the putting to work. It denies the resistance of materials (here all the words ending with the sound R: the earth [*la terre*], the matter [*la matière*], the stone [*la pierre*], the glass [*la verre*], the iron [*la fer*], without which, it is thought, there is no architecture that holds up, only *analogical* discourses on architecture). To verify it does not mean that one should be satisfied with what Hegel says about architecture itself, but take account of the fact that architecture is nothing once it is withdrawn from the teleology of absolute knowledge. In the same way, aphorisms can only multiply or be put in a series if they either confirm or contradict each other.

45. There is always more than one aphorism.

46. Despite their fragmentary appearance, they make a sign towards the memory of a totality, at the same time ruin and monument.

47. In their contradictory multiplicity they can always once more become dialectical moments, the absolute knowledge held in reserve in a thesis or antithesis. Preface to a short treatise on negativity in architecture. How an architectural interruption regathers a meaning, a function, a finality, (work of the negative) in a new edification.

48. Contrary to appearances 'deconstruction' is not an architectural metaphor. The word ought and will have to name a thought of architecture, it must be a thought at work. From the start it is not a metaphor. It is no longer possible to rely on [*se fie*] the concept of metaphor. Next, a deconstruction, as its name indicates, must from the start deconstruct the construction itself, the structural or constructivist motif, its schemes, its intuitions and its concepts, its rhetoric. But it deconstructs as well the strictly architectural construction, the philosophical construction of the concept of architecture. The concept is governed by the model both in the idea of the system in philosophy as well as in the theory, practice and teaching of architecture.

49. Superstructures are not deconstructed in order finally to reach the basis, the original soil, the ultimate foundation of an architecture or of a thought of architecture. There is no return to the purity or to the propriety/property [*propriété*], to the essence of architecture *itself*. One begins with the scheme of the foundation and with the oppositions that it induces: 'base/surface', 'substance/quality', 'essence/accidence', 'inside/outside' and especially 'foundational research/finalised research'; this last opposition is of great consequence here.

50. The engagement, the wager: taking account of the architectural or anarchitectural necessity without destroying it, without drawing only negative consequences from it. The baseless ground [*le sans-fond*] of a 'deconstructive' and affirmative architecture can cause vertigo, but it is not the void [*le vide*], it is not the gaping and chaotic remainder, the hiatus of destruction. Inversely it is no longer the Heideggerian *Destruktion* even if its project must be supposed. Still less is it the improbable *desobstruction* which has recently been dressed up in our language.

51. Neither Babel, nor Nimrod, nor the Flood. Between *kora* and *arche* perhaps, if there was an architecture which was, in the *between* neither Greek nor Judaic. A still unnameable filiation, another series of aphorisms.

52. Maintaining [*maintenir*], despite the temptations, despite the possible reappropriation, the chance of the aphorism, is to keep within the interruption, without the interruption, the promise of giving place, if it is necessary/ if it is missing [*s'il le faut*]. But it is never given.

JACQUES DERRIDA IN DISCUSSION WITH CHRISTOPHER NORRIS

BERNARD TSCHUMI, PARC DE LA VILLETTE, FOLIE DETAIL

JACQUES DERRIDA
In Discussion with Christopher Norris

Of circumstantial detail it is perhaps enough to record that this interview was conducted at Derrida's home near Paris during a two-hour session in March, 1988. He had wanted to attend the Tate Symposium and participate in a panel discussion with Bernard Tschumi, Peter Eisenman, Charles Jencks and others. In the event he was unable to make the trip and instead arranged with Symposium organiser Andreas Papadakis to do a video interview, screened as part of the Symposium proceedings. There was no time to submit questions or do much in the way of advance planning, but as it turned out this was no problem: the interview covered all the main points I had hoped to raise, along with various related topics. Derrida kindly agreed to speak in English, which helped a great deal when it came to the screening and subsequent audience discussion. In editing the transcript I have slightly expanded some of my questions to improve continuity and to offer some signposts or contextual cues for readers unfamiliar with Derrida's work. I have taken this opportunity to reconstruct one or two passages where the meaning wasn't altogether clear, but I have kept editorial intrusions to a minimum and trust that those who have seen the taped interview will judge this a faithful presentation of its content.

*   *   *

In so far as one can define, explain or summarise the Deconstructionist project, one's account might go very briefly as follows. Deconstruction locates certain crucial oppositions or binary structures of meaning and value that constitute the discourse of 'Western metaphysics'. These include (among many others) the distinctions between form and content, nature and culture, thought and perception, essence and accident, mind and body, theory and practice, male and female, concept and metaphor, speech and writing etc. A Deconstructive reading then goes on to show how these terms are inscribed within a systematic structure of hierarchical privilege, such that one of each pair will always appear to occupy the sovereign or governing position. The aim is then to demonstrate – by way of close reading – how this system is undone, so to speak, from within; how the second or subordinate term in each pair has an equal (maybe a prior) claim to be treated as a *condition of possibility* for the entire system. Thus writing is regularly marginalised, denounced or put in its place – a strictly secondary, 'supplementary' place – by a long line of thinkers in the Western tradition, from Plato and Aristotle to Rousseau, Husserl, Saussure, Lévi-Strauss and the latter-day structuralist human sciences. But just as often – as Derrida shows in *Of Grammatology* – writing resurfaces to assert its claim as the repressed other of this whole logocentric tradition, the 'wandering outcast', scapegoat or exile whose off-stage role is a precondition of the system. And this curious 'logic of supplementarity' operates wherever thinking is motivated by a certain constitutive need to exclude or deny that which makes it possible from the outset.

Now it is not hard to see how such a Deconstructive reading might affect the discourse of current (Post-Modern) architectural thought. Thus Peter Eisenman suggests that: 'the traditional opposition between structure and decoration, abstraction and figuration, figure and ground, form and function could be dissolved. Architecture could begin an exploration of the "between" within these categories.' And Derrida has likewise written of an architectural 'supplementarity', a movement of *différance* between and within concepts that would open up hitherto unthought-of inventive possibilities. The interview has a good deal to say about this in relation to Derrida's collaborative venture with Eisenman and Tschumi. His book *The Truth in Painting*

also has essays on Valerio Adami and Titus-Carmel. In their work – as in Derrida's recent texts – one can make out the signs of a close and reciprocal exchange between Deconstruction and a certain problematics of writing and graphic representation. But critics have also applied the term 'Deconstruction' to other artists like Duchamp, Jasper Johns and Francis Bacon. Derrida himself makes mention of Magritte in the context of 'citationality' and the deconstruction of mimetic illusion through effects of juxtaposed image and text. And again there is his essay 'Restitutions' raising the question of painterly 'truth' by way of Meyer Schapiro's quarrel with Heidegger over the true significance of Van Gogh's *Old Shoes with Laces,* the question – seemingly so vital to each of them – as to whether they were peasant's shoes or those of a man-about-town.

So the interview asks what relation might exist between these various forms of deconstructive activity: that is to say – for want of better terms – 'creative' Deconstruction on the one hand, and diagnostic or critical commentary on the other. To pose the question like this is of course to fall back into just the kind of value-laden binary thinking that Deconstruction sets out to challenge. But it is equally mistaken to believe that, having once seen through their delusory appearance, one can finally come out on the far side of all such 'metaphysical' categories. What is required is a vigilant awareness of the way that they inhabit all our thinking about art, about criticism, philosophy and the human sciences, while also giving rise to problematic tensions within and between those disciplines.

In *The Truth in Painting* Derrida writes: 'We must sharpen the points, the blades or the edges of a certain *chiasmus.*' This figure – the trope of crossing or exchanged attributes – is one that plays an important role in his reading of Kant and the 'parergonal' discourse that frames Kant's thinking on questions of aesthetic judgement. It is also important to Eisenman, this and other tropes (like catachresis) that push beyond the bounds of reason or representation by radicalising language in its figural aspect. Thus Eisenman: 'the way to catachresis is not to suppress metaphor but to find the catachresis repressed in metaphor, and the way to another architecture is not to suppress the Classical but in fact to cut in . . . to surgically open up the Classical and the Modern to find what is repressed'. This interview may be read as an improvised commentary on the way that Deconstruction has opened up such questions for philosophy and the visual arts alike.

Christopher Norris

*   *   *

Perhaps I could start by asking a perhaps rather naive question: can there be such a thing as 'Deconstructivist art' or indeed 'Deconstructivist architecture'? That is to say, do these terms refer to a given style, project or body of work? Or do they not rather signify a certain way of looking at various works and projects, a perception that would break with (or at least seek to challenge) established ideas of form, value and aesthetic representation?

Well, I don't know. . . I must say, when I first met, I won't say 'Deconstructive architecture', but the Deconstructive discourse on architecture, I was rather puzzled and suspicious. I thought at first that perhaps this was an analogy, a displaced discourse, and something more analogical than rigorous. And then – as I have explained somewhere – then I realised that on the contrary, the most efficient way of putting Deconstruction to work was by going through art and architecture. As you know, Deconstruction is not simply a matter of discourse or a matter of displacing the semantic content of the discourse, its conceptual structure or whatever. Deconstruction goes *through* certain social and political structures, meeting with resistance and displacing institutions as it does so. I think that in these forms of art, and in any architecture, to deconstruct traditional sanctions – theoretical, philosophical, cultural – effectively, you have to displace . . . I would say 'solid' structures, not only in the sense of material structures, but 'solid' in the sense of cultural, pedagogical, political, economic structures. And all the concepts which are, let us say, the target (if I may use this term) of Deconstruction, such as theology, the subordination of the sensible to the intelligible and so forth – these concepts are effectively displaced in order for them to become 'Deconstructive architecture'. That's why I am more and more interested in it, despite the fact that I am technically incompetent.

– Could you say a little more about your work with Bernard Tschumi and Peter Eisenman, and some of the collaborative projects under way in Paris at the moment?

Well, what I could do is just a narration of the way things happened. Once I had a phonecall from Bernard Tschumi, who I didn't know at the time, except by reputation. Tschumi told me: 'Some architects today are interested in your work and would you be interested in working with some of them, or one of them, on a project in La Villette?' As you know, Tschumi is responsible for all the architecture at La Villette. Of course I was surprised, but my answer was 'Why not?' And so I had my first encounter with Tschumi and I began to look at those projects and to read some texts, by Tschumi and Eisenman. Then I met Eisenman many times in New York. We worked together, we co-ordinated everything in discussion, and now there is a book which is soon to be published on these collaborations. My proposal was that we start with a text that I had recently written on Plato's *Timaeus* because it had to do with space, with Deconstruction, so to speak, 'in the universe'. It also had to do with a problem that I was interested in and that concerned, let us say, the *economic* determination of the way we usually read Plato. This strategic level was extremely important for me. So I gave this text to Peter Eisenman and in his own way he started a project that was correlated with but at the same time independent of my text. That was true collaboration – not 'using' the other's work, not just illustrating or selecting from it . . . and so there is a kind of discrepancy or, I would say, a productive dialogue between the concerns, the styles, the persons too. And so, after about 18 months' or two years' work, the project is now ready to be 'constructed', you might say. . . to be realised . . .

– So it would be wrong to see this as a new 'turn' in your thinking, a sudden recognition of connections, affinities or common points of interest between Deconstruction and the visual arts? In fact there are many passages in your earlier writing – and I am thinking here of texts like Force and Signification *or* Genesis and Structure *– where the argument turns on certain crucial (let us say) metaphors of an architectural provenance. The context here was your joint reading of the structuralist and phenomenological projects – more specifically, of Saussure and Husserl – as two, equally rigorous but finally incompatible reflections on the character of language and meaning. Thus you write: 'the relief and design of structures appears more clearly when content, which is the living energy of meaning, is neutralised. Somewhat like the architecture of an uninhabited or deserted city, reduced to its skeleton by some catastrophe of nature or art. A city no longer inhabited, not simply left behind, but haunted by meaning and culture'. And of course these architectural figures and analogies occur more often in your later writings on Kant and the tradition of Classical aesthetics (for instance, 'The Parergon' in* The Truth in Painting*). Thus for Kant,* architectonic *is defined as the 'art of systems', that which articulates the various orders of truth-claim and ensures their proper (hierarchical) relationship one with another. So in a sense one could argue that your work has always been crucially concerned with 'architectural' models and metaphors. Do you perceive a clear continuity there, or am I just imagining all this?*

No, not at all. But I would like to say something about the concept of analogy or metaphor you rightly used a moment ago. Of course there is a lot of architectural metaphor, not only in my texts but in the whole philosophical tradition. And Deconstruction – the word Deconstruction – sounds very much like such a metaphor, an architectural metaphor. But I think that it's more complex than that, since the word appeared or was underlined in a certain situation where structuralism was dominant on the scene. So Deconstruction shared certain motifs with the structuralist project while at the same time attacking that project. . . .

But Deconstruction doesn't mean that we have to stay within those architectural metaphors. It doesn't mean, for example, that we have to destroy something which is built – physically built or culturally built or theoretically built – just in order to reveal a naked ground on which something new could be built. Deconstruction is perhaps a way of questioning this architectural model itself – the architectural model which is a general question, even within philosophy, the metaphor of foundations, of superstructures, what Kant calls 'architectonic' etc, as well as the concept of the *archè* . . . So Deconstruction means also the putting into question of architecture in philosophy and perhaps architecture itself.

When I discovered what we now call 'Deconstructive architecture' I was interested in the fact that these architects were in fact deconstructing the essentials of tradition, and were criticising everything that subordinated architecture to something else – the value of, let's say, usefulness or beauty or living – '*habitation*' – etc – not in order to build something else that would be useless or ugly or uninhabitable, but to free architecture from all those external finalities, extraneous goals. And not in order to reconstitute some pure and original architecture – on the contrary, just to put architecture in communication with other media, other arts, to *contaminate* architecture . . . And notice that in my way of dealing with Deconstruction I suspect the *concept* of metaphor itself, in so far as it involves a complicated network of philosophemes, a network that would always lead us back at some point into architecture . . .

– Yes, this is a topic you raise in your Fifty-Two Aphorisms for a Foreword. *There you explicitly disown the idea that Deconstruction is in any sense an 'architectural metaphor', a figure that would serve obliquely to name or to specify some ongoing project in the field of building and design. And this for the reason, as you say, that it is 'no longer possible to make use of the concept of metaphor'. But might we not say with equal force (as you did some years ago in 'White Mythology') that there is no possibility of doing without some residual 'concept of metaphor'; that if indeed all concepts come down to metaphors – as Nietzsche argued – then it is also the case that we possess only concepts of metaphor, ideas that have always already been worked over by the discourse of philosophic reason, from Aristotle on? I take this argument as one more example of the firm insistence, on your part, that 'Deconstruction' is not be treated as a break with 'Western metaphysics', a leap outside the logocentric tradition that thinks to land on some alternative, radically different ground. Is it not this acceptance of the need to work patiently* within *and against the structures of inherited thought that has chiefly distinguished Deconstruction from other, less exacting and rigorous forms of Post-Modern thought? I ask this question – as you may by now have guessed – in the hope that you will be drawn into offering some account of what specifically sets Deconstruction apart from the broader Post-Modern project.*

As you know, I never use the word 'post', the prefix 'post'; and I have many reasons for this. One of those reasons is that this use of the prefix implies a periodisation or an epochalisation which is highly problematic for me. Then again, the word 'post' implies that something is finished – that we can get rid of what went *before* Deconstruction, and I don't think anything of the sort. For instance, to go back to the first point of your question, I don't believe that the opposition between concept and metaphor can ever be erased. I have never suggested that all concepts were simply metaphors, or that we couldn't make use of that distinction, because in fact at the end of that essay ['White

Mythology'] I deconstruct this argument also, and I say that we need, for scientific reasons and many reasons, to keep this distinction at work. So this is a very complicated gesture.

Now as for architecture, I think that *Deconstruction* comes about - let us carry on using this word to save time – when you have deconstructed some architectural philosophy, some architectural assumptions – for instance, the hegemony of the aesthetic, of beauty, the hegemony of usefulness, of functionality, of living, of dwelling. But then you have to *reinscribe* these motifs within the work. You can't (or you shouldn't) simply dismiss those values of dwelling, functionality, beauty and so on. You have to construct, so to speak, a new space and a new form, to shape a new way of building in which those motifs or values are reinscribed, having meanwhile lost their external hegemony. The inventiveness of powerful architects consists I think in this reinscription, the economy of this reinscription, which involves also some respect for tradition, for memory. Deconstruction is not simply forgetting the past. What has dominated theology or architecture or anything else is still there, in some way, and the inscriptions, the, let's say, *archive* of these deconstructed structures, the archive should be as readable as possible, as legible as we can make it. That is the way I try to write or to teach. And I think the same is true, to some extent, in architecture.

– *You have stressed your suspicion of 'post-' movements in philosophy and art, whether Post-Modernist, Post-Structuralist, or post-humanist (as in your early essay 'The Ends of Man'). And this for the reason – as I take it – that all steps beyond in the name of this or that radical new way of thinking are liable to find themselves unwittingly reinscribed within the terms of that same oppositional order of thought which they hope thereby to escape. Do you not see a risk of something similar happening with current attempts to break with the so-called 'Modernist' paradigm and its associated structure of concepts and values? Thus Peter Eisenman: 'For architecture to enter a post-Hegelian condition, it must move away from the rigidity and value-structure of these dialectical oppositions' (ie figure and ground, ornament and structure, form and function etc). Or would it perhaps be true to say – as some like Gregory Ulmer have claimed – that things have moved on during the past decade or so from 'Deconstruction' as a species of meticulous textual critique to 'applied grammatology' as a practice of creative reinscription that goes beyond such basic, preliminary work? Would this be borne out by what you have recently achieved in your collaborative enterprise with artists like Eisenman and Tschumi, or would you perhaps consider this a wrong understanding, a false opposition?*

I wouldn't say 'false' opposition. It is an opposition which, I would say, is pertinent for some forms of appropriation in so far as it amounts to a critical method within texts, within literary texts or even philosophical texts. But I insisted from the beginning that Deconstruction was not *simply* a method, was not a critique, or not simply critical. The concept of critique or criticism is deconstructive somewhere... It is not negative – it was linked from the beginning with affirmation, with the 'yes', an affirmation which is not a 'position' in the Hegelian sense. So the move which is described by Greg Ulmer is not so much a move *in* Deconstruction. It is a move we can identify in some places – I wouldn't say 'in' my work, from that point of view at least. And of course the variety of fields, of disciplines, of texts, of publishers – this variety was necessary from the outset, philosophical and literary texts and painting and now architecture and some others too, legal texts and many other things.

So I think it is important, this way of opening up the boundaries, and mainly the academic boundaries between texts and disciplines; and when I say academic boundaries I'm thinking not only of the humanistic disciplines and philosophy, but also of architecture – the teaching of architecture. This crossing, this going through the boundaries of disciplines, is one of the main – not just stratagems but *necessities* of Deconstruction. The grafting of one art on to another, the contamination of codes, the dissemination of contexts, are sometimes 'methods' or 'stratagems' of Deconstruction, but most importantly they are moments of what we call history. And that is why I don't think Deconstruction belongs to an epoch or a period, even a modern one.

I don't think Deconstruction is something specifically modern. There are some 'modern' features of what we identify as Deconstruction in some academic contexts, but what makes Deconstruction *unavoidable* has been at work a long time, even with Plato or Descartes. So we have to distinguish between, let us say, some phenomena which are not the entirety of Deconstruction and which give rise to methods, to teaching, to thematic treatment, and something more hidden, more persistent, less amenable to system or method which makes this thematic Deconstruction possible in discourse and in teaching and the arts.

– *Isn't it a problem that the term 'Modernism' (let alone 'Post-Modernism') means such very different things for philosophers on the one hand, and literary critics or art-historians on the other? And doesn't Deconstruction need to adopt a somewhat different stance with regard to these two phenomena? I am thinking here of your recent essays on Kant, on the 'Principle of Reason', and on the Enlightenment tradition in general. There you make it plain that we cannot simply break with that tradition; that any criticism must come (so to speak) from inside and avail itself of the concepts and categories of enlightened critique while questioning their claims to ultimate truth. And I think this places some considerable distance between your own thinking and the kinds of project pursued by [for instance] Lyotard or Baudrillard. Whereas the Post-Modern 'turn' in literature, art and cultural theory has a different set of historical coordinates and a different relation to issues of truth, reason and ideological critique. Haven't these distinctions become rather blurred in recent debate?*

I wouldn't want to call Deconstruction a critique of modernity. But neither is it 'modern' or in any sense a glorification of modernity. It is very premature to venture these generalisations, these concepts of period. I would say that I just don't know what these categories mean, except that of course I can tell more or less what other people mean them to signify . . . But for me they are not rigorous concepts. Nor is Deconstruction a unitary *concept*, although it is often deployed in that way, a usage that I find very disconcerting. . . Sometimes I prefer to say deconstructions in the plural, just to be careful about the heterogeneity and the multiplicity, the necessary multiplicity of gestures, of fields, of styles. Since it is not a system, not a method, it cannot be homogenised. Since it takes the singularity of every context into account, Deconstruction is different from one context to another. So I should certainly want to reject the idea that 'Deconstruction' denotes any theory, method or univocal concept. Nevertheless it must denote *something*, something that can at least be recognised in its working or its effects. . .

Of course this doesn't mean that Deconstruction *is* that 'something', or that you can find Deconstruction everywhere. So on the one hand we have to define some working notion, some regulative concept of Deconstruction. But it is very difficult to gather this in a simple formula. I know that the enemies of Deconstruction say: 'Well, since you cannot offer a definition then it must be an obscure concept and you must be an obscurantist thinker'. To which I would respond that Deconstruction is first and foremost a suspicion directed against just that kind of thinking – 'what is . . . ?' 'what is the essence of . . . ?' and so on.

– *Could we perhaps take that point a bit further? Some theorists of the Post-Modern (Charles Jencks among them) have rejected what they see as the negative, even 'nihilist' implications of the Deconstruction movement in contemporary art. According to Jencks, 'Architecture is essentially constructive. It builds up structures, depends on joint endeavours of mutual confidence, the combination of foresight, good-will and investment – all of which Deconstruction undermines, if not totally destroys.' I thought you might like to comment on this and similar responses, especially in view of current debates – taken up in the American and British press – about the 'politics of Decon-*

struction' and its supposed nihilist leanings. I'm sure you would say that they have misunderstood.

Absolutely, absolutely. . . There has been much criticism, many objections that we find in the newspapers, in the bad newspapers . . . Which doesn't just mean that the people who write such things are jealous. Often they are academics who don't read the many texts in which not only I but many people insist on the fact that Deconstruction is *not* negative, is not nihilistic. Of course it goes through the experience and the questioning of what nihilism is. Of course, of course. And who knows what nihilism is or isn't? Even the people who object don't raise the question 'What is nihilism?' Nevertheless, Deconstruction is or should be an affirmation linked to promises, to involvement, to responsibility. As you know, it has become more and more concerned with these concepts – even Classical concepts – of responsibility, affirmation and commitment . . . So when people say it's negative, nihilistic and so forth, either they don't read or they are arguing in bad faith. But this can and should be analysed . . .

– In the Aphorisms *you refer to an 'ageless contract' that has always existed between architecture and a certain idea of dwelling or habitation. And of course this points toward Heidegger and a whole thematics of building, dwelling, and poetic thinking. You also remark – in a slightly different but related context – that 'there is no inhabitable place for the aphorism', that is to say, no place within the kind of large-scale conceptual edifice that philosophy has traditionally taken for its home. Thus: 'the aphorism is neither a house, nor a temple, nor a school, nor a parliament, nor an* agora, *nor a tomb. Neither a pyramid nor, above all, a stadium. What else?' Could I ask you to pursue this particular line of thought in whatever direction you wish, and perhaps suggest also what connections it might have with your latest writings on Heidegger?*

Ah, that's a very difficult question . . .

– Yes, I'm sorry . . .

No, no, not at all. Difficult questions are necessary. The fact that architecture has always been interpreted as dwelling, or the element of dwelling – dwelling for human beings or dwelling for the gods – the place where gods or people are present or gathering or living and so on. Of course this is a very profound and strong interpretation, but one which first submits architecture, what we call architecture or the art of building, to a value which can be questioned. In Heidegger such values are linked with the question of building, with the theme of, let's say, keeping, conserving, watching over, etc. And I was interested in questioning those assumptions in Heidegger, asking what this might amount to, an architecture that wouldn't be simply subordinated to those values of habitation, dwelling, sheltering the presence of gods and human beings. Would it be possible? Would it still be an architecture? I think that what people like Eisenman and Tschumi have shown me – people who call themselves Deconstructivist architects – is that this is indeed possible; not possible as a *fact*, as a matter of simple demonstration, because of course you can always perceive their architecture as again giving place to dwelling, sheltering, etc; because the question I am asking now is not only the question of what they build, but of how we interpret what they build. Of course we can interpret in a very traditional way – viewing this as simply a 'modern' transformation of the same old kinds of architecture. So Deconstruction is not simply an activity or commitment on the part of the architect; it is also on the part of people who read, who look at these buildings, who enter the space, who move in the space, who experience the space in a different way. From this point of view I think that the architectural experience (let's call it that, rather than talking about 'buildings' as such) . . . what they offer is precisely the chance of experiencing the possibility of these inventions of a different architecture, one that wouldn't be, so to speak, 'Heideggerian' . . .

– The Aphorisms *have a good deal to say about the International College of Philosophy and its work in promoting inter-disciplinary exchange. They also make a point of* not *talking about 'projects' in this or that field, as if the work undertaken could be staked out in advance,*

or in accordance with some governing scheme or teleology. Thus you write, in Aphorism 36: *'To say that it does not have a project does not amount to denouncing its empiricism or its adventurism. In the same way an architecture without a project is engaged perhaps in a more thoughtful, more inventive, more propitious work . . .'*

Could you say something more about the kinds of new and productive thinking that have emerged from this bringing-together of people from hitherto separate disciplines? Just what goes on when you 'exchange ideas' – to put it very crudely – with artists like Eisenman or Bernard Tschumi; an enterprise without clear-cut aims and ambitions, without some teleological goal?

I was referring to the French meaning of the word 'project' in the code of architecture. I don't know whether it has the same meaning in English. A project is something which is prior to the work, which has its own economy, a governing role which can then be applied and developed . . . And you have the same kind of relation between the project, or the concept, and its carrying-out in practice as between, say, the transcendental signified and its incarnation in the body, in writing etc. So there is a critical reflection on this concept of the 'project' going on among a number of French architects. When I say there is no project in the College, I don't mean to say that we start without any idea of where we're going, but that the relation between the project and the experience, the act, has no Classical or philosophical equivalent. For instance, the College could be seen from one aspect as having the character of a new foundation. And of course a 'foundation' is something with strong philosophical, as well as architectural links. It has its building, its forms, its shape, its place . . . But in fact, within this College we ask questions – sometimes, not always, in a deconstructive way – about what grounding means, what the foundation means, what the space of the community means, what hierarchy means, in terms not only of academic authority but also in terms of the pedagogical scenography, the organisation of the classroom, the way we appoint people, elect people, the way the hierarchies are stabilised or destabilised, and so forth. And all these things have their architectural models. So since our model was not the Western university as it is organised now, or the philosophy that lies behind this modern university, we had to invent also the symbolic and physical architecture of this new community without referring to any previous, given model.

Of course all the time we have to negotiate, we have to compromise with previous, given models – that's the political strategy, and I think that architects also have to negotiate with norms and practical constraints and so on. Nevertheless, these tactics are oriented toward something that would be new, or that would bring about a real alteration in the old structure. And I think that from the beginning we had, my friends and I, this certainty that first it was something new – something new to be built in the architectural sense, new commitments, a new space, a new field of knowledge . . . But also, more specifically, the sense that we *had to* work with architects, that the teaching and experience of architecture would be an important aspect of our work at the College. So even though my collaboration with Eisenman and Tschumi was not officially a part of the programme, it had to do with the College and indeed gave rise to various conferences, meetings and communications . . . events that led on to a close involvement between philosophers and architects. The one for which I wrote my *Aphorisms* was an example of it.

– You have talked about the relationship between 'modernity' in art, architecture, philosophy etc, and a certain idea of the modern university, one that took hold in Germany a couple of centuries back and which still exerts a great influence on the way we think about disciplines, subject-areas, questions of intellectual competence, and so forth. And this would perhaps take us back to what you said previously about Kant's 'architectonic', his doctrine of the faculties, that which enforces a proper separation of realms between pure and practical reason, theoretical understanding, aesthetic judgement and their various modalities or powers . . . To some extent your work in the International College is a way of deconstructing those relations,

showing how they give rise to endless litigation or boundary-disputes, often played out in very practical terms as a matter of institutional politics . . .

Oh yes, I agree with your definition of what is going on. Deconstructing not only theoretically, not only giving signals of the process at work, but trying to deconstruct in a practical fashion, that is, to set up and build new structures implying this work of Deconstruction. It's not easy, and it is never done in or through a single gesture. It takes a long time and involves some very complicated gestures. It is always unfinished, heterogeneous, and I think there is no such thing as a 'pure' Deconstruction or a deconstructive project that is finished or completed.

– Isn't there a risk that Deconstruction might become mixed up with that strain of Post-Modern or neo-pragmatist thought which says that philosophy is just a 'kind of writing', on a level with poetry, criticism or the 'cultural conversation of mankind'? That these distinctions are merely 'rhetorical' or imposed by an obsolete 'enlightenment' doctrine of the faculties, so that we had best get rid of them and abandon any notion of philosophy as having its own special interests, distinctive truth-claims, conceptual history or whatever? Do you see that as a constant risk?

There are many risks and this is one of them. Sometimes it is an interesting risk, sometimes it opens doors and spaces in the fields which are trying to protect themselves from Deconstruction. But once the door is open, then you have to make things more specific, and I would say, following your suggestion, that no indeed, philosophy is not *simply* a 'kind of writing'; philosophy has a very rigorous specificity which has to be respected, and it is a very hard discipline with its own requirements, its own autonomy, so that you cannot simply mix philosophy with literature, with painting, with architecture. There is a point you can recognise, some opening of the various contexts (including the philosophical context) that makes Deconstruction possible. But it still requires a rigorous approach, one that would situate this opening in a strict way, that would organise, so to speak, this contamination or this grafting without losing sight of those specific requirements. So I am very suspicious – and this is not just a matter of idiosyncracy or a matter of training – I am very suspicious of the over-easy mixing of discourses to which your question referred. On the contrary, Deconstruction pays the greatest attention to multiplicity, to heterogeneity, to these sharp and irreducible differences. If we don't want to homogenise eveything then we have to respect the specificity of discourses, especially that of philosophical discourse.

– There is one particular essay of yours which I think may help to focus some of these questions. It is called 'Of an Apocalyptic Tone Recently Adopted in Philosophy', a title that you borrow (or cite) almost verbatim from Kant, and it strikes me that there are two very different things going on throughout this text. In fact it is often hard to know whether you are writing, as it were, 'in your own voice' or whether the passage in question is sous rature *or to be read as if placed within quotation-marks. Sometimes you write of the need to maintain 'Enlightenment' values, to preserve what you call the 'lucid vigil' of Enlightenment, critique and truth. In this sense the essay appears to side with Kant against the adepts, the mystagogues, the fake illuminati, those who would claim an immediate or self-present access to*

truth by virtue of their own 'inner light', without submitting their claims to the democratic parliament of the faculties. Elsewhere you adopt your own version of the 'apocalyptic tone' – a series of injunctions, apostrophes, speech-acts or performatives of various kinds – as if to defend the right of these characters not to go along with Kant's rules for the proper, self-regulating conduct of philosophic discourse. It does seem to me a profoundly ambivalent essay. On the one hand it is establishing a distance – even an antagonism – between Deconstruction and the discourse of Enlightenment critique. On the other it is saying that the Kantian project is somehow indispensable, that it is bound up with the very destiny of thought in our time, that we cannot simply break with it as certain Post-Modernist thinkers would wish – or have I misread your essay in some fairly basic way?

No, no, you read it very well. I agree with everything you said. It is a very, very ambivalent essay. I tried – as I often do – to achieve and say many things at once. Of course I am 'in favour' of the Enlightenment; I think we shouldn't simply leave it behind us, so I want to keep this tradition alive. But at the same time I know that there are certain historical forms of Enlightenment, certain things in this tradition that we need to criticise or to deconstruct. So it is sometimes in the name of, let us say, a *new* Enlightenment that I deconstruct a given Enlightenment. And this requires some very complex strategies; requires that we should let many voices speak . . . There is nothing monological, no monologue – that's why the responsibility for Deconstruction is never individual or a matter of the single, self-privileged authorial voice. It is always a multiplicity of voices, of gestures . . . And you can take this as a rule: that each time Deconstruction speaks through a single voice, it's wrong, it is not 'Deconstruction' any more. So in this particular essay, as you rightly said a moment ago, not only do I let many voices speak at the same time, but the problem is precisely that multiplicity of voices, that variety of tones, within the *same* utterance or indeed the same word or syllable, and so on. So that's the question. That's one of the questions.

But of course today the political, ideological consequences of the Enlightenment are still very much with us – and very much in need of questioning. So a 'new' enlightenment, to be sure, which may mean Deconstruction in its most active or intensive form, and not what we inherited in the name of A*ufklärung, kritik, siècle des lumières* and so forth. And as you know, these are already very different things. So we have to remember this.

– I suppose I'm looking for some kind of equivalence between what we call 'Modernism' in philosophy, let's say Kantian philosophy, and the term 'Modernism' as conventionally applied in architecture and the visual arts. You might compare the attitude that Deconstructivist architects take toward Modernism – not simply one of rejection or supercession, but a critical attitude directed toward that particular form of Modernist critique . . .

Of course. That's why I'm reluctant to say that Deconstruction is Modern or Post-Modern. But I should also be reluctant to say that it's not Modern, or that it's anti-Modern, or anti-Post-Modern. I wouldn't want to say that what is Deconstructive, if there is such a thing, is specifically Modern or Post-Modern. So we have to be very careful with the use of these epithets.

—————— * ——————

Discussion and Comments

The following discussion took place after the showing of the Christopher Norris, Jacques Derrida interview in the auditorium of the Tate Gallery on the 11th May, 1988. The participants are Stephen Bann, Chairman [SB] with Andrew Benjamin [AB], Geoff Bennington [GB], Christopher Norris [CN] and Michael Podro [MP].

SB: I shall start with a very brief cautionary story. There has been recently in New York an artistic movement called 'Neo-Geo'. A few months ago a visiting philosopher and sociologist, Jean Baudrillard, was called to account for the sins of the 'Neo-Geo' movement at a dreadful occasion at the University of Columbia. He disclaimed any connection with it and said that their assertion to use his concepts was totally misplaced. I think that what we've seen of this interview so far is quite an interesting and perhaps significant instance of Derrida's intellectual generosity, particularly in relation to architecture. He said in the interview very little about art, but perhaps that is something that might come up at a later stage.

Some of you may not know the context in which the original collaboration between Derrida and the architects (Tschumi and the others) took place. The competition for La Villette on the outskirts of Paris brought together an immense number of architects, philosophers, sociologists, intellectuals, to take part in teams. Derrida's counterparts were present in nearly all the other teams, producing one of the major architectural competitions of the recent period in France.

Now what I would like to begin by doing, and possibly I can ask Christopher Norris this, is to concentrate on one of the essential aspects of Derrida's discourse. Architecture for him is not merely analogical. It's not simply transferring a concept out of his own discourse into architectural terms. Why is architecture special for Derrida?

CN: I suppose because he has been using architectural analogies (I don't know what term you could use them apart from analogy or metaphor or concept) in his work from the early 1960s. Without some notion of structure, architectonic, building or construction it's virtually impossible to think in a sequential way. Obviously there are analogies as architects such as Eisenman and Tschumi are convinced that Deconstruction has a relevance to architecture.

But I went with a certain degree of scepticism, partly because I felt that Deconstruction has been exported, or imported perhaps, into too many contiguous disciplines. Very often it doesn't preserve much of its original rigour or specificity; that is partly why I was trying to turn the questions around towards the specific nature of Deconstruction and the difference between philosophy and other discourses. But Derrida was constantly nudging me back to architecture, so I think there was a degree of tension there.

SB: It seems that Derrida implies that architects are the real Deconstructionists and that he is taking a back seat as linguistics are, in a sense, secondary.

CN: Charles Jencks made a very good point when he asked what it would be for an architect to make a mistake. In a Deconstructionist reading of a text you can make a mistake. Deconstruction depends on the tension between logic and rhetoric, or the tension between what are visibly an author's 'intentions' and what actually turns out to be his or her 'meaning' in the text. Now you can't have a mistake in that sense in a building. You might have a gross error of judgement, you might have a totally disfunctional window . . . but not *that* kind of mistake, or significant error that Deconstruction talks about. This is a peculiarly linguistic thing.

Now it may be you can't have that in fiction. A good deal of Deconstructionist criticism of fiction states that what looks like a realist text on the surface is, in fact, a tissue of metaphors. There is no such thing as realism, no such thing as a transparent access to the world through language. Well, we all know that already.

Post-Modernism makes a lot of sense in connection with architecture because what you have there are various collages and quotations, citations, the mixture of styles. But a Deconstructionist idiom in architecture gives me problems. Derrida, however, clearly believes in it and so does Tschumi, so who am I to say there's no such thing?

AB: Part of the difficulty with this is trying to locate Deconstruction in an object. In other words, to say of a specific work of art or a specific architectural form that this is an instance of Deconstruction. Now there are two reasons why that is difficult. The first is the old philosophical problem of naming. What is fascinating about this aspect of Derrida's work is that he refuses to answer the question: what is Deconstruction? Now the question 'what is' anything is the question that comes into philosophy from Plato. It's a question that demands an answer that has an essential nature. What Derrida is refusing is the possibility that Deconstruction has an essential nature. That point is only

important because establishing an essential nature allows for re-identification.

The refusal to answer the question 'what is?' must be understood within this historical dimension. What Derrida is doing in this instance is presenting a fundamental challenge to the dominance of a certain theory of naming within philosophy; this has put the question of the object to one side. The question of the object returns in another way and it goes back to the point put to Derrida as to whether or not Deconstruction is something that comes to be enacted within an object or is a way of reading objects or a way of reading texts. As is always the case with these things, it's clearly both; the question of enactment is problematic.

In the interview, and in his writings on Tschumi and Eisenman, Derrida uses the word 'affirmation'. What Derrida means from my understanding of 'affirmation' is that it is the consequence of that 'space of interruption' that holds the deconstruction of a binary opposition and the privileging of the subordinate term within the opposition and the privileging of something else. That privileging does not take place within the opposition itself, it takes place within what he calls this 'space of interruption'. It is that privileging which is 'affirmative'. This is a mode of thinking that's not enacted, it governs the analysis in projections, in the project as the projection and the project as the act of interpretation. There is a clear link here between what he says about Tschumi's architectural work and what he says about the novels of Roger Laporte. I mean, Laporte novels are ones which he argues disallow the possibility of their being encapsulated within any metalanguage. They project themselves outside of that and in so far as they do that they are affirmative.

The danger and the scepticism, which I take as being a very important part of this, can be calmed by recognising that what is at stake here is a mode of thinking. The question is how that mode of thinking becomes enacted; enactment itself becomes both a philosophical and an architectural problem. That goes back to what Derrida said about sheltering and the need to dwell on sheltering. In other words the question of enactment is the possibility of an architecture that takes place within that space of interruption that holds within it sheltering but, at the same time, deconstructs sheltering.

SB: One of the points that one could say is held in common between the architectural project and the Collège Internationale de Philosophie, I think, might also be the word 'interdisciplinarity'. Tschumi's initially worked with projects involving *Finnegan's Wake*.

AB: Interdisciplinarity is problematic. Let's establish the relationship between philosophy and architecture, philosophy and literature, philosophy and whatever. The question is: from where are you establishing that relationship? On what terms is that relationship being established? Deconstruction, in a sense, puts the onus back on philosophy to answer this question of relationships. What Derrida is saying is, 'I'm not an architect, I'm not a literary critic, I'm interested in what architects and literary critics do when they think within literature or within architecture. I am trying to think about the relationship between philosophy and architecture from within philosophy, and thereby to question philosophy.

MP: I take Andrew Benjamin's last point but, perhaps, not altogether what he said before that. I'm not clear, however, how far we diverge. Three things strike me as coming out of this discussion relatively clearly. The first and, in a way, the most obvious, is the relative specificity, the autonomy of philosophy. Whatever else, whatever misgivings we may have, however impossible it is to be 'univocal', to keep inside Derrida's mode there are always going to be, even when we are doing philosophy, voices which tell us that our modes of procedure have gone rigid and have become alienated. Nevertheless, we recognise that what we do, when we engage in philosophy, is continue a discussion that goes back to Hegel, Kant, the Enlightenment, Plato and Aristotle.

The important point is that one doesn't identify what one is doing by answering the question 'what is?' – by offering a definition. One identifies what one is doing by exemplification; there is a strong philosophical tradition in taking this view – 'don't look for the meaning, look for the use' would be the simple modern analogy. The closeness here of Derrida to Wittgenstein is apparent in the conception of language as explicable to a degree by watching how we behave with it.

CN: Wittgenstein is a conspicuous absence in Derrida's writing. He mentions Russell and Austin and various other analytical philosophers, but not Wittgenstein. Many people have made a case for reading Derrida as a kind of crypto-Wittgensteinian. Derrida's texts, they say, boil down to homely and recognisable Wittgensteinian doctrines. In Wittgenstein's case there are very close connections with architecture as he was himself an architect. But I think perhaps the Heideggerian connections might be more rewarding to follow up.

GB: I think the link with Wittgenstein is interesting in the sense that I think

L TO R: ILSE BING, *SELF-PORTRAIT IN MIRRORS*, 1931; AGNES BONNOT, *SELF-PORTRAIT*, 1981

Michael Podro is indeed wrong. Noticeably Derrida transcribes Wittgenstein's statement that 'whereof one cannot speak, thereof one must be silent' into that 'whereof one cannot speak, thereof one must write.' I think the basic problem for Wittgenstein in *The Philosophical Investigations* is that language is a matter of how we behave with it, which presupposes that we are doing the 'behaving' with it. We play language games, if you like. Derrida certainly does not presuppose the humanist notion of us as the players who then play the game. The players are in the game in a way in which the game metaphor can't, in fact, handle.

There are some rather misleading translations of Derrida that have used the notion of game when they should have used the notion of play. This, I think, is rather different. Also, so far as I remember at the beginning of *The Philosophical Investigations*, the example of slabs is Wittgenstein's analogy for language *if* you took on the traditional philosophical view of it. This was an attempt to show just how limited that view was; we need many more things before we can begin to have an account of language. So the connection with architecture is a little bit odd.

If you have a radical notion of exemplification without the notion of an essence of which the example is an example, then, strictly speaking, the notion of example is insufficient and in a traditional deconstructive way would need to be crossed out. And possibly the same with analogy, which I think is an interesting term to pick up in Derrida's essay. Analogy for Derrida has the notion of logic and logos lurking in there. The *Ana* prefix, which is something that Derrida has specifically written about and uses a great deal, probably includes or suggests the type of ambivalence that Michael Podro was wanting to get at. This could imply a more or less 'againstness' with respect to the logos but not a simple anti-logos. I think there is much work that needs to be done precisely on the uses of terms like 'exemplification' and 'analogy' as these can easily lead into trouble. Finally I want to endorse Andrew when he says that Deconstruction is not in objects. I want to add the corollary that objects are in Deconstruction.

MP: I disagree with the way you take the simple model of language in *The Philosophical Investigations*. Clearly Wittgenstein is not saying: 'Yes how marvellous the structures can become, how plastic human life is' but he's trying to say: 'Look, don't look for the nature of the thing in some remote realm; look for it as part of a way in which human life, communal human life, develops itself.' Now, it may be the case that this is deeply anti-derivative; is that what you would be saying?

GB: I don't think so. It's obviously fairly possible and presumably unavoidable for that type of exemplification to take place pedagogically with respect to Deconstruction. But that wouldn't necessarily have said anything particular about the place of examples in Deconstruction. That could easily be a question of approach and strategy with a whole set of pedagogical imperatives, which wouldn't necessarily prejudge the question of the example as such. For instance, it may well be necessary to rely on concepts and oppositions which Deconstruction would – perhaps later on in the pedagogical process – call into question. That is why Derrida might be interested in the *Tractatus* which has something of that movement about it.

I certainly wouldn't want to say that there's anything deeply anti-Derridean about the later Wittgenstein, I'm not sure I've got an opinion about that. But I take it that Wittgenstein's point is to say: 'Sure, don't look somewhere else in the mysterious realm for the essence of language', but, on the other hand, he is certainly not saying: 'Look at the language game played by the builders or the slabs, that's the essence of language.' It's saying that in no form of life

or modern language is the essence of language apparent. I take that to be the radical point of view of *The Philosophical Investigations*. To that extent I cannot see that that's anti-Derridean at all.

SB: Could I raise another question, and that is the question of art. If one were to be the devil's advocate, I think one could say that many post-war French thinkers have had a really extraordinarily positive feeling for art. I could mention Sartre, Foucault, Kristeva. I myself always feel that Derrida tends to treat these subjects at arm's length, but I may be wrong.

GB: No, I think probably your intuition is right. It would be inaccurate to suggest that Derrida has the type of intuitive feel for painting that some of the people you've mentioned have, and I think the reasons for that aren't necessarily accidental or personal or psychological. One of the reasons is that in those people's thinking about art there would at some point be (and perhaps most complicatedly worked out in some of Lyotard's recent writings about painting), however subtle the analysis, however complicated the mediations and so on, a reliance on something like a moment of sensory or perceptual presence. And this is indeed something that Lyotard happily stresses and wants in a sense to salvage – which is to say that when you stand in front of a painting, look at it, there is something which he wants in a provocative way to call presence. This is extremely difficult to talk about using traditional philosophical discourse. Derrida of course is suspicious in all his work of that type of appeal, however modest or however grandiose, to something like a founding moment of presence of any type. I suspect that what we say about having a feeling for art presupposes the very things that Derrida is busily undoing in one way or another. Now, it may be that that suggests different ways of talking about painting which may in the end, I suppose, become in some way intuitive or familiar. I'm not at all sure that *The Truth in Painting* provides a very clear sense of that, but that would be predictable if it really were new. The essay on Adami I think is a genuine try and maybe the fact it is Adami is something that one can talk about. Most of the essay is explicitly written without reference to colour. And yet colour is certainly the most surprising and striking thing about Adami's work, and is that which would immediately have the 'presence' built into it.

SB: Perhaps Andrew Benjamin would like to comment on that.

AB: It seems to me that part of what's at stake here is as I mentioned before, trying to find Deconstruction in an object. What Derrida is doing in writing about Adami, Titus-Carmel and so on is to concentrate on two particular points. On the one hand an attempt to deconstruct a certain pretention, on the other a recognition that the painting or the work of art affirms the impossibility of that pretention. If we could assume just for a moment that the idea of self-representation is marked by the impossibility of presence, it would provide a way of reading autobiographical, or rather, self-portraits at both the level of photography and of painting. I'm particularly interested in photography, therefore I'll just make a few comments about that.

In one of Ilse Bing's self-portraits there is the standard gesture of the photographer photographing herself. Yet there are two heads within the frame. One is the head of the act of photographing and the other head is the photographed head. Between these two heads there is a necessary non-correspondence. They are different and yet of course they are the same. The frame therefore contains sameness and difference inscribed within the same. Now what I would argue following Derrida is that this particular photograph by Ilse Bing can be 'interpreted' as affirming the impossibility of self-presence. That, for me, would be the opening move in any discussion of this work. On the other hand there is a photograph of Agnès Bonnot photographing herself. It 'shows' her standing over a mirror. A reading of this photograph would begin by arguing that it works within the impossibility identified by Deconstruction – the photograph seems to accept the idea of a pure self-presence, of making oneself present to oneself. The act of self-representation is inscribed within the frame itself. However, you could then launch a Deconstructive reading of that photograph to show in what way this act of pure self-presence, the pure side that one represents to oneself, became impossible. What I would take from Derrida's writings is an interpretative framework in which to talk about affirmative literature or affirmative art or affirmative photography, and that which works within the seduction of unity.

There is therefore a critical dimension. That is, one can identify what he calls the affirmative. I think that exists in art and in literature.

CN: There is a problem with that, though, in that the two photographs you offered as examples are, in a strong sense, exemplifications of Deconstruction; they wouldn't be analogies, so they answer that difficulty. Deconstruction as a philosophy of language is not criticism of interpretation. It is not merely pointing out self-reflexive elements in literary texts. De Man on Proust makes a point about allegories of reading. He chooses a scene from *A La Recherche du Temps Perdu* where Proust writes about the act of reading and notes a whole series of oppositions between indoors and outdoors – being indoors with a book, and outdoors playing, or whatever, metaphor versus metonymy. This is the opposition between the virtues of imaginative self-absorption and creativity and the continuance of everyday life.

De Man states: 'But you can do this with any passage of Proust, you can do this with any piece of fictional language. The fact that this describes a scene of reading is neither here nor there, it's merely fortuitous, really.' Now I don't believe that. I think one needs to call his bluff, and I think the same applies to Derrida. He is very good at passing off authors or particular texts that often thematise the particular effects of language on the history of art. This is so in Rousseau, Derrida notes, when he is writing about language, music, history, political economy and so on. It therefore must be something more than a mere theme. It is an effect of language but it is also to a degree thematised.

Now it strikes me that the example of those photographs would be an example of self-reflexive, thematic reading. It's an example of Deconstruction in that sense, but in a strong sense and a weak sense: strong in that it's not just an analogy, it's more than a metaphor: it's weak in the sense that it's explicit. The photograph presents itself to be read in those terms.

AB: But it also presents itself to be read in other terms, I would resist the fact that these photographs are Deconstructive in any sense. The interesting question here is the way an object sustains conflicting interpretations. But that is a separate issue.

Member of audience: I cannot find out the relation between the buildings in the Parc de la Villette and Deconstruction.

AB: Could I reply to that? The question is what could count as an answer to your question? And in a sense it seems to me that it's worth dwelling, if I could use that word, on what would count as an answer. It goes back to the point that Michael Podro raised of exemplarity or exemplification. Do you want to go to the Parc de la Villette and say: 'there is an example of Deconstructive architecture.' If that is the sort of relation for which you're looking, you're not going to find it. A bridge is provided by Derrida and Eisenman's own writing on architecture.

It's precisely these writings that provide the way of understanding how architectural thinking can be exemplified. We must allow the question of exemplification to be heterogeneous and recognise that exemplification within architecture is not purely a question of applied theory in practice. There is a different link between a philosophical dwelling on architecture and an architecture that takes up and sustains that philosophical thinking.

MP: Tschumi has spoken in a similar vein. One of the things that struck me was the particular way of proceeding with the development of buildings as the Parc de la Villette site progressed. As the project changed its own objectives, a building which started off as one thing turned into a fast food place at the next stage of the development. The accidents of contiguous structures then become things that Tschumi tries to utilise. What was striking to a layman like myself was that an attempt appears to have been made to utilise the period of building. In a city building, the changes of use, the deposits, the economic and social pressures which bring about complexity and diversity make themselves felt and give us this sense of the rich tissue of human activities.

Though Tschumi was trying to include this contingency and revision and utilisation of the changes during the building process, it has itself a mini-history. Now, you may say: 'Well that hasn't shown us any connection with Deconstruction' or, alternatively, you might say: 'Yes, that has shown us a possible kind of connection with Deconstruction's own or Derrida's own,

curious self-consciousness, self-revisionary, self-interruptive, self-adaptive procedure.

Member of audience: There were suggestions that there are two different ways of looking at analogy, and it's gratifying to hear Derrida say something like 'if there's only one voice, it's wrong.' Perhaps one can see analogy as a way of looking at two things at once and therefore seeing the tension between them. That seems to me to be combining analogy with metaphor. Affirmation can then be said to be an added feature.

GB: There is certainly a whole imagined contention in Derrida as to the notion of the 'between'. One of the best pedagogical approaches to his work is precisely to try and think less in terms of the 'this and that' than in terms of the tension 'between'. What Derrida has looked at most explicitly is metaphor in philosophical texts, although metaphor is traditionally looked for in literary texts. There's no simple and automatic exportation of that work into fiction and poetry. Therefore a certain amount of caution is needed.

The point that Derrida makes is that a traditional philosophical use of metaphor – and this would correspond to one of these views of analogy – is that metaphor is used to illuminate an unfamiliar 'this' with a more familiar 'that'. The traditional philosophical view is that language is a rather difficult and complex thing to get to grips with. The house metaphor is much more immediate and familiar and will help us understand the concept more fully. Derrida shows that the way this is deployed in Heidegger is not the way the metaphor works, that is it doesn't work the other way round. And it's not simply that you can't know what a house is even though you might think you do. The terms language and house are held in such a way that neither has that simple priority over the other, neither can help you understand the less familiar.

Member of audience: It seems to me that the implicit subtext of all this is that Derrida doesn't have very much to say to art and architecture. All he is doing is questioning assumptions and asking us to be suspicious about nothing can be definitive, everything changes. Deconstruction involves – a point made by Derrida – an endless struggle between the enlightened on the one hand, and the rest on the other. Despite Derrida's pragmatic caution and caring, the enlightened side always wins in the struggle. An exemplification of that is the presentation today. Nothing can be more traditional than having five people sitting at the front telling everybody else what they think, then inviting questions. You don't say 'What does everybody else think?' but, 'Has anybody got any questions?'; you act as sources of authority in residence.

GB: The notion of Deconstruction having things to offer obviously sets up an extremely familiar and comforting view whereby it offers itself as a new intellectual product on the market place, trying to win over customers. Its latest attempt, its latest market research, takes it out towards art and architecture, trying against resistance to sell its product. I think that in no sense, however, as Derrida very clearly states, can Deconstruction be considered a new intellectual movement of that type. As for enlightenment always winning out, I would say that the opposite occurs – enlightenment never wins out; there is no winning out in Deconstruction. There is a necessary and endless tension. Saying that is not a prediction about the future, it is a statement of necessity. The basis of the question, which is extremely common and which I think is probably at the root of a lot of misunderstandings, is to suggest that Deconstruction presents itself as a radical break. This is obviously of a piece with the language of marketing and selling, with the product and so on, with a brand new language. Derrida's comments on this are absolutely clear – Deconstruction occurs in Plato as well as in Derrida.

The last thing I want to say is that probably at least five of us up here on the stage regret the absence of any architect among us. And as for the position of authority, answerability, and so on, I suspect that most of the people here, including myself, feel rather uncomfortable about that. On the other hand, again within the rather simple notion of a radical break, shift etc, the idea that this type of structure can simply be got away from, that for example (which I take to be the tone of the question), if Deconstruction were really so radical as it pretends, we wouldn't need any such structure of authority, any such structure of pedagogy and so on, is obviously quite untenable. .

But there *is* a relationship of tension between what's teachable, and what is not, what is exemplifiable, and what is not. There are also degrees of authority that anybody, including Derrida, can have with respect to Deconstruction, of which he's certainly not a subject or author in any traditional sense. These are all limits and tensions which need to be negotiated. And I agree with the questioner on one thing, and I think one thing only, which is that this particular format negotiates them rather badly. But I suspect that we're as sorry about that as you are.

PETER EISENMAN, WEXNER CENTER FOR THE VISUAL ARTS, OHIO STATE UNIVERSITY

ANDREW BENJAMIN
Derrida, Architecture and Philosophy

BERNARD TSCHUMI, PARC DE LA VILLETTE, PARIS

The history of philosophy has always demonstrated a two-fold concern with architecture. The first is by philosophy either addressing architecture as an aesthetic form (eg in Hegel's *Aesthetics*), or deploying architectural examples in a more general discussion of aesthetics or art (eg Heidegger's discussion of the Greek temple in *The Origin of the Work of Art*). The second is the presence of architectural forms (eg Kant's architectonic) or architectural metaphors in the develop-

ment or construction of a philosophical argument. The second of these is, in this instance, the more relevant. To delimit a specific terrain of discussion into which Derrida's writings on architecture can be articulated, I will concentrate on the justly famous architectural metaphor developed by Descartes in the second part of the Discourse on Method. Despite the length of this passage I will quote it in full in order that its force may be made clear:

> . . . there is not usually so much perfection in works composed of several parts and produced by different craftsmen as in the works of one man. Thus we see that buildings undertaken and completed by a single architect are usually more attractive and better planned than those which several have tried to patch up by adapting old walls built for different purposes. Again, ancient cities which have gradually grown up from mere villages into large towns are usually ill-proportioned, compared with those orderly towns which planners lay out as they fancy on level ground. Looking at buildings of the former individually, you will often find as much art in them if not more than in those of the latter; but in view of their arrangement – a tall one here, a small one there – and the way they make the streets crooked and irregular you would say it is chance rather than the will of men using reason, that placed them so. And when you consider that there have always been certain officials whose job it is to see that private buildings embellish public places you will understand how difficult it is to make something perfect by working only on what others have produced.[1]

This passage refers, if only initially, to Descartes' attempt to justify both his own philosophical project as well as establishing the necessity of its being undertaken by a single philosopher working alone.

Descartes is attempting neither a reworking nor a refurbishing of past philosophy but a radical departure that thereby establishes a new and original philosophical system. Descartes' aim therefore is two-fold. On the one hand he wants to establish a total and unified system, and on the other, one that breaks fundamentally with past philosophical systems (in particular, of course, the Scholastics) and is thus not tainted by earlier mistakes and prejudices. It is this two-fold aim that is expressed in his metaphor of the activity of architects and builders.

The elaborate metaphor opens with a juxtaposition of the one and the many. Works produced by one craftsman have a greater degree of 'perfection' than those produced by a number. Buildings designed and built by a single architect are, as a consequence, far more attractive than buildings whose refurbishing has involved the participation of a collection of architects working over a number of years and inevitably with different intentions. Having made this point Descartes then extends the range of the metaphor, moving from a single construction to a city. Here the contrast is between a city which has developed through time, through consecutive and perhaps overlapping stages and which therefore contains ill-proportioned and irregular components, and a city or town conceived and built within an extended single moment. The force of this opposition is then reinforced by the further opposition between chance and reason. If there is anything attractive about the buildings, or even the quarters of an ancient city, then it is the result of chance. The beauty of a city designed and built during the single extended moment is the result of the application of reason. Before taking up the important opposition between reason and chance, it is essential to dwell on this single extended moment.

The moment is the enactment of that which reason dictates. The regulation of reason extends through the conception, the enactment and its completion. Reason has what could amount to a universal and to that extent an atemporal extension. The singularity of the construction (a singularity excluding plurality), the singularity of the architect (excluding pluralism and thereby erecting the architect as God – one replacing the other within similar hierarchic principles) is reinscribed within the singularity of this moment.

The lack of order in the ancient city is marked by – as well as being the mark of – the lack of reason. It has the consequence that not only is the city in some sense 'mad',[2] it can also be thought within the totalising purview of reason, except of course as mad. Therefore when taken to its logical extreme the architectural metaphor indicates both the possibility of a unified totality – to be provided by the application of reason – as well as that which stands opposed to this possibility, namely, madness; presented here as the untotalisable plurality of the ancient city. The opposition between reason and madness is introduced by, and within, an architectural metaphor.

The triumph of reason over madness, Descartes is insisting, is the path to be followed by the philosopher as architect and the architect as philosopher. The activity of each is delimited not by reason as such, but by the oppositions between reason and chance, and reason and madness. There is of course an imperative within Descartes' metaphor. It indicates his understanding of the philosophical task. For Descartes the totality and necessary unity engendered by reason can be attained. Within the metaphor the old city can be razed to the ground. The new city will emerge without bearing the traces of the old. There will be no traces of the old to be remarked. As will be seen it is precisely the possibility of the absence of any remark, or rather the impossibility of its absence that is taken up, amongst other things, when Derrida writes of 'maintaining'. The chance of architecture is maintained by the 'interruption' between the traditional and the affirmative. This point will be pursued.

There are two important components of Descartes' architectural metaphor and the ensuing philosophical practice to which it gives rise. The first is the functional opposition between reason and chance (reason and madness). The second, far more difficult to discern, involves the opposition between the inside and the outside. The metaphor of the city, in order that it further Descartes' philosophical end, must be understood as a structured space, and therefore as a place to be re-deployed in the construction of the city of reason. Furthermore it must be constructed to allow the philosopher or architect the possibility of a place outside its own wall. Regulation and control must take place from the outside. The metaphor of the city is therefore also ensnared within the further opposition of inside and outside (as well as the one between theory and practice). I want to develop these two elements.

The intriguing element that can be seen to emerge from within the metaphor of the city is the implicit recognition that if the city of reason has an outside, then it is madness. The haphazard chance of *déraison* is constrained to take place outside the city walls. The consequence of this is that the architect must be written into the city in order to avoid madness and yet the philosopher or architect must be outside the gates in order to exert control. The architectonic needs to be regulated from outside. Present here is the problem of the before and in front of. The philosopher (or architect) would seem therefore to be placed – and to have placed themselves – within a double-bind, that can, in historical terms, perhaps only be resolved by God.

The importance of the description of the opposition between reason and chance (reason and madness) as functional lies in the fact that it indicates that the opposition is neither arbitrary nor simply a result or conclusion, but plays a structuring role in the text. However in the present context it is the second component that is the more relevant. In spatial terms the distinction between the inside and the outside is perhaps best understood in relation to the labyrinth. The labyrinth is obviously the sign of the city. It is also the sign of writing.[3] Both the labyrinth and writing are concerned with, if only because they give rise to, firstly the problem of the place, and secondly an epistemology of

the place. A philosophy of totality and unity positions itself, of necessity, outside the place – outside the labyrinth and writing – and as such, knowledge is invariably linked to the transcendental. In Cartesian terms this distinction finds its most adequate formulation in terms of the distinction between the understanding and the imagination. Only the understanding working with transcendental rules can determine and yield certainty. The understanding is always positioned outside and then comes to be applied in the world. This is not to suggest that for Descartes knowledge is empirical; rather knowledge is of the empirical. The conditions for the possibility of knowledge – the method to be applied and the rules governing clear and distinct perception, etc – are themselves transcendental. The imagination on the other hand is trapped in the labyrinth. The problem of the imagination is that in itself it lacks a limit. The imagination is essential for knowledge but only when its results can be controlled by the understanding. For Descartes the typology of consciousness necessitates a divide between the domain of the understanding and the domain of the imagination. It is clear that this distinction – one that is repeated and reinforced in other of his writings in terms of the distinction between the understanding and the will – has specific ontological and temporal considerations.

In tracing the implications of the architectural metaphor in Descartes' *Discourse on Method* what has emerged is a series of oppositions that play a structuring role within the presentation of his philosophical position. It is quite literally constructed in terms of them. It is of course precisely in relation to these oppositions that the force of Deconstruction can be located. It is by tracing through their implications – allowing their unstable logic to unfold – that the work of Deconstruction begins to take place. Derrida details this aspect of Deconstruction in the following terms:

> De-construction . . . analyses and compares conceptual pairs which are currently accepted as self-evident and natural, as if they had not been institutionalised at some precise moment, as if they had no history. Because of being taken for granted they restrict thinking.[4]

Deconstruction, in this instance, is therefore a beginning. However Deconstruction is not the simple reversal of the dominant term within an opposition. This becomes increasingly clear in Derrida's writing on the work of Bernard Tschumi.[5] A fundamental strategy of that paper (*Point de folie – Maintenant l'architecture*) is the retention of both madness and chance and yet they are not part of a simple opposition. They are not merely the other side of reason.

The work of Tschumi under consideration by Derrida is his plan of the *Parc de la Villette*, and in particular a series of constructions within the park known as *Les Folies*. Of this title, name, signature, Derrida makes the important point that they are not 'madness (*la folie*), the allegorical hypostasis of Unreason, non-sense, but the madnesses (*les folies*)'. In sum what makes Derrida's writings on architecture of particular interest is the way he tries to indicate in what sense a philosophical argument or position can be incorporated into a different activity. Two elements need to be stated in advance. The first is that Derrida is emphatic that despite appearances Deconstruction is not itself an architectural metaphor. Not only is he suspicious of metaphors; it is also the case that Deconstruction does not amount to a simple dismantling, it is at the same time – and in the Nietzschean sense – affirmative.

The second point is that logocentrism is evident in the way in which architecture, habitation, dwelling, living, etc are understood within both philosophical and architectural thinking. It is the evident presence and structural force of logocentrism that provides a possible entry for Deconstruction. It enters via the rearticulation of metaphysics. It is of course a rearticulation that is housed architecturally and yet extends beyond architecture. It is at home in the history of Western metaphysics. As Derrida suggests, the 'architectonics of invariable points . . . regulates all of what is called Western culture, far beyond its architecture.' However it also takes place – and finds a place – in its architecture. It is this that makes a Deconstruction of architectural thinking possible. It is furthermore what makes an affirmative architecture possible. Derrida says of Tschumi's *folies* that they: '. . . affirm, and engage their affirmation beyond this ultimately annihilating, secretly nihilistic repetition of metaphysical architecture.'[6]

There is an interesting parallel here between Derrida's discussion of architecture and his discussion of literature. Without returning to the question – what is literature? – it is essential to point out that in Derrida's work there is no privileging of the literary as opposed to the philosophical. Both can be and usually are logocentric. They are both sites, inhabited and constructed by the repetition of metaphysics. For Derrida literature is something to-come. It is this element that he locates in the work of the French writer Roger Laporte. Derrida writes of his work *Fugue* that '. . . in inscribing itself in an historically, libidinally, economically, politically determined field . . . no metalanguage is powerful enough today to dominate the progress [*la marche*] or rather the un-folding [*la dé-marche*] of this writing.'[7] He goes on to add: '*Fugue* . . . takes away in advance all metalinguistic resources and makes of this quasi-operation an unheard music outside of genre.'[8]

Taking into consideration Derrida's own writings on genre[9] – his Deconstruction of the possibility of genres as all-inclusive – further serves to indicate that in the place of texts dominated by logocentrism and which therefore count as a rearticulation of metaphysics, as well as themselves being inscribed within 'conceptual pairs', Laporte's text *Fugue* is, in the sense alluded to above, affirmative. It is *as* a work – and *in* its work – the literature-to-come. There is therefore, within Derrida's own philosophical undertaking, an important connection between the works/writings of Tschumi and Laporte. Their futural dimension, their being works-to-come, is located in their connection to that which proceeded. The hinge connecting them marks a type of sublation.

What has to be traced in Derrida's understanding of Tschumi is this affirmative dimension. The point of departure is provided by the oppositions between reason and chance, and reason and madness. It is already clear in what sense these 'conceptual pairs' are operative in Descartes' architectural metaphor. The question is how are madness and chance taken over by Derrida?

The first point to note is that Tschumi's *folies* are not, as has already been mentioned, simply the other side of reason. They are marked by the opposition reason/madness and yet not articulated in terms of it. Connected to the act of affirmation is the equally important process of what could be called a form of displacement or distancing. The process of distancing is found in Derrida's description of the *folies*:

> Tschumi's 'first' concern will no longer be to organise space as a function or in view of economic, aesthetic, epiphanic, or techno-utilitarian norms. These norms will be taken into consideration, but they will find themselves subordinated and reinscribed in one place in a text and in a space that they no longer command in the final instance. By pushing architecture towards its limits, a place will be made for 'pleasure'; each *folie* will be destined for a given 'use', with its own cultural, ludic, pedagogical, scientific and philosophical finalities.[10]

The distancing or displacement – and indeed the hinge marking or remarking their connection to logocentrism/metaphysics/'conceptual pairs' – is captured by Derrida when he writes of 'norms' being 'taken into consideration'; being 'reinscribed'; present but no longer in 'command'. Norms become, in Nietzsche's sense, 'fictions'[11] – thereby opening up, though always in a way to be determined, the possibility gestured at in what Derrida calls 'transarchitecture'.

Distancing is still connective. There is no pure beyond. In any adventure there is still the remark. The Cartesian desire for the absolutely new, for the completely unique, is, for Derrida, an impossibility. It forms part of logocentrism's desire for a self-enclosed totality. The remark can always be remarked upon. It is in terms of 'maintaining' that this interplay is described. In addition however it is

also exemplified, stylistically, in the aphorisms which Derrida chose to preface a collection of recent papers on philosophy and architecture. The uniqueness and self-referring nature of the aphorism is deconstructed via that aphorism itself. Self-reference is an impossibility. Perhaps even the act of citing the following aphorism (its citation rather than its contents, especially as it is incomplete) is sufficient to make this point:

> An authentic aphorism must never refer to another. It is sufficient unto itself; world or monad. But whether it is wanted or not, whether one sees it or not, the aphorisms interlink here as aphorisms, and in number, numbered. Their series yields to an *irreversible* order . . .[12]

Derrida locates the work of Tschumi within a paradox and also within the *maintenant*. The presence of what could be described as a logic of paradox within Derrida's work is too large a theme to be taken up here. It is, however, at work in his discussion of Tschumi. When, for example, he argues that the 'red points' (deployed by Tschumi as part of his project) both disperse and gather, they become and articulate this logic. However the dispersal and gathering is held together and is maintained: 'The red points space, maintaining architecture in the dissociation of spacing. But this *maintenant* does not only maintain a past and a tradition: it does not ensure a synthesis. It maintains the interruption, in other words the relation to the other *per se*.'[13] It is of course precisely in terms of 'maintaining' that an affirmative conception of architecture is allowed to take place. Furthermore it is one that involves and deploys chance and madness in the 'interruption' with the 'conceptual pairs' within which the history of philosophy has placed them. Chance becomes the wager. And madness, that which by a fascinating etymological gamble is freed from one madness, becomes, amongst other things, the 'madness of an asemantics'. The importance of chance lies in its breaking of a conceptual closure. 'Disassociation' takes place – yet it takes place in the 'space of reassembly'. Maintained, it could be argued, within a logic of paradox.

The oppositions within which Descartes' architectural metaphor took place are no longer either authoritative or central. Madness and chance have been freed not just from their subordinate place within those oppositions, they have also emerged as affirmative 'concepts' within which to think the possibility of a Deconstructive architecture. The nature – and, it must be added, a nature beyond essentialism – of such an architecture is described by Peter Eisenman in the following way:

> What is being proposed is an expansion beyond the limitation presented by the classical mode to the realisation of architecture as an independent discourse, free from external values; that is, the intersection of the meaningful, the arbitrary and the timeless in the artificial.[14]

The challenge presented by Deconstruction to architecture is the 'same' as the challenge it presents to all the arts, and of course to philosophy, literary criticism, etc. It is a challenge that, initially, takes place on the level of thinking; here in the example of architecture thinking maintaining. Thinking that comes to be enacted – or can be seen to be enacted – in the architectural work of Eisenman and Tschumi amongst others.

Having come this far it is worth pausing to try and place Deconstruction before architecture, or architectural thinking before Deconstruction. In either case the 'before' does not mark the presence of a universal and transcendental law – eg the work of the understanding within the Cartesian texts, or Hegelian 'absolute knowledge' – that would regulate architecture or Deconstruction as philosophy. Does Deconstruction allow for what within traditional aesthetics is of fundamental philosophical importance; namely, evaluation? Derrida has tried to delimit the relationship between Deconstruction and architectural thinking: 'Architectural thinking can only be Deconstructive in the following sense: as an attempt to visualise that which establishes the authority of the architectural concatenation in philosophy.'[15]

The 'architectural concatenation' is itself repeated within the history of metaphysics. A repetition that is found throughout the texts – and in part structures the texts – that are included within the history of philosophy. (It has been observed in Descartes' *Discourse on Method*, though it could just have easily been traced in a diverse range of texts, including Aristotle, Kant, Hegel and Heidegger.) Its authority is precisely the object of Deconstruction. Deconstructed authority is retained but without its authority, although when it comes to the question of evaluation, the criteria are themselves articulated in terms of that authority. In *The Critique of Judgement* Kant subsumes the evaluation of architecture under the rubric of design which is then joined to taste. Taste becomes the universal and self-referential form of legitimation working before, during and after the construction: 'In painting, sculpture, and in fact in all the formative arts, in architecture and horticulture, so far as fine arts, the design is what is essential. Here it is not what gratifies in sensation but merely what pleases by its form,

that is the fundamental prerequisite for taste.'[16]

In other words the vocabulary of evaluation – the language of aesthetics – does itself form part of the philosophical architectonic. The consequence of this is that if there is to be a language of evaluation stemming from Deconstruction then it will necessitate what Nietzsche described as a 'revaluation of all values'. Even though Derrida may appear to privilege the uniqueness of a specific work, this is not a recourse to a fundamental pragmatism. In fact the thing/event can never be unique and sel-freferential; hence gathering and dispersal; hence *maintenant/maintenir*; hence the always already-present remark. A Deconstructive aesthetic and the plurality of a Deconstructive criteria for evaluation are yet to be written. Derrida's writings on architecture, while on architecture, are also an aesthetics-to-come. The potential for a Deconstructive aesthetics is to that extent always already written.

Notes

1 R Descartes, 'Discourse on Method', in *The Philosophical Writings of Descartes*, Vol 1, Cambridge University Press, 1985, p 116.

2 Derrida has written a number of texts on 'madness', including critiques of Foucault's *Madness and Civilisation* and Blanchot's *La folie du jour*.

3 Derrida makes similar points in an interview, 'Architetture ove il desiderio puo abitare', *Domus*, No 671, April 1986. While it is perhaps a transgression, I have rewritten some of the arguments he presents so as to link them with more general, if not conventional, philosophical concerns. Perhaps, again, this is translation as transgression.

4 A point made by Derrida in the above-mentioned interview.

5 'Point de folie', trans Kate Linker, *AA Files*, No 12, 1986.

6 *ibid*, p 69.

7 J Derrida, 'Ce qui reste à force de musique', *Psyché*, Galilée, 1987, p 96, (my trans). For an amplification of the point made about literature see R Gasché, *The Tain of the Mirror*, Harvard University Press, 1986, pp 255-318. I have discussed the importance of Gasché's book in 'Naming Deconstruction', *History of the Human Sciences*, Vol 1, No 2, 1988.

8 *ibid*, p 96.

9 J Derrida, 'The Law of Genre', *Glyph*, 7, 1980.

10 Derrida, *op cit*, p 69.

11 See F Nietzsche, *Beyond Good and Evil*, trans by W Kaufman, Vantage Books, New York, 1966, Section 21.

12 J Derrida, 'Cinquante-deux aphorismes pour un avant-propos', *Psyché*, Galilée, 1987, p 513 (my trans). This text formed the preface to *Mesure pour mesure: Architecture et philosophie*, Cahiers du CCI (Centre Georges Pompidou), 1987, a book emerging from a meeting between philosophers and architects organised by the Centre International de Philosophie.

13 Derrida, *op cit*, p 75.

14 P Eisenman, 'The End of the Classical', *Perspecta*, No 21, 1984. Derrida has written on Eisenman in, 'Pourquoi Peter Eisenman écrit de si bons livres', Psyché, pp 496-508. For an introduction to Eisenman's work see *Investigations in Architecture: Eisenman Studies at the GSD*: 1983-85, Harvard University, 1986, and P Eisenman, *Fin d'Ou T Hou S*, Architectural Association, 1985.

15 See the interview with Derrida mentioned above.

16 I Kant, *The Critique of Judgement*, trans J Meredith, Oxford University Press, 1986, p 67.

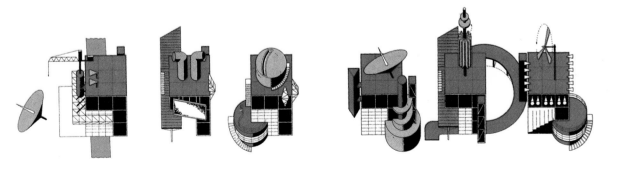

BERNARD TSCHUMI, PARC DE LA VILLETTE, PARIS (LA CASE VIDE, DETAIL, 1985)

GEOFF BENNINGTON
Deconstruction is not what you think

1. Deconstruction is not what you think.

[...]

1.3. Deconstruction is not what you think. If what you think is a content, present to mind, in 'the mind's presence-room' (Locke). But that you think might already be Deconstruction.

2. Deconstruction is not (what you think if you think it is) essentially to do with language.

2.1. Nothing more common than to hear Deconstruction described as depending on 'an extension of the linguistic paradigm'. 'There is nothing outside the text' (Derrida): proves it, obviously.

2.1.1. Everybody also knows this is not quite right. 'Text' is not quite an extension of a familiar concept, but a displacement or reinscription of it. Text in general is any system of marks, traces, referrals (don't say reference, have a little more sense than that). Perception is a text.

2.2. Think of recognition. Two requirements: that the object of recognition be in principle repeatable as the same object in a different context; that in the given context it be identifiable as different from the other elements of that context. (If it helps, think of the first as a temporal requirement, the second as spatial: but space and time do not determine the text, they are made possible by it.)

2.2.1. Presence would be that there be no difference, nor referral, no trace. Which is impossible. So presence would not be were there no difference, or referral, or trace. Presence is made possible by the trace, which makes pure presence impossible: each present moment is essentially constituted by its retention of a trace of a past moment. This is just as true of the 'first' present moment as of any other, which thereby has a relation with a past that never was present: absolute past.

2.3. 'Referral' is not reference in the linguistic sense. Deconstruction does not have a place for language over here, and a world over there to which it refers. Elements in the language refer to one another for their identity, and refer to non-linguistic marks which refer in turn for their identity and difference. There is no essential difference between language and the world, the one as subject, the other as object. There are traces.

2.3.1. Think of Deconstruction as extending the world paradigm if you like. It makes no difference, so long as you don't think of the world set up out there over against.

2.4. Of course text does not mean discourse. Perception is not a discourse, it is a text. Discourse is a text. (But nobody thinks you can separate Deconstruction from language. Nor from the world. Text is not a mediation between language and world, but the milieu in which any such distinction might be drawn.)

3. Deconstruction is not a theory or a project. It does not prescribe a practice more or less faithful to it, nor project an image of a desirable state to be brought about.

3.1. Deconstruction is necessary.

[...]

4. Painting. Not just that painting is probably unthinkable without language. Certainly not that painting is 'like a language'. But there's no trouble thinking about painting as difference and trace. The 'event

of presence' (Lyotard) which a painting presents would be quite unpresentable otherwise.

4.1. A painting is a text, of course. The problem is that of knowing what sort of text. Deconstruction is not at all to do with treating a painting like a 'written' text, 'reading' it etc. (Unless 'reading' is displaced in the same way as text.)

4.1.1. Reading is not a simple process of deciphering, nor of interpreting, for Deconstruction. It is neither entirely respectful nor simply violent. 'Secure production of insecurity' (Derrida). Reading is not performed by a subject set against the text as object: reading is imbricated in the text it reads. Leave a trace in the text if you can.

4.2. Write about the way painting has been written about (in its supposed relation to the truth, especially), more on painting's side than on the attempts to speak its truth. That's one thing to do.

4.3. But be very careful before writing on painting.

4.3.1. Writing on painting is easy if you think writing and painting don't mix. So long as painting's not writing and writing's not painting, easy enough to keep writing (or painting). But it's just as bad to think that writing and painting are simply the same sort of thing (*ut pictura poeis*).

4.3.2. But in the referrals of the text, the security of the divisions gives way and with it the security of the passages across those divisions. It's not great drama to cross a frontier so long as you know where it is.

4.3.3. Writing can no doubt do things painting can't, and vice versa. But don't make too much of iterability and ideality on the side of writing, singularity and materiality on the side of painting. Of course there are differences between a literary text and a painting: but the latter is also essentially reproducible. The age of mechanical reproduction (Benjamin) does not befall painting like a catastrophe: aura is always already being lost.

[...]

5. Colour. Where is the colour in Deconstruction?

5.1. Colour is a question of differential values, and therefore traces. This is not a point about colour vocabulary, but about colour. Deconstruction is not linguistic relativism. Colour is, in Deconstruction.

[...]

6. 'Deconstructionist painting' could not be the result of a successful 'application' of Derrida's theory (see 3.).

6.1. Deconstruction in painting has always already begun.

6.2. Of course painting can be 'influenced' by Derrida's writing. This does not *ipso facto* make it 'Deconstructive'.

6.2.1. It is quite possible that the most 'Deconstructive' painting should (have) happen(ed) in ignorance of Derrida's work, though knowledge of Derrida's work might help us to talk about that painting, and others.

[...]

7. A painting could try to be a 'reading' of texts by Derrida. Adami. Leave a trace in the text if you can.

GEOFF BENNINGTON
Deconstruction and Postmodernism

Deconstruction just might, I suppose, become the name for an artistic 'movement'. It is reasonable enough to suppose that behind the organisation of the symposium, for example, lies a suspicion that the time for such a naming and recognition has come, or at least a desire that the time has come. We have by now a sense of 'deconstruction' at work not only in philosophy and literary studies, but also in architecture and architectural criticism, so why not in painting too?

By naming artists and critics who would claim or accept the label 'deconstruction', and proceeding to pin that label on others in spite of their protests; by seeking out antecedents' thought either to foreshadow (and consequently deny the apparent novelty of) this deconstruction or, more subtly, as in Borges' essay on Kafka, antecedents recognised as having been created as precursors through this process of naming deconstruction; by quarrelling over dates at which the movement might be said to have started, over 'the first deconstructive painting' and so on, we can get going quite happily generating discourse and argument, staging (or stage-managing) what are called 'debates', eventually publishing manifestoes, organising exhibitions, writing catalogues, engaging in polemic, and generally enjoying ourselves – *if* that's what we enjoy.

These activities, which are I imagine in some way necessary to the institutions of art, thrive on confusions of various sorts, if the recent and I suppose still current example of the so-called 'debate' around 'post-modernism', 'postmodernity' and 'the postmodern' is anything to go by. Clearly something is going on here, but there is a perhaps unusual degree of disagreement as to what it is, and even as to whether it is 'really' going on, or somehow 'manufactured' by those who find their advantage in saying that it is. Perhaps the disagreement *is* all that is going on. And if disagreement (or dissensus) be taken as a sign of the postmodern, then it would indeed seem reasonable not so much to look for a 'true state of affairs' *behind* that disagreement as to take the disagreement as the true state of affairs. In this sense, disagreement about the meaning or existence of the postmodern would *itself* be the postmodern, and we would have enforced at least the consensus that there is a dissensus. And if a corollary of the conception of the postmodern as disagreement is that the disagreement (which becomes a *différend* in Lyotard's sense) cannot be dominated and resolved by one of the parties to the disagreement (and Derrida, who has in general been extremely prudent about the term, has linked postmodernism to the end of a project of domination), then it follows that it would be naive to attempt an 'overview' of the so-called 'debate'. (A supplementary complication would arise from the suspicion that the major items in the 'debate' *are* nevertheless attempts at overviews.) The situation is complicated further still by a recent tendency, in my own field at least, to conflate postmodernism with so-called post-structuralism and even deconstruction. Some people try to put some order into this by saying that deconstruction and post-structuralism are merely part of a more pervasive postmodernism (and Stephen Melville has suggested that one of the effects of the translation of *The Truth in Painting* is that it will bring deconstruction more obviously into the field of the visual arts, thus connecting with postmodernism), but the general aim of such conflation is usually to lump a lot of things together the better to celebrate or get rid of them without in either case having to think very hard.

Rather piously, perhaps, I'd like to hope that some of the more frenetic features of the post-modern debate might be avoided in the case of deconstruction. There are a number of reasons why this hope might not be absolutely pious. For example, unlike 'deconstruction', the very term 'postmodernism' implies a fairly simple linear or at best dialectical conception of history which is difficult to avoid. A cautionary tale of some of the difficulties this can lead to is provided by Charles Jencks' pamphlet, *What is Post-Modernism?* In the course of his remarks, Jencks suggests that the reaction of committed Modernists to post-modernism (a reaction he calls 'The Protestant Inquisition') is as 'paranoic, reactionary and repressive as their Beaux-Arts persecutors were before them' (p 14). On the one hand, Jencks rather welcomes this: 'I do believe that these characterisations have not done what they were supposed to do – stem the tide of Post-Modernism – but rather have helped to blow it up into a media event' (*ibid*), and goes on: 'My nightmare is that suddenly the reactionaries will become nice and civil' (Before moralistically condemning Jencks for what seems to be a complacent welcoming of 'media hype', we might pause to wonder what sort of 'event' today – including today's 'event' – (and indeed what sort of event in general) would *not* be in some sense a 'media event', and to wonder also if this might in addition be a component of a 'postmodern condition', and an object of deconstructive negotiation). In any case, having apparently welcomed this violence of reaction and the consequent 'media event', Jencks goes on to deplore it too, because it has hidden what he calls 'the root cause of the movement'.

Jencks then proceeds to offer the reader the 'true story' of the movement called postmodernism. Despite the claims made on the pamphlet's cover-note about 'typical Post-Modern devices of exposition' (irony, parody and so on), this story is in fact academic and classical enough, maybe just because it's a story. Jencks in fact defines Post-Modernism in the most traditionally dialectical way imaginable, as 'the continuation of Modernism and its transcendence' (p 7): cancellation and preservation in a nice Hegelian *Aufhebung*. In view of this, it perhaps comes as no surprise to find Jencks at the end of his text endorsing and appropriating Peter Fuller's call for 'the equivalent of a new spirituality based on an "imaginative, yet secular, response to nature herself", seeking '"a shared symbolic order of the kind that a religion provides", but without the religion' (p 48). Jencks explicitly sets this against the 'relativism' he suggests must inevitably result from Lyotard's arguments: but the result is that the 'disagreement' I was suggesting might be constitutive of the postmodern is here rapidly defused and absorbed into the pious projection of a horizon of consensus and even redemption, beyond current rows and media events. Nothing could be less postmodern than this type of schema of argument, and nothing could more invite deconstruction than the unquestioned value of 'nature herself', which is of a piece with the simple view of history I have described: let me quote from *The Truth in Painting* to illustrate this difficulty:

If one were to consider the *physis/tekhné* opposition to be irreducible, if one were to accredit so hastily its translation as *nature/art* or *nature/technique*, one would easily commit oneself to thinking that art, being no longer nature, is history. The opposition nature/history would be the analogical relay of *physis/tekhné*. One can thus already say: as for history, we shall have to deal with the contradiction or the oscillation between two apparently incompatible motifs. They both come under one and the same logical formality: namely, that if the philosophy of art always has the greatest difficulty in dominating the history of art, a certain concept of the historicity of art, this is, paradoxically, because it too easily thinks of art as historical. What I am putting forward here obviously assumes the transformation of the concept of history, from one statement to the other.[2]

The problems this would raise for Jencks' conception show through most clearly in his attempt to re-describe as 'Late-Modern' (exaggerating properly Modernist tendencies) what other writers would call 'post-modern' (which Jencks wants to describe in the dialectical way I have mentioned). His main object of disagreement here is Jean-François Lyotard, whom he appears to be quite simply unable to read: I would suggest that this illiteracy is quite consistently programmed by Jencks' own simple historicising and dialectical argument. Jencks is quite unable to make any coherent sense of the relationship between the three following propositions in Lyotard:

1. That the 'grand narratives' of legitimation are in decline, leading to a situation of generalised 'delegitimation'.

2. That a 'sensitivity to differences' and a 'war on totality' might be called for in this situation.

3. That, *in a certain sense*, the postmodern might be said to *precede* the modern (just as I would want to say that *in a certain sense* deconstruction is prior to construction).

I do not propose to dwell on Jencks' failure to distinguish in Lyotard between a description of a state of affairs as 'slackening' (of which the work of Charles Jencks might be taken as an example – Lyotard links Jencks' notion of the postmodern to an eclecticism attuned to the demands of capital)[3] and a prescription as to the appropriate (affirmative) way to think about that situation. The problems that arise from the third proposition I have isolated are more difficult and thereby more interesting, and closer to what we might understand by deconstruction. Jencks finds the idea of the postmodern somehow coming 'before' the modern 'amazing' and 'crazy' (although 'original'), and suggests that it leads Lyotard to 'confuse' postmodernism with 'the latest avant-gardism': he goes on to admit that 'it's embarrassing that Post-Modernism's first philosopher should be so fundamentally wrong', and to suggest rather condescendingly that because Lyotard is a philosopher (which indeed he is) and sociologist of knowledge (which he certainly isn't), he is simply not sufficiently attuned to cultural differences to make sense of what is going on.

Lyotard is, happily, philosopher enough to be suspicious of the sort of view that would reduce what he is trying to think (provisionally and, I think he would agree, imprudently) under the name of the 'postmodern' to the simple terms of much of the debate. If Lyotard is right to insist on the temporal complexities of what he calls the event of presentation or even of presence, which can be said to make the post-come first,[4] then we can be quite certain that standard sociologising and historicising accounts of what he is doing must be reductive at the very least. Our problem is and will be that what I would call journalism (with no pejorative intent), in its constitutive preoccupation to identify 'news' *now*, will almost necessarily reinforce that sort of reduction.

The same sort of point can be made of Derrida and deconstruction. The term 'deconstruction' does not carry the immediately unfortunate periodising connotations of the term 'postmodernism', although it is in some ways an unfortunate and misleading label (as Derrida himself has often said) for the work he and those inspired by him have done. Even accepting the label 'deconstruction', it would, for example, be quite inaccurate to suppose that this simply names something like a method or a technique or a theory or even a philosophy invented by Derrida in Paris at some ideally datable moment in the 1960s. There are important and specifiable reasons why it is wrong to think of deconstruction as something Derrida or anyone else does or has done to a text or an argument or even a painting. Let me quote briefly from Derrida's short text, 'Letter to a Japanese Friend', which discusses, with a view to its translation into Japanese, the status of the term 'deconstruction':

> In spite of appearances, deconstruction is neither an *analysis* nor a *critique*. . . It is not an analysis, in particular because the dismantling of a structure is not a regression towards the *simple element*, towards an *indecomposable origin*. . . No more is it a critique, whether in a general or a Kantian sense. . . I'll say the same thing for *method*. Deconstruction is not a method and cannot be transformed into a method.

Our historicist and subjectivist or objectivist impulses are so ingrained that it is difficult to think this, but we have to try to understand that deconstruction is neither something done at a given date by an active and willful or even heroic subject to a more or less resistant or complicit object, nor quite something that that subject is shown to do to itself anyway, whether we like it or not. Here's Derrida again, in the same text:

> It is not enough to say that deconstruction cannot be reduced to some methodological instrumentality, to a set of rules and transposable procedures. It is not enough to say that each "event" of deconstruction remains singular, or in any case as close as possible to something like an idiom or a signature. We should also make clear that deconstruction is not even an *act* or an *operation*. . . Deconstruction takes place, it is an event which does not wait on the deliberation, consciousness or organisation of the subject, nor even of modernity. [p 391(5)].

In *The Truth in Painting*, for example, Derrida does not more or less perversely deconstruct Kant's *Critique of Judgement*, but nor does Kant's *Critique of Judgement* deconstruct itself. The point is rather to locate in Kant's text elements which the overall argument has difficulty in containing satisfactorily and which have unsettling effects on that argument in its entirety: what Kant calls the *parergon* cannot adequately be described as either inside or outside the work of art, although without *parerga* the work of art would have no inside and outside. (*Mutatis mutandis*, this questioning of the frame – in the most general sense of the word – is also what interests Lyotard in the work of Daniel Buren, which is why Buren's 'installations' are difficult to locate as either inside or outside the institution of art: and one can be sure that if we were to try to frame Buren by deciding to call him a deconstructionist, he would respond by sticking his striped pieces of paper all over that frame too.)

If deconstruction is not, strictly speaking, a theory (given what Derrida calls the 'singularity' of its events: I suppose this is what gives some obscure motivation to Merquior's rather crass characterisation of it as a 'dismal unscience'), then it cannot be taken to prescribe a practice. It is hard to imagine a painter scouring *The Truth in Painting* for instructions as to how to proceed. The two central essays, on Adami and Titus-Carmel, which can indeed be taken to express some admiration for the work discussed, hardly amount to a manifesto of what art should be up to now. But if deconstruction has effects on certain philosophical determinations of art, and if art has always been more or less complicit with its philosophical determination, never separable from busy discursive activities of all sorts, then of course deconstruction might give rise to artistic events of various types, to be invented. But insofar as deconstruction does not simply question the philosophical determination of the work of art from within, say, aesthetics, but questions the coherence of the systematic philosophical organisation in which the domain of the 'aesthetic' is located, then just as Derrida is no longer strictly speaking writing philosophy, so deconstructive art would no longer strictly speaking be art, and just as deconstructive literary criticism is no longer strictly speaking literary criticism, so deconstructive art criticism would no longer strictly speaking be art criticism, even if its object was work which appears to fall happily within the traditional determination of art. These consequences follow quite rigorously from the argument I quoted above from *The Truth in Painting*, where they are linked to the *form* of the question 'What is Art?' Whence the comments in the essay on Adami on the 'silliness' of discourse on painting insofar as it is compelled by a drive to philosophical or poetical 'mastery', and the effort made in that text to respond to Adami's work differently, answering the *trait* of Adami's line with a proliferation of words beginning in *tr*, producing a text which escapes our familiar sense of assessment, academic value and translation. The claim would be that something is happening in Adami's work: the academic response to that event is to bind it tight in the strictures of commentary and explication and historical location (including the strictures of the label 'deconstruction'). Derrida tries to let something happen in his text which is certainly not purely independent of Adami's event, but which bears a relationship to that event which is not simply servile and therefore masterful, not trying to sublate the sensuousness of paint into the truth of the concept. Despite appearances, this is not essentially different from what Lyotard is attempting to do when he writes about attempting to respect or bear witness to the event of presence given in painting, the 'that it happens' of the event which is what he is attempting to write in the 'post-' of the postmodern: such an event is 'prior' (and in this sense perhaps art is indeed 'a thing of the past') to the temporal organisation of history as a narrative which Jencks has to presuppose.

According to the generalised sense of 'text' with which Derrida works, this type of approach also blurs the frame between work and commentary. Adami reads Derrida as much as Derrida reads Adami – no established criteria are going to decide which of these two 'texts' deserves priority in any sense. And Titus-Carmel's work is *already* as 'philosophical' as Derrida's discussion. There is no claim here that this situation is radically new or unprecedented: the most traditional

philosophical views of art as *mimesis*, and its most academic practice, have always necessarily left uneasily open a sense of art as a dangerous event in which something happens to disturb the integrity of 'nature herself' (and not just respond to her), somewhere resisting the grasp of concept and commentary, and through the insufficiency of attempted explanations of this event in terms of talent, inspiration or genius something of this deconstructive edge or 'point', as Derrida says, has always been at work. To this extent, art has always already been in excess of its concepts. already deconstructive, and deconstruction the motor or movement or element of art, whether in the relatively and historically variably unstable domain of painting or in the equally unstable domain of criticism, just as much as in philosophy. If there were ever to be a deconstructive movement in art, it would be a movement already dissolving its determination and resisting the restitution of its events to anything so stable as a nameable movement: Derrida again:' *Of Grammatology* places in question the unity of the 'word' and all the privileges with which it is in general credited, especially in its *nominal* form' (p 392 [6-7]) – the messy and tense area left between determination and indeterminacy, where odd things happen, is where deconstruction is at work.

Nothing whatsoever guarantees that a painting which explicitly translated or adapted or thematised Derridean ideas or operators would be in the least successful in letting something happen, and that lack of guarantee (which also explains why deconstruction could never prevent the formation of a historically identifiable 'movement' or school invoking it in manifestoes and maybe spawning its own academicism), which is not an unfortunate insufficiency but the rigorous consequence of an irreducible radical chance, is where its interest lies. 'Deconstruction' might just, I suppose, by an inflection of that chance, become the name for an artistic movement: but it is in any case a provisional and necessarily improper name for the movement one of whose traditional names has been 'art'.

Notes

1 Charles Jencks, *What is Post-Modernism?*, Academy Editions, London, St Martin's Press, New York, 1986, page references are given in the text.
2 Jacques Derrida, *La Vérité en peinture*, Flammarion, Paris, 1978, p25; trans *The Truth in Painting*, University of Chicago Press, 1988, p21.
3 Jean-François Lyotard, 'Réponse à la question: qu'est-ce que le postmoderne?', in *Le postmoderne expliqué aux enfants*, Galilée, Paris, 1986, pp 13-34 (p 22); trans in *The Postmodern Condition*, Manchester University Press, 1984, pp 71-82 (p 76).
4 I have argued for this understanding of the post, which is also implied by

Derrida's *La Carte Postale*, Aubier-Flammarion, Paris, 1980 [trans University of Chicago Press, 1988], in 'Postal Politics and the Institution of the Nation', forthcoming in Homi K Bhadda, ed *Nation and Narration*, Methuen, London, 1989.
5 'Lettre à un ami japonais', in *Psyché. Inventions de l'autre*, Galilée, Paris, 1987, pp 387-393 (p 390); trans in Wood and Bernasconi, eds, *Derrida and Différance*, Parousia Press, Warwick, 1985, pp 1-8 [pp 4-5]: page references will be given in the text (I have modified the translation a little here and there).

VALERIO ADAMI, *CAMERA DA LETTO*, 1970, ACRYLIC

DAVID LODGE
Deconstruction: A Review of the Tate Gallery Symposium

By far the best and most comprehensive review of the Tate Gallery Symposium, this article, first published in the 'Review' section of the Guardian, Friday, April 8th, 1988, is included here because of both the context it gives to the event itself, and the clear and general overview of the subject as a whole. Beginning with the Derridean notion of Deconstruction in philosophy and literature, it goes on to question the wider application of such ideas in the fields of art and architecture.

The only way you could get into the auditorium for the Tate Gallery's one-day symposium on Deconstruction in Art and Architecture was through a swing door clearly marked with the international 'No Entry' symbol. Whether this was planned or accidental, it seemed appropriate that we should be transgressing the conventional meaning of this familiar sign all day long (and it was a long day), as we shuffled backwards and forwards between the auditorium and the lobbies; for one of the axioms of Deconstruction is that the bond between the signifier and the signified is not as stable as is generally supposed, but on the contrary 'always already' subject to slippage and the play of *différance*.

Some who pushed their way through the No Entry sign were hoping to find out what Deconstruction was. Others of us were curious to discover what it could possibly have to do with Art and Architecture.

Deconstruction is the brainchild of the French philosopher Jacques Derrida. Over the last 20 years it has been an important – some would say the dominant – element in that general movement in the human sciences known as post-structuralism. It's not so much a method, more a frame of mind – one that has tirelessly questioned the nature and possibility of meaning through *analysis* of and commentary upon texts – originally philosophical texts, then literary texts.

Taking their cue from Derrida's assertion that 'language bears within itself the necessity of its own critique', Deconstructionist literary critics, especially at Yale, have demonstrated, to their own satisfaction and in the teeth of traditional scholarship, that any text inevitably undermines its own claim to have a determinate meaning. Since this procedure opens up the text to multiple interpretations, its appeal to literary critics is perhaps obvious.

But how could a movement so deeply invested in the analysis of verbal language be relevant to art and architecture? My first reaction to the announcement of the Tate Symposium was incredulity.

Well, we live and learn. I soon discovered that Derrida himself had published a whole book about the aesthetics of the visual arts, recently translated into English as *The Truth In Painting*, and that he has taken a keen interest in architecture, to the point of collaborating with Bernard Tschumi and Peter Eisenman on projects for the Parc de la Villette, a kind of post-structuralist theme park now under construction (or should one say, under deconstruction?) on a cleared industrial site in the northern suburbs of Paris.

Tschumi and Eisenman are among seven architects whose work is to be exhibited at the Museum of Modern Art in New York this summer under the heading of Deconstruction or Deconstructivism (there is some mystery and controversy about the exact title), an event awaited with keen interest and the audible sharpening of knives in the architectural fraternity. The Tate Symposium was in some sense a preliminary skirmish in the controversy this show is bound to provoke.

Peter Eisenman indeed complained that it would be the first time in history that an exhibition was being commented on before it had happened. What he was registering was the crucial place of the international conference as an institution in modern intellectual life.

New trends now start not from exhibitions or publications but from conferences. It was, after all, the 1966 conference at John Hopkins University, Baltimore, 'The Languages of Criticism and the Sciences of Man,' attended by Derrida and other Parisian savants, that first put the ideas of post-structuralism into circulation in America, where they were developed, institutionalised, and ultimately re-exported to Europe and the rest of the academic world.

* * *

Not surprisingly, therefore, the Tate Symposium (jointly sponsored by the Academy publishing group, who are publishing two useful special issues of their handsomely illustrated journals *Art & Design* and *Architectural Design* in conjunction with the event) was over-subscribed long before the day, especially as Derrida himself was advertised as a participant. Cynical veterans of the international conference circuit were equally unsurprised when Derrida didn't show up.

Instead we were shown an edited videotape of an interview with him recorded a few days earlier by Christopher Norris, Professor of English at Cardiff and the leading British expert on Deconstruction. Perhaps after all it was fitting that the relentless critic of the idea of 'presence' in Western metaphysics should be a palpable absence at the gathering he had indirectly provoked.

On this fuzzy, jerky bit of video (Deconstruction, as I discovered last year in the process of making a film for Channel 4 about a similar conference, seems to have a bad effect on the focal properties of TV cameras) Derrida, seated in a glazed study surrounded by lush greenery, admitted that he had himself once been doubtful about the application of Deconstruction to architecture, but the persistence of architectural metaphors in philosophical and theoretical discourse ('foundation', 'supersturcture', '*architectonice*' etc) had encouraged him to investigate further. Architects, he suggested, used Deconstruction to challenge the hegemony of architectural principles such as 'function' and 'beauty' reinscribing this challenge in their work.

What does this mean in practice? Well, it means warped planes, skewed lines, exploded corners, flying beams and what Dr Johnson, describing metaphysical verse, called 'heterogeneous ideas yoked by violence together'.

Take, for instance, Frank Gehry's house in Los Angeles. This is an ordinary suburban shingle house, painted pink by the previous owners, to which Gehry added a visually disorientating extension made of corrugated steel, glass, chain link, black asphalt and cheap timber posts, full of skewed angles and unexpected gaps, and generally suggestive of a school playground or the back of a film set.

It is unpopular with Gehry's neighbours, one of whom has described it as 'a dirty thing to do in someone else's front yard', but a source of intense interest among architects and designers – indeed it is possibly the most written-about house to have been built in the last decade.

Gehry himself is cheerfully untheoretical about his work – his answer to the question, what is the difference between art and architecture, being that 'the architect is willing to put a toilet in his structure' – but his exploitation of discord, discontinuity and distortion, to break down accepted architectural distinctions between form and function, beauty and ugliness, inside and outside, have made him willy-nilly a sort of figurehead in the Deconstructionist movement, and his work will feature in the MOMA exhibition.

Peter Eisenman is a more self-consciously theoretical architect, who has based his work (especially a series of houses known austerely as House I, House II, House III etc) on linguistic models. His early work was inspired by Chomskian generative grammar, entailing a series of 'transformations' of a geometrical deep-structure with total indifference to the comfort and convenience of his clients.

His House VI, for instance, has non-functional columns which separate people sitting at the dining table, and a slit in the floor of the master bedroom that makes twin beds mandatory. When climbing the stairs you must take care not to bang your head on a second inverted staircase stuck on the ceiling. The architect's conversion to Deconstruction was marked by House X, which has a cantilevered transparent glass floor and no identifiable centre.

Eisenman was the first of a panel of speakers on architecture in the morning session of the Symposium, introduced by Charles Jencks, an American art critic resident in England, with a special, some would say proprietorial, interest in Post-Modernism. This he defines not merely as an architectural reaction against the severely functional cubic shapes of Corbusier and Gropius, but as a wider cultural phenomenon of 'double coding' to be found across the board of contemporary innovative art.

Whether Deconstruction is part of or the same as Post-Modernism was one of the recurrent issues of the day's debates. Jencks' view seemed to be that insofar as Deconstructionist architecture was distinguishable from Post-Modernism it was probably not architecture, but a kind of aesthetic joke. His introductory discourse was entitled 'Deconstruction: the sound of one mind laughing.'

Eisenman was not amused. 'I'm quite fond of Charles,' this feisty New Yorker drawled into the microphone, 'but enough's enough. Next time could we have an introducer who knows what he's talking about?' To have blood on the carpet so early in the proceedings was a good sign. The audience clapped and sat up expectantly. Jencks, who is used to being the man other people in the art world love to hate, didn't seem unduly disturbed.

Though Eisenman's buildings sound fairly loony in description, his ideas are interesting. His version of Deconstruction has a psychoanalytical slant: it breaks down dialectical oppositions to reveal what they have repressed. In the past, visual artists told us truths about architecture that architects preferred to conceal. Munch's paintings reveal the fear and loathing entombed within the bourgeois house. Piranesi deconstructed perspective and point of view by the insoluble riddles of his vaulted staircases. The medieval cathedrals acknowledged what they repressed in the form of decorative gargoyles. 'We want to make the repressed structural,' said Eisenman – to 'cut into the areas of greatest resistance.'

Then Bernard Tschumi (Swiss in origin, American-based), sombrely dressed in shades of black and dark grey, showed slides of his prize-winning plan for the Parc de la Villette. Its chief feature is a series of eccentric-looking red buildings, vaguely reminiscent of Russian Constructivism in shape, scattered over the flat site at 120 metre intervals according to a point grid, and called *folies* – a Derridean pun on the English architectural folly and the French word for 'madnesses'.

Derrida himself has given the enterprise an approving commentary: 'the *folies* put into operation a general dislocation: . . . they deconstruct first of all, but not only, the semantics of architecture.'

The functions of the *folies* are flexible and ambiguous. One, Tschumi told us, originally earmarked as a children's centre, is now a video studio. Another has been designated at different stages a restaurant, a garden centre and most recently an art gallery. Another was designed with no specific function in mind.

Tschumi's approach to architecture is fiercely historicist in the Popperian sense. The speed of modern communications, he assured us, has made traditional measure redundant. It is no use trying to disguise the abolition of permanence. We live in a period of deregulation – of airlines, of the Stock Exchange and the laws of classical physics. The Parc de la Villette used permutation and substitution to attack the obsolete logic of cause and effect. This, Tschumi claimed, was a truly Post-Modernist architecture – the eclectic revivalism which claims that name being merely regressive, a desperate attempt to recuperate a discredited notion of meaning.

There is a bleak, fanatical consistency about Tschumi's vision which seems all too likely to be realised in the Parc de la Villette. Looking at the slides I kept imagining little groups of disconsolate people wandering through the Parc on a wet Sunday, staring numbly at the meaningless red buildings as the rain dripped from the functionless flying beams onto their umbrellas, wondering what was expected of them.

According to Zaha Hadid, a London-based architect of Persian extraction, who spoke next, the new architecture affirms that 'much about the 20th century is very enjoyable,' and for me her stunning architectural paintings, drawn as if viewed from the cockpit of a low-flying jetplane, expressed this hedonistic principle more successfully than Tschumi's *folies*.

Hadid's architecture has been described as 'anti-gravitational'. The prizewinning design for a club on top of a mountain overlooking Hong Kong is in her own words, 'a horizontal skyscraper.' but the cunning arrangement of its slabs and ramps makes it look as if it is about to slide down the side of the mountain. It's a pity the client has suspended the project because of some unspecified trouble with the Hong Kong authorities: it would be interesting to see if it could be built.

Mark Wigley, the young co-organiser of the impending MOMA show, stressed that the exhibits (they include Hadid's) were not utopian fantasies. Walls might be 'tormented', structure and materials brought to the very limits of tolerable stress, but they could all be built. Contrary to Tschumi, Wigley claimed that architectural Deconstruction was not a new 'ism' or avant-garde, but an effort to uncover the problematics of all architecture. It administered 'the shock of the old'. On that note we adjourned to a buffet lunch.

* * *

Later in the afternoon, the session devoted to art and sculpture was rather more subdued, perhaps because the speakers were all scholars and critics rather than practitioners, perhaps because the quiche lorraine and chocolate gateaux they were digesting slowed them down, but mainly, I think, because the relationship of Deconstruction to the visual arts is less specific than in the case of architecture.

There are a few artists, such as Francis Bacon , who claim to have been influenced by Derrida, and some, like Valerio Adami and Gérard Titus-Carmel, on whom he has commented sympathetically and at length. But so much modern art is concerned with the interrogation of its own processes and the questioning of *a priori* assumptions about perception and the world, that the term Deconstruction can be applied loosely to almost anything, and precisely to almost nothing, from Post-

Impressionism onwards.

Geoff Bennington of Sussex University, the co-translator of Derrida's *Truth in Painting* (a task comparable in difficulty to serving spaghetti with a knitting needle) asked rhetorically whether to name a movement in art 'Deconstructionist', and gave the impression that only politeness restrained him from giving a negative answer.

The fact is that the term Deconstruction is in danger of being appropriated indiscriminately by artists and art critics searching for impressive-sounding theoretical concepts with which to explain and justify the varied assaults of modern art upon common sense. Derrida is on record as saying that 'Deconstruction is a word whose fortunes have disagreeably surprised me', and one suspects that he would get some unpleasant shocks browsing through the special issue of *Art & Design* on 'Deconstructive Tendencies in Art'.

Arguably the application of the term to architecture is just as specious, but the existence of a number of practising architects with some understanding of the theory behind it makes a focused debate possible. This was perhaps one reason why the audience at the symposium rebelled against the organisers' provision for two discussion panels, one on painting, one on architecture, to close the day, and insisted on a single panel of all the speakers. (Another reason was that because the programme was running late, they would have had to miss their tea to attend both panels. Of course, the audience always objects to the way things have been arranged towards the end of such events: enforced silence for hours on end while being lectured at generates a kind of collective resentment which has to be discharged somehow.) It became clear in the last session that the key to the whole symposium was another event that, as Eisenman pointed out, had not yet happened: the MOMA exhibition. What makes this show potentially so important is that it has been 'instigated' and co-organised by Philip Johnson, the doyen of American architects.

When he was a young man, in 1932 to be precise, Johnson co-organised another exhibition at MOMA called 'The International Style,' which launched the work of Corbusier and the Bauhaus in America, and thus in due course changed the face of the modern world. In the late 1970s Johnson was spectacularly converted to Post-Modernism (he is the architect of the notorious 'Chippendale' skyscraper for AT&T in New York), and now it seems he is putting his enormous authority behind a group of architects previously thought of as marginal and eccentric. Is it conceivable that Deconstruction could become the new International Style?

A lady of mature years in the audience obviously expressed the misgivings of many when she observed that the architecture diplayed in the course of the day had seemed to her both 'elitist and sprawling' –what relevance did it have to today's overcrowded world?

In reply, Tschumi said his architecture was expressing a revolution that had already happened (he meant an information revolution). Eisenman said his architecture was a critique of architecture. Hadid said architects could inject new ideas into society by rewriting the architectural brief. In short, they retreated behind a shield of professionalism.

It was interesting, and perhaps predictable, that the attack on Deconstructionist architecture should have had a political slant, because the same thing has been happening in the field of literary studies. Deconstructionist criticism is in retreat, especially in America, from something called the New Historicism, a quasi-Marxist, quasi-Foucauldian situating of literature in its socio-economic context–so much so that J Hillis Miller, one of the luminaries of the Yale School of Deconstructionists, felt impelled to rally the troops in a remarkable presidential address to the Modern Language Association of America in December 1986,'The Triumph of Theory, the Resistance to Reading, and the Question of the Material Base', in which he affirmed that 'the future of literary studies depends on maintaining and developing that rhetorical reading which today is called 'Deconstruction.'

In the scholarly journals, however, there is an increasing sense that Deconstruction is on the wane. Derrida's own late work has become increasingly whimsical, fictive and difficult to methodise (he himself always denied that it was a method).

More recently, the prestige of Deconstruction has sustained a blow from which it may never recover in American academic circles: the discovery (noted recently in these columns by Desmond Christy) that Paul de Man, the most revered and authoratative member of the Yale School of criticism, who died, much mourned, in 1983, had, as a young man in occupied Belgium, published a great many newspaper articles sympathetic to the Nazi cause.

Imagine that F R Leavis was discovered, shortly after his death, to have once been a member of Mosley's blackshirts and you will have some idea of the impact of this revelation on American academics.

It has been a gift to those on the intellectual left who have always suspected that Deconstruction is dangerous to moral health, that its critique of reason is a pretext for evading social and political responsiblities.

Architects, in short, appear to be scrambling onto the Deconstructionist bandwagon just at the moment when literary intellectuals are jumping off. It remains to be seen whether this will save the cause of Deconstruction or consign the architecture to limbo.

PETER EISENMAN, PITTSBURGH TECHNOLOGY CENTER OFFICE BUILDING, 1989-, MODEL

PART III

DECONSTRUCTION AND ART

FRANCIS BACON, *STUDY FOR PORTRAIT OF JOHN EDWARDS*, 1986, OIL AND PASTEL

JOHN GRIFFITHS
Deconstruction Deconstructed

DAVID SALLE, *SHOWER OF COURAGE*, 1985, ACRYLIC, WOOD CHAIRS AND FABRIC

John Griffiths traces the origins of Deconstruction, looking at the impact it has made on trends in contemporary culture. He surveys the fundamental connections between Heideggerian and Derridean philosophical notions of human existence and examines Deconstruction's counterparts in current art, describing the various ways in which artists as diverse as Francis Bacon and Dan Graham have related to this modern theoretical idiom.

'Deconstruction' is above all a term drawn from and conditioned by changes in the philosophy of Jacques Derrida, (born Algeria 1930). Since the early 1970s, his talks and publications, those of his contemporary, the not-dissimilar philosopher and cultural analyst Michel Foucault (born Poitiers 1926), and those of various disciples and associates, such as Jean-François Lyotard and Daniel Buren, have influenced practitioners of the human sciences, especially literary critics and social-psychiatric pundits, in various ways.

Over two decades this influence has spread from thinkers to makers; from critics to poets, novelists, architects, painters and sculptors. As always happens, such cultural effects, founded variously (on various persons, times, places; on followers loyal and disloyal, with the rise or fall of political interests, or alongside and in disparate cultures), have been wholly, hardly, or not at all affected by orthodox Deconstruction.

Since some critics, many writers and most artists thus influenced, even those hinting at or flaunting their adherence to the 'movement', are very wide of the Derridean mark, almost every interested party will find fault with any account of the concept and its history with special reference to the visual arts.

That, in a way, is as it should be. Works of art often have the oddest relations to the ideas which they cite, manipulate, and even proclaim as their origin and goal. Measured by the yardstick of loyalty to the supposed originating philosophic, theological or political system, artworks which a number of people agree are very worthwhile are usually cheap heresies. Strange to say, however, they often would not exist, or exist in precisely

that appealing way, without the impetus and sometimes vaguely correct but usually mistaken quotation of the ideological system which is their *apparent* structuring principle.

This is all the more difficult when, as with Deconstruction, the philosophic method or system itself happens to be split into numerous, sometimes warring, schools or factions.

The main problem, however, is that orthodox Deconstruction, even more than the 20th-century philosophies from which it derives by a kind of abreaction, is a highly refined system of double-takes. It is to the Cheshire cat's smile as the smile is to the Cheshire cat. It suspects not only the declared aims, apparent narrative structure, obvious ethos, and so on, of the phenomena it is used on, but also whatever anything, even its own ongoing Deconstruction, may suggest is the actual substrate of the object of analysis. To reveal an innermost or fundamental concrete blunder which Deconstruction, *ab initio*, would avoid.

Deconstruction derives from a context of ideas and idea systems, including psychoanalysis and Structuralism, all of which have grand aims. They want to say something momentous about big issues; about the really big issues concealed by the issues we think are big. They are interested above all in human 'being', and in the unity of human experience. Wishing to unify, they put asunder. Freudianism breaks through the apparent and rational to find real significance. Neo-Marxism looks not for a psychic but for an economic infra-structure, and for associated interests which condition the meaning of social events and products, including art.

In a great Western tradition the foregoing, and similar methodologies, claim to be able to say what is really going on. They express their interest in unified human experience above all by making distinctions about specific aspects of a supposed or desired whole. They try to interpret creations of the human mind: whether language, dream or myth; whether works of art or even social systems. Often the objects examined are not instances of factual discourse or even of 'unconscious' dreamwork, but highly refined, labyrinthine and unpredictable aesthetic constructs.

The interpretative methodologies in question agree that the most fruitful way to understand such phenomena is to study their relationship to reality, yet not by the out-dated and untrustworthy method of discovering a history to which they belong and then uncovering their traces in it.

They also reject 'logical' approaches in as much as they refuse both the assumption that (linguistic) forms straightforwardly reflect factual reality, and the assumption that logic can be straightforwardly applied to such forms (of language) so as to reveal that underlying reality.

The best thing to do instead is to isolate and decipher the relevant code or set of conventions which the phenomenon as part of an institution (philosophic, literary or artistic, but always social) appears to use and actually uses; or actually uses while pretending to use another; or actually itself is, even while representing itself as another. If the object is embedded in many sets of interactive and overlapping conventions, most of which the observer ignores while one of them is accepted as an illusory context for originator and recipient, then deciphering the code will be a form of demystification of the text or image and so on. Once that code or set of codes is deciphered, we begin to uncover the human perception of reality; then the relationship between that perception and the structure of the human mind; and finally, perhaps, our mental structure itself.

In the case of a literary work, the writer and the reader, and in the case of a painting, the painter and the viewer, are examined not as independent selves over and above the sign-system of the work, but as entities jointly subject to the authority of that system and of its meaningful sub-systems and connotations. Their freedom is the knowledge of the necessity of the signs that join them. The desire and pursuit of the whole have found a temporary horizon. Of course, there can be no question of any other 'precedent', let alone ordaining reality. Yet precedence there must be, for the phenomenon examined can never be seen 'in itself' but always in relation to the unified experience of the originator of the phenomenon, the phenomenon itself, and the examiner.

Naturally, all these systems of analysis pay more or less attention to their own status and standpoint, to their own codes and their relation to those of the phenomena studied, and to the perennial question of the privileged observer: 'For we are ourselves the entities to be analysed'. And Deconstruction is possibly the most conscientiously self-conscious of these analytical systems. It owes its self-consciousness mainly to its refinement and rejection of the ideas of two forerunners: those of Lévi-Strauss and Heidegger.

Lévi-Straussian Structuralism requires a set of presumably neurologically conditioned human universals somehow in the unconscious and in the psyche. These are said to be precedent to and constitutive of languages and cultural phenomena. Such mental universals determine our unified experience. All languages, all codes, all classifying systems, all myths and all works of art whatsoever derive from them. Perhaps we can work through rules, systems, codes, myths to the structural laws of each type or group. Then we can look not only to the past but to the future of that group's development. By examining the structural laws of structural laws we may discover the nature of

human nature. The particular structure and integrity of a specific painting will be like others in other specific paintings not because they are superficially, perhaps 'figuratively' loyal to some mundane or 'natural' phenomenon, but because ultimately they obey the same unifying principle: the innate laws of the human mind. The way in which cultural products are structured, not their evident meaning, declares their hidden, common human meaning. Different phenomena can be compared not by picking out observable similarities, but by discerning the differences between them and showing how those differences enable phenomena to interact meaningfully in an organised whole, which is no mere monotonous pattern or regular repetition of the same elements.

The relation of Derridean Deconstruction and its key notion of *différance* to the emphasis on significant differences in Lévi-Straussian Structuralism is complicated. Even more chequered is the path from Heidegger to Derrida, though an important link is Heidegger's reminder that we enter into any form of meaningful discourse only by learning and obeying a set of conventions which adopts us and controls us and which we can neither adopt nor control. The meaning of our meaningful text or image is subject to the predetermined meanings of the codes which constitute it as well as to the new connotations and intensities of meaning which that text or image teases from the conventional weave.

Another similarity between Heidegger and Derrida is the looming conviction of their impressionable common reader that the human condition is merely to be there, having to be there, not being there, never having been there. Certain painters – especially Francis Bacon, or Francis Gruber, or Lucian Freud – like certain writers – especially Beckett, or Céline, or Malcolm Lowry, who seem to favour obviously bloody, angst-ridden, dusty, cynical or solitary topics – have been superficially identified as Heideggerian-Existentialist or Derridean-Deconstructivist. Pictures which seem to demonstrate the non-Being of human Being, or to erode vestiges of human imagery, have been seen as 'Deconstructions' in this very crude sense. The actual association is somewhat more complex and has to do with the creative process.

A basic theme in both Heidegger and Derrida, considered as philosophers, is the importance of experiencing Being 'as presence': that is, perhaps as meaning; perhaps as oneself; and so on. For Derrida (in his earliest, still most influential works of the 1960s, at least), the history of philosophy is the history of philosophers fruitlessly trying to offer in writing (that is, in rational discourse) their experience of the presence of Being. But the wrong medium has been used for this essential task. Only the living, not the written, word can convey that presence. Rational discourse obfuscates the real presence of Being. The living word indicates Being by showing the 'difference' or distance between the 'rational' self, or object, or meaning, and the 'unthinkable' thought or self. Not rational discourse but literary, creative discourse or psychoanalysis may disclose this pre-rational, pre-conceptual, original, radical, extreme thought. This 'archi-écriture', or aboriginal writing, is unlike us and ours in its freedom from the finite condition, from death – the pathos, the even tragic note, of Derridean philosophy comes in with its stress on that human finitude which inevitably deprives us of the full presence of Being. We sense full Being as somehow present to us (for we do sense it), but as obscure, as neutral, as different from our own incomplete, condition-unto-death. We are condemned always to see through a glass darkly, enigmatically – *per speculum in aenigmate*.

The echoes of biblical and religious discourse are not accidental. The 'irrational' tendency of Deconstruction and Derridean talk in general, has certain affinities with Christian and above all

Jewish cabbalistic analyses that refuse or even break the conventions to reach back before the assimilation of Aristotelian logic. They rely on quasi-magical, narrative and lyrical discourse, arrangements of signs and emotive affinities to apprehend what the latter kills. In esoteric Lurianic cabbalism, for example, the task of man is 'the restoration of his primordial spiritual structure or *Gestalt*. That is the task of every one of us, for every soul contains the potentialities of this spiritual appearance, outraged and degraded by the fall of Adam, whose soul contained all souls. From this soul of all souls, sparks have scattered in all directions and become diffused into matter. The problem is to reassemble them, to lift them to their proper place and to restore the spiritual nature of man in its original splendour as God conceived it' (Scholem). For radical cabbalists of all times and all persuasions, however, the offensive conventions of our present context must be shattered before that devout recovery can begin.

The vatic tone of Derrida's *Of Grammatology*, with its encapsulated critiques of Western thought from Plato to the heirs of Hegel, through the rise and fall of book culture, and on to the betrayal of the living word which 'writing' represents, is characteristic of much Deconstructionist discourse: 'Patient meditation on and a strict inquiry into what is still provisionally known as writing ... may be the odyssey of a way of thinking which is loyal and attentive to the world which is to come, and which proclaims itself in the present, beyond the closure of knowledge. The future can be anticipated only as radical danger. It breaks absolutely with normality as it is constituted; therefore it can make itself known, present itself, only in a monstrous form. There is as yet no epigraph for this future world, for those aspects of it which make the values of sign, word and writing quake, or for what guides our antecedent future here and now'. The anti-idealistic idealism and apocalyptic tone of this way of talking can be very congenial for pundits as well as artists who are tempted to equate the mere depiction of a vile or imperfect condition with following a philosophic programme of some complexity.

The sense of eliciting a style from a despair afforded not only by Derrida but by other French Post-Structuralists whose criticism has approached the condition of art (for instance, Barthes on the pleasure of the text, or on the peculiar forms of unease evoked by photography) has seemed appropriate to the work of artists whose visual stuff includes the distress or nastiness of being human. Francis Bacon, for example, has said that he finds what might be called Derrida's 'uncongeniality' congenial. This criticism's awareness of beauty and simultaneous wrestling with human powerlessness and finitude, its abandonment of self-will and courting of the happenstance, has much to do with the modern way of things for certain painters: '... you don't know how the hopelessness in one's working will make one just take paint and just do almost anything ... to try to break the willed articulation of the image, so that the image will grow, as it were, spontaneously, within its own structure and not my structure. Afterwards ... you begin to work on the hazard that has been left to you on the canvas ... Certainly one is more relaxed when the image that one has within one's sensations – you see, there is a kind of sensational image within the very, you could say, structure of your being, which is not to do with a mental image – when that image, through accident, begins to form'. (FB in David Sylvester, *Interviews with Francis Bacon*, 1980).

The apparent concept of the human condition in Bacon's works seems admirably summarised by Post-Structuralist pronouncements on the status of the human being as a disappearing figure in a transient conceptual system: 'The archaeology of our thinking demonstrates clearly that man is a recent invention. Perhaps also his approaching end' (Foucault, *Les mots et les choses*). It would be odd indeed if a sensitive artist and a sensitive aestheticising philosopher in the Continental European sense did not respond appropriately, that is formally, to the culmination of a scientific tradition that has treated the human being as an object among objects: one that has paused only to sigh with its supreme works of art at the poignancy of that image of humanity (itself) as determined by mechanisms unknown in a process of beginning and end unknown, for reasons unknown. Then, but only then, a concern with formal relations unites the supremely 'Deconstructionist' artist and thinker: '... intention involves such a small fragment of our consciousness and of our mind and of our life. I think a painting should include more experience than simply intended statement. I personally would like to keep the painting in a state of "shunning statement", so that one is left with the fact that one can experience individually as one pleases; that is, not to focus the attention in one way, but to leave the situation as a kind of actual thing, so that the experience of it is variable' (Jasper Johns in 1965 BBC interview with David Sylvester).

Post-Structuralist Deconstruction, like the Structuralist method before it, has always been especially interested in contemporaneous and avant-garde art. The Structuralist linguist Roman Jakobson, whose studies of form and structure were among the earliest inspirations of Structuralism pure and simple, took as a watchword Braque's 'I do not believe in things but in relations between things'. Among the most profound influences on his thought was Braque's and Picasso's Cubist wrestling with form to the point where it so predominates that the illusion of artist's and observer's existence is all but cancelled, and the work itself seems self-sufficient as an interactivity of elements whose kinship to anything real has long been systematically eroded.

Derridean Deconstruction has directly affected artists' declared practice – that is, *has* been 'adopted' as the structuring principle of the works themselves – most recently in architecture. In 'art' this has happened for the most part in similar instances, such as Dan Graham's critiques of American suburban tract housing developments.

This trend accords with the politico-philosophical implications of Deconstruction first associated with the left-wing awakening throughout Europe in the late 1960s. They were openly declared during the heady events of May 1968 in Paris, and during the student debates which often invoked the wholly novel Post-Structuralists as the avant-garde of morally committed scrutiny.

Before looking briefly at art and related architectural practice directly affected by Post-Structuralism, and by Deconstruction in particular, I shall try to describe those aspects of Derrida's general critique of Structuralism as weak-kneed which took him out of the ranks of Structuralism, proclaimed him a latter-day Phenomenologist and even Existentialist, and made him most attractive as an inspiring and provocative force for applied artists, for socio-critical minimalists, and for architects.

Derrida saw that the 'within-without', or *word*-as against-*writing* dualism advanced by Structuralists from Saussure to Lévi-Strauss (and by philosophers from Plato through Rousseau to Hegel and Husserl – but not Nietzsche or Heidegger), concealed a light-dark opposition with strong religious overtones.

Writing had been thought of as the dress in which speech was clad. But it has its own presence. Within and without, soul and body, spirit and form, word and letter; 'Western tradition has always conceived writing, the letter, and so forth, as the body and matter located somehow outside the spirit, the breath, the word and the logos' (*Of Grammatology*). One side of the opposition was pure spirit; but the outer form was sinful and contaminated. Western tradition has long conceived truth as what is signified – *content* – apart from how it is signified – *form*. The result is an inauthentic metaphysics of what Derrida calls 'presence': one which supposes that we can directly know a definite, concrete reality without. There would then be an ultimate signified to which we could undoubtedly aspire. But that world-picture, says Derrida, is obsolete. Our suspicions about a fixed ultimate are so strong that we realise that forms of 'writing' are not sign-systems which reflect and point out anything specific or concrete. They do not stand for 'the real thing'.

The essence of a sign has been its own disappearance in favour of what it signifies. Paradoxically, the sign can be saved only by destroying it as understood in our obfuscating tradition. Instead we must insist that the organisation of thought is its very condition; and that a sign-system is a formal play not of similarities but of 'differences'.

'Differentiation' or 'differing' (*différence*), which may also and simultaneously be understood as 'defer-ment' or 'postpone-ment' (*différance*), is the authentic condition of an on-going structural process. The elements of such a process are interrelated by their distinctions, by their 'removes', 'distances' or 'intervals' from the reality they 'represent', and by previous acts of representation whose 'traces' they bear. These interactions, differences, defer-ments and traces deprive all texts of an ultimate 'external' and immutable meaning.

In the new world-view, then, a text may be liberated from slavery to an inevitable significance. Now it is free to offer a new reality, to be creative. Text or artwork can create the new. Deconstruction examines the peculiar logic of this intrinsic beauty, showing what is 'framed' or 'intrinsic', rather than what is merely inside not outside: 'When we ask "What is a frame?", Kant replies, "It is a parergon, a composite of within and without, but a composite which is no mere amalgam or half-and-half – an outside which is summoned within the inside in order to constitute it as inside"' (Derrida, *The Truth in Painting*).

Here Deconstruction becomes finely tuned practice. The Deconstructor scrutinises the paradoxes of 'parergonal logic'. He or she detects 'frame slippage': those moments when aspects of the signified move over to become parts of the signifier; when content fragments into form; and so on.

Creating and using a sign-system (including a visual artwork) means manipulating a 'transformative apparatus', or sign-system, a set of interactive elements defined by its own internal distinctions. The play of differences which make up the sign-system is 'inscribed' in each of its elements: 'Each element is constituted by virtue of the trace in it of the other elements of the chain or system' (*Sémiologie et Grammatologie*). Moreover, any meaningful system is a network or 'texture' of intervals and delays. The system and its inward play are organised by a 'centre' which paradoxically is both within and without the structure. There is none of the reassuring immobility and certitude of the outdated notion of a centre. Moreover, the trace of each difference appears in every other difference. There is no absolute general 'origin' of meaning. Each trace exists by virtue of another.

In architecture some of the foregoing basic Derridean ideas have been used critically and creatively. Bernard Tschumi's project for the development of the vast Parc de la Villette site in Paris (competition announced 1982; initial phase, representing approximately half the project, under construction) is directly indebted to Derrida's ideas. Here they are applied in a conjunction of aesthetic, moral and philosophic energies that provisionally realises what seemed mere uplift and at best wishful thinking in the 1960s-70s.

The communally functional and the creative aspects of classi-cal Deconstruction are no longer confined to the will to reconstruct an existing (literary) text but are given creative rein as utopian differentiation. Derrida has contributed an article, 'Point de Folie: Maintenant l'Architecture', to Tschumi's book (itself a utopia) on the project (*La Case Vide*, Paris, 1986).

The project manipulates numerous elements, from an art gallery to a science museum, from a rock concert hall to performance workshops, which reciprocate by creatively structuring the whole. Its elongated yet varied layout and visible discontinuity are designed flexibly to exploit contemporary 'disjunctions and dissociations'. Revisions, combinations and replacements of the architectural and social elements, the buildings, within and athwart the main conceptual framework, are not only possible but called for, so that the differences of future contributions by architects, other professionals and the actual users, would decide individual contributions and interact without harm to the democratic, uncentred, structural principle. It is an attempt to make planning usefully unplanned. It is a superb example of a socio-creative philosophy of the future in action, of art as open-ended social planning.

A regular point grid is used so as to refuse precedence of programme over architecture and vice versa, and so as to eradicate the architect as the eternally privileged director of building function. Classical rules of composition, hierarchy and order have been refused. The competition programme, even the architect's programme, has been 'deconstructed', and fruitful 'intertextuality' and 'anticontextuality' have replaced an ever-immanent directive 'meaning'. Each observer and user will, it is hoped, add to the never-fixed meaning of the whole. ' . . . what is questioned is the notion of unity . . . The idea of order is constantly questioned, challenged, pushed to the edge' (Bernard Tschumi, 'Disjunctions' in *Yale Architectural Journal*, 1987).

Moving from Deconstructionist architecture to Deconstructionist Conceptual Art, the work of Dan Graham, because of its obvious architectural-environment and unscripted performance interests, provides the best link with the multitude of supposed and actual Deconstructions in painting and sculpture.

Graham's work is 'Deconstructionist' in a less orthodox sense. It deliberately presents then complicates and fractures a meaning or set of meanings. It does this to disclose the possibility of a desirable basic meaning, but one which is never reached in the creation or 'active contemplation' of the work, because it remains to be created by observers and artists in the posited new context and society. Graham rearranges elements of one style or of several familiar styles, and thus 'defamiliarises' or alienates them so that the observer begins to perceive the possibility of a, if not actually 'the', very different reality 'underlying' the seemingly secure conventions by which we are said/shown to be enslaved. By superimposition, the work may go on to suggest other conventions, more appropriate to our condition. In some cases it is content to carry out the first step of defamiliarisation.

Graham's pieces have ranged from art magazine contributions subverting the art magazine as a form of commodity fetishism, through film and video, to performance and installation projects, all in their ways attacking the conventions of context (the art gallery is a favourite target). The observer is brought to re-experience typical enclosures stripped down to a set of meanings which reveal their unsatisfactory location in an unfulfilling society, yet one replete with promising buildings and artefacts intended for the ease of living and human fulfilment which that society preaches in its self-publicity.

Graham derives from a vaguely Minimalist, definitely Neo-Marxist background (more explicitly Marxist than Derrida for some time has allowed himself to be). He also owes much to 1960s critical-Pop ventures such as the Richard Hamilton *et al* Whitechapel show. He shares interests with Minimalists such as

Claes Oldenburg, John Knight, Kawara, and the early Dan Flavin, but more recently with John Chamberlain and his smashed automobiles and with Robert Venturi and his revelatory couches and interiors. *Interior Design for Space Showing Videotapes*, 1986, involves the observer with mirrors and glass walls, cushions, couches and so on, and in the consequent ongoing, shifting creation of the work and its critique of contemporary art galleries as part-showroom part-business office.

Graham was much taken by achievements like Venturi's showroom design for Knoll in New York in 1982, which alienate while attracting the observer by casting an unholy sheen on the sacred chairs themselves; or Venturi's games with Chippendale, Art Deco and modern office furniture in order to create a shifting critique of the corporate modern style, then the theory and practice of capital management in a redesigned office suite for Capital Management. Graham's own glasshouse installations (eg, *Two Adjacent Pavilions*, 1982) mimic and criticise through viewer participation the slick US back-to-nature illusion of the country house whose owner is closeted from, yet constantly views, a sanitised nature without; nature becomes part of the furnishings.

Other projects extended the 'glass' critique of Philip Johnson-style houses to the Mies van der Rohe Manhattan glass tower and its negative aloofness. The links with 'purist' Parisian Deconstruction should be clear: with critiques of the work as a

> sumptuous artefact, wholly subject to the sober rules of beauty, pleasing thus. Yet it is by that very perfection that it deceives us. It makes itself attractive to the architect lusting for the absolute who has slumbered in the European and possibly the international art patron since Palladio, Bramante, Mies van der Rohe and Gropius. It awakens in him the old and always ready dream of absolute imperial rule over space and time, tracing as it does the lines, surfaces and volumes of that domination (Jean-François Lyotard, *Que Peindre?*, Paris, 1987, p 76).

Various artists labelled 'Deconstructionist' are merely so because they conjoin fashionable forms provoking and sifting dangerous dreams. The artist so rearranges them as to evoke profound irony, distrust, nostalgia, a dizzymaking sense of randomness or nullity, and possibly an unsatisfied longing for timeless form and content. Such works seek to 'denude' (*dénudation*) the observer of illusions, and in advanced instances invite him or her to create the longed-for new order. Such works ask to be deciphered not as substitute structures corresponding to the formal structure of the external world, but as experiences in which gaps, puns, differences, 'slips', destroy any immutable appearance and meaning.

It is not too fanciful to see these, the whole Deconstructionist project, and its Constructivist, Cubist and Dada as well as Minimalist forebears, as part of the same complex of uncertainties as our late 20th-century mathematics and physics of indeterminacy and uncertainty. Even 'populist' Deconstruction looks back with learned yet ironic nostalgia to the age of linear order; it rejects all certainty and privilege, yet operates as if an overwhelming certainty were in the offing.

In this extra-Derridean sense, Deconstructionist works are disconcerting, iconoclastic, irreverent, subversive of complacency, eclectic, pretend an interest in the ruling order, face several ways, are streetwise, apolitically political, trust no one, nothing, not even themselves, declare all multinational efforts criminal while decrying the solipsistic individual, use only to explode it the imagery of the electronic and previous technological decades.

The Deconstructionist *avant la lettre* is therefore Marcel Duchamp, whose *The Bride Stripped Bare by her Bachelors Even* (1915-23) and some of its mechanico-erotic avatars (see Michel Carrouges, 'How to identify bachelor machines' in *Le macchine Celibi*, by various hands, Milan, 1975, pp 23-38), perfectly reveals the dangers of Deconstruction's subversion of all categories. Here reason and emotion erode one another to the point where all ambiguous forms are suspended in nullity, and painted and transparent surface areas are perfectly balanced, asking an overwhelming question which they answer neither with humanity nor with the machine but with incomprehensibility. In the *Large Glass* all legends the observer recognises are stripped bare; they are deconstructed unto death: ' . . . everywhere the mark of sharp-edged negation, this reversal of a proof carried to absurdity, since the absurd is, on the contrary, reinstated here' (Michel Leiris).

Duchamp's enigmatic retirement from art has been vastly dangerous to all clean-cut Modernism. Few of the great artistic questioners of this century who involve spectators in their ever-fresh processes are without debt to him. René Magritte's and Doukapil's puns on visual illusions; De Chirico's and Picabia's 'metaphysical' and physical disconcertments; Haacke's anti-icons of the commercial world; Joseph Beuys' uninstructional blackboards, no-possible-where; menacing tablets of no law cast down as soon as displayed.

All may be said to exemplify the understanding of an artwork as an assemblage of instructively engaging ruses that is the LCD of Deconstruction.

L TO R: BARBARA KRUGER, *YOUR FACT IS STRANGER THAN FICTION*, 1983, PHOTOGRAPH; DAVID MACH, *HARD TO SWALLOW*, 1987, MIXED MEDIA

PAUL CROWTHER
Beyond Art and Philosophy
Deconstruction and the Post-Modern Sublime

To understand recent fundamental changes in the practices of 'art' and 'philosophy', and their common sublimicist character,[1] it is first necessary to trace parallel patterns of development in both spheres, during the Modernist epoch. Beginning with art, Clement Greenberg has argued[2] that Modernism was a response to a crisis. To resist being absorbed by entertainment, each art form adopted a kind of self-critique wherein it attempted to ground itself on those features which produce effects unique to itself. Now the basic impetus of this argument is correct, in so far as since the time of Manet, artists have seemed preoccupied with features and effects taken to be unique to the visual arts, and this has led, in the case of painting, to the production of flatter-looking works. However, what is more problematic is the question of which of these features and effects *are* in fact actually unique or essential to art. There are two broad approaches here. First, from a formalist direction, critics such as Fry and Bell, and Greenberg himself, hold that through the possession of significant form or declared flatness (respectively), art gives rise to a unique mode of experience – the aesthetic. Second, a substantial number of both artists and critics have suggested that the visual arts' distinctiveness lies in the way they give expression to what, in the broadest sense, might be termed states of 'spiritual' reality. Cubism's early theoreticians and Mondrian, for example, see their art as exemplifying visual reality *as conceived*, ie, in its essence, rather than as given in the particularity of direct sense-perception. Others, such as Malevich and the Surrealists, see the uniqueness of their work as consisting in its privileged access to deep-seated subjective states – 'pure feeling' in the case of the former, and the 'unconscious' in the case of the latter. Yet others – such as Duchamp, the Dadaists, certain Pop and Minimal artists, and the protagonists of Conceptual Art – see the distinctive feature of the art-object as consisting in the creative 'idea' which underpins it.

There are several things to note about these points. First, we find that through striving to achieve self-presence, Modernist art divides into two broadly opposed tendencies (formalist and 'spiritual') which themselves contain diverse and conflicting approaches. When art explicitly orientates itself towards some assumed unique or privileged features or effects, it 'deconstructs': its historical development differentiates a variety of putatively 'essential' art features and effects. Now if it should still be claimed that one of these putative essential and unique features should be privileged above all the others (ie, that one artist, critic, or 'school' has got it right and the others have got it wrong) then this requires theoretical or better still philosophical justification in order to establish the claim and to orientate the audience towards it. But surely if *the* feature or effect supposedly unique to art requires this sort of philosophical back-up (in Derrida's terms a 'supplement') in order to be recognised as such, then art's claim to uniqueness becomes a mere formality. It becomes dependent on the interventions of theoretical discourse.

It is this conflict, of course, which Joseph Kosuth's Conceptual Art paper 'Art after Philosophy' (*Studio International*, 1970) makes manifest and consummates. The end of Modernism is marked by art's characterisation of its own definitive features in terms of those of the supplement – philosophy.

This trend is paralleled (with the protagonists reversed) in the development of 20th-century philosophy. Existential phenomenology, as exemplified by its three major figures – Heidegger, Sartre and Merleau-Ponty – defines itself as the search for a method that will differentiate philosophy from scientific and technological understanding. Broadly speaking, modern philosophy from Descartes onwards has tended to interpret reality on the basis of mechanistic models derived from the scientific domain. However, whilst such mechanistic models have proven value in the scientific context as a means for controlling and utilising reality, they result only in distortions when applied to philosophy. In general terms, the world is construed as a kind of intellectual construction – a function of the mind's organisation of sense-data. Indeed the human subject itself is reduced to a pure subject – the disembodied organiser of such sense-data. Now against these abstractions Heidegger, Sartre and Merleau-Ponty all assert (albeit with different emphases) the primacy of 'being-in-the-world'. The human subject does not organise sense-data through mere intellectual acts of mind as such, rather our knowledge of the world (and of our own subjectivity) is constituted from the totality of our practical, emotional, social and linguistic interactions with it. This complexity of the sensuous and the intellectual underpins all knowledge, but it is difficult to articulate because the traditional philosophical language of abstract concepts and systematic arguments oversimplify and, thereby, distort. How, then, can this sustaining complexity be adequately expressed? In this respect, it is interesting that having posed this problem in their early work, the existential phenomenologists all offer, in effect, the same answer through their subsequent development. Sartre's existential phase, for example, is followed by that which contains the bulk of his literary production. In their later works, Heidegger and Merleau-Ponty move towards an increasingly idiosyncratic and metaphorical mode of expression. This mode, it should be noted, does not merely act as an accompanying illustration to more discursive structures of argument, rather it embodies the very substance of Heidegger's and Merleau-Ponty's texts. By introducing an artistic dimension of style and metaphor into their work they are able to fuse the sensuous and the intellectual in a play of language which shows rather than simply states the complexity of our 'being-in-the-world'. As Merleau-Ponty puts it 'Philosophical expression assumes the same ambiguities as literary expression, if the world is such that it cannot be expressed except in "stories" and, as it were, pointed at.'[3]

Surprisingly, even two of the major contemporary thinkers in the Anglo-American tradition of 'analytic' philosophy have (albeit by a rather more circuitous route) recently arrived at some similar conclusions. In his book *Philosophy and the Mirror of Nature*, for example, Robert Rorty rejects traditional epistemology and its idea of truth as a correspondence with the essence of reality. Instead he demands an 'edifying hermeneutic' where 'as opposed to the epistemological point of view, the way things are said is more important than the possession of truths.'[4] Even more emphatic is Robert Nozick in his *Philosophical Explanations*. The last section of this work is entitled 'Philosophy as an Art Form', and in the very final paragraph, we are told that 'We can envision a humanistic philosophy, a self-consciously artistic one, sculpting ideas, value, and meaning into new constellations.'[5]

I am suggesting, then, that philosophy's search for its own distinctive method has led thinkers in both its major traditions to identify with the methods of art. Those elements of stylisation and metaphor which were once regarded as supplemental, as mere accompaniments to, or illustrations of, discursive argument, are now shown to embody fundamental traits of philosophical 'method' itself. We find, in other words, a parallel to the self-Deconstruction which is revealed through the historical development of Modernist art in its striving towards self-presence.

The moral to be drawn from these mutual convergences of art and philosophy is that forms of discourse are not independent of one another. They must conflict, displace, converge, and overlap, because our engagement with the world is historical – a shifting complex – a perpetually developing interaction. Now I would suggest that the moment of Post-Modernism in 'art' and 'philosophy' occurs when their practitioners turn back and ask what conditions enable the myth of autonomy in their respective modes of discourse to come about, ie, (in a sense) how is Modernism itself possible? To explore this moment, I will reverse the order of exposition adopted in the first part of this essay, and will consider 'philosophy' first – since it is in this domain (broadly defined) that the Post-Modernist question is most insistently asked. In the work of Michel Foucault and Jacques Derrida, for example, we find it approached from two different directions. Foucault makes it his task to reveal the closures and concealments which have determined the historical formation of different intellectual disciplines and social institutions. He insists, indeed, that all discourse is a function of the play between desire and power, and that the reification of discourse into supposedly autonomous modes is determined by the exercise of the latter. In the case of Derrida, a similar disclosive strategy is undertaken, but in relation to the truth-claims embodied in specific 'philosophical' texts. He asserts that the 'objective' truths supposedly revealed by the impersonal non-figurative 'philosophical' use of language involve an unacknowledged 'metaphysics of presence', ie, such truths are grounded on metaphors of speech – in so far as it is construed as embodying a perfect coincidence of meaning and signification with thought. This self-presence, however, itself conceals (whilst all the while presupposing) what Derrida terms '*différance*'. As he puts it, ' . . . the signified concept is never present in and of itself, in a sufficient presence that would refer only to itself. Essentially and lawfully, every concept is inscribed in a chain or in a system within which it refers to the other, to other concepts, by means of the systematic play of differences. Such a play, *différance*, is no longer simply a concept, but rather the possibility of conceptuality, of a conceptual process and system in general.'[6]

We find, then, that no textual meaning or truth can achieve total coincidence with the 'thoughts' it expresses. Meanings in language are only present in so far as they are definable in relation to a background network of other elements which are implicit, but not present. It is this which constitutes *différance*. Now such a denial of the possibility of enclosed self-presence is carried over by both Derrida and Foucault as a characterisation of the self. Their justification for this consists in the fact that we can only have experience in so far as we are the subject of language and its play of *différance*. Hence, Derrida says, 'Subjectivity – like objectivity – is an effect of *différance*, an effect inscribed in a system of *différance*. This is why the *a* of *différance* also records that spacing is temporisation, the detour and postponement by means of which intuition, perception, consummation – in a word, the relationship to a present reality, to a *being* – are always deferred. Deferred by virtue of the very principle of difference which holds that an element functions and signifies, takes on or conveys meaning, only by referring to another past or future element in an economy of traces.'[7]

On these terms, then, whatever individual emphases and uses the human subject gives to language, he or she is at the mercy of it as an acquired and inherited system and tradition that exceeds the particular subject – with all the tensions, paradoxes, and concealments that this entails. Such linguisticality cannot be transcended. There is no meta-discourse which will fully describe how, through language, the human subject articulates self and world. Rather we are left with the writings of Derrida and Foucault, whose play of style, ellipses and displacements (characterisable neither in terms of philosophy nor literature) disclose those foundational closures and concealments which have sustained the illusory claims to autonomy made by philosophy and other modes of discourse. This Deconstructive interrogation of history and its texts is the Post-Modern approach. It would seem, at first sight, that its justification is simply negative – as an ongoing vigilance against unjustified claims to autonomy. Indeed in this respect Jürgen Habermas has observed that 'Nothing remains from a desublimated meaning or a destructured form; an emancipatory effect does not follow.'[8]

However, contra Habermas, there *is* also a positive dimension. To Deconstruct history or texts in the style of Derrida or Foucault is to make evident that play of *différance* – that ungraspable network of relations, which sustains but is concealed by claims to self-presence. It is, in other words, to offer an insight into, or partial presentation of, a totality which *as a totality* is unpresentable. This, as Derrida remarks, 'gives great pleasure'.[9] But what sort of pleasure could this be? The answer, I would suggest, is that of the sublime:[10] Jean-François Lyotard has explicitly attempted to link Post-Modernity with the experience of the sublime – defined as the 'presentation of the unpresentable'. However in his writings it is not only sometimes unclear what is meant by the unpresentable (and its synonyms, the 'invisible' and the 'undemonstrable') but, more importantly, Lyotard is unable to offer an adequate explanation of why the presentation of the unpresentable should be a pleasurable experience at all. The source of his difficulty here arises from a very partial utilisation of Kant's theory of the sublime, and one which overlooks the aesthetico-moral significance of the experience – a significance which remains, even if we remove the more philosophically dubious aspects of Kant's explanation (such as the notion of the 'supersensible').[11] Such a reconstructed version of Kant's theory might (briefly) read as follows: if an object exceeds or threatens our perceptual and imaginative capacities, through its totality of size or *complexity*, or potentially destructive character, this can nevertheless still cause us pleasure, in so far as we are able to *present* it as excessive or threatening – in thought, writing, or visual representation. The fact, in other words, that what transcends us can be *represented as transcendent*, serves to make vivid the scope of our cognitive and creative powers. We inscribe the dignity of our rational being even on that which overwhelms or which threatens to destroy. Applying this theory, then, one might say that by making that ungraspable totality of *différance* (which sustains yet exceeds any discourse) visible in their texts, Derrida and Foucault strikingly affirm the dignity of the rational project through a symbolic presentation of the unpresentable. To fully engage with the Deconstructive surge of their writing, therefore, is to experience the sublime. Indeed we are thus made aware of a hitherto repressed aspect of philosophy – namely its justification in terms of pleasure.

This leads us to a crucial point. The tendencies I have just described in relation to theoretical discourse, are, I think, paralleled in much recent artistic production. A major figure here is Malcolm Morley – an instigator of that photorealism which inaugurates the explicit critique of Modernism from within art practice. Morley, however, soon goes beyond even this with *Race Track* (1970) a painting which replicates a poster advertising a South African race course, but which is crossed out by two diagonal lines in red. The work invites both a political and a Deconstructive reading. The political one is too obvious to require comment, and it is perhaps this obviousness which has led Morley himself to stress the work's significance as a moving beyond photorealism. The diagonals erase the closures and pressures inherent in working within a genre that has become over-determined by critical discourse and market approval. For the audience, matters are more complex. The two alternative readings open up a space of indeterminacy which is experienced as a displacement and a threat. It does not simply present a borderline case – a style 'in transition', rather the violence of the erasure challenges existing categories of meaning and pleasure. It refuses to repeat the cool aesthetic surface of Late-Modernism, yet at the same time refuses to replace it with a homage to radical chic. Morley's subsequent works achieve similar displacements on the grand scale. Pictures such as *School of Athens* (1972) or *Arizonac* (1981) decentre our notions of 'finish', history painting, Surrealism, and (even) Expressionism. We customarily conceive art history in terms of an enclosed systematic totality – a succession of definable schools and genres, with corresponding 'individuals' made present to themselves and their audience through distinctive styles – each with its own definable 'phases' of development. Morley, however, disrupts our sense of the enclosed and intelligible nature of this totality. His rapid transitions from lyricism to violence, broken brushstrokes to stable masses, fantasy to reality, make it impossible to locate him. Familiar categories are loosened and made strange; the horizon of *différance* appears.

What Morley achieves on the large scale is manifest in a more localised form in many other works of the late 1970s and 1980s. Especially interesting in this respect is the late Philip Guston. For most, Guston is an important figure in the lyrical phase of American abstraction during the 1950s. However his more recent works open up an entirely different prospectus; not simply a return to pictorial representation, but an extreme of it – grotesque exaggerations, cigarette butts and the like, gummy colours, forms which are things – but of an unrecognisable sort. To mark this displacement of lyrical abstraction more particularly, to signify our shock at it coming from 'Guston', the term 'realism' is introduced. But can these parodies of 'bad painting' really be realist? 'Really be realist'. The phrase sticks. We are caught in the play of possible realisms. 'Goofy' realism? 'Neo'-realism? Perhaps 'lumpen' realism? 'More realist than . . . ' 'Realist as compared to . . . ' With his insistence on the caricature, the incidental, and the miniscule made gargantuan, Guston not only dislocates our customary scalar readings of the world, but also displaces any tidy sense of realism. Its rational character becomes manifest . . .

Similar disruptions can be found in the work of Georg Baselitz. 'Expressionist' is here the ready-to-hand-term, the instrument of familiarisation and closure. Do not his upside-down paintings relate to this tradition? Are they not justifiably labelled 'neo-Expressionist'? Here the prefix 'neo-' at once signifies and neutralises time. What, in effect, separates Baselitz from full 'Expressionism' is a passage of time – which must be noted, but is nevertheless insignificant if we pick out the affinities. He's German; he uses a lot of paint; he's a bit extreme – angst-ridden even. But Baselitz is post-Dresden, post-Auschwitz, post-Berlin Wall, post-'Ost Politik'. The term 'neo-' erases this matrix and makes Baselitz stylistically safe. His inversions do not connote a potential discourse with these ultimate inversions of moral values and security, rather they are continuations of our stereotype of the style 'Expressionist' – the angst-ridden creative genius, on the road to profound self-expression. Suppose, however, that we erase the 'neo-' and let the conjunction of Baselitz, Expressionism, Germany, history, and inversion, engage in a serious play. What then? Perhaps Baselitz now reads as a disruptor of the stereotype. He presents a sense of the futility of Expressionism construed as a project for the deepening or totalisation of individual selfhood. It becomes, rather, a dissemination of the self in so far as, through its articulation in paint, the world is disrupted and inverted in the light of history, rather than possessed.

The final works I want to discuss in relation to this brief sketch of the Deconstructive trend (though there are a great many others)[12] are David Mach's assemblages. The threat to good taste is clear. Not only does a frustrated artist incinerate himself whilst attempting to burn *Polaris* (1983) (the submarine assembled from tyres) but the *Daily Mirror* features the artist standing by his spherical shoe assemblage *Foxtrot* (1984) and sums up its reaction in one word – 'Balls'. This latter attack is the more sinister and significant of the two. The very fact that the *Daily Mirror* should even mention a contemporary artist signifies an extreme displacement. There are two related aspects to this. First, an assemblage such as *Polaris* is one which is confined to its original site, although this comforting intersection with the point of physical origin issues in no aura of self-presence. Assemblages usually disguise their assembled character under the label 'installation'. This term connotes settledness – a fixity, even though we may know from the exhibition catalogue that this fixity is of limited temporal duration. Mach's works, however, have transience inscribed in the very spaces of their structure, and in the untoward elements – be it tyres, magazines, or liquid-filled bottles – which are the stuff of that structure. A second and more radical displacement arises from the fact that such untoward elements are used as a means of representation. This disrupts one of our most deep-seated yet lazy attitudes towards representation, namely that through it we possess and preserve the world, ie, we translate a transient subject-matter into a permanent and enduring form. This issues in an aura of timelessness – the more so if the representation is encountered in a secure context such as a gallery or a bank vault. The sense of timelessness gradually distorts our sense of artifice. The work was not created in a dirty studio from mundane materials. It 'happened' – as a mysterious emanation from the unfathomable depths of genius. Gradually the myth of 'art' as a privileged realm apart takes shape. We are drugged with false ontology. It is, of course, delusions such as these which Mach disrupts. His assemblages not only manifest the fact that to represent is to transform the subject-matter, but also disclose the customarily concealed facts of art's finite and mundane origins and destinations, ie, that it was put together, and will ultimately come apart. Artistic representation is thus restored to the real world. To put all this in Derridean terms, in Mach's work we again have a 'supplement' – something which the conventional mind (eg *Daily Mirror*) would regard as a marginal and ridiculous form of representation, but one which discloses both the repressed dimensions of representation as such, and some of the assumptions about 'artistic' representation which are implicated in this repression.

I am suggesting, then, that much recent art is characterised by a Deconstructive approach which parallels the discourses of Derrida and Foucault and the experience which arises from them. Not only do all the artists I have mentioned radically 'dislocate' their subject-matter in a way that questions the nature of representation and vision's correspondence with the world but more fundamentally, they Deconstruct those assumptions about personal styles and genres which are reified in labels such as Realist, Expressionist and the like. The essentialising attitude which makes Modernism possible, in other words, is subjected to a remorseless critique. 'Art' is recognised as a play of *différance*. It is a sense of this complexity, this immense 'art' totality, its past and its possible future, its overlap with other discourses,

which is thrust upon us by the works I have discussed. But whilst such a totality is ungraspable from the viewpoint of a finite imagination, the artist at least presents it as such. It is he or she who, in de-constructing the subliminal closures and concealments of 'art' and its history, inscribes this overwhelming complexity upon our sensibility. We are thus transformed. The pain of that which exceeds us gives way to the pleasure of achieved understanding. It is this common transition from the subliminal to the sublime which warrants the term 'sublimicist' in relation to both contemporary 'art' and 'philosophy'. Indeed, this term may have a rather more general significance, for (as Lyotard's recent Pompidou Centre exhibition *Les Immatériaux* strikingly shows), the availability of techno-scientific equipment and data is so pervasive in contemporary life that 'reality' itself is readily Deconstructed into an overwhelming network of macro and microscopic processes and relations, which are customarily concealed, but which make 'reality' as we know it, possible. This suggests, in other words, that sublimicism may be a definitive feature of Post-Modern culture *as such*.

Notes

1 To my knowledge J F Lyotard was the first person to make a link between Post-Modernism and the sublime, in his essay 'What is Postmodernism', included in J F Lyotard, *The Postmodern Condition: A Report on Knowledge*, trans G Bennington and B Massumi, Manchester University Press, 1984. However I have a number of strong disagreements with Lyotard, not least of which is that the sublimicist artists who I consider in this essay, would not, in so far as they work in representational modes, count as artists of the sublime in Lyotard's sense of the term.

2 In his essay 'Modernist Painting', included in *Modern Art and Modernism*, ed Francis Frascina and Charles Harrison, Harper and Row, London, 1984, p 510.

3 Maurice Merleau-Ponty, *Sense and Non-Sense*, trans Hubert and Patricia Dreyfus, Northwestern University Press, 1984, p 28.

4 Robert Rorty, *Philosophy and the Mirror of Nature*, Basil Blackwell, Oxford, 1978, p 359.

5 Robert Nozick, *Philosophical Explanations*, Oxford University Press

Oxford, 1981, p 647.

6 Jacques Derrida, *Margins of Philosophy*, trans Alan Bass, The Harvester Press, Brighton, 1982.

7 Jacques Derrida, *Positions*, trans Alan Bass, The Athlone Press, London, 1981, pp 28-9.

8 Jürgen Habermas, 'Modernity – An Incomplete Project', included in *Postmodern Culture*, ed Hal Foster, Pluto Press, London, 1984, pp 3-15. This reference, p 11.

9 Derrida, *Positions, op cit*, p 7.

10 See, for example, the essay 'Answering the Question "What Is Postmodernism"' included in Lyotard *op cit*, pp 71-82. Also 'Presenting the Unpresentable: The Sublime', *Art Forum*, April 1982, pp 64-9.

11 See for example, Immanuel Kant, *The Critique of Judgement*, trans J C Meredith, Oxford University Press, Oxford, 1973, especially pp 259.

12 I would mention in particular the paintings of Anselm Kiefer, Theresa Oulton and Julian Schnabel.

THERESE OULTON, *SONG OF DECEIT*, 1988, OIL.

ABOVE: *ICONOCLASTIC CONTROVERSY*, 1980, MIXED MEDIA; BELOW: *ICARUS – MARCH SAND*, 1981, MIXED MEDIA

ANDREW BENJAMIN
Anselm Kiefer's *Iconoclastic Controversy*

The question of memory, the presence of a past – its reality and possibility – cannot be posed outside of tradition. And yet far from giving the question a fixity, such a location, while accurate, only serves to compound the question's problematic nature. Tradition lacks a specific determination. Tradition can be incorporated within history – it may even be 'history' – nonetheless neither tradition nor history are thereby finally determined and allocated a semantic and heuristic structure. There are further difficulties since memory, tradition, history all encounter the problem of time. Each is unthinkable without time. (This will be true even in the weak sense in that their being thought will always contain within it, either implicitly or explicitly, a temporal dimension). Rather than attempting to give greater specificity to these complex interrelationships in advance, they will be allowed to emerge within a consideration of the interpretative problems posed by Anselm Kiefer's work *Iconoclastic Controversy*.[1]

Kiefer's title names the painting. It is a title which is thought to exhibit Kiefer's concern with history. Within his own history the title has been repeated and thus has been thought to name a preoccupation. In addition, of course, the title also names the dilemma at the heart of titles; the arguments within and over the image. The difficulty for interpretation – perhaps also as an interpretation – that emerges even within these opening and tentative deliberations is twofold. The first is the problematic nature of the naming relation. (The relationship between name and named). The second is connected to the first since it stems from that element within any representation, (and therefore within mimesis) that yields the possibility of representation at the same time as calling into question the viability of representation; ie of permanently establishing and fixing the relationship between the representation and the represented. It takes place, of course, within the terms – the conditions of possibility – representation sets for itself. This element is succinctly captured in the following question: Can the painting, *Iconoclastic Controversy* be viewed as a representation of the Iconoclast controversy? If it were to be asked – what is the Iconoclast controversy? (What is named by the term 'Iconoclasm'?) – then the twofold problem, already identified above, would have been merely repeated.

The factual co-ordinates of Iconoclasm are relatively straightforward.[2] The ban on the production of religious images was brought into existence by Emperor Leo III in 726. It was challenged and altered at the Second Council of Nicaea and finally overturned in 843. The latter part of the period coincided with a struggle for power between Empress Irene and her son Constantine. The ban concerned religious images rather than secular ones. During the period in question painting, engraving and the illustrating of manuscripts were practised; as was the construction of mosaics. Indeed abstraction flourished. While it is always possible to fill out the factual detail of Iconoclasm this would neither address nor answer the question of whether or not it was this 'detail' that was named by the painting's title and

therefore which was represented within the frame. If this state of affairs is the case then the simple recitation of the factual, while providing an adumbration of elements, will, of necessity fail to allow for a significant interpretative approach to the frame. The shadow of images endures. It is possible to go further and suggest that what seems to emerge here is a rift for which there is no obvious bridge insofar as regardless of the quantity of information that was amassed concerning Iconoclasm, it would always fail to form the interpretation. In fact, though perhaps ironically, it is precisely this problem that already informs interpretation since it brings to the fore the question of history, of access to the past and therefore of memory. It is for these reasons that it is essential to return to the difficulties posed by naming and representation. History – understood in this instance as the 'detail' of the past – does not provide any direct access to history as a problem within interpretation and thus as figure within the frame.[3] The emergence of naming and representation as problems does not take place in isolation. They are brought into play by the frame and moreover by its name. However it is, as always, more complex. In order to trace this complexity it will be necessary to approach these problems under two different headings. The first is 'Representation Titles' and the second 'Memory History'.

Representation Titles

The question of titles is an element of the larger problem of naming.[4] However what is demanded and expected of a title is different from the demands and expectations made of name. Nonetheless while the naming relation is more rigorous than the one at work within the title, it is still the case that the title in some sense names. The painting is entitled to a name which then comes to be its title. (The legal and moral aspect of titles and entitlement should not be overlooked). The title designates the frame in at least two senses. Firstly it allows it to be named within any discussion; be that discussion legal, aesthetic, referential or even the opening moves within an interpretation. In this sense the title names the frame; the tableau. It is not, as yet, intended to name what is framed. This will be the second designation. The first is exact. It exemplifies the accuracy demanded by the conventions of citation. (The viability and possibility of the fulfilment of this demand is a separate issue). The question that must be answered is, what takes place in the move from the title as designating the tableau – the painting qua material object – to its designating the painting qua object of interpretation? This shift in register is not a simple redescription of the 'same' entity. The painting as material object involves fixity. Its being is exhausted in and by its objectivity; its 'everydayness'. The object of interpretation will lack exhaustion as it is continually open to reinterpretation. This is why it is preferable to speak of the continual becoming-object of the object of interpretation. It is within this shift – this fundamental change in the nature of the object – that the title as designating the content of the frame needs to be approached.

It is however in relation to the becoming-object that the question of representation and titles becomes more complicated. The reason for this is straightforward. What is at stake here is that if the object of interpretation is the site of interpretation as well as the site of the continual possibility of reinterpretation, then it follows that the title – any title – can always be read as designating the actuality of interpretation in addition to this inherent possibility within any actual interpretation. (Where the actual is defined as the present; ie the locus of the task of interpretation and from which it comes to be enacted).

Now it is clear that the title cannot be thus interpreted within the field of intention – ie in relation both to what is intended for the title as well as to what the title itself intends – it is rather that the interpretation of the title, the interpretation of the frame and the interpretation of the relationship between title and frame, all sanction this reworking of the title's function. The intriguing element here is that while this is a general claim about titles it is also possible to argue that the title *Iconoclastic Controversy*, the content of the frame and the relation between them, inscribe these considerations within the frame of *Iconoclastic Controversy*. In sum therefore beginning to interpret the frame, the painting, *Iconoclastic Controversy*, involves recognising that part of its content is this enacted rethinking of titles. This does not occur in addition to the painting's content but as part of its content; as *it*. (It goes without saying that, at this stage, it is its content thus interpreted). There are important implications of this inscription for an understanding of memory and history. However prior to taking up this task it is vital to plot the way this inscription takes place.

The ostensible issue within Iconoclasm was the worship of images. There is a sense therefore in which this historical moment, even though it is coupled with the division between the Eastern and Western church, and the more general question of power within the Byzantine empire, is also an integral moment within the history of mimesis. (These two moments are not mutually exclusive). The problem raised by the worship of images refers on the one hand to the Judaic and Islamic traditions in which God could not be made present, while on the other it invokes the Platonic argument that a mimetic presentation within both the visual arts and literature, by definition, is always going to be unable to present the 'reality', or 'essential being' of the (*to on, ousia*) of the represented. When the argument to do with the limits of mimesis concerned a trivial example – the 'bridle' in the *Republic* (Book X) – then the significance of the limits lay within mimesis itself and not the example. In the case of God however it is different. Now the example is of central importance.

The problem of the presentation of God has both its origins as well as its conditions of existence in Platonism. When for example Augustine in *The Confessions* (Book XI, VII) poses the question of how God's word can be represented because it takes place at one time and therefore cannot be articulated within the temporality proper to human speech, he is drawing on the distinction established by Plato between the ontology and temporality proper to the 'Forms' and that proper to the domain in which things come into existence and pass away. The problem generated by the Platonic conception of mimesis is that it may lead to the transgression of God. This risk is *both* sustained and generated by mimesis. Understood as a moment within the history of mimesis, Iconoclasm therefore involves, at the very minimum, two significant elements.

The first is that it has to be assumed that what is not present has a fixed reality which by definition cannot be represented as itself, ie presented in itself, and secondly that purported representations of God led the 'faithful' to conflate the image with reality. Once again this is precisely the problem Plato identified

within mimesis. (It informs, for example, the careful consideration in *Republic* Book II and III, of which stories should be told to children). The important element is not God as such but the non-present. For once the presence of Iconoclasm comes to be inscribed with the frame titled *Iconoclastic Controversy* it is then possible to interpret the non-present as history. In addition the presentation of history – the coming to presence of the non-present – would seem to involve a painting that was enacted as memory; ie as an act of remembrance. As with any beginning the specificity of these terms is far from clear. What must be pursued therefore is not simply the relationship between history and memory, but rather a reworking of memory and remembrance such that they could in the end be situated beyond presence. In other words reinscribed in order that they be maintained but not as purveyors of presence.

Memory History

The inscription of the problem of non-presence within the frame indicates that the question at hand concerns how the presence of that non-presence is to be understood. This problem is not reducible to establishing the possibility of a remembrance in which the non-present becomes present. (However, as shall be seen, remembrance brings with it the questions of what is remembered and for whom?) Iconoclasm was a movement that resisted this possibility though it was a resistance formulated within mimesis. The *Iconoclastic Controversy* as a title does not name a problem within mimesis. Rather the past does not emerge out of mimesis, but on the contrary as a problem for mimesis. Therefore the criteria of interpretation cannot themselves be articulated within mimesis. There are wider implications as the painting does, in addition, pose the question of the possibility of history – the coming to presence of the non-present – even of history as the narrative of continuity given the nature of that history.

The frame itself contains a number of important components that can be seen as enacting these considerations. The first is the combination of media, ie photography and paint. It is often assumed that it is the presence of mixed media within the frame that is referred to by the painting's title, or at least that the title questions the 'reliability' of the photograph. On their own it is extremely unlikely that these possibilities could account for the relationship between title and contents, let alone the inscription of the title's dilemma (the dilemma of the title) into the frame itself. The way towards an understanding of the co-presence of both photography and painting is provided firstly by the presence of the palette outlined in black and secondly by the words written in the bottom right corner, *Bilder-Streit*.

The palette figures in a number of Kiefer's paintings. There are at times slight variations. In *Icarus – March Sand*, for example, the palette has a wing. This painting also involves a combination of media. Moreover, its title is written within the field of the painting. Invariably within his work the palette exists in outline only. The palette is at the same time empty and full. This is especially the case in *Iconoclastic Controversy*. It is empty of its specific content and yet is filled by what it outlines. The paradoxical palette is both a part and yet apart. The palette opens a rift within the frame that the painting does not try to heal. It is precisely the presence of the 'a part/apart' that indicates the impossibility of a retrieval or recovery of a past which is no longer present. The present within this paradox becomes the site – the witness – to a continual remembrance. It is however one where remembering demands neither the continuity of narrative nor of tradition. (The temporal dimension that is displaced as well as the one that emerges in its place, pose interpretative questions of considerable importance). The rift, the holding apart, that signifies without mimesis – apart from mimesis and therefore without a fixed and determined signified (the represented) – is the possibility which while not being contained within Iconoclasm, is nonetheless the risk within mimesis that mimesis itself attempts either to restrict via the introduction of truth or circumvent via what could be called a generalised iconoclasm. It is in this sense that the palette is connected to the words that also stage the argument over images; *Bilder-Streit*.

The frame, the painting *Iconoclastic Controversy* has therefore inscribed within it – 'within it' becomes of course 'as it' – a questioning, if not a reworking of titles and of representation. The presence of this activity within the frame works to reinforce the rift opened by the palette. Since both suggest that, on one level at least, neither representation, nor mimesis are adequate to the task of providing an interpretation of the painting. Indeed this emerges, in part, as an interpretation of the painting. In other words the problems of interpretation, mimesis etc, are not anterior to the painting but take place within the frame. They do have a specificity. The point is that history, memory, remembrance, etc, do not just happen, they form part of a tradition; a dominant tradition. Contests, even a controversy, that take place within the tradition concern dominance. It is the way in which the tradition has come to dominate, taken in conjunction with the consequences of that dominance, that it becomes essential to house tradition but not within the house of tradition.

In *Iconoclastic Controversy* the presence of the tanks and the wall gathered within the paradoxical palette form a part of historical continuity and yet are at the same time held apart from it. They thereby signal the necessity that emerges when history, memory and tradition can no longer be thought within representation and mimesis, ie within the very terms that tradition demands that they be thought. In addition what also emerges is time, since the temporality proper to memory and continuity is the temporality of the ordered sequence. A break within that sequence – a rift – can always be healed by memory. Memory is understood as creating a narrative within the temporality of sequential continuity. It is this conception of memory that the painting suggests is no longer possible. Memory is not to be linked to the past. The painting gestures towards a present remembrance; a witness to the rift.

Undertaking this task – present remembrance – is done for the most part within Kiefer's work by deploying figures and events from 'history'. However each one works in a particular way such that it calls into question the possibility of its own use as the creator of a true history in which the past comes to be either retrieved or restored. Present remembrance thus opens up the possibility of thinking the temporality of the rift and also of developing a conception of tradition as rift. Tradition and time (though only the time of tradition) now have a determination. It is, of course, one that is not handed down within and as tradition. The determination is the rift. It is in sum the actualisation of the risk within mimesis.

———— * ————

Notes

1 This paper is part of a work-in-progress on the paintings of Anselm Kiefer. It takes up, but does not complete, an interpretation of Kiefer's work that was begun in *What is Deconstruction?* pages 50-54. The sketch offered here is, as was the earlier one, connected to the philosophy of Deconstruction without being reducible to it. I have retained the ambiguity suggested by the co-presence of the English and German titles: *Iconoclastic Controversy/Bilder-Streit*. See the catalogue, *Anselm Kiefer*, published by The Art Institute of Chicago and the Philadelphia Museum of Art, 1987.

2 Even this claim, without of course being misleading, is problematic since the primary sources are themselves split between the opposing factions. Even conventional histories are torn between the East and the West. For an overview see E J Martin, *A History of the Iconoclastic Controversy*, SPCK, London, 1930. A general discussion of the arts of the period is provided by David Talbot Rice in *Byzantine Art*, Pelican Books, London, 1954.

3 I have discussed the problem of naming in *Translation and the Nature of Philosophy: a New Theory of Words*, Routledge, London 1989. See in particular Chapter 6.

4 I am not denying the importance of evidence and the factual content of history. Indeed it is at times essential to have access to such material. A clear example concerns the polemic around the 'existence' of the death camps. The two points that emerge here are different. On the one hand it involves the recognition that evidence can never exist *in vacuo* but is deployed and redeployed and thus ordered within the different, and at times, conflicting narratives in which it appears. On the other hand it is significantly more complex. It refers to the problem of representation (and hence mimesis) in the sense that it refers to the problem of understanding what it is that is presented in the present as history. The question is: what form does the presence of the past take? Moreover is it constrained to take a particular form? The question therefore does not concern the 'that' of history – its content – but history itself. The point at issue here is whether or not Kiefer's painting raises these questions from within its content or, more radically, are these questions its content. It is precisely the tension between these two possibilities that will be explored in this paper.

BACK TO BOMBAY, 1977, ACRYLIC

VALERIO ADAMI
The Rules of Montage

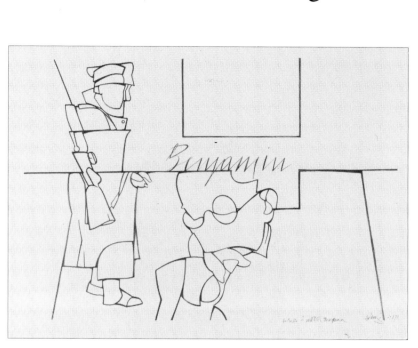

RITRATTO DI WALTER BENJAMIN, 1973, DRAWING

Valerio Adami's work has recently attracted much critical attention from deconstructionist philosophers. In his paintings and drawings, Cubism and Pop Art rival each other in a fragmented system where different sections are juxtaposed yet by their intrinsic shape allude back to their origins, and result in an almost nostalgic quality being bestowed upon the subject. The following text consists of a series of extracts taken from the artist's book: *Les règles du montage.*

The discrepancy between our daily life as we see it and the stories that the media make about it where it is only a matter of war, misery, riots, etc. To give evidence of this reality's experience without giving free rein to its subjectivity, or even to confused mysticism. To finish thus with a quasi-neurotic painting produced by sexual drives or by the will of taking one's desire for power for reality, etc. We must look for methods to establish an order. A picture is the recording of a very precise reality, even in the succession of his contradictory actions: man who, at every moment, would question his existence.

No reality is separate, each thing is conditioned and conditions in turn. As I see it, this dynamic is constitutive of *facts*, in the Wittgensteinian sense. Every fact results from actions and objects in a symbolic union – the fact places itself in the succession of time etc. It is the process of life. Thus its representation obeys its own language. An open structure, as rich in potential as human life.

In its materiality, the real dissolves into figures in constant evolution. It relinquishes its place to new, autonomous structures, but which take their form from the first reality. These will be the precipitated chemical of the real, its definition even. Let us rid ourselves of every pre-existing schema and open up to this new dimension of narrative.

New objects appear, which claim another space and another item and their form will result from their support, from which we have a system composed of inexhaustibly detailed elements, open to infinite variations, to the limits of the irrational. Because of this temporal characteristic any proposition that defines a picture as a self-determined, autonomous object is false, for it is involved in an infinitely open time, a globality etc.

We are far from being able to make a psychological analysis of the object-course to find the origin of our 'deeds' in their intimate projection. I am thinking about an objectivation of its own mechanisms in its relations with the inside and the outside. The mastery of form, in this sense, ought to lead us to the phenomenon of the real. Toilets, hotels, private slaughters are ways of life, another nervous system like mine when I go out with my camera. 'Hey painter, don't cut your ear off!' shouts a taxi-driver to me.

*　　*　　*

Arona. My lacustrian love. Place marked with questions and answers. Drawing is a literary occupation, reading is a matter of the eyes. A drawing must give all the information about itself. The hand follows its subject which detaches itself from us, impelled by an energy which is contained in the sign itself and returns at the end of the route against the author. We abandon a drawing when we are ready to add the final work, the finishing line being the point of suspension. I would like to be able to use the terms 'prose' and 'poetry' and define my work as a prose painting. The narrative departure point is essential, etc. But the form alters my conviction and my doubts, just as a curved line and a broken line influence the signified. Following that it is drawn with a continual or broken line, the same object is different. Chance intervenes in all composition, even in the most rigorous. The fortuitous element hides behind every movement of the hand. A painter goes from one surprise to another. If, while painting, a drop of paint drips onto his paper, nothing prevents him from using it. In any case, he must settle his accounts with it, whether he effaces it or paints it in again. The unexpected changes representation and shifts it to a metaphysical register. The order of a picture is different to that of nature, it corresponds to another type of logic: I would say that the picture is emancipated. A drawing is, neither more nor less, sketched lines: the spectator must not complete it by referring to what it represents. Fixing a form is something that occurs in the mind. The picture is a plural representation. Each line defines two arenas, a concave space and a convex space. We often find ourselves in the convex space. We first see the drawing in its entirety, it is not until after the event that we discover its details. We do not read a picture like a book or a film. Each shape is part of a whole, which after all includes its negative.

*　　*　　*

Rudyard Kipling with *early morning tea bags*. How do you invent a text? A centripetal action that follows a centrifugal movement. The whole is the text. The hand, while moving, also explains something about itself. To draw with the metronome, etc. Prolegomena of a journey to India.
21.04.77. I draw: *Back to Bombay*.

When the area of a surface found itself covered by colour, the idea of art was born, etc.

23.04.77. I draw: *Monument à la poésie immortelle*. The figure in profile is wearing a hearing-aid.

Etude pour la dissidence. Modèles pour un récit. Artiste qui travaille à son autoportrait. Sphinx. Chaises et ballons rouges.
24.04.77. I recall a note by Leonardo writing on the subject of the work of art, that it must not base itself on nature but on natural laws. The school of the nude teaches us how to lay bare. To draw from memory. Memory is a model to look at as one regards a landscape. The unity of a drawing is the infinite number of parts which make it up. I have proof that my drawing does not have total confidence in its maker and that it wants at all cost to submit me to its will. The idea changes going through the drawing. Questions in blank hypnosis, etc.
Schifanoia's ritual shape. Emotions dating from the Renaissance. Objectivity, virtue of precision. There is a wasteland between the signified and the signifier, the painter must appropriate it. Paint without too many adjectives. But how do you represent the whistling of the wind in the chimney? Colour, drawing's phoneme. Conjunction, fixing of a system, passage from one line to another through involuntary confessions, police dogs and searches, etc. The arbitrariness of the hand that takes hold of the pencil. System can become theory. Reuniting, assimilating, effacing, confronting, receiving, finding, refuting . . . (identity papers) and painting begins in identity. But what is theory and practice? The vices of definitions. Images as things. To invent a new body for these things, etc. Things as angels, in the equation angels-objects. Poetic manufacture. Where can we start? Painting interests me when it ceases to be sensitive . . . to draw a muscular body. The sign has its own, characteristic, muscular system which takes the place of the model's anatomy . In contrast with Italian Renaissance painting the anal side of all Flemish painting seems to me to be clearly evident. Precious faecal acts, excrement of an incurable nervous system. (I tell Damisch this about the catalogue . . .)
Every day painters announce the death of painting and yet painting can only come out of the belly of the painter.

2.08.77. *In apendice alla villa dei misteri (sinopia)* Cabaret Voltaire. Post-scriptum. Two invented portraits. Flagellating demon found in the guide. Extasies. Voltaire leaning against metaphysic (winged figure at the bottom right of the painting).
We find ourselves facing the theme like the audience at the cinema: in the dark, we are always ready to identify with the hero.

*　　*　　*

The imperfections of the table beneath the pencil alter a sign, then someone enters the room and the drawing changes again, I leave it for a few moments, I go back to where I had left off, but something has now stepped in, anti-figuration.

*　　*　　*

Art for art's sake. The art of war. *Non ci sono guerre giuste* (E. Pound) There are subjects into which blue cannot enter. Colour is within what one thinks about and not in what one sees. This is why acrylic is the most adaptable medium. To think yellow in urine is a symptom of illness. Seagulls are flying over Brooklyn bridge in the evening, a primate of art, domination exercised by power over nature.

*　　*　　*

Attentato secondo (sinopia). A policeman on horseback goes through the 41st decuman gate. A golden sky over New York's *agora*, perfect sign of a religious art. The balance of the painter between personal and impersonal with the coming and going of the view. Facts deprived of apparent relationships between themselves, but really composed like a film sequence. The movements of a picture that correspond to a myth and the myth that corresponds to the totality of its movements.
How do we look at a picture? To understand the beauty of it whatever it may be. To pass through painted figures and stop to live a moment with them. A series of tasks must be carried out before taking a photograph: focusing, exposure time, aperture. This is how we must proceed so as to look in an effective way. In short we search, we search in all the corners of the picture as if we have lost something: there is an image to find, there is the indication of a symbolic body, the hypothesis of an angel, etc. There are figures who live in heaven, etc. In many paintings, space is not a description of a place, but a mental aura. In fear of speaking in the first person, we create metaphors. At Arezzo, I lived among Piero's characters, etc. The true interpreter of the drama is the plastic value of the painting. The cross in Adam's mouth (Arezzo) half-way between knowing and seeing.
Reflections on classical virtues, etc. Painting which considers man, man and his nude body, the relief of the body in drawing, etc. Past and future equidistant. *Exploded drawings* etc. I dream of the Pontormo nudes, etc. Aphorisms on the body: learn to know yourself but to represent your neighbour. Look into yourself if you wish to find the other, etc. 'Recherche de paternité' in the Appiani cartoons (at the Louvre), the illusion of being impregnated, the imitator of classics with us, the mind painted. Without 'style' we turn, sweep round and lose our balance. Images that are never composed in advance, they invent themselves, we manipulate them in the course of work; a picture is finished when the process is finally recomposed. Harmony exists in the connection between detail and the whole. There is a physical seeing and a political seeing. We must ask ourselves: what do we see? A window, a radiator, a dog. Is that the whole

scene? But is it autumn or spring? (We know that the angle between the walls of a room and the floor is a right angle, but we do not see it as such . . .)

From where do we choose subjects? I look between the lines. I start from literature, then invention will begin . . . Beatrice, Fidelio, Loreley, etc, are female nudes. A great ball with the past . . . But Don Juan didn't like his time either. In the lake of memory (*Mnémosyne*, Hölderlin)

* * *

Anagrammi is possibly my best painting, but it is also the one which consoles me the least; the liberating knock-out has not happened. And yet the method of a drawing, the chain-reaction between the images and the themes which adapt and combine the working time that repeats lived experience, etc, should have a calming effect, put order into disorder and clear away pain, etc.

What attracts me nowadays is a painting of metamorphoses, that of cubism and of perspective. Firstly the drawing, genital organ of my picture, etc. What is then the finish and what is its opposite? – for the form is not the 'chiaroscuro'; when dealing with chiaroscuro we only ever seek to fill it etc. The image which is not closed by the borders of the painting is in any case influenced by their horizontal or vertical parallelism. By removing all the unnecessary and superfluous lines we reach the perfect form, etc: the eyes' work consists of examining and correcting the hand, finding straight lines, curved angles, etc. I draw the outline of a mountain with a single line. The modern has concentrated on 'expression', unknown expression of the classics, expression of life, etc. But the moment does not lend itself to nostalgia . . .

* * *

19.02.87. *Tema dell'erica*. If I make many paintings from the same drawing it is because its theme contains the obsession of memory and, by repetition, I expel and exorcise it. Form and progress: this is the cover beneath which the young artist will find himself, and this against disorder. This notebook is only the diary of disorder which goes from one group of drawings to another, it is only the confessional grille (as I am unable to draw it someone is watching me).

At the end of each painting you always lose something but you also grow richer, you see the past through different eyes and, rediscovering yourself, you become liberated, you follow expectations, remorse, sadness, nostalgia, etc. You search for expression because, without it, a drawing is merely a piece of paper that can easily fly away. Passion is created within expression, but passions are multifarious and one is never expressed in another. And what if one wants to represent it? – For my part, I do not think that passion can express passion. More than emotion, what counts when faced with a painting, is the idea that it is born inside us, the construction of states of mind, etc.. Language presents prefigured feelings, painting has given faces to heros and images to myths, but if we face the past we have our backs to the future. In my old paintings the object made its way towards man and a nude stretched out on the sofa made a body from the sofa; these days, the opposite occurs: a nude, in a landscape, becomes the lines of hills or merges with a lake so as to affirm itself as a part of the whole. The style comes forward again and again, it is repeated from painting to painting, but it is always more or less rich in varied intentions etc.

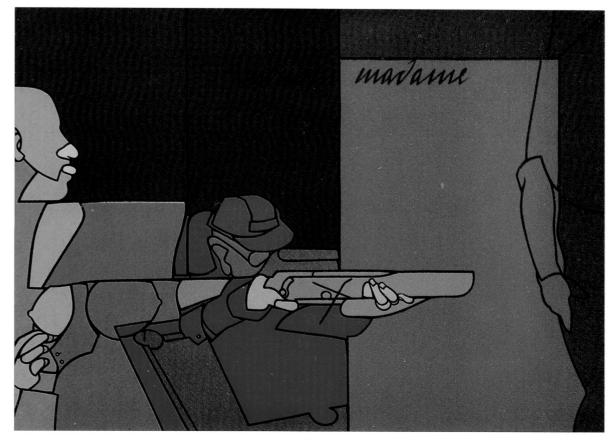

MONSIEUR MADAME, 1976, ACRYLIC

REFRACTIONS, 1988, MURAL FOR A HOUSE IN ETON PLACE, LONDON, ACRYLIC

ZOE ZENGHELIS:
The Elegance of Balance: An *Art and Design* Interview

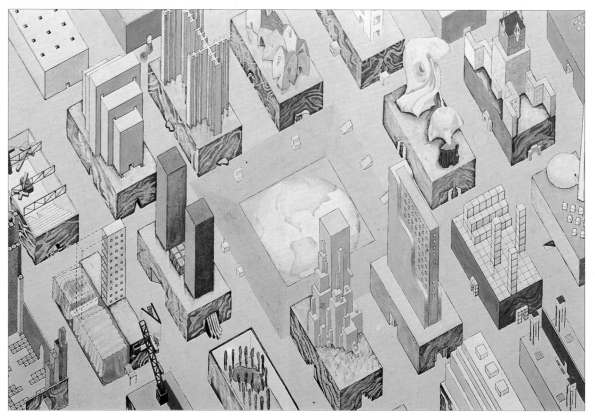

CITY OF THE CAPTIVE GLOBE, 1972, MIXED MEDIA

Zoe Zenghelis established herself as a painter during the 70s with a series of visionary architectural fantasies for the Office for Metropolitan Architecture. Her work is characterised by a dual sense of pure visual and architectural form. In an interview with *Art & Design* she discusses her work, which ranges from pure abstraction to representations of projects, in the light of its unique combination of formal analysis, balance and mystery.

–Could we start with some of the pictures you did for OMA (Office for Metropolitan Architecture)? If you take the City of the Captive Globe *for instance, would you say that picture is a representation of an architectural vision or does it stand as a picture in its own right?*

The *City of the Captive Globe* painting is both a representation of our architectural vision and in my opinion a painting in its own right. Paintings are done at all stages of OMA's designs, sometimes on an exploratory basis, others on a purely representational level. Besides techniques, my job is to create the correct mood and effect, for example to prove the seductiveness of a building or the polemics of its architecture, its blending, its contrast etc. Sometimes, looking at a drawing, I get inspired for a painting and it is then that my OMA work is at its most abstract.

–Is the work you've done for OMA an important part of your work?

It was a very important part of my work. Painting for OMA in fact gave me the confidence and drive to become a painter in my own right. Lately I have too many commissions, exhibitions etc so I paint less for OMA. I like alternating from painting for OMA to teaching, to painting my own pictures, sometimes in oil, sometimes in acrylic, abstract one moment, realistic the next. In

other words there is a continuous need to tackle something different all the time.

–How do you go about doing a painting with OMA? Do they say to you 'We want this particular view of a building?'

We usually think about the painting together. We discuss different ideas, I make some rough sketches and together we take the final decision on the type of drawing, the angle, whether it will be a day or a night scene etc.

–To what extent is architecture an important influence on your painting?

To a great extent, although my work deals with what architecture evokes rather than what it is.

–So you are concerned with the atmosphere it creates as well as its formal qualities. It seems to me that you have some pictures that are almost close representations of buildings in a setting and others that are more abstract, drawing on elements of forms.

That's right. I never know how the painting will end, what it will finally look like. The beginning of a painting itself is different every time. I could start from an image that for certain reasons has an impact on me and try to recreate it in painting, but I could just as well start by doodling on an already used paper and from then on by adding and subtracting, create a new set of relationships of lines, shapes and colours.

–What kind of things do you want to suggest?

Melancholy, longing, mystery, vagueness. No coherent messages, no symbolic meanings.

–So it's a variety of style and mood that attracts you?

Yes, indeed, I thrive on the possibility of different choices. The choice leads to the media and vice versa. My most atmospheric and dreamy work is done in oil. When I use acrylics, because of the perfect surface and texture that this medium offers I get obsessed with precision and my paintings become a game of geometry. Architecture is the perfect subject for both aims.

–What interests you particularly when you work with shapes or on an abstract? What governs your imagination when you work in that mode? Is it in your head that you are deconstructing a structure or a pattern or a harmony, or is the combination dictated by your imagination when you create it?

I suppose I deconstruct a pattern or a harmony step by step, sometimes I add or superimpose, always balancing and contrasting lines with shapes, shapes with colour. It is intuition rather than intention and ideology.

–When you've achieved the final image, do you see something in

Yes, I am a painter of the built landscape although I could never be an architect. I started studying interior design as a concession to Elia's insistence that I should study architecture as he did. I soon changed to stage design for my Intermediate and did just painting for my NDD – all this at the Regent Street Poly in the sixties. We did not work together at that stage. Anyway hardly anyone was using colour in architecture then. I think that OMA introduced architectural paintings in the early seventies. Maddy [Madelon Vriesendorp] and I are the only painters, I think, who are partners in an architectural group.

– It's interesting that you talk about liking balance, particularly in an age in which given notions of balance have been rejected. I suppose that must partly come from what you know about architecture?

Yes, I guess so. I enjoy working with architects and teaching architectural students. As you know, Maddy and I run the colour workshop at the Architectural Association. I think that it is the only School of Architecture in England that teaches painting. Function, use of materials, choice of drawings and techniques, precision etc, in other words the plurality of problems, demands careful balancing. The more you abstract the greater the impor-

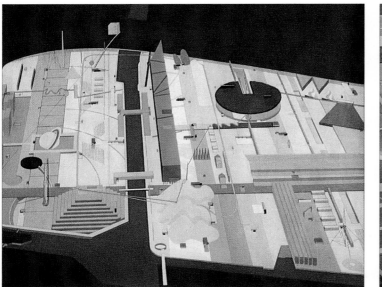

L TO R: PARC DE LA VILLETTE, 1984, ACRYLIC; HAGUE TOWN HALL, 1987, WATERCOLOUR

it then?

I see something in it all the way but the final image as you call it is the first moment in the process that I can stop and let it be.

–Do your more abstract works draw in any way on the tradition in abstract art, say the Russian Constructivists?

Yes, there is a lot of influence from them in their preoccupations with geometry and the elimination of the unnecessary. Also Cubism I would say, but mostly the Russians. I can add to this that my less abstract work, the work that contains more yearning and drama, has an affinity with some modern Russian architectural pictures of the last decade.

–What kind of things are not necessary?

Most things.

–So you are a Deconstructionist?

I think there is some connection. I hope people will not translate Deconstruction as dismantling.

–Do you like visual purity and simplicity?

Yes, very much so – and balance. I'm almost neurotic about getting the right proportions and relationships, the right colour on the right material with no waste.

–Do you think that comes from your interest in architecture?

tance of balancing becomes.

–Do you think that abstraction helps in any way for the students' understanding of architecture?

Yes, to start from a given image and to successfully subtract and abstract in different stages till you reach the final abstraction that nevertheless still holds the intrinsic messages of the original image is a very important disciplinary exercise for the student.

–Is this a process that you use yourself?

Simplifying and controlling excess surely helps the artist not to lose hold of what is important in a design.

–Is the balance you try to achieve in the more abstract paintings similar to the balance you want to achieve in the realistic ones?

Of course! Balancing is a manifestation of your ability to choose and use only those elements, ideas etc that will best express your intention. Abstraction or realism in this case are the same.

–Do you combine the two elements, realistic and abstract, at all?

Yes, I use realistic figurative images in an abstract way.

–Do you think that removes your work from the strict distinction some people create between the abstract and the realistic?

Possibly! To tell you the truth I don't mind what my paintings are labelled as. It just happens that they are really completely abstract (I am Greek after all). As for myself, I like all forms of art.

–Does the use of architectural forms give you a structure which you can break away from and can play with imaginatively?

Over and over I am inspired by the architectural form. You couldn't have described it better. I like to take a structure and let my imagination play around with it.

– Are there any particular things derived from your association with architectural projects that you have gone on to use in other ways in your own work?

Yes, many of my paintings derive from architectural projects we have done in the office. These belong to the type of paintings that I mentioned earlier, the ones that start on an already used paper and develop from there usually to something totally different from the original picture.

–How did your involvement with Parc de la Villette, for example, influence your work?

There are four paintings that I call Parc de la Villette. In two of them you can still recognise some elements of the original design.

–So the visual forms you come across in your work for something

question mark.

–Did you consciously abstract from the plan?

Yes, I shaded the background of the painting so that there is a distinct concentration of colour and movement in the centre. I placed the plans of the houses that surrounded the centre to form the curved top of the question mark then I arranged the next lot of houses to describe the straight line of the question mark and the single plan disappearing in the sea is the sign of the full stop.

–So what appealed to you initially, was it the image of the plan?

It was the hurricane-like movement of the houses in contrast to the geometry of the roads' black lines.

–It's interesting that the kind of balance you talk about is a balance that someone else, say someone who likes traditional perspective, would say isn't balance.

Traditionalists would say that, wouldn't they!

–Do changes in contemporary art and criticism affect you at all? For instance, does it matter to you when people say Modernism is dead?

Yes it does. I am a Modernist and consider modern architecture and art alive now just as much as in the 20s, 30s or 60s. It might shock people that some of the so much hated 'high rise blocks' of

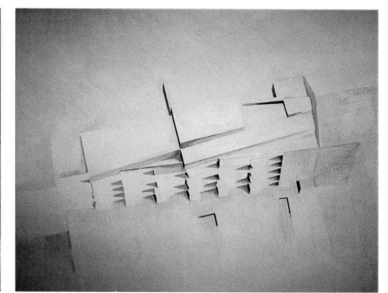

L TO R: LUTZOWSTRASSE NIGHT, 1983, OIL; CHECKPOINT CHARLIE, 1986, OIL.

like that appeal to you more than the particular ideology or theory affecting a project?

Modernism is the only ideology I would subscribe to and this I have in common with OMA. Otherwise, I use forms as a starting point from which to develop my paintings.

–With La Villette did any of the talk about the philosophical ideas inspiring architectural participants inspire you?

They interested me but they certainly did not inspire me!

–Do projects like La Villette exist as visual images for you rather than buildings, I suppose part of a building's nature is that it is a visual image as well as a concrete structure?

The La Villette projects exist for me as visual images rather than buildings or ideologies.

–Do you ever abstract from a plan?

Yes, I have done once or twice. The painting that comes to mind is the one from the Antiparos housing plan that looks like a

the 60s I find visually stimulating, dramatic and haunting! Their appalling built quality and inability to function properly socially was political and economic.

–Would you agree with some definitions of Post-Modernism that by taking some elements from the past and combining them with Modernist styles you achieve a modern style that is contemporary?

Post-Modernism is not a modern contemporary style. It is retrogressive and very alive, like a private joke between friends. It is not only Modernism gone wrong but also even like elitism gone wrong ... if that is possible!

– Some people would say the influence of Deconstruction was a new shot in the arm for Modernism or that it was a development; would you say so?

It will take time, I think, until it becomes clear what Deconstruction is.

———— * ————

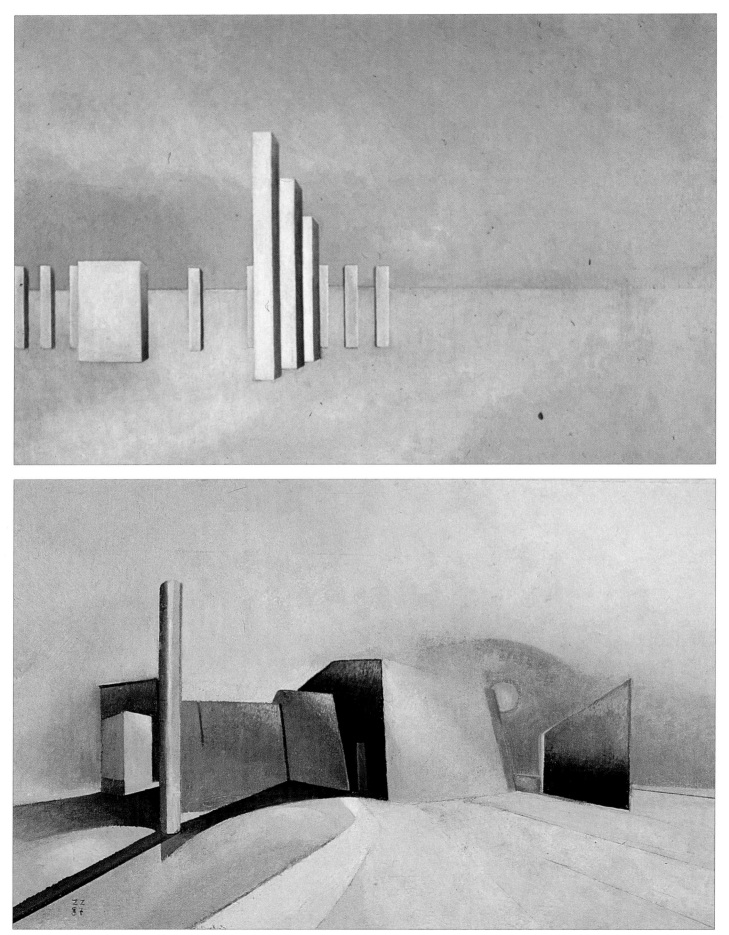

ABOVE: URBAN LANDSCAPE, 1983, OIL; BELOW: BUILDINGS IN THE MOONLIGHT, 1987, OIL

ABOVE: TALL RED, 1989, ACRYLIC; BELOW: SILENT SEA, 1989, OIL.

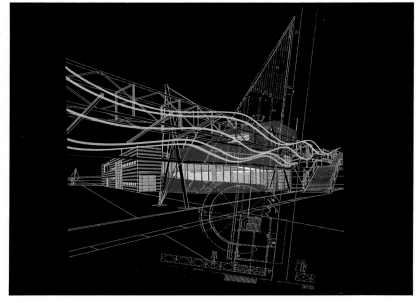

BERNARD TSCHUMI, PARC DE LA VILLETTE, FOLIE L2 AND GALLERY

PART IV

DECONSTRUCTION AND ARCHITECTURE

DANIEL LIBESKIND, BERLIN 'CITY EDGE', MODEL ALPHA

CHARLES JENCKS
Deconstruction: The Pleasures of Absence

OMA, BOOMPJES HOUSING PROJECT, ROTTERDAM

If there really is a 'Neo-Modern' architecture, as many architects and critics have been quick to claim, then it must rest on a new theory and practice of Modernism. The only such development to have emerged in the last 20 years – known as Deconstruction or Post-Structuralism – takes Modernist elitism and abstraction to an extreme and exaggerates already known motifs, which is why I would continue to call it 'Late'. But it also contains enough new aspects which revalue the

suppositions of cultural Modernism to warrant the prefix 'Neo'. 'New' or 'Late' – it *is* a matter of debate, and of whether the emphasis is on continuity or change: but the fact of a Deconstructionist movement in architecture has to be accepted. Reflecting changes in the literature of the 60s (Roland Barthes' 'death of the author' and, later, 'pleasures of the text') and changes in philosophy (Jacques Derrida's notions of critical 'deconstruction' and '*différance*'), the movement has been most comprehensively developed by Peter Eisenman as a theory and practice of negativity ('*not*-classical', '*de*-composition', '*de*-centring', '*dis*-continuity'). Eisenman, always on the lookout for linguistic and philosophical justifications for architecture, and having exhausted his use for Structuralism and Chomsky in the 70s, has tirelessly moved on from one metaphysics to the next, an indefatigable Ulysses in search of his non-soul, a wandering Modernist who has found momentary respite in Nietzsche, Freud and Lacan, before pushing on to further points of ennui and alienation. The Second World War, the Holocaust, the atom bomb, and any number of other inescapable horrors become for him, as they do for a hero in Woody Allen's universe, the essence of Modern life, the data to be represented in architecture. For some people nothing has more credibility than the Great Void and the seriousness with which certain New Yorkers pursue this *nihil* would suggest it is located near midtown Manhattan. But since architecture is supposed to be a constructive art with a social base, an architect who designs for emptiness and non-being is slightly humorous. Who's to say? A Deconstructive, anti-social architecture has as great a right to exist as the same traditions in art, literature and philosophy (as long as one builds it for oneself or a knowing client) and it should not come as a surprise that all are equally Mandarin. The

ultimate *différance*, Derrida's coinage for the 'difference that escapes language', the eternal unknowable and 'otherness', is the individual isolated from the group and now even removed from himself in schizophrenia. Although it may seem absurd to base building on this solipsism and scepticism, architecture always represents general cultural values, and no one will dispute that these are current, even fashionable, motives in the other arts. There is even an aesthetic, pleasurable side, a developed formal language which might be discussed prior to the theory: certainly the style of Deconstructive Abstraction preceded its intellectual formulation by Eisenman and others.

Frank Gehry and the Deconstructionist Style
Frank Gehry has developed the Post-Modern space of Charles Moore and others with a Late-Modern, abstract vocabulary. This phase of his work, consolidated in his own house conversion of 1978, has become increasingly self-conscious as it has become a popular genre and professional norm. With Gehry's production of cardboard furniture and Formica fish lamps, his many building commissions and art installations, his travelling exhibition originating at the Walker Art Gallery in 1986, his fish restaurants in Japan or fish skyscraper proposed for New York, and his acceptance as the leading American avant-gardist by *Progressive Architecture* and *House and Garden*[1] – with all this production and acclaim one can speak of a widespread acceptance of the Deconstructionist aesthetic. Like the clothing of *Esprit* and post-Punk music, it is an informal style appealing to a substantial taste for the discordant and ephemeral, the unpretentious and tough. It's a style for everyday street life and in this sense a direct

heir to the Modernism of Baudelaire's Paris, of Duchamp and Le Corbusier.

Gehry's method of Deconstruction can be quite literal at times, since he will smash an existing building into parts, leave elements of his own work unfinished and, as in his disintegrating cardboard furniture, make an aesthetic virtue of rough, crumbled surfaces. The roots of this approach probably stem, as they do with Eisenman, from his complex attitude to his ethnic identity, a Jewish past at once denied and accepted as an emblematic role. Gehry changed his surname from Goldberg in his 20s, but now regrets it and would like to reconstruct his name again and wear his Jewishness openly.[2] Extensive psychoanalysis has helped him, as it has Eisenman, to understand his double motives and how they are quite normal in American life: a youthful renunciation of Judaism, a turn to atheism and then a return to ethnic identity, even the role of professional outcast, the *different*. 'Being accepted isn't everything', he says as the opening proverb to his life's work, as long as one's unacceptance is accepted.[3]

These ironies partly explain his extensive use of the fish motif. As a young boy he suffered several humiliations for being a 'fish eater', for 'smelling of fish', in short, for being a Jew in a tough Catholic neighbourhood in Toronto. 50 years later he was asked to design

or flared keystone, or any motif which cannot be explained by function and cost. In this sense the fish is the perfect symbol for Deconstructionist architecture, precisely because it is an absurd *non sequitur*. If, following Nietzsche, there is an arbitrary base in all cultural form, and if architects can never prove their choice of style and ornament, then why not fish? They 'deconstruct all our assumptions' and show, if it needed showing, that there is no natural and absolute base to architectural style.

I have discussed this marine animal at such length because its implications for design are more revealing than the abstract Deconstructions of Eisenman, Tschumi *et al*. They force us to confront 'otherness' in an unambiguous form: you can sublimate fractured grids and abstraction, but not this recognisable scaly friend. For 'The Shock of the New', Gehry substitutes 'The Shock of the Fish' and in this sense, and others, his Deconstruction is a kind of Ultra-Modernism: '. . . if everybody's going to say that classicism is perfection [Gehry is attacking Post-Modern classicism here] then I'm going to say fish is perfection, so why not copy fish? And then I'll be damned if I don't find reasons to reinforce why the fish is important and more interesting than classicism. That's intuitive . . .'[5] Here we have the Gehry dialectic, which like Eisenman's is a form of 'anti-classicism',

FRANK GEHRY, *L TO R*: LOYOLA LAW SCHOOL, LOS ANGELES, 1981; FISH RESTAURANT, KOBE

objects for the Formica product called Colorcore, a pristine plastic laminate which always looks fastidious no matter how you cut it. In a mood of inspired desperation Gehry threw his uptight material at the floor and it deconstructed into pieces with ripped or fractured edges. From these imperfect/perfect parts he made the scales of his fish lamps – art objects rather than reading lights, which sell in a gallery for well over 10,000 dollars. (I mention this inflated price because it contradicts Gehry's usual cheapskate aesthetic and shows his typical ability to move across categories.) The breakage, the transformation, the puns ('fish scales are the right scale for buildings') all have their counterpart in Eisenman, who will superimpose layers of glass and then break them to generate new, non-human forms of a transformational order.[4] The parallel is obviously with Duchamp's *Large Glass*, 1915-23, which wasn't finished until it was broken.

The fish as Gehry's representational sign has been analysed for its Christian-Freudian overtones, but these are probably less important than two more obvious meanings. It's a friendly image which people will respond to with affection, as they do to elephant and dinosaur buildings (other animals which have been constructed many times as habitable volumes). Moreover, in its sheer gratuity it becomes Gehry's emblem for the artist and architect, his version of a Corinthian capital

always having the enemy close at hand, depending on it for oppositional definition.

This brings us to the crux, and what is perhaps veiled hypocrisy, of Deconstruction: it always depends for its meaning on that which is previously constructed. It always posits an orthodoxy which it 'subverts', a norm which it breaks, an assumption and ideology which it undermines. And the minute it loses this critical role, or becomes a dominant power itself (as in so many academies), it becomes a tyrannical bore. The same is true of Deconstructionist architecture: it works best as an exception within a strongly defined norm.

Gehry's additions to and transformations of the Loyola Law School are a case in point. The urban context may not constitute a strong norm – it's a near slum close to downtown Los Angeles – but Gehry has borrowed the adjacent morphology of towers and industrial fabric, just as he has adapted the small-block planning and *Collage City* of the Post-Modern classicists whom he otherwise disdains. These norms are then fractured and eroded to create an ensemble of three (non) temples and one (non) palazzo surmounted by a central (non) aedicula of glass. The client saw a classicising typology as suitable for the study of law, which has its roots in Greece and Rome, and it's Gehry's simultaneous acceptance and resistance of this which gives the scheme a rough tension. Columns and colonnades are built with a primitive solidity lacking base, capital and entasis; a freestanding portico is built in aluminium and repeated on a larger scale – both versions without pediments; a belfry has no visible bell; a 'Romanesque' chapel is made from rough Finnish plywood and glass; and three grand stairways – contemporary Baroque flourishes – are constructed without mouldings or balusters. The windows of the (non) palazzo are the typical punched voids of Adolf Loos, rectangles that are classically proportioned but missing their 'eyebrows' and other articulations. These absences may have annoyed the Viennese, 70 years ago, but here, however, critics and the public admire the pleasure of these missing elements and find them suitable for the informality of Los Angeles. The architecture breaks up and frames social activity very effectively, and allows many opportunities for sitting down or moving through and over the space. Altogether it's a successfully scaled and punctuated urban place which owes a lot to the classical typology it deconstructs.

Gehry's Wosk House additions, a penthouse 'village' placed on top of an apartment in Beverly Hills, uses one fractured language to contrast with a second, conventional one. A village typology subverts the pristine pink base in the Hollywood International Style. Gehry has again appropriated and deconstructed the classicism of Michael Graves,

In the Wosk penthouse the space flows freely between volumes, yet is partly divided by subtle articulations. The client's brightly coloured paintings, tiles and artefacts are sympathetically framed and set off by the background, yet contrasted. Indeed, since Miriam Wosk contributed so much of her own style to the design, it is 'finished' and detailed to a degree rare in Gehry's work.

Deconstruction is most effective when norms of construction and ornament are also there to be resisted. The danger for Gehry, which he hasn't altogether avoided with his increase in commissions and attendant poetic license, is that his work becomes completely arbitrary and hermetically sculptural, referring only to his whims of composition. His most successful interventions, such as the attachment to the Aerospace Museum in Los Angeles, relate directly to the function and urban context – here, the celebration of flight and the mixed, semi-industrial landscape. On the exterior a Lockhead F 104 Starfighter takes off at an angle, both an icon in the Constructivist tradition and in the vernacular of LA billboards and giant donut buildings. The broken volumes in whites, greys, and silvers suggest the anonymity of aeroplane hangers and their collisions capture the energy of explosive movement. They also suggest the contradictory aims of the defence policy where billion dollar weaponry is built and destroyed for

FRANK GEHRY, *L TO R:* WOSK HOUSE, BEVERLY HILLS, 1982-4; STATE OF CALIFORNIA AEROSPACE MUSEUM, SANTA MONICA, 1982-4

the Post-Modern classicist he often chides, whose initial Portland scheme also had a village of primitive temples surmounting a giant base. Thus the temples of Graves become a greenhouse/dining room, a mute pink elevator shaft and a corrugated metal studio with bowed roof. Some interior spaces are elided – thus denying the representational truth of these volumes – while others do indeed hold discrete functions. For instance, and quite oddly, Gehry puts the kitchen under a dome borrowed from Nero's Golden House, and then paints it baby blue! The intentional 'bad taste' of this gesture is repeated on the other side where a ziggurat shape is painted with an industrial colour known as Golden Cadillac. In effect Gehry is not only sending up Graves and classicism, but the whole neighbourhood, the pre-existing building, his client, and himself.

Yet this is not a radical critique or subversion, but, as with much Deconstruction, something closer to music hall satire – a wry, complicitous insinuation, a joke made from within the system and told with a wink. Deconstructionists often assert that one must operate inside the language, (or 'text' of society) in order to break down its assumptions, and this is certainly Gehry's tactic. He usually tries to work with some of the assumptions and taste of his client, to bring the building in on time and budget, and to come up with ingenious functional solutions.

symbolic purposes: it's an effective analogue of the baroque cacophony of the Cold War. However, the Aerospace Museum has a characteristic Gehry problem: it assaults the rather drab building to which it is attached, thus denying the possibility of a gentle discourse and continuity. This is the classic stance of most Deconstruction, which makes contact with what exists by contrast and aggression.

Rem Koolhaas and Neo-Constructivism

The Neo-Constructivist aesthetic unites the work of Gehry with that of such designers as Rem Koolhaas, Arquitectonica, Zaha Hadid and Bernard Tschumi into a clearly identifiable 'school'. Whereas Gehry tends to revive Early-Constructivism, especially in his exhibition structures on the Constructivists, Koolhaas and Hadid lean towards Late-Constructivism (the work of Leonidov), and Tschumi towards the most ripe practitioner of the style – Chernikhov. As with most revivals there is an ideological component and here it is an attempt to continue a Modernist tradition of the 30s and 50s which was heading towards both mass-popularity and hedonism. Koolhaas looks to the 50s populism of Wallace Harrison and, at the same time, to the programmatic inventiveness of Manhattan, the 'culture of congestion' which produced the delirious superabundance of piled-up life-styles and functions. *Delirious New York* is a form of Surrationalism, a surreal and rational polemic for building our cities. Ideologically opposed to Post-Modernism, it is nevertheless historicist: its revivals are just confined to the post-20s.

Koolhaas and his group called OMA (Office for Metropolitan Architecture) have produced many city projects which illustrate their theories and have won several competitions – only to find themselves placed second after political intervention.[6] OMA's work is not so much Deconstructionist as combinatory, combining typologies of many different Modernists – Hilberseimer, Mies, Cedric Price, Malevich, Leonidov – but doing so in a way which is discontinuous with the existing fabric, as in the scheme for the Parc de la Villette. This layering of opposed systems so that they are randomised and discontinuous amounts to a formal Deconstruction and OMA's work has had a significant effect on Hadid, Arquitectonica and Tschumi, who are more obviously within the general trend.

For the Parc de la Villette Koolhaas proposed an interesting new landscape strategy to deal with an overly complex and detailed brief. He divided the long site into a series of lateral 'bands' of different activities and planting. These thin bands have small elements or 'confetti' sprinkled randomly over the site. Then comes a layer of large elements, including the existing buildings, then circulation and connecting layers. Thus the superimposition of five separate systems results in a rich texture which copes with the complex programme and its uncertain growth and funding. This flexibility and indeterminacy, indebted to Cedric Price's 'non-plans' of the 60s, has an elegance and humour not often found in the genre. Because there is no overall figural shape, the scheme is disorienting, as is all good Deconstruction, but the staccato of repeated bands does provide a minimal coherence for the delightful 'confetti' of buildings and gardens to play against. It's very much the urban garden demanded in the brief and ultimately a new model for Deconstruction, as challenging and convincing as anything Tschumi and Eisenman have proposed. No doubt something like it will be built some day.

One scheme, the Churchill Plan for Rotterdam, uses a Deconstructionist method of composition where skyscraper volumes are cut up and inverted. Thus inclined planes and columns lean in counterpoint to each other (Hadid takes this distortion to a further extreme). Another scheme, for Checkpoint Charlie, takes the Berlin Wall as its departure point and rings the changes on repeated elements: not only the wall, but the courtyard house, chimney, stairway, curtain wall and what Koolhaas provocatively calls 'the limp curve of humanism'. One of their many paintings displays the kind of intricate, abstract planning that J J P Oud and other Dutch Modernists practised in the early 20s. It shows an urban tissue which is continuously varied and effectively pared into nicely scaled domestic fragments. Koolhaas might be reluctant to attribute this to his Dutch background and the tradition of De Hooch, but it is implicitly here, and it mediates effectively the overconcentration inherent in his 'culture of congestion'. This is no small matter since the major problem of mass-culture is its anomie; its lack of divisible, defensive space, and its absence of small-scale identity.

Koolhaas's first major completed building, the National Dance Theatre in The Hague, is more reticent than his paintings, partly because of the site and budget constraints, and partly because he advocates a 'new sobriety'. The Minimalism of Mies disciplines all the abstract shapes which rise and fall in happy agitation – as in Gehry's penthouse. They are organised loosely in a spiral of materials and colours that run from black stucco to gold leaf. This starts at the back with the most utilitarian forms, and the tempo picks up as one moves around the site giving way to glazed motifs, sloping aluminium piers (fat 'cocktail sticks'), a mural of dancing figures on the stage tower, and then the most sensuous shape – an inverted cone in gold – which marks the entrance and restaurant. The wavy roof, the interior ovoid satellite suspended by cables and the swimming pool suggest a counter-theme, the programmatic hedonism which underlies OMA's theory. The foyer has the dynamic spatial quality conveyed in a Koolhaas painting. A ceiling slides down into the wall, giving perspectival distortion, while the suspended ovoid champagne bar and curving balcony add further accelerations of movement. Colour contrasts increase the speed and, taken together, all the moving forms convey the feeling of a very swift and controlled dance. The anti-gravitational architecture of Leonidov is used here effectively as forms are held as 'tension in space', bodies which are frozen in mid-leap. As usual Koolhaas contrasts stereotypes the way a Surrealist plays the game 'exquisite corpse' – that is, as a series of cool disjunctions and deadpan collisions. There is a built-in alienation to this method because each language game confronts the next with no implied integration or meaning, winner or loser, linkage or resolution. As in *Delirious New York* it's a stand-off between separate, equally valid fantasies, phobias, ideologies and ways of life.

Unlikely as it may at first seem, Arquitectonica has turned Koolhaas' approach into a very successful commercial formula in Miami, but then this Florida city has essentialised New York trends in the past, most importantly for this team the style known as Skyscraper Deco. Laurinda Spear and Bernardo Fort-Brescia, the wife-and-husband leaders of Arquitectonica, assume Modernist typologies for their work – such as the repetitive glass box – and then break it up with an assortment of graphic motifs: red triangle, yellow balcony and blue square (a void of space known as a 'skycourt'). The three Bauhaus primaries are thus used to deconstruct the dumb box, in this case a rectangle of expensive condominiums disguised as offices behind slick, black mirrorplate. The name of these luxury condominiums, 'The Atlantis', is as much a *non sequitur* as a question of styling and one is bound to question whether the motives are not more commercial than artistic. Arquitectonica might well protest that this opposition is unfair; after all, their flamboyant art is inspired by commerce and its fantasies. Hence the names, 'The Palace', 'The Babylon', 'The Miracle Center' (on Miracle Mile, Coral Gables); hence the attachment to 30s shapes such as kidneys and boomerangs; hence the 'cocktail' colours and chic surfaces, the design from outside-in.

This last method, a reversal of Modernist doctrine, still relates closely to the Modernism of holiday architecture, to their love of Rio de Janeiro, and for this reason their style might be called, with only slight exaggeration, 'Miami-Niemeyer'. Because they turn 20s Modernism on its head and sometimes literally on its side (walls are treated as roofs and vice versa), they are more directly subversive to the movement than are outsiders. Their commercial play with the grammar of social responsibility deconstructs, as it were, 'the ideological assumptions of socialism from within'. Or does it? Perhaps their work is more a continuation of the Miami vernacular, an unlikely mixture of Morris, Lapidus, Moderne and marketing. The intentions and results are deeply ambiguous, even diffused in oppositions. For public buildings, such as the North Dade Courthouse, they adopt a more serious version of Neo-Constructivism; for shopping centres and marina/condos they proffer a mixture of the flamboyant and the dumb. The graphic invention of Spear is evenly balanced by the astute salesmanship of Fort-Brescia, a man who has gained the confidence of developers not only in Florida and Texas, but Peru as well. This combination allows the very programmatic density and opposition which OMA seek: at the Miracle Center a shopping mall is set off by functions which Koolhaas finds essential for the 'culture of congestion': the swimming pool, theatre and health club. But the variety and opposition which these functions imply, their schizoid dynamism, is smoothed over by an accommodating version of Neo-Constructivism.

Zaha Hadid's Neo-Constructivism, by contrast, is more extreme and closer in spirit to its source, the mystical Suprematism of Kazimir Malevich and his block compositions known as Tektonics. Like Arquitectonica and Tschumi, Hadid has been strongly influenced by Rem Koolhaas, who was her tutor. For several years in the late 70s she was a member of OMA and since then she has taught at the Architectural Association in London, a centre, if there is one, for this decentring movement, providing show space for the Deconstructionists' very exquisite drawings.[7] Indeed these drawings, and sometimes paintings, which express an energetic, sometimes explosive and usually optimistic form of anti-gravitational architecture, are the essence of the movement, more influential than the few completed buildings and divergent theory.

Zaha Hadid's winning entry for the Peak competition in Hong Kong exemplifies this. The idea of the luxurious club is conveyed through a dynamic painting that seems to be exploded apart in a series of fractured planes: actually it's based on an 'exploded isometric' projection which is virtually impossible to figure out. Blue and grey facets abstract the mountainous topography and Hadid imagines that several rock outcrops will be polished so that her flying beams would tie in with a shiny new nature. With this rocky architecture we are close to Domenig's Expressionism and his Stone House. But Hadid's elements are rectilinear, the tectonic beams of Malevich made extra long, rotated off the grid and combined with slight curves and dissonant angles. The new feeling of explosive, warped dynamism comes from the acute angles she chooses to use for laying out the perspective, an anamorphic projection which gives a distorted view except from one point. This graphic dislocation then becomes the basis for her programme and metaphysic. As she says, functional elements of the club 'hover like spaceships' or 'suspended satellites'.[8] The club itself is a void 13 metres high suspended between the roof of the second layer and the underside of the penthouse layer.[9] In other words 'layering', common to both Late- and Post-Modernists, is being used as an anti-gravitational device. And had it been built, the engineering to hold the building up would have been a series of box trusses and box beams flying slightly at angles towards each other – the 'cocktail sticks' of Koolhaas. The end result resembles a Malevich Tektonic which has been elongated and skewed by an earthquake.

Such 'Planetary Architecture', as Hadid calls it, is placed in opposition to historicism by her and critics such as Kenneth Frampton. For him the work continues the 'unfinished project of Modernism', implying that Modernism was fundamentally concerned with 'machine eroticism' and 'hedonism'. Except for a few Constructivist and Bauhaus designers this characterisation sounds unlikely. Equally bizarre is the notion that this 'Neo' style, a revival of the 20s and 50s, isn't historicist. Frampton is much closer to the mark when he characterises the whole oeuvre as a kind of 'cursive script' and says 'This inscription is so hermetic as to defy decoding'. This comment is offered as praise and it's one that might be applied to Deconstructionist architecture in general. One thing that defines it as Neo-Modern is precisely this personal symbolism, the text which only its author understands and controls.

Here we touch on a paradox of Deconstruction. Having, with Roland Barthes, announced the 'death of the author', 'the pleasure of the text' and the joint creation by many texts, or 'intertextuality', designers such as Hadid, Libeskind and Eisenman nevertheless create the most individual symbolism possible, one where only the author has the authority to tell you what it means. This ultra-poetic use of language is virtually private and therefore authoritarian; fully architectural language must, by definition, be more public.

And yet certainly there are shared meanings to the style. Many of the young have a developed taste for dynamic abstraction and the majority of the profession are still Late-Modernists. This architecture may be impossible to decode in specific instances, as Frampton avers, but in general it signifies the determination to continue Modernism as an elite discourse and it has a very strong ideological component. Hence the constant references to Le Corbusier, Terragni and the Constructivists used not so much as quotes, but as the final meaning.

Hadid's work signifies quite clearly the continuation of Modernism as a distorted abstraction. Her office project for Berlin is almost the normal slab block, but is gently warped, skewed and bent. Just as the Rococo style made very small variations on an essentially economic structure, she twists functional elements and extends walls at the corners to give the appearance of a wilful exuberance. The plans of this building show a few boomerang walls and leaning piers, the customary 'cocktail sticks'; the transparent curtain wall shows gently curving skin that tilts out as it rises; and the sequence of space is punctuated by layered wedges and cantilevered beams. In other words, a refinement of dynamic expression is made by warping a no-nonsense Modern block. This is a piecemeal heightening of an existing aesthetic, not something radically new, yet the subtle articulations feel entirely fresh: balconies fly about like half-finished slices of brie; glass planes are faceted by thin, elegant cuts which taper so delicately they look like incisions made by a surgeon. The accumulation of many such warps and cuts results in a totality which feels new.

Deconstruction Goes 'Public'

The feeling of the new, created by combining forms of the old Modernism, is nowhere so strong as in Bernard Tschumi's winning competition masterplan for the Parc de la Villette in northern Paris. Combining images and tactics from the 20s and 60s, his series of red buildings called *'folies'* are meant to signify at once the British 'folly' in the 18th-century garden and the French notion of 'madness' (as elucidated by Foucault in his *Histoire de la folie*). This conjunction of irrationalities, proposed as a 'Park of the 21st century', has a certain mad logic to it since it replaces part of the 60 million dollar meat market that was recently built and then never used, a mega-folly on the scale of one of NASA's greater accomplishments in the genre. And when President Mitterand, who presided over this *grand projet* among others, had to announce that the winning competition design consisted of more *folies*, with a price in the multimillions, French intellectual life suddenly woke up to the era of official, built Deconstruction. The government naturally asked Tschumi to change the name to something less embarrassing such as 'fabrique' and he, equally naturally, refused.

Tschumi's plan, as mentioned, makes a fresh combination of previous formulae which are acknowledged as historical: the layering of three systems – points, lines and surfaces – explicitly recalls Kandinsky's and Klee's aesthetics; the transformation of *folies* resembles Chernikhov's '101 architectural fictions' in method and style; the graphic abstraction of the aerial perspective owes something to Cedric Price, Archigram and OMA. This last is recalled by the dislocation of red dots, green lines, and cinematic swirls which float on an abstract grey and black background, the representation of 'any city'. This non-place could be the flatscape of a parking lot, or a suburban sprawl littered with supermarkets, parkways, little houses and garden plots. In this sense it's an abstraction of social reality, an attempt to make high art from the heterogeneous fragmentations that surround any major city, particularly Paris, and it's no small irony that Tschumi aims his paintings of this conceptualised nowheresville at the art market, selling them at the Max Protech Gallery in New York. This, after all, is a knowing *praxis* which once again works within the system it purports to deconstruct.

If completed as planned, the Parc de la Villette will have over 30 *folies*: fire-engine red constructions of enamelled steel, located every 120 metres on a grid. Their use, an ideal Koolhaas mix, combines hedonistic and educational activities. Baths, cinema, restaurant, health club, music and science centres are set amongst a host of small gardens. These will be connected by a three-kilometre randomly snaking gallery which Tschumi calls the 'cinematic promenade' because it is a montage of images with a layout that takes the form of an unrolled filmstrip. The list of garden designers reads like a roll-call of Late-Modernists and it includes John Hejduk, Dan Flavin, Jean Nouvel, Gaetano Pesce, Daniel Buren in association with Jean-François Lyotard, and the long-awaited collaboration of Peter Eisenman and Jacques Derrida. If they all do their own thing, the result could be one of the oddest agglomerations of the 20th century: a type of avant-garde Disneyworld which will be, final surprise, integrated through abstraction and the internalised references of the art and architectural worlds. Here Eisenman will be commenting on Libeskind's comments on Eisenman's previous work, where nearly everyone is a

Neo-Constructivist, harmony of a kind prevails.

This, of course, contradicts basic Deconstructionist theory and the intentions of Tschumi which are always concerned with *différance* not unity. It is true the layout favours chance and coincidence, the incongruities and discontinuities which result when three different systems are layered randomly and at angles to each other. The superimposition of many more Late-Modern gardens will further the disjunctions. But unless the designers and formulae are chosen from a wider spectrum – and this would mean the inclusion of Post-Modernists and traditionalists – the result will be unintentionally monistic, recalling Harold Rosenberg's ironic characterisation of the avant-garde liberal intellectuals as 'a herd of independent minds'.

Such orthodoxy, it goes without saying, differs from Jacques Derrida's reading of the scheme. He writes specifically of *les folies* in the plural and emphasises throughout his text that: 'We will have to account with this plural.'[10] It is worth quoting from this text at length since it is a rare example of *the* Deconstructionist philosopher writing on architecture, and it illustrates the main tenor of this philosophy. One should note, in reading the following, that Derrida places special emphasis on the atemporal now, *maintenant*, which implies the dislocation of an event that is still occurring:

was infinitely anaesthetised, walled in, buried in a common grave or sepulchral nostalgia . . .

These *folies* do not destroy. Tschumi always talks about 'deconstruction/reconstruction'. . . By pushing 'architecture towards its limits', a place will be made for 'pleasure'; each *folie* will be destined for a given 'use', with its own cultural, ludic, pedagogical, scientific and philosophical finalities . . . the structure of the grid and of each cube – for these points are cubes – leaves opportunities for chance, formal invention, combinatory transformation, wandering.

What could a deconstructive architecture be? . . . Deconstructions would be feeble if they were negative, if they did not construct, and above all if they did not first measure themselves against institutions in their solidarity, *at the place of their greatest resistance*: political structures, levers of economic decision . . .

One does not declare war. Another strategy weaves itself between hostilities and negotiations . . . Architect-weaver. He plots grids, twining the threads of a chain, his writing holds out a net. A weave always weaves in several directions, several meanings, and beyon dmeaning. A network-strategem, and thus

OMA, RESIDENCE OF THE IRISH PRIME MINISTER, DUBLIN, 1979, AERIAL VIEW

The *folies* put into operation a general dislocation; they draw into it everything that, until *maintenant*, seems to have given architecture meaning. More precisely, everything that seems to have given architecture over to meaning. They deconstruct first of all, but not only, the semantics of architecture.

. . . An always-hierarchising nostalgia: architecture will materialise the hierarchy in stone or wood (*hylè*); it is a hyletics of the sacred (*hieros*) and the principle (*archè*), an *archi-hieratics* . . .

These folies destabilise meaning, the meaning of meaning, the signifying ensemble of this powerful architectonics. They put in question, dislocate, destabilise or deconstruct the edifice of this configuration . . . We should not avoid the issue: if this configuration presides over what in the West is called architecture, do these *folies* not raze it? Do they not lead back to the desert of 'anarchitecture', a zero degree of architectural writing where this writing would lose itself, henceforth without finality, aesthetic aura, fundamentals, hierarchical principles or symbolic signification; in short in a prose made of abstract, neutral, inhuman, useless, uninhabitable and meaningless volumes?

Precisely not. The *folies* affirm . . . they maintain, renew and reinscribe architecture. They revive, perhaps, an energy which

a singular device . . .

There are strong words in Tschumi's lexicon. They locate the points of greatest intensity. These are the words beginning with *trans* (transcript, transference, etc) and, above all, *de-* or *dis-*. These words speak destabilisation, deconstruction, dehiscence and, first of all, dissociation, disjunction, disruption, *différance*. An architecture of heterogeneity, interruption, non-coincidence. But who would have built in this manner? Who would have counted on only the energies in *dis-* or *de-*? No work results from a simple displacement or dislocation. Therefore invention is needed . . . it gathers together the *différance* . . . A transaction aimed at a spacing and at a *socius* of dissociation.[11]

At moments in this analytical panegyric to Tschumi, especially when he asks rhetorical questions to answer them in the negative, Derrida sounds like Nietzsche; at other times his thinking is inspired by alliteration and analogy, as if poetic thought would deconstruct rationality.[12] If he flirts with nihilism ('meaningless volumes') it is only to reject it and thereby assert a generalised affirmation, and thus he switches back and forth quickly between many possible '*de-s*', the deconstruction/ reconstruction antinomies of Nietzsche. Behind this stalemate of oppositions it is possible to find two defining accents: the emphasis on the *pleasure* of wandering in an unstable permeable 'weave', to use his metaphor, a kind of in-between or liminal state, and the idea that Tschumi's Parc forms a '*socius* of dissociation' which gathers together *différance*.

As already mentioned I would dispute that the latter constitutes a real pluralism, which must be founded on a wider set of public languages than a restricted abstraction, but there can be no doubt about the pleasure of Tschumi's constructions and layout: the tilted walls which recall the anamorphic projections of Hadid, the undulating tensile walkways (engineered by Peter Rice), the flying cantilevers and skewed 'cocktail sticks', the juxtaposed space frames in blood-red steel, the collision of different plants and curving *allées* of trees. In short, Neo-Constructivist aesthetics are played with considerable invention and skill.

As for the 'point-grid' plan and the random sprawl, this is meant to be interpreted as emptiness (what Tschumi calls *la case vide* or 'empty slot'), the kind of urban reality already created by Modernism, industrialisation and the 'dispersion' of contemporary life.[13] The critic Anthony Vidler juxtaposes this decentring with the work of what he calls the Post-Modern 'nostalgics' and their concern for recentring urban life.[14] The *folies*, or *cases vides*, are on this reading 'open

rately conditioned and externally controlled ciphers who have lost their identity and history.[16] And so we have the Deconstructionists' abhorence of meaning and hierarchy, sentiments shared by Tschumi, Eisenman and Derrida, and their corresponding elevation of the Empty Man, the nomadic 'man without qualities' who can weave his way through all hierarchies showing them to be temporary and nonsensical. Empty Man, or Orgman, as Rosenberg also notes ironically 'is, with necessary additions and disguise, none else than the new intellectual talking about himself'[17]: the nomadic international traveller without family attachments or long-term commitments or a past that he cares to recognise. In brief it's a picture of that *beau-ideal* of the 20th century, the Futurist and Existentialist who defines his goals and changes them without much sentiment or angst.

And yet this ideal type, the Empty Man, has another aspect to his character which may come as something of a surprise: he always seeks and then predictably finds, like a 13th-century pilgrim pursuing the Holy Grail, the empty centre at the heart of society, the self-contradiction of all texts, the Great Void of Extinction – and this cheers him up. For what he has discovered is a religion without faith, a positive nihilism,[18] or in Derrida's terms an affirmative Deconstruction. This certainty of meaninglessness is very bracing: it also leads to a very

ARQUITECTONICA, *L TO R*: AXONOMETRIC FOR THE ATLANTIS, MIAMI, 1979-82; NORTH DADE COURTHOUSE, FLORIDA, 1985-7

structures for the nomadic *banlieue*', elements which have no meaning in time and space, perfect receptacles for an uprooted, anarchic and confused mass-culture, and in this sense hardly a utopian prospect. But then Tschumi intends a celebration of the status quo: 'I would say that La Villette is not about the way things should happen in the future, but the way things are now today. There are no utopias today.'[15] Such arguments sound, ironically, like the Post-Modernist Robert Venturi explicating Las Vegas for its lessons 15 years earlier, but now Venturi's 'decorated sheds' have lost their decoration, or rather had it abstracted to a red hue, a colour meant, like the white and black used elsewhere, to be a non-colour. Empty slots, non-hierarchies and non-colours, de-this and that, oh the pleasures of the absences!

That we are seeing here the style of urban anomie raised to a high art should come as no surprise, since it is one of the most recurrent archetypes of Late-Modernism and has been so since Cedric Price's 'non-plans' of the 60s. It's important to stress the historical nature of this idea since it is so central to the Deconstructionist enterprise. The sociology of alienation, developed by William H Whyte (*The Organisation Man*) and David Reisman (*The Lonely Crowd*), has led to the spectre of a world populated by 'other-directed' automata, what Harold Rosenberg has sarcastically termed 'Orgmen', that is, corpo-

coherent style of absence, something equivalent to the great styles of iconoclasm and self-renunciation of Cistercianism of the 13th century and Zen-Buddhist art.

Hiromi Fujii, in part a follower of Eisenman, is one master of this genre who produces many buildings which signify the beauties of absence: missing walls and windows, cut planes, uncoloured surfaces, etc. As he describes it, his method of 'metamorphology alters acquired meanings (customary codes) for the sake of producing non-conforming relationships'.[19] A set of mechanical operations, different from Tschumi's and Eisenman's in operation but similar in their random mechanism, is performed to alter the customary codes: 'disparity, gapping, opposition, reversal'.[20] Characteristically the grid marches all over the building in black and white reversals to destroy the conventional relations of up/down, roof/wall and furniture/ room.

Another master of this cryptic religious style is John Hejduk whose bleak and beautiful constructions often resemble a functional mechanism that is deconstructed and reconstituted on a new scale. For Berlin he has designed a scenario and set of 67 structures called *Victims* which are intended to be placed, one each year, on the site of the former Gestapo Headquarters. Each one is named with a label that is both functional and associative and then placed on a point-grid with no discernible overall geometry of layout. A related mechanism, *The Collapse of Time*, was built by the Architectural Association for a London Square, an odd choice of site for this structure because, as an adjacent plaque indicated, it too commemorated the victims of the Gestapo. Passers-by could watch over a four-week period while Time, represented by a set of stacked cubes (coffins?) numbered one to 13, fell to 45 degrees and then collapsed onto their bier. The image of railroad tracks, five pairs of wheels and the bleak wood containers was both poetically childlike and disturbing, humorous and remorseless, a vivid memorial to those who took their last journey on a wooden train. The blocking of the '12th hour' implies that we are now Post-Holocaust and the presence of the number 13 is a funny/mordant reminder of that floor which is usually missing in skyscrapers. Hejduk combines word, scenario and Minimalist image in a unique style, but his work relates to that work of Libeskind and Eisenman in having an almost nihilistic metaphysical origin.

Peter Eisenman, the Positive Nihilist

No architect is more committed to the faith of dogmatic scepticism, the importance of the gaps and contradictions within the text, than Peter Eisenman. In about 1978 he became a Deconstructionist and at the

series of mechanical processes which destroyed the centre of the house (decentring), anthropomorphic scale (scaling), and customary usages (a glass wall is used as a floor and is cantilevered over space). House X itself was not built, but a version of it was, a squashed-down axonometric model which looked from every angle except one as though it had been carefully blown down by a very precise tornado. This violent anamorphic act ('an attack on representation') was, in its sheer gratuity, just one more distancing means among many others that Eisenman was to deploy in order to reveal the arbitrary, non-natural mechanism of design, its possible anti-humanist, anti-classical bias. That the abstract results were also quite beautiful and sensuous was admitted, but this unfortunate human vestige was soon to be expunged – a computer would see to that. The world must be alienated after all.[22]

Fundamental to Eisenman's notion of alienation is his understanding of the Modern *episteme*, as outlined in a 1976 article called 'Post-Functionalism'. Using Foucault's idea of an underlying thought pattern or iconology for every period, he generalises the 'Modern' as an anti-humanist epoch which leads stylistically to a series of 'non-s' ('non-objective abstract painting of Malevich and Mondrian', 'non-narrative, atemporal writing of Joyce and Apollinaire', 'non-narrative

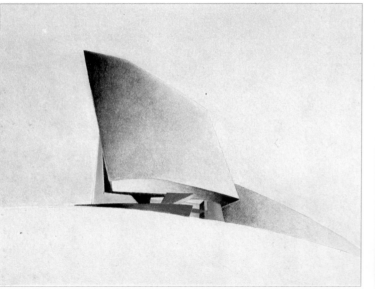

ZAHA HADID, *L TO R*: KURFURSTENDAMM 70, BERLIN, 1985-6, VIEW FROM KURFURSTENDAMM; HONG KONG PEAK, 1981-3, ELEMENTS OF THE VOID

same time underwent psychoanalysis; two events that have no doubt reinforced each other and his own dogmatic scepticism. It's illuminating to give a brief summary of his development, partly based on his own words, because it shows how much he is attracted to current philosophies and theories of the moment and how he intentionally 'mis-reads' them for his own purposes to give his work what he rightly calls a 'didactic energy'.[21] His buildings, writings and theories all have a frantic energy and are compulsively mixed together as if this might produce a real breakthrough, a new non-architecture which is part writing, building and model. Paradoxically his aesthetic has remained much the same white-gridded abstraction as his first houses, although several tactics such as the L-shape and half-buried building have been added to the repertoire.

The first houses, numbered I and II, were carrying forward the Modernist syntax of Le Corbusier and Terragni. Houses III and VI were Late-Modern exercises in 'pure formalism', influenced by the art-historians Rosalind Krauss and Clement Greenberg, Structuralists such as Lévi-Strauss and Chomsky, and Minimalists such as Donald Judd. House X, 1978, is the 'last formalist work' and the 'first use of decomposition which is opposite to a rational transformational process'. The building was designed by subtracting elements and by a

films of Richter and Eggeling') and it leads philosophically to a series of 'dis-s' ('a displacement of man away from the centre of his world').[23] Thus '[Man] is no longer viewed as an originating agent. Objects are seen as ideas independent of man' and therefore they can be dislocated in scale and totally abstract. These ideas dovetail nicely with Roland Barthes and lead Eisenman to a new series of rhetorical strategies to represent the loss of centre: *L-shapes*, or 'els', which signify partness and instability, *excavation* which signifies digging into the past and unconscious, *scaling* which results in decreasing or increasing an element successively to non-human proportion, and *topological geometry* which provides an alternative to the more anthropomorphic Euclidean geometry. We will find Eisenman adopting still further methods of decentring, with what could be called his rhetoric machine, but the important point is that each method is based on his metaphysics of nihilism, the *episteme* he presumes underlies the Modern project. (Perhaps it should be mentioned at this point that there *was* a humanist Modernism, a truth he conveniently overlooks; in any case it is his intention to subvert and deconstruct it.)

House 11a, initially designed for his friend Kurt Forster, now head of the Getty Center, is based on a series of L's which are part above and below ground and also rotated with respect to each other. These eroded cubes are meant to 'suggest a more uncertain condition of the universe. House 11a takes this condition of uncertainty as its point of departure . . . We live in an age of partial objects . . . the whole is full of holes'.[24] From this stage, according to Eisenman, there is a shift in his work towards the bigger scale – he seeks out urban projects – and towards considering the site. The Cannaregio project for Venice, 1978, indicates this shift towards what I would call his 'Non-Post-Modernism', that is his use of Post-Modern norms in an inverted or Deconstructed way.

Thus responding to Contextualism, he both denies the fabric and history of Venice and asserts the *absence* of Le Corbusier's hospital project for this city, by using its grid as an ordering device. The scheme is a positive bouquet of 'non-s' ('non-mimetic, non-narrative and non-vertebrate') and it takes the decomposed House 11a for its non-scale. This is to be

> built as three differently scaled objects. One of the objects is about four feet high, it sits in the square and is the model of a house. You can look at it and think 'well, that is not a house; it is the model of House 11a.' Then you take the same object and put it in House 11a; you build House 11a at a human scale – and you put this same model of it inside . . . the larger object

folies, as a pure intellectual condition which has begun to dominate his work, life and mental state. In the early 80s the Institute for Architecture and Urban Studies, which he had co-founded, began to deconstruct as he turned his efforts towards a larger practice without altogether extricating himself from its control.[26] He became alienated from some of his friends and, for a time, his wife and children. Even his students at Harvard, where he taught from 1983 to 1985, went through traumas of de-stabilisation and momentary withdrawal as he introduced Deconstruction as a practising method.[27] After several written attacks on classicism and Post-Modernism,[28] he took direct aim at his former friend and ideological enemy, Leon Krier, the exponent of classicism and defender of Albert Speer. Krier's revivalism was dismissed as nostalgic, out of touch with modern science and equated with the anti-Semitism of Speer and other Nazis. As Krier apparently once confessed to Eisenman that the 'homeless Jewish intellectual' was not the starting point of his urbanism, this lapse on his part is once again taken as the authoritarian nature of classicism. 'Any woman', Eisenman said pointing at the audience, 'who subscribes to classicism is self-denying'.[29] 'Logocentrism', the favoured sin of Deconstructionists, anthropocentrism, hierarchy, anti-feminism, anti-Semitism and nostalgia were all rolled up together into one paranoid

BERNARD TSCHUMI, PARC DE LA VILLETTE, PARIS, 1983-, FOLIES

minimalises the smaller one. Once the object inside is memorialised, it is no longer the model of an object; it has been transformed . . . into a real thing. As a consequence, the larger house, the one at anthropomorphic scale, no longer functions as a house . . . Then there is the third object, which is larger than the other two, larger than reality, larger than anthropomorphic necessity . . . It becomes a museum of all these things.[25]

One is reminded here of Mozuna's houses-within-houses, his *Anti-Dwelling Box* of 1971, based on *The Mother Goose* rhyme, and Borges' endless library of self-referring books, both examples of an eternal process of self-referentiality.

These devices, later called 'scaling' and 'self-similarity' by Eisenman, decrease the power of the user just as they increase that of the architect and it's not surprising that Eisenman later produced even more solipsistic works, such as 'House El Even Odd' (a pun on House 11a as an odd one) and 'Fin d'Ou T Hou S' (a deconstructed set of puns on 'find out house;' 'fine doubt house' and 'fin d'août' – the 'end of August' 1983, when he designed it). Broken puns and scrambled sense, his psychoanalyst must have assured him, constitute our normal, psychic state.

It is Eisenman's determination to represent this madness, Tschumi's

ball and hurled at Krier. Needless to say this caricature missed its mark and, since it assumed a totalising ideology, was in any case a very non-Deconstructionist act.

Eisenman's scepticism and dislike of the classical has found expression in many recent articles and urban projects.[30] Primary among the latter was his winning entry for social housing in Berlin, an IBA project located near the Berlin Wall and Checkpoint Charlie. The traumatic past of this city afforded Eisenman, as it did Hejduk and Libeskind, a good opportunity to represent catastrophes and discontinuities of the past and present: 'Germans killing Germans trying to flee from Germany to Germany' as one circular and mordant proposition put it.[31] Eisenman's first scheme, produced in 1982, postulated the redevelopment of a whole block with additions (a museum and walkways) and subtractions (an 'artificial excavation' down to 18th-century foundations), but in the event only 37 apartment units were constructed on the southwest corner. His intention here was to provide an alternative to Post-Modern historicism with its emphasis on continuity, wholeness and patching up the fragmented Modern city. This last approach is dismissed as an attempt to 'embalm time', or 'reverse or relive it' – 'a form of nostalgia'.[32] Instead Eisenman proposes in a disinterested way a neutralising 'anti-memory', something akin to

Tschumi's reproduction of the status quo:

Anti-memory does not seek or posit progress, makes no claims to a more perfect future, or a new order, predicts nothing. It has nothing to do with historicist allusion or with values or functions of particular forms; it instead involves *the making of a place that derives its order from the obscuring of its own recollected past.*

In this way memory and anti-memory work oppositely but in collusion to produce a suspended object, a frozen fragment of no past and no future, a place. Let us say it is of its own time.[33]

'Our time', judged from the completed building, is where a light green wall with a white grid *appliqué* represents the remaining buildings on the site, while another grid shifted from the first one by 3.3 degrees represents 18th-century foundations and the Mercator grid, that abstract ordering pattern which 'ties Berlin to the world'. Above all, it represents the Berlin Wall just to the north. In effect then, like Richard Meier's 3.5 degree shifts at Frankfurt, we have a Late-Modernist dealing with a Post-Modern theme, the representation of site requirements. The problem is, however, that no one could possibly know this without reading Eisenman's explanations several times because so much is intentionally obscured and left abstract, without any visual cues or conventions. This 'difficulty' of reading is an essential part of

west corner. There is no semantic reason for this and it seems simply an aesthetic decision, to harmonise the colours and forms of this facade. And such harmonies, banal integrations for Eisenman, are precisely what he seeks to deconstruct in his pursuit of an honest 'anti-classicism'. Also, and perhaps more importantly, the 3.3 metre base is meant to refer to the height of the Berlin Wall, but it is treated as a *glass* wall of cheerful squares, or on the southwest corner, an exercise in perky setbacks. In other words the 'memory' of this, the most traumatic wall in the West, is aestheticised and trivialised, the accusation that Eisenman levels at Post-Modern historicism.

The confirmed sceptic might answer that no Deconstructionist can be perfect; there's always incoherence in the text. So how do we judge the difference between good and bad Deconstructionist building? Again there is no clear answer to this, as Eisenman has said: 'Looking at the corrosion of formal categories, the work [of mine] suggests that there is no such thing as the good or the beautiful'.[34] If the work is thus not meant to be 'good', it still remains 'not-bad', either; otherwise I wouldn't write at such length on these tortured inconsistencies. For this is the subject of Eisenman's art, systematic doubt, and it takes considerable effort and courage for him to pursue it. On the other hand, it would be naive not to recognise such scepticism as a reigning fashion

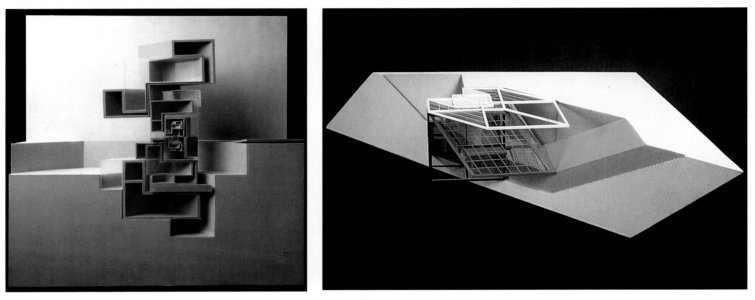

his theory of the totality – writing/architecture/ world/text – and it makes no concessions to how the inhabitants might 'mis-read' the building if they just look at it or live in it.

However from this man-in-the-street view the fragmentations and destabilisations are very clear. The L-shapes rotate slightly, the tilted block seems to smash through the greenish block to re-emerge on the corner, only then to dissolve its figural identity. This tilted block, in fragmented grids of white, grey and red, provides a welcome syncopation and identity for each flat: all the windows here vary and the double-storey white grid successfully contrasts with the more predictable rhythms of the background green. In conventional terms it's a delightfully moving set of volumes, lines and coloured grids which provide individuality and anonymity in equal measure, and the skew of grids provides just enough tension to relieve what might have been a ponderously large block. So far, for the man or woman-in-the-street, so good.

But what about the deeper reading for the cognoscenti, the man-with-the-Eisenman-text-in-his-hand, the Empty Man? Here there are problems of inconsistency which cannot be deconstructed away. The greenish grid, which represents the street line and previous buildings, unaccountably changes its colour to the grey-red-white grid on the

of our time, with graduate schools and Parisian salons full of Doubting Thomases.

Eisenman's winning entry for an Arts Center in Columbus, Ohio, takes his rhetorical strategies a stage beyond the Berlin scheme. Again it is based on the shift between two grids, 'artificial excavation' and complex, fragmented figures – signs of doubt. Again it eschews beauty and harmony for the abstract layering of white and grey grids. Again it exhumes an old building – in this case the foundations of a former armoury – and uses it as a 'fiction' to be built as a 'ghost' tower, another narrative and formal device borrowed from Post-Modernists. But whereas a Post-Modernist might have stitched together past, present and future, Eisenman builds the abstracted fragment of this armoury as a ruin. Red masonry towers built from a new 'non-brick' material tie down a jumble of canted rectangles, one of which, a long white grid of galleries and the main spine, smashes between the existing buildings and then rises up 'like a north arrow', and even more like one of Hadid's skewed flying beams.

Obviously Eisenman has been influenced here, as elsewhere, by other Deconstructionists, and in this sharing of certain conventions we are witnessing the growth of a new convention and set of rules, however short-lived. The long thin rising spine – the skewed box beam

– deconstructs the hierarchies and harmonies of the two rather dull buildings to either side and, like one of Frank Gehry's bumptious wedges driven into a classical cliché, this act of contextual murder brings a certain life to boredom. One may question the frenetically fragmented confusion, but the Arts Center explicitly asked for a building which would represent the experimental nature of contemporary art and in this sense they have achieved their goal: a tilted Sol LeWitt anchored by a Cubist ghost armoury next to an earthwork *à la* Michael Heizer. One may also question the reference of the tilted grid. After all, is the city grid really worth representing, or is it merely a pretext to convince the client that this 13 degree shift and its costly collisions are necessary? As usual Eisenman proffers a set of paradoxes: 'We used the site as a palimpsest: a place to write, erase and rewrite [history]'; 'Our building reverses the process of the site inventing the building [Post-Modernism]. Our building invents the site'. The resurrected, abstracted armoury 'affirms the significance of a major lost landmark on the Ohio State Campus and refers the University to a piece of its own history'.[35] But is a destroyed armoury really that important to anyone at the university; was it perhaps once a military academy?

As Eisenman faced such questions of content and introduced new

tation: 'I am the worst person to ask, because it is a very unconscious project for me. It's a very interesting project for my psychoanalyst who thinks it's a very interesting insight into my psychology. He understands it much better than I do, in a certain sense'.[37]

Since architecture is a public art and Romeo and Juliet will not be built, we'll leave its analysis to others more highly paid for the task. But its extension of previous ideas should be mentioned, the method of layering and cracking glass planes to introduce non-anthropomorphic tropes – 'scaling', 'superimposition' and 'self-similarity'. These, in Eisenman's words, create a 'scale-specifity in that it is a recursive scale: it relates to its own being. Its scale is internal. In this work, we are talking about the loss of God, the lack of belief in the incarnation, and the need for an incarnate mediator. We are talking about the loss of self as the only identifying metaphor . . . Recursive, self-similar, discontinuous geometry is potentially a scale non-specific to man's geometry'.[38]

Why the 'need for an incarnate mediator' isn't another vestigial sentiment of 'Post-Modern nostalgia' is not explained; but the absence of God is, of course, the ultimate reference for all this de-centred work. It brings up the point of whether the feeling of loss – so powerful in Tschumi, Hejduk, Libeskind and Eisenman – isn't a form of Nietzsch-

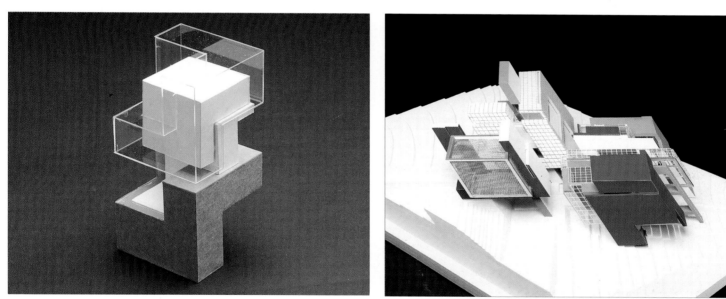

PETER EISENMAN, *L TO R*: MODEL OF HOUSE 11A, AXONOMETRIC MODEL OF HOUSE X

rhetorical tropes into his own armoury – 'fiction', 'anti-memory', 'representation', 'figuration' – he became much closer to the Post-Modernists he spurned. But to save himself from this unspeakable fate, he inverted their primary methods and turned miraculously into a 'Not-Post-Modernist'. Thus for Post-Modern 'simulation' of ruins, for instance, Eisenman proposed a 'dissimulation' of ruins, that is counterfeit excavations and false foundations that either pretend to be real ones, or represent in some phoney material the fact that they're false. One scheme of his, the Romeo and Juliet project for the Venice Biennale, 1985, takes the texts of Da Porto and Shakespeare, among others, as its departure point for showing the inherent conflicts between the two famous families of Verona. It makes this the pretext for a 'superposition' of conflicting scales and endless mis-readings – hence part of its title, 'Moving Arrows, Eros, And Other Errors'.[36] 'Scaling', Eisenman's method of amplifying or diminishing a grid or figure so that it relates only to itself ('self-similarity') is the rhetorical figure used and it results, for instance, in a diminished model of the city of Verona being inserted in the citadel of Romeo's castle. So many such shifts and 'superpositions' and 'excavations' are used here that Eisenman quickly loses his privileged role as the author of this text and, in an amusing and revealing admission, says this of its represen-

ean, or at least Existentialist, revivalism. Whatever the case, Eisenman and Derrida's garden for Tschumi's 'park of the 21st century' is where all this absence comes together and becomes recursive, referring to itself in a kind of silent ping-pong game of nothingness. First of all there was a cryptic battle going on over precedent: which 'author' – Tschumi with his 'Joyce's Garden' of 1977, or Eisenman with his Cannaregio project of 1978 – first invented the famous Deconstructionist 'point grid', a dispute rendered void in the scholar's mind by Archizoom's 'Non-Stop City' of 1970, or Barsch and Ginzburg's 'Green City' for Moscow, 1930. Eisenman no doubt wanted to take the credit for discovering Le Corbusier's 'point grid' for his Venice Hospital of 1964-5, and this is referred to in the layout of the garden which combines both Le Corbusier's and Tschumi's grid with his own Cannaregio project: its eroded L-shapes, a diagonal cut and positive and negative 'excavations'. In the garden another diagonal is added to pick up Tschumi's and then two grids are rotated at an angle to suggest to the cognoscenti that Eisenman had the idea before his friend (ie Tschumi's Parc is based on Eisenman's Cannaregio). Then the ground plane is tilted at an angle and (perhaps) made from Corten steel (a reference to Hadid's polished rock planes?). This incline deconstructs solid ground and disorients the viewer, who has to observe this topsy-

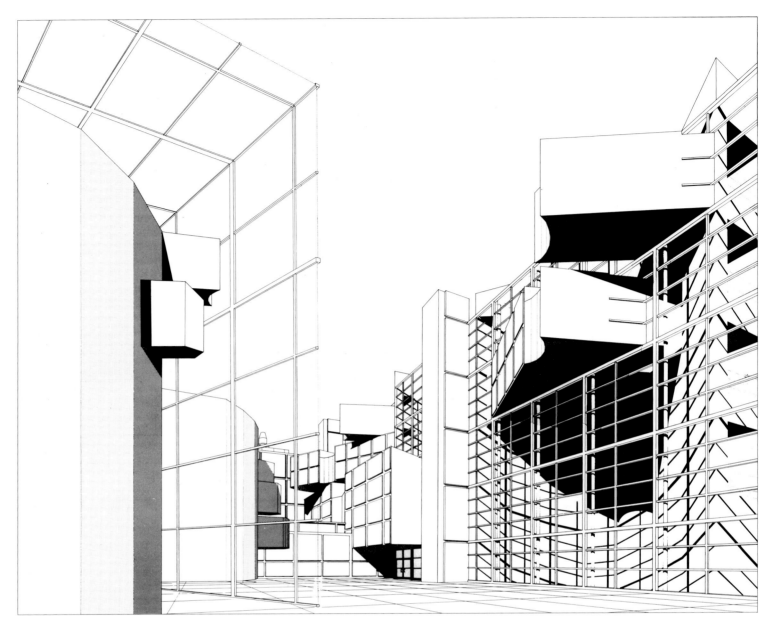

PETER EISENMAN, BIO-CENTRUM, FRANKFURT, PERSPECTIVE

turvy miniature of the world from outside.

Again the three basic levels represent time: underground excavations, the past; tilted plane, the present; and elevated L's, the future. The 'self-similarity' of the L-shapes further breaks down human scale and reference, but a touch of comprehensible Post-Modern representation is permitted in the fragmented images of the Paris ramparts (elevated) and abattoirs (sunk). These are 'traces' from the site and its history of constant destruction and reconstruction, the most recent being in the 80s when the slaughterhouses were transformed at great political and economic expense (represented by the gold colouring?). Binary oppositions are signified – Parisian abattoir/Italian slaughterhouse (site of the Venice Hospital), Tschumi/Le Corbusier, house/folly, life/death – as well as the simultaneity of past, present and future. The whole garden is called 'Choral Works', a collaboration of Derrida and Eisenman, who sing their sacred and metrical hymn in unison to an audience of knowing Empty Men; other Deconstructionists who will contemplate with reverence their need for an 'incarnate mediator' they cannot have – the pleasures of sacred absence.
Eisenman explains:

The idea of the quarry becomes a very interesting notion. That is what we are using in La Villette. We are using two pieces: the

quarry and the palimpsest . . . Now you take the stones and build one project. Someone else will take the stones from our project and build something else . . . We start from the palimpsest which is the superposition of two pieces [Cannaregio and Tschumi?] which then becomes a quarry and then you subtract from the palimpset leaving the trace of the former superposition, but also the trace of the subtraction, so in other words we are talking about 'chora'. The combination of the superposition of palimpsest and quarry gives you 'chora' which is the programme that Derrida set for the La Villette project. So we are into some really very crazy things at La Villette . . .[39]

Eisenman's rhetoric machine seems to have dominated Derrida's programme[40] – 'excavation', 'palimpsest', 'quarry', 'self-similarity', 'superposition', 'scaling', 'textual figuration', 'dissimulation', 'point grid' and 'ghost representations' – these are the tropes from his armoury which are evident in the garden. His adoption of categories from rhetoric may also have been influenced, unlikely as it is for both of us, by my earlier work.[41] In any case, by 1987 Eisenman was adopting many more terms which generated a Not-Post-Modern ornament – 'catachresis', 'fractals', 'arabesques' and 'grotesques' – and moving towards the paradoxical position of joining the enemy he was leaving, actually producing an ornamental and representational architecture. Yet several dispositions kept him free of this fate, above all his commitment to abstraction and hermeticism and the Deconstructionist emphasis on continual process, constant change. Like Nietzsche's man of the future he is committed to the restless task of deconstructing and reconstructing all categories of thought and building, and he is becoming more and more aware of the 'giant paradox' this poses for architecture, something that should have a little more permanence than fashion, and something which has a 'presence', as well as a reference to ideas and absence.

By 1987, Eisenman's definition of the 'Rhetorical Figure' asserted that architecture must convey its simultaneous 'presence' (as an existing object) and 'absence in presence' (those things which are 'repressed' by building and destroyed or missing).[42] In effect, like Derrida's 'affirmative Deconstruction', his positive nihilism makes an expressive virtue of its own fallibilities and destructions. It also conveys the optimism and enjoyment which attend any breaking of habitual categories, the creative exuberance apparent also in the best work of Gehry, Koolhaas, Hadid and others. If one values Deconstructionists from a sceptical position, as I do, then it is for their inventive freshness, their bringing of new rules and conventions to the tired game of Modernism, for making it truly 'Neo'. If one has doubts about the generality of approach, they concern the 'dogmatic scepticism' which is always sure of the negative results and the anti-political and anti-public nature of the activity. As a Mandarin style Deconstruction is, as Manfredo Tafuri wrote of the New York Five and others in 1974, 'architecture dans le boudoir'.[43] Like a Rococo boudoir it can be sensual and engagingly complex, but it's fundamentally undemocratic. And here is the real contradiction in Deconstruction: in spite of the claims to pluralism, différance, 'a war on totality' and defence of 'otherness', this hermetic work is often monist, elitist, intolerant and conveys a 'sameness'. Perhaps, in architecture, this is a result of staring into the Void for too long: it has resulted in a private religious language of self-denial. Because of such suppressions and contradictions one could argue that a real Deconstructionist architecture of variety and humour has yet to exist.

Notes

1 See *The Architecture of Frank Gehry, 1964-1986*, exhibition, Walker Art Center and book, Rizzoli, New York, 1986; *Progressive Architecture*, October 1986; *House and Garden* (US ed) award for architecture, August 1987.
2 See Thomas S Hines 'Heavy Metal, The Education of FOG' in *The Architecture of Frank Gehry, op cit*, pp 10-11, 16, 18.
3 *ibid*, frontispiece.
4 See the discussion of the 'Three Glass Incident' in *Investigations in Architecture: Eisenman Studies at the GSD, 1983-5*, Harvard GSD, Cambridge, Mass, 1986, pp 44-5 and 'Moving Arrows, Eros and Other Errors', *Box 3*, Architectural Association, 1986.
5 Frank Gehry in conversation with Adele Freedman, *Progressive Architecture*, October 1986, p 99.
6 Notably the Parc de la Villette, 1985, and the Hague City Hall, 1987. They were announced winners one day and semi-finalists later.
7 See the large black *Folio* books published for events at the Architectural Association and see *AA Files* 2-14, 1979-1987, for critical articles and reviews.
8 Zaha Hadid, 'The Peak Hong Kong', *AA Files* 4, July 1983, p 84.
9 *ibid*.
10 Jacques Derrida, 'Point de Folie-Maintenant Architecture', *ibid*, p 7. Also printed in *AA Files* 12, Summer 1986, p 65.
11 *op cit, AA Folio*, pp 4-19, *AA Files* 12, 65-75, translation by Kate Linker.
12 Jacques Derrida, *AA Files* 12, p 70.
13 Bernard Tschumi, 'La Case Vide', *AA Folio* 8, 1986, p 3.
14 Anthony Vidler, 'Trick-Track', *ibid*, pp 20-21.
15 Bernard Tschumi, *op cit*, p 26.
16 Harold Rosenberg, 'The Orgamerican Phantasy', *The Tradition of the New*, McGraw-Hill, 1965, pp 269-285.
17 Rosenberg, *op cit*, p 284.
18 See my 'The Perennial Architectural Debate, Abstract Representation', *Architectural Design*, Vol 53, No 7/8, 1983, pp 10-16.
19 Hiromi Fujii, 'Architectural Metamorphology: In Quest of the Mechanism of Meaning', *Oppositions* 22, Fall 1980, pp 14-19.
20 *ibid*.
21 See interview between Peter Eisenman and Carsten Juel-Christiansen, *SKALA*, No 12, October 1987, p 10.
22 *ibid*, p 12.
23 Peter Eisenman, 'Post-Functionalism', *Oppositions* 6, Fall 1976, pp ii-iii.
24 'A Poetics of the Model: Eisenman's Doubt', interview with Peter Eisenman by David Shapiro and Lindsay Stamm, 1981, in *Idea as Model*, IAUS, Rizzoli, New York, 1981, pp 121-5.
25 *ibid*, p 123.
26 Kenneth Frampton was the Director of the IAUS for several months in 1985 before resigning.
27 See *Investigations in Architecture: Eisenman Studies at the GSD: 1983-85*, Cambridge, Mass, 1986, especially articles by Whiteman and Kipnis.
28 His attacks on Post-Modernism start with 'The Graves of Modernism', 1979, also see the references in the publication cited in the previous note.
29 These remarks by Eisenman were made at an Architectural Association lecture, May 29, 1985.
30 'The End of the Classical', 'The Futility of Objects', 'The Beginning, the End and the Beginning Again', or most recently 'Architecture and the Problem of the Rhetorical Figure', in *A+U*, 87:07, pp 17-22.
31 For this quote see Susan Doubilet, 'The Divided Self', *Progressive Architecture* 3, 1987, p 82.
32 See Peter Eisenman, 'The City of Artificial Excavation', *Architectural Design*, Vol 53, 7/8, 1983, pp 24-7.
33 *ibid*, p 26.
34 See interview in *SKALA*, note 37, p 11.
35 Eisenman quoted in *GSD News*, Cambridge, Mass, Nov/Dec, 1983, p 9.
36 Peter Eisenman, 'Moving Arrows, Eros And Other Errors', *op cit*.
37 'Interview Peter Eisenman + Lynn Breslin', *Space Design*, 86:03, p 65.
38 Quoted in *Investigations in Architcture, op cit*, note 43, p 62.
39 'Peter Eisenman + Lynn Breslin', *op cit*, note 53, p 65.
40 'If anything he [Derrida] doesn't push me enough', *ibid*, p 64.
41 I first spoke on 'Rhetoric and Architecture' at a conference on semiology in Barcelona 1972, also attended by Eisenman. My *Late-Modern Architecture and Architecture Today*, 1982, may have influenced his rhetoric machine.
42 Eisenman, 'Architecture and the Problem of the Rhetorical Figure', *A+U*, 87:7, pp 19-20.
43 Manfredo Tafuri, 'L'Architecture dans le Boudoir: The Language of Criticism and the Criticism of Language', *Oppositions* 3, IAUS, May 1974, pp 37-62.

MARK WIGLEY
Deconstructivist Architecture

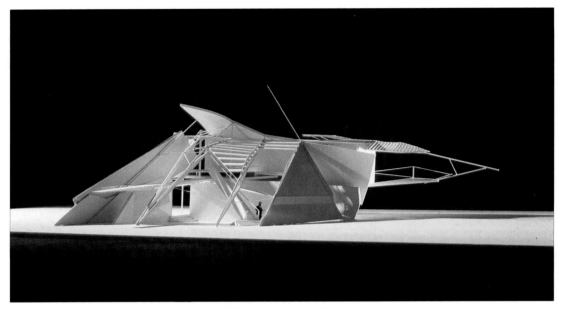

Last week, to escape a conference in Miami on architecture, I went into the Everglades. We went on an airboat with a big fan at the back in which one had the sense of floating on a plane, which completely ignored the context. We were literally passing through the context – a Yuppie experience, no doubt, but thrilling nonetheless. We stopped in a kind of spooky pool, which was an alligator pool, and up from the deep came a pair of extraordinarily menacing eyes – underneath the

water one could see a long, slippery, slimy shadow. Quite nervewracking – we all leaned towards the inside of the boat.

The alligator was important to me because it lives so far away from culture in that completely artificial landscape of the Everglades in which every plant and every animal has been imported. The animal was then lured up from the depths with pink marshmallows. I was struck in a kind of fetishistic way with the encounter between the most trivial, insignificant object of consumption in the twentieth century – the fluffy, sugary, pink marshmallow – and this slippery, slimy demon of the deep, who in the moment of very delicately snatching this pink marshmallow, for the first time its full length and horror emerged. The reason I mention this story is that consumption is of issue here, except today what I've seen is the reverse: I have seen the marshmallows attempt to consume the alligator.

I think Deconstruction deserves a seriousness with its now long history. I am very disturbed by a casual glance upon both the strongest work in contemporary theory and, in my view, the strongest work in contemporary criticism. We have constantly experienced [this morning] references to a non-existent show, a show fabricated here in London, a show which has different players in it than the Museum of Modern Art show in New York. It's a show which apparently should have included a whole lot of other people, a show apparently about a movement, a show indeed with a title that I hadn't heard before – Deconstructi*vism* – a show that is a style, a show that has some reference to some ideas, some old ideas about a new spirit, seems to me to be a show that cannot be distinguished from what I'd known of and tried to forgive as Post-Modernism. It's a show concerned primarily with a banal sense of fragmentation and explosion, a show, above

all, about traditional artists. It seemed to me that what I was seeing was a sugary sweet English marshmallow.

First, a crass generalisation. Architecture has always been a central cultural institution, valued for its stability and order. These qualities seem to arise from the geometric purity of its formal composition. The architect has always dreamed of pure form, producing objects from which all instability and disorder have been excluded. Buildings are constructed by taking simple geometric forms and combining them into strategic ensembles following compositional rules which prevent any one form from conflicting with any other. No form is permitted to distort another. All conflict is resolved; the forms contribute harmoniously to a unified whole. This geometric structure becomes the physical structure of the building and its formal purity is seen as guaranteeing its structural stability. Having produced this structure, the architect then elaborates it in a way that preserves its purity.

Any deviation from the structural order, any impurity, is seen as threatening the former values of harmony, unity and stability, and is therefore insulated from the structure and regarded as mere ornament. Architecture is a conservative discipline that produces pure form and protects it from contamination. I believe the projects in the Deconstructivist Architecture exhibition at MOMA mark a different sensibility, one in which the dream of pure form has been disturbed. Form is no longer simply pure, it has become contaminated. The dream has become a kind of nightmare. It is this ability to disturb our thinking that makes these projects Deconstructive. It is not that they derive from the form of contemporary criticism known as Deconstruction, they are not an advocation of Deconstructive theory, rather, they emerge from within the architectural tradition and happen to exhibit some Deconstructive qualities.

Deconstruction is often misunderstood as the taking apart of constructions. Consequently, any provocative architectural design which appears to take a structure apart by the simple breaking of an object – as in James Wines or the complex dissimulation of an object into a collage of traces, as in Eisenman and Fujii – has been called Deconstructive. These strategies have produced perhaps the most formidable projects of recent years, but remain simulations of Deconstructive work in other disciplines because they do not exploit the unique condition of the architectural object.

Deconstruction is not demolition or dissimulation. While it diagnoses certain structural problems within apparently stable structures, these flaws do not lead to the structure's collapse. On the contrary, Deconstruction gains all its force by challenging the very values of harmony, unity, and stability, and proposing instead a different view of structure: the view that the flaws are intrinsic to the structure and cannot be removed without destroying it. They are, indeed, structural. A Deconstructive architect is therefore not one who dismantles buildings but one who locates the inherent dilemmas within buildings – the structural flaws. The Deconstructive architect puts the pure forms of the architectural tradition on the couch and identifies the symptoms of a repressed impurity. That impurity is drawn to the surface by a combination of gentle coaxing and violent torture. The form is literally interrogated. But this violence is not external to the form, it is not a fracturing, or slicing, or fragmentation, or piercing. To disturb a form from the outside in these ways is not to threaten that form, only to damage it or decorate it.

This damage produces, perhaps, a decorative effect, an aesthetic of danger – an almost picturesque representation of danger – but not a tangible threat. Instead, the kind of architecture I'm describing disturbs figures from within; it is as if some kind of parasite has infected the figure and distorted it from the inside. The roof-top re-modelling by Coop Himmelblau is a form distorted by some alien organism, a roving, disruptive animal breaking through the corner. Some twisted counter-relief infects the octagonal box. It's a skeletal monster which breaks up the elements of the form as it struggles out. Released from the familiar constraints of octagonal structure, the roof splits, shears, and buckles. The distortion is peculiarly disquietening because it seems to belong to the form, to be part of it. It seems to have always been latent there until released by the architect. The alien, emerging out of the stairs, the wall, and the roof plan, not from some dark pool, or even alligator pit, is given shape by the very elements that define the basic volume of the attic. The alien is an outgrowth of the very form that it violates; the form distorts yet does not destroy itself. In a strange way the form somehow remains intact.

This is an architecture of disruption, dislocation, deflection, deviation, and distortion, rather than of demolition, dismantling, decay, decomposition, or disintegration. It displays the structure instead of destroying it. It should be noted that the 'de-s' work both ways. What is finally so unsettling about such a work is precisely that the form not only survives its torture, but appears to be all the stronger for it. Perhaps the form is even produced by it; it becomes unclear which comes first – the figure or the distortion, the host or the parasite.

At first glance, the difference between the form and its ornamental distortion appears clear, but, on closer examination, the line between them breaks up. The more carefully we look, the more unclear it becomes where the perfect figure ends and its imperfection begins. They are found to be inseparably entangled; a line cannot be drawn between them and no surgical technique can free the form, no clear incision can be made. To remove the parasite would be to kill the host as they comprise one symbiotic entity. This produces a feeling of unease, of disquiet, because it challenges the sense of a stable, coherent identity we associate with pure form. It is as if perfection had always harboured imperfection, that it has always had certain undiagnosed congenital flaws which are only now becoming visible. Perfection, perhaps, is secretly monstrous. Tortured from within, the seemingly perfect form confesses its crime, its imperfection.

This sense of dislocation occurs not only within all the projects in the MOMA exhibition, it also occurs between those forms and their contexts. In recent years, the modern understanding of social responsibility as functional programme has been superseded by a concern for context. But contextualism has been used as an excuse for mediocrity, for a dumb servility to the familiar. Since Deconstructive architecture seeks the unfamiliar within the familiar, it displaces the context rather than acquiesces to it. The projects in the exhibition do not ignore the context, they are not anti-contextual. Rather, each makes a very specific intervention in which elements of the context become defamiliarised. Each project activates some part of the context to disturb the rest of it, drawing up unnoticed disruptive properties and making them thematic. Each assumes an uncanny presence, alien to the context from which it derives, strange yet familiar, a kind of sleeping monster which awakes in the midst of the everyday.

This estrangement sets up a complicated resonance between the disrupted interior of the forms and their disruption of the context. This analogy between the two functions calls into question the status of the walls that define the form. The division between inside and outside is radically disturbed, the form no longer simply divides an inside from an outside as the geometry proves to be much more convoluted. The sense of being contained, whether it be by a building or a room, is disrupted, but not by simply removing the walls; the closure of form is not simply replaced with openness. This is not freedom, liberation, but stress – not release but even greater tension. The wall breaks open in a very complex way. There are no simple windows, no regular openings puncturing a solid wall. Rather, the wall is tormented, split and folded so that it no longer provides security by dividing familiar from unfamiliar, inside from out. The whole condition of enclosure breaks down.

Even though it threatens this most fundamental property of architectural objects, Deconstructivist architecture does not constitute an avant-garde. It is not a rhetoric of the new. Rather, it exposes the unfamiliar hidden within the traditional. It is the shock of the old. It exploits the weakness in the tradition in order to disturb rather than overthrow it. Like the modern avant-garde, it attempts to be disturbing, alienating, but not from the traditional retreat of the avant-garde, not from the margins. Rather, it occupies and subverts the centre. This work is not fundamentally different from the tradition it subverts. Deconstructivist architecture inhabits the centre of the tradition in order to demonstrate that the tradition is always infected, that pure form has always been contaminated. It speculates that architecture has always been riddled with these kinds of enigmas, that they are the source of its force and its delight, that they are the very possibility of its formidable presence.

By inhabiting the tradition fully, obeying its inner logic more rigorously than ever before, these architects discover certain dilemmas within the tradition that are missed by those who sleep-walk through it. Deconstructivist architecture, therefore, poses problems to both the centre and the margins of this discipline. Neither can simply appropriate the work. It cannot simply be imitated by the margins because it demands such an intimate knowledge of, and therefore complicity with, the inner workings of the tradition. But neither can it simply be appropriated by the centre; it cannot be so easily assimilated. It invites consumption by employing traditional architectural forms. It tempts the profession and the critical establishment to swallow it whole. But because it infects those forms, it always produces a kind of indigestion. In this moment of critical resistance, it assumes its full force.

Much supposedly radical architectural work of recent years has neutralised itself by maintaining itself on the margins, the position of the historical avant-garde. A tradition of brilliant conceptual projects has developed which look more radical than the work which will go on display in the exhibition, but I believe lack its force because they do not confront the centre of the tradition. They marginalise themselves by excluding building. They do not engage with architecture, but make a sophisticated commentary upon it. They produce a kind of commentary on building without entering into building. Such drawings have written into them the detachment of the historical avant-garde. They inhabit the margins, the ones up front, at the frontier. They are projections of the future, brave new worlds, utopian fantasies. In contrast, the work in this exhibition is neither a projection into the future nor simply a historicist remembrance of the past. Rather, it attempts to get under the skin of the living tradition, irritating it from within.

Deconstructivist architecture locates the frontiers, the limits of architecture coiled up in everyday forms. It finds new territory within old objects. This work carries out the kind of subversion usually regarded as possible only at a distance from the reality of built form. The projects are radical precisely because they do not play in the sanctuaries of drawing, of theory, or sculpture. They inhabit the realm of building. Some have been built, some will be built, and others will never be built. But each is buildable; each aims at building. They develop an architectonic coherence by confronting the basic problems of building, structure and function, even if they do so in an unconventional way. In each project, the traditional structure of parallel planes stacked up horizontally from the ground plane within a regular form is twisted, the frame and even the ground plane is warped.

Pure form pushes structure to its limits, but not beyond. The structure is shaken but does not collapse. It is just pushed to the point where it becomes unsettling. This work produces a sense of unease when floors and walls move disconcertingly, tempting us to cross something closer to the edge. But if these structures produce a sense of insecurity, it is not because of flimsiness. These buildings are extremely solid. The solidity is just organised in an unfamiliar way, shifting our traditional sense of structure. Though structurally sound, at the same time they are structurally frightening. This displacement of traditional thinking about structure also displaces traditional thinking about function. The Modernists argue that form follows function, and that function in the efficient forms necessarily had a pure geometry. But their streamlined aesthetic disregarded the untidy reality of actual functional requirements. In Deconstructivist architecture, forms are distributed and only then are given a functional programme.

The distortion of pure form provides a complexity of local conditions congruent with functional complexity. Function follows deformation. Despite calling into question traditional ideas about structure, these projects are rigorously structural. Despite calling into question the functionalist rhetoric of Modernism, each project is rigorously functional. For most of the architects, this commitment to building is a recent shift that has completely changed the tone of their work. They have left behind their complex subtractions and confronted the materiality of built objects. This shift gives their work a critical edge. Critical work today can only be done in the realm of building. The object becomes the site of all theoretical enquiry. Theorists are forced out of the sanctuary of theory; practitioners are roused from sleepwalking practice. Both meet in the realm of building and engage with objects. This should not be understood as a rejection of theory but, on the contrary, indicates that the traditional status of theory has changed.

No longer is it some abstract realm of defence that surrounds objects, protecting them from examination by mystification. Architectural theory generally pre-empts an encounter with the object. It is concerned with veiling rather than exposing objects. With these projects, all the theory is loaded into the object and propositions now take the form of objects rather than verbal abstractions. What counts is the condition of that object, not the abstract theory that produced it.

The force of that object makes the theory irrelevant. Consequently, these projects can be considered outside of their usual theoretical context. They can be analysed in strictly formal terms because the formal condition of each object carries its full ideological force.

Such an analysis brings together highly conceptual architects with pragmatists. They join together in the production of describing objects which interrogate pure form in a way that exposes the repressed horror of architecture. This is not to say that they participate in a new movement. Deconstructivist architecture is not an *ism*, but neither is it simply seven independent architects. It is a curious point of intersection amongst strikingly different architects moving in completely different directions. The projects are about brief moments in the independent programme of the artists. Clearly they influence each other in complex ways, but this is not a team. It is, at best, an uneasy alliance. I think each of the seven architects argues that at least two of the other architects should be removed. Each architect chooses a different tune, and this seems to me the ideal combination today.

I think this episode will probably be short-lived. The architects will proceed in completely different directions. Their work will certainly not simply authorise a certain kind of practice, a certain kind of object. This is not a new style. The projects don't even share an aesthetic. What they share is the fact that each produces an unsettling object by exploiting the hidden potential of Modernism. What they share is the sense of disquiet that their objects produce by locating the impurity within pure form. This sense of disquiet is not simply a perceptual response, it is a cultural disquiet – the disquiet the culture feels when its assumptions are being slid sideways. It's a sense of slippage, the perceptual response is completely different. For most people it's just a feeling of 'there is a beautiful object' in the traditional sense. So it should be understood that this is not a discussion of how to alienate the viewer – it is as removed from the author as it is from the receiver, at least, I think, at the level of cultural assumptions.

And these cultural assumptions are millenial in character. The convoluted relationships between the architectural discourse and the philosophical discourse would, I think, provide the suitable framework for discussing where this work actually impinges. Certainly the disquiet produced by these objects is not some new spirit of the age. It is not that an unsettled world produces an unsettled architecture – here, of course, I guess I'm disagreeing with Catherine Cooke and Bernard Tschumi. It's not even the personal *angst* of the architects; it's not a form of Expressionism. The architect expresses absolutely nothing here. The architect only makes it possible for the tradition to go wrong, to deform itself.

The nightmare of Deconstructivist architecture inhabits the unconsciousness of pure form rather than the unconsciousness of the architect or the perceiver. The architect merely countermands traditional formal inhibitions to release the suppressed alien. Each architect releases different inhibitions in order to subvert the ideas about form in radically different ways. Each makes thematic the different dilemma of pure form. In so doing, they all produce a devious architecture, a slippery architecture that slides uncontrollably from the familiar into the unfamiliar, prompting an uncanny sense of the alien hidden within the familiar, an architecture, finally, in which form distorts itself. But it's not an architecture with any special epistemological basis; it is not an architecture which is fundamentally different from any of the works of the tradition. It is merely an architecture which makes thematic certain problematical conditions of all architectural objects and suggests that those problems are the source of architecture's force.

———— * ————

JAMES WINES
The Slippery Floor

First, the good news. The Museum of Modern Art's Department of Architecture and Design, under the new and able leadership of Stuart Wrede and sponsored by the generous patronage of Gerald Hines, launched a series of architecture exhibitions intended to survey current tendencies and influential designers. Although still reflecting former curator Arthur Drexler's Modernist/formalist bias, these shows explored the work of architects as varied as Ricardo Bofill, Leon Krier, and Mario Botta. The exhibition I shall talk about assembled a group of contemporary architects whose work derives from Russian Constructivism and De Stijl – most specifically from the work of early Soviet revolutionaries like Melnikov and Chernikhov and the Dutch Moderns Rietveld and Van Doesburg. What distinguishes this recent work is the use of certain formal devices – rotated axes, shattered grids, crossed beams, tilted walls, and radical juxtapositons of materials – that appear to violate the more orderly and ideological tenor of the original sources. It is open to question whether, in fact, these distortions are more extreme than those of the past; but let us assume that these advocates of revised Constructivism demonstrate an irreverence for the traditions of post-and-lintel structure and conventional equilibrium that were not characteristic of the work of Chernikhov and Rietveld.

Since the MOMA show included practitioners of considerable accomplishments with ideas in common, it would have been appropriate to title this event 'neo-Constructivism' or 'architects working in the Constructivist tradition'. Nary an eyebrow would have been raised in distrust.

This brings us to the bad news. Instead, the exhibition was called *Deconstructivist Architecture* and supported by some of the most specious rationales and self-serving political strategies that New York (a climate accustomed to thinly veiled hype) had witnessed since the abortive attempt to claim Op Art as a major movement in the 1960s.

Organised by architects Philip Johnson and Peter Eisenman, the MOMA show was not simply a thoughtful assembly of brilliant architects with mutual formal concerns, but an event destined to result in what critic Michael Sorkin so candidly summarised as 'the reduction of an architecture of polemic, contention, and vitality to the necrophiliac realm of motif, the transmutation of research into fashion, the liberation of form from content so as to make it useful for appropriation by hacks'.

For an explanation, it is necessary to return to architectural politics on the local scene. Philip Johnson, it must be remembered, made his auspicious debut into the world architectural arena in 1932 as the co-curator (with Henry-Russell Hitchcock) of MOMA's International Style exhibition. Always a generous supporter of youthful innovation in architecture, an eclectic in his own work, and an art collector of consummate taste, Johnson often helped younger professionals get their first commissions or come to the attention of museums and the media. It was in this role as catalyst that, in recent years, he embraced the historical references of the Post-Modernist style and went on to promote the work of Michael Graves, Stanley Tigerman and Robert Stern.

Enter Peter Eisenman as director of the Institute for Architecture and Urban Studies in New York during the 1970s. This institution –

originally connected to MOMA but later separated because of divergent agendas and a reported friction between director Eisenman and the museum's Arthur Drexler – was dedicated to architectural discourse and polemical exhibitions. For the first few years the IAUS seemed truly ecumenical in its approach, albeit with a strong tendency to favour ideas that were directly traceable to Modernist/formalist origins. At the same time the Institute was shaping its philosophical strategies, Robert Venturi's thesis supporting 'complex and contradictory' architecture and forms derived from 'the everyday world, vulgar and disdained' was catching fire with an ever-widening student constituency. Soon it seemed inevitable that the Modernist thrust of the IAUS risked falling from grace. Loyal early members like Graves, Stern, Tigerman, and Frank Gehry defected to more hybrid ways of thinking. Soon the formalist ranks – including Eisenman (who was then somewhat like an anxious dog trying to gain traction on a slippery floor) – needed to re-establish a conceptual foothold joining with hardline Modernist supporters like critic Kenneth Frampton and architects Mario Gandelsonas and Diana Agrest, Eisenman retrenched and shaped the Institute more firmly as a bastion against the untidy wave of Venturiites and Po-mo historicists by emphasising the bulwarks of Modernism – rationalism and structuralism. Eisenman left the directorship for professional practice, and the inheritors, lacking his inspired guidance, continued the institution by cranking out endless models and endless drawings, endlessly reminiscent of the Villa Stein, the Villa Savoye and the Schroeder House. All of this activity was arduously defended by opaque theoretical discourse predicated on the conviction that Modernism was still very much alive and that its seeming decline was nothing more than a lack of strict enough enforcement, not a failure of inspiration among the followers. The redoubled effort proved fruitless against the rising popularity of decorative Post-Modernism and the tendency of the press to favour the most audacious and photogenic kinds of architecture for attention.

Eisenman had tried to align his work with conceptual art and linguistic theory with moderate success. Even though such artists as Joseph Kosuth, Lawrence Weiner and Douglas Huebler (then much admired by Eisenman) tended to reject the efforts of all architects as traditional formalism and unsuited for inclusion within conceptualism's ephemeral and cerebral objectives, Eisenman persisted, rationalising his work in structuralist terms and equating it with the theories of linguists and philosophers like Chomsky, Saussure, Lévi-Strauss, Foucault, and, more recently, the Deconstructivist literary critic Jacques Derrida.

Philip Johnson's connection to IAUS was as a staunch early supporter with vague hints that he might award a sizeable grant to the institution at some future time. When the Institute began to decline, he tried,in vain to help it survive. Finally, around 1981, when it collapsed, both Johnson and Eisenman appeared to concede that its day had come and gone and they went on to other endeavours.

Several years passed and it became apparent that the architectural scene was again in a restless state of change. A great deal of new work was taking the form of fragmentation and disjunction, and student drafting tables (an architectural trend's truest barometer), instead of being populated by the entablatures, pediments, and columns of Post-

Modernism, had begun to sprout models of crumbling, disjointed, and warped edifices, without a trace of historicism (except for an obvious debt to Constructivism).

There were rumours of a planned exhibition developed by several designers in academia – Paul Florian, Stephen Wierzbowski and Aaron Betsky – that was supposed to deal with this new phenomenon. Entitled *Violated Perfection: The Meaning of the Architectural Fragment,* this show never managed to generate the necessary funding or the political clout to get off the ground, but it seemed convincingly like the wave of the future. Neither Johnson nor Eisenman was going to let the failures of the IAUS thwart a fresh incentive to make history. Eisenman had been anxiously awaiting the fall of the Po-mo star (especially since the movement had inconveniently obscured his career for a time and made his colleague and rival, Michael Graves, into a celebrity). Johnson, for his part, needed a cause to round out his career as an arbiter of taste and style. So, with a little weeding out of non-formalist participants, he and Eisenman simply stole the *Violated Perfection* show idea and renamed it *Deconstructivist Architecture.* The timing was perfect. With Eisenman's interest in linguistic relationships in architecture and his awareness of the popularity of French literary criticism and philosophy, he could identify in this new wave

a similar methodology applied to architecture would call for the identification of an 'archetype', to serve as an equivalent for the archetext. In the absence of written words, a comparable tool must be substituted. In architecture, this language would most logically derive from the methods and materials of building and un-building – or, in other words, its history of archetypal components, systems, and forms.

Without detracting from the importance of an exhibition of this particular group of Constructivist-influenced architects – their talent and deservedness are unquestioned – the issue of greatest concern in the MOMA show was its premise. The politics of die-hard Modernist design notwithstanding, there was a fundamental problem with the intellectual side of this entire endeavour. As a philosopher friend of mine remarked when told about the exhibition, 'Deconstructivist architecture? You must be joking!'

My friend's point was that Deconstruction – a form of literary criticism with implications in philosophy because it questions the reliability of language itself – is not a term that can be facilely attached to an art movement. In the work of Deconstruction's leading protagonist, Jacques Derrida, the universal tendency to read literature in terms of cultural bias, conventional syntax, structuralist logic and rhetorical

GORDON MATTA-CLARK, *L TO R*: OFFICE BAROQUE, BRUSSELS, 1977; POMPIDOU MUSEUM, PARIS, 1977

both an interesting revision of Modernism and a conveniently esoteric connection to Derrida. Also, Eisenman's earlier description of his work as 'structuralist' could, with a slight twist of linguistic license, be converted to 'deconstructivist'. There were enough formal similarities in his architecture to that of such colleagues as Frank Gehry and Coop Himmelblau to make a creditable case for his inclusion in a show featuring pioneers of the new fragmentation, the new Constructivism-cum-Deconstructivism.

Derrida's vastly intricate propositions have exerted a great influence on today's writers and philosophers, but Deconstructivist reading translates self-consciously and awkwardly into the description of an architectural movement. This is not to say that Deconstruction's ideas cannot be applied to buildings, but that there should be some cautionary ground rules. Derrida has pointed out that his complex readings of literature are best accomplished by starting out with certain classic narrative structures because of the reflex identifications in the language and the conventional perceptions of its use. What he has called 'archetexts' form a matrix for his game of analysis and a source of operative meanings to be altered. If words are used to critique words, then it is obvious that some starting point is essential to set the stage for the Deconstructivist process. It stands to reason that

assumptions about an author's intentions are brought into question. Inspired by the observations of physics, which has increasingly abandoned the orderly model of the universe for one conceived in chaos, Derrida has taken his cues from scientific research because it no longer depends on a traditional 'centre' as a point of departure for its investigations. Recognising that the human brain is merely a fragment of a larger scheme of infinite disorder (and a rather crude instrument for filtering speculations about the phenomena of which it is made), scientists and philosophers have also come to regard language as a rather tentative tool. Derrida took this to mean that there was no 'absolute truth' and has returned to such dialecticians as Hegel and Heidegger in order to read their ideas in this revised context. In doing so, it became apparent that the ambiguities of language matched the ambiguities of philosophy and science and required an entirely new system of reading that would embrace the concept of universal chaos and its absent centre. It has been Derrida's purpose to show that literature is just another manifestation of indeterminacy, he has proposed that life itself is a text and that there is no meaning outside of this text.

Returning to the Johnson/Eisenman event, one of the exhibition's assumptions, according to Mark Wigley's catalogue text, was that certain formal characteristics passed as Deconstructivist, while others did not. For example, fragmented and dematerialised elements in buildings were *not* legitimate (thereby excluding the work of seemingly appropriate contributors like Gordon Matta-Clark, Nigel Coates and SITE), whereas rotated axes, disrupted grids, slanted walls, and anything directly traceable back to Constructivism qualified. Inherent in this argument is the cardinal sin of critical analysis in any form – that is, the reading of superficial appearance as the meaning of an art object, or, in Wigley's case, the notion that buildings showing evidence of fragmented and dematerialised sections refers specifically to demolition and ruin. On superficial reading, obviously they do; but consistent with any intelligent reading of an art language, the surface imagery must be read not *as* the content but as a means of signification that invites interpretation. To assume that Gordon Matta-Clark's dissected buildings are about demolition is as erroneous as believing that sculptor Alberto Giacometti's dematerialised figures are nothing more than the artist's rendition of emaciated, war-torn people. Referring back to the context of Deconstruction, the point of this kind of reading is to reach beyond surface appearances; thus both dematerialisation and disjunction of form might be disqualified. Deconstruction is not about form but about attitude. Wigley's ration-

ping centres. Surely one of the justifications of Post-Modern historicism has been based on the conviction that certain past references evoke popular response and are, accordingly, archetypal.

If the MOMA show's view of Deconstruction proclaimed that certain buildings can be subjected to a new form of reading, the examples included could have been expanded. Instead, the organisers' massive misconception was to mistake style for archetype. In its final shape, the show became what Philip Johnson so aptly described in the press as 'an exhibition of architects whose work uses forms that look like Constructivist drawings'. What was passed off as Deconstruction was, to the contrary, extremely skilful abstractionist design based on Constructivist form-making, shape-making and space-making. The so-called 'violations' and 'pleasures of unease' were simply too positivist in their objectives, too rational from a structuralist ethic, to be considered Deconstructivist. Also, none of the work at MOMA demonstrated the strong element of narrative so essential for Deconstructivist reading.

To follow the Derrida model a little further in architecture, the major ingredient that must change is perspective. The purpose of Deconstruction is to alter perception. It is particularly fortuitous that, at the same time the Johnson/Eisenman show was on at MOMA, the

GORDON MATTA-CLARK, *L TO R: SPLITTING*, WORK IN PROGRESS, ENGLEWOOD, NJ, 1974; *SPLITTING*

ale was obviously a poorly camouflaged tactic to promote a slightly altered version of Modernist aesthetic for one more crack at the limelight.

Here is where the MOMA show's interpretation of Deconstructivist architecture broke down. Assuming that a Derrida-like reading can be adapted to building, the first hypothesis would seem to require some archetypal structure to serve as the subject of analysis. For Derrida, in literature, this has always been some pivotal text, like Rousseau's *Les Confessions* or Mallarmé's *Mimique*. He prefers such works because they are conditioned by time with certain built-in notions of meaning and, therefore, function as ideal foils for inversionist reading. To propose that stylistic devices borrowed from the highly personalised and ideological work of Melnikov and Chernikhov represent archetypal sources is absurd. Very few, if any, Modernist or Constructivist-derived building images produced in this century have been sufficiently integrated into the unconscious mind of society to qualify as archetypal. Study after study of the public's reflexive selection of archetypes has produced only Tudor and colonial houses and Greco-Roman banks and civic buildings. Occasionally, confirming Venturi's theories about certain commercial iconography, people will identify with high-rise housing blocks and shop-

Brooklyn Museum held a major retrospective of the work of the late Gordon Matta-Clark. This architect turned-artist, if any figure in the past fifteen years deserved to be called Deconstructivist, fits the definition (although he probably would have rejected such a categorisation). His omission from the MOMA show had to be one of the most narrow-visioned and irresponsible in curatorial history.

Matta-Clark invariably used existing archetypal buildings as targets for his interventions. His 'cuttings' utilised inherent construction/demolition processes and materials (or its unique language) as the means of critique in architecture. His work, like Derrida's readings, evolved into an entirely new interpretation of its subject. Matta-Clark's approach was the opposite of formalist design and thus radically new in attitude; he used indeterminacy and chance as raw ingredients, and finally, he exerted considerable influence on the MOMA show's most talented participant, Frank Gehry. Specifically, it is generally felt among critics that Gehry's personal house in Santa Monica, where he invaded a typical 1950s California bungalow with a series of Constructivist forms, was the closest parallel to Matta-Clark's ideas and Gehry's finest work to date.

The most important aspect of Matta-Clark's work was his constant awareness of narrative in architecture and the need for a social/

political conscience when working in the public domain. As Derrida has pointed out, there is no purpose in Deconstructivist reading unless the results inform and enhance our knowledge of the human condition. Otherwise, the focus of reinterpretation can be used to justify irresponsible uses of power and even fascist thinking. Strongly opposed to the Modernist-derived caricatures that passed for architecture during the 1970s – particularly those sterile pastiches of the Bauhaus – Matta-Clark always intended that his sculptural incisions in buildings should both change perceptions about 'the functionalist aspect of past due Machine Age moralists,' and respond to 'the ever less viable state of privacy, private property, and isolation'. He wanted to let the light penetrate, philosophically, metaphorically and architecturally.

The greatest power of his art was the aspect most related to Deconstruction: its capacity to change our perceptions on the most basic level. For example, in his famous project *Splitting* in Englewood, New Jersey, he used a small suburban dwelling scheduled for demolition, with all of its archetypal associations. Since this house was to be removed anyway, his dissection of the structure converted it from death to life – preservation by demolition. The artist's intervention shifted the course of economic events, social significance, and the cultural status of a building in a single gesture. This would seem to be the essence of Deconstructivist reading in architecture.

Because Matta-Clark always operated on existing buildings (like existing texts), a good argument could be made that he was the only true Deconstructivist architect. Architecture is, after all, systematically made from the assembly of ponderous materials, controlled by functional requirements and oppressive bureaucracies. It is difficult, therefore, to make a case in favour of Deconstructivist meaning in newly-built edifices. By stretching the point about archetypes as equivalents for archetexts, it could be contended that an architect might utilise widely accepted building types as the raw material for inversionist interpretations.

There are a number of architects whose work has utilised highly associative building archetypes with fertile narrative implications, and, by the insertion of illogical fragments, has introduced new areas of meaning. These include Nigel Coates, Michele de Lucchi, Ugo La Pietra, Gianni Pettena, Tatsuhiko Kuramoto, Morphosis, Eric Moss, Gaetano Pesce, Stanley Saitowitz and SITE. Whether their ideas should be classified as Deconstructive or narrative is up for debate, but as the term Deconstruction is also questionable when removed from its legitimate literary context, these architects seem well qualified for examination in an alternative exhibition.

Unfortunately, the MOMA exhibition was not about content, debate and criticism. It was about politics. Its greatest virtue was that it displayed the work of some exceptionally talented professionals, whatever their philosophies and the show's dubious premises. Otherwise, it was a belated attempt to resurrect the moribund agendas of the defunct Institute for Architecture and Urban Studies and to revive Modernism (this time in Constructivist guise) for its final round. Whether this strategy worked or not still remains to be seen. In the meantime, the reputations of a very gifted group of individuals seem to be left to the mercy of an omnivorous media that misunderstood the already shaky intellectual pretentions and buried the style with over-indulgence. From all indications, Johnson and Eisenman preserved that slippery floor at the IAUS and moved it to MOMA. The question is who, if anyone, gained traction?

———— * ————

SITE
Frankfurt Museum of Modern Art and Recent Projects

FRANKFURT MUSEUM OF MODERN ART, 1983
For practical and philosophical reasons, SITE decided to place a rectangular building on a triangular site. In order for the spectator to understand this inversion of the rectangle, the site area is defined by an abstraction in glass which penetrates the structure of the museum. The convention of the rough architectural cutaway is used to allow the street to part freely, thereby heightening the dominant 'inside/outside' theme of the project.

COSMO WORLD WATERFRONT DEVELOPMENT, YOKOHAMA, 1988
This project for a public park treats the entire site as a metaphor for the cosmos, the architecture melting into the site rather than existing as an intrusion.

PERSHING SQUARE, LOS ANGELES, 1988
A 'peoples' park' for downtown LA on the theme of a metaphorical 'magic carpet', a visual and participatory microcosm of the geometric landscape.

TOP TO BOTTOM, L TO R: FRANKFURT MUSEUM OF MODERN ART, 1983; COSMO WORLD, YOKOHAMA, 1988; PERSHING SQUARE, LOS ANGELES, 1988

SOCIAL HOUSING, KOCHSTRASSE, IBA, BERLIN, 1982-7

PETER EISENMAN
An *Architectural Design* Interview by Charles Jencks

BIO-CENTRUM, FRANKFURT, COMPUTER DRAWING

This special interview with Peter Eisenman was conducted over the telephone to New York from the offices of *Architectural Design* in London, spring 1988. Eisenman discusses the ideological background to his architecture, his early houses attacking structural formalism, his recent collaboration with Jacques Derrida, his belief that only now is he really tackling the problem of 'the between' and his views on the Deconstructivist exhibition at the Museum of Modern Art, New York.

The Modernism of Alienation and Dislocation

First of all I'm going to explore your theology. It seems to me that you believe in a Modernism of alienation.

There is no such thing as believing in a 'Modernism of alienation'. Modernism was a *condition* of alienation because the questions of truth, value, origin and substance were called into question in science, philosophy and theology. In fact, it is this calling into question of the supposedly natural truths and the exposition of disjunctions in each discipline that Modernism is about. This produced a condition of some anxiety and dislocation and it is dislocation that is called alienation.

–But surely you agree that it is different in architecture from the other Modernisms, so that there would be a Modernism of alienation in let us say religion and the philosophy of someone like Nietzsche, but there hasn't been a similar architectural Modernism.

In architecture, there has never been an articulation of a theory of Modernism, that is a theory concerning the dislocation of the truth that has occurred in other discourses. Now for the first time we are going to be able to articulate that theory. I don't know if it is possible to believe in it, I think I practise it because I think it is the only thing that one can practise. Of course the Modernism that you speak of, as opposed to what I practise, is really a continuation of the classical tradition.

–Right. Now I'd like to look at some of your early work and see it as continuous with your later, Deconstructionist, work. It seems to me your early Terragni-based work and Le Corbusier-based work was even then Deconstructionist, in the sense that it was concerned with the 'presence of the absence' – like Wittgenstein's house in Vienna – the presence of the absence of capitals there is articulated, just as the

presence of the absence of columns was in this early work. So in the very beginning you were, in a sense, concerned with those absences.

I want to correct your phrase 'Deconstructionist work'. I am not certain that my work is Deconstructionist. It is possible to read my early work in the way you seem to be saying, even though I do not think it was clear to me then that that's what I was doing.

–Your early houses are very disorienting, I mean they're upside-down!

Yes, but that is not what I was doing consciously.

–Yes you were, your Cardboard Architecture is consciously disorienting.

I might have been doing it but I was not articulating it theoretically. I used to call it 'formalism'. I believed that I went from the kind of Modernism of Le Corbusier in House I, to say Terragni in House II, to a different kind of space in Houses III, IV and VI, where there was a more pure formalism. Then I went through a Structuralist period characterised by House X.

–Well that's really Post-Structuralist and your early Chomskian work is more Structuralist, surely?

I am obviously the last one to be able to articulate truth about what I do.

–But there were a lot of anti-s. You were very anti-functional in those formalist houses, and in a sense your later work is anti-classical. The anti-s, the dis-s and the de-s, your language has in a sense shifted but what I'm trying to say is that there is a great deal of continuity all through the work.

I would say 'anti-' is the wrong word, it was about not making function thematic.

–No, no, come on. You know that in your House VI, the stairs and the famous kitchen table are polemically anti-functional and . . .

No, they were against the symbolism of function.

–No, no, they don't work . . .

People live in them.

–But the hole cut in the bedroom floor and having to add rails on the stairs and having a stairway that doesn't work, all of that was polemically anti-functional – I think it's useless for you to pretend it isn't – you said it, critics said it. You were even proud that your House II was not lived in by the mathematician it was built for, so why the sudden denials?

It is not a denial, I am merely trying to make it clear I was never anti-functional. I believe there is a difference between being anti-functional, and being against making function thematic.

–But there was a part of you which was proud of the fact that that mathematician couldn't live in the house, and often you seem to be against content and against things working.

Again I would argue that the work was certainly not anti-functional but against symbolising function. Those houses keep the rain out, you can sleep in them . . .

–Yes, but with great difficulty.

wanted to start that summer and I said 'No, I want to do Cannaregio' and when I came back the house had been abandoned. It is then that I felt I needed to go into therapy. I was really upset, having spent so much time on a house and then not having it built. It was when I started to go into my unconscious in my analyses that I became less oriented to the head. This caused a shift in my architecture: it went into the ground. I mean House IIa, House El Even Odd, Fin d'Ou T Hou S, all of those projects were in the ground in a sense, they were digging into the unconscious, as were the projects for Cannaregio and Berlin. They were all grounded projects. Before, none of my houses had any grounding; they were all in the air. Yes, the shift came in '78, when I started analysis. It came at the same time as the split from the Institute. I needed to establish another identity for myself. I think the identity for me as the Institute-man, as not myself, was something I found very problematic in my analysis. It took a few years, but certainly by 1980 it was clear to me that I would not continue at the Institute.

–All of your life has been very much a conscious moving from position to position and in a sense a perpetuation of crises, maybe unconsciously, and then consciously confirmed and seen straightforwardly. In other words you don't shy away from naming them and then acting them out in a completely honest and straightforward way. If we can

L TO R: HOUSE I, EXTERIOR VIEW; HOUSE III, EXTERIOR VIEW

No, with different attitudes towards what it means to function as a house.

–OK, I won't press the point.

My work attacks the concept of occupation as given. It is against the traditional notion of how you occupy a house.

–Right, and the holes in the floor of the room attack the notion of how you occupy and how you step across the living room?

And having a column in the middle of the bedroom so you could not put a bed in it certainly attacked the notion of how you occupy a bedroom.

Psychoanalysis and Excavation

–In theorising about yourself, Peter, you've always pointed to this 1978 shift which is a kind of compound shift as I understand it. It's when you started undergoing psychoanalysis in an extended way and it's at the time when you produced House X and the Cannaregio project and became conscious of Deconstruction, and decentring in particular. Would you agree with that?

I think I would almost agree. You have the sequence wrong. House X was the end of a certain phase. I started psychoanalysis when I went to Venice to do Cannaregio – instead of building House X. The clients

shift to the crisis in the Institute, that occurred in around 1982?

The crisis occurred before that, during the tenth anniversary of the Institute in '77. The high period of the Institute was '76, '77, '78 – that's when Rossi, Tafuri, Scolari, Tschumi, Koolhaas and Fujii were there. And then my practice, as it was then constituted, started to go downhill and I knew by 1980 that I really wanted to get out. The crisis came in '82. First of all, nobody believed that I wanted to leave and that I would walk away. I kept telling everybody that I was going. It was very clear to me that I was going, I do not think anybody was prepared for that. It was this that many people resented.

–You hung on too, let's not over-emphasise your leaving. You remained in New York to influence your followers like Frampton, Vidler and Stephen Petersen and that became a problem for them.

Perhaps, but what was I supposed to do? Leave New York so that Frampton, Vidler et al could feel relieved?

–Let me say that there are many ways of going about divorce from an institute, and one is just to leave town and be out of touch.

But why should I have left?

–I'm not prosecuting, I'm just saying that your ghost was very much there. Maybe it was a clean break for you but you seem to have influenced things behind the scenes, enough so that Frampton felt he

had to withdraw.

But I think that was one of Frampton's problems.

–It may be Frampton's problem, but it was perceived as one of your manipulations.

It is always perceived as one of my manipulations, as is the new museum show on Deconstruction. But I have to deal with it. I have to face what people say about me whether it is true or not. I think right now I am very much engaged in the practice of architecture while a lot of people think that I am engaged in the practice of politics.

–But you are.

To some extent, but to a lesser degree than you are.

–Alright, it's good you acknowledge it, that's all you have to say. Do you have anything further to add on the crisis in the Institute. When did it actually start to close down?

Between '82 and '84. I really thought that Stephen Petersen was not the person for the job. I had my own candidate and this was seen as a problem.

–Did you lose a lot of friends in this period? In a sense, to put an overly cryptic interpretation on it, you 'Deconstructed' the Institute and a lot of friends at that time, didn't you?

I would say that inadvertently that was probably true.

last bastion of location. I think this is the real problem. Architecture represses dislocation because of the paradoxical position it maintains. You don't have that problem with theology or philosophy or science.

–It seems to me that you're trying all the time to reconcile people to alienation and to present being a Jewish outsider as a universal state. You're trying to take the homeless Jewish intellectual as Kant's imperative and say that everybody should be, or is, a homeless Jewish intellectual, either openly admitting it like yourself, or inadvertently.

I do not think it is inadvertent, but rather sub-conscious. I do not think that you have to be a Jewish intellectual to be desperately lonely, an island of the unconscious. Architecture has repressed the individual unconscious by dealing only with consciousness in the physical environment that is the supposedly happy home. I think it is exactly in the home where the unhomely is, where the terror is alive – in the repression of the unconscious. What I am trying to suggest is that the alienated house makes us realise that we cannot be only conscious of the physical world, but rather also our own unconscious. Psychoanalysis is talking about this. Psychoanalysis is partly a Jewish phenomenon, understandably for a people who need to be in touch with their own psychological being. I would argue that we all have a bit of a Jew in us; that the Jew is in our unconscious; that's why there is anti-

L TO R: HOUSE VI, VIEW OF WEST ELEVATION; HOUSE X, ORTHOGONAL MODEL

–Did your psychoanalysis allow you to do that without too much heart-rending pain?

My psychoanalysis was very important for me to become myself. Before the analysis, I was always a political animal reacting to public pressure. After analysis for the first time I was really able to do deal with myself, not as the public wanted me to be, but as I needed to be. Therefore it really did not matter what other people thought. I knew what I had to do for myself. I never thought very much about what it was doing to other people because it was more important to work out my own problems.

The Jew and Outsider in Us

–In the Krier interview you say 'as a Jew and an outsider I have never felt part of that classical world, I feel that Modernism was the result of an alienated culture with no roots'. So your definition of Modernism as alienation is first of all, as you have already admitted, only really possible outside architecture, it isn't true of architecture.

It has not been true of architecture, but I think it should be. I think it's more difficult in architecture because, as I have said on many occasions, architecture is so rooted in presence and in seeing itself as shelter and institution, house and home. It is the guardian of reality. It is the

Semitism, because we do not want to face our unconscious, we do not want to face our shadow; the Jew stands for that shadow. We do not want to face the issue of rootlessness. I am from New York but I do not necessarily feel more at home here than in many other places. However, I do not feel any more alienated here than I would in any other place. But this is not necessarily a Jewish problem, but rather one of Modern man in general.

–Well, I would agree that to be in New York is to feel alienated and alone, and at the same time to be a Jew in New York is to feel everybody is alienated and alone, so that it's a kind of universal New York experience. I think a certain amount of irony should creep into your view of yourself in that light. I mean you get a lot of Woody Allen films made on precisely that subject. In a way, it's a fact of being in New York and you can be considered canonic, you are actually acting exactly as Harold Rosenberg claimed – 'a herd of independent minds' – you are very independent, but you are still part of a culture which is, at least seen from the outside, so strong that it's overpowering.

I think that New York is the one place where the subconscious and the lack of a collective is very much on the prowl. I would not say 'universalised' because I do not think we can ever universalise. There are some people who will never see the haunted beings in their houses, the ghosts that inhabit all of our homes.

–Don't you think there's a danger that by emphasising alienation and the Holocaust and the Second World War and the atom bomb and all of the things that are, if you like, dis-locating and disorienting, your position becomes a kind of terrorist tactic, that forces a closure of discussion; that in its own way is just as repressive of the true otherness of pluralism as classicism?

I think we ought to be careful about pluralism. I do not believe that pluralism is at issue here. Although I certainly believe in 'the other', I do not believe in the dismissal of classicism.

–You don't dismiss classicism? You've changed again then, when did you stop being anti-classical?

Where my position has slightly changed is in the fact that repression of any kind comes to haunt us. For example, if you are interested in catachresis you do not throw away metaphor but rather you try to find the catachresis repressed in metaphor. If you are against classicism you do not throw it away, you try to find the hidden other that has been repressed in classicism. In other words, it is what I call the anaconda strategy: you squeeze classicism, suffocate it as it were until you squeeze out of it what was repressed. I believe that this is a big difference, I am no longer talking about alienation because I believe that politically it is a loaded word, that kind of terrorism is exactly what I found in Krier's position and I agree with you that the kind of demagogic condition that I accused him of is exactly what I had to be careful of myself. The way to another architecture is not to suppress the classical but in fact to cut into it, to use the previous metaphor: to be a surgeon in Tafuri's terms rather than a magician. Not to repress but to surgically open up the classical, the modern, and to find what is repressed. I think that is really an account of Deconstruction if you want. It is about multivalency.

–I agree, I think that is canonic to Derrida too.

Derrida and others say 'Let's not throw these things away, let's find out why we want to throw them away.'

–Which is a way of hanging on to them too.

Post-Functionalism and Post-Modernism

–In your article 'Post-Functionalism' of 1976 it was a kind of Not-Post-Modernism, it was your answer to Robert Stern and me and ever since then you've slid in and out of Post-Modernism. As you know, in our debates over the last 12 years, I've always thought of Post-Functionalism as a kind of ultra-Modernism or Late-Modernism, and I'm aware you declared Post-Modernism dead and appalling three or four times particularly in 1981 when you were interviewed by Stephen Gardiner in the Observer *over here. You announced its death at least a year before the British did.*

The death of what you would have called Post-Modernism.

–Well it's not just me, Peter.

I mean the Post-Modernism of eclecticism and Neo-Classicism, of people like Robert Stern, Michael Graves, Charles Moore, and I still believe that that will not be seen by history to be Post-Modernism. I think that what we are talking about now is another postmodernism.

–That goes back to a much bigger debate as you well know, back to the origins of Post-Modernism and its essence or if you like, its idea, its agenda and of course the court is still out on what that agenda really is, whether it's what you and the Deconstructionists do. By the way, of course, you are very aware that the Post-Structuralists don't want to be called Post-Modern by and large.

It's an occupied term in architecture. I have been for several years telling you that I thought I was a postmodernist.

–In the sense of someone like Ihab Hassan, yes. You have consistently been a Hassanian-Post-Modernist although you've slipped in and out, even about that you've shown great scepticism.

Being slippery by the way is the trait of a postmodernist.

*–Not my kind of Post-Modernist, I value consistency and you value slippage, what greater word is there in Deconstruction than slippage? The phrase 'slippery' is used by Mark Wigley à propos Deconstructiv-*ist architecture.

That's right. I agree that your kind of Post-Modernism is not at issue in this interview. You asked me to define my position and that is what I'm saying. For me when you're saying there's been slippage, I would say that being slippery is part of the discourse.

–Well you know the famous remarks of Karl Popper and others: 'from contradiction in philosophy anything follows'. There are no rules of the game, if you start slipping, if you can both claim to be a Post-Functionalist and a Post-Modernist, align them at some times, distinguish them at others and operate in an ad hoc way. I find that kind of slippage anti-philosophical and just pure opportunist pop-gun politics.

Well if that was the case I would agree with you, but that's not quite what I've done.

–You insist on certain positions on Post-Modernism one day and then others another day and you aren't quite clear.

It struck me when I read your work Architecture and the Problem of the Rhetorical Figure *(1987) that it was perhaps influenced by, God help us both, my* Rhetoric and Architecture *(1972) and* Current Architecture *(1982) – a lot of rhetorical terms appear, like oxymoron, anastrophe and chiasmus – not catachresis – was there any influence?*

Well Charles I read a lot and I am not saying I do not read you. I don't think I dredged these things up from you however. I also read Derrida and Kipnis and Vidler and Wigley and Nietzsche. It's not clear to me how much is consciously or unconsciously present. To me the question of who wrote it first is of little value. It does not matter to me if Philip Johnson says Frank Gehry originated the Deconstructionist movement, because I know that Frank Gehry did not 'originate' it.

–I'm not trying to claim priority, I'm just trying to clarify the overlapping funny dialectic. Let me put another case to you, to go back to Post-Modernism; all of a sudden in your reminiscences of the Armoury at Ohio and the ramparts and the abattoir in the Paris garden project, are they not my *kind of Post-Modernism?*

I think that they are not trying to be. Your historical imagery returns architecture to itself. Mine tries to move architecture away from itself – to be disjunctive with its past. It tries to move architecture to what I call 'between', between its old past and a repressed present.

–You can say between simulation and dissimulation, but they are very much like the ghost buildings of Venturi, and Jim Stirling at Stuttgart. In other words they are very much in the Post-Modern tradition, whether you intend them to be something else is your affair, but they are very much like Post-Modern ghosted signs which allude to the past.

They allude to a past without nostalgia or the necessary continuity proposed by both Venturi and Stirling.

–Well nostalgia's probably in the eye of the beholder.

I think that all continuity and tradition deals with a nostalgia for a tradition that is no longer possible.

–Well what's this fear of nostalgia?

Not fear, because I think nostalgia leads to what can be called 'the aestheticisation of the banal' which is what Post-Modernism is also about.

–Nostalgia can be perfectly healthy or perfectly radical. In the case of the French Revolution, Roman dress and recalling Republican virtues was positive radical nostalgia. In the case of someone recalling his parents, or his background, or his race, or his Jewishness, or his position, or his memory, it's perceived as a very functional and real thing, it's talking about having a feeling about something that was and isn't now. How can memory not be involved with an element of nostalgia, why repress it?

I am not against memory as a tissue of forgetting. There is a difference between this kind of memory and the sentimentalising of memory which is nostalgia.

–The word nostalgia is so corrupt for you, but a lot of people, even tough-minded people, have a place for nostalgia, as long as it's recognised as a part of memory.

Well, I guess Charles, my new position would be (as opposed to the way I would have answered you six months ago) that you're right; what one must do is find out why one is so much against nostalgia, ie to thematise the problem of nostalgia which is what I am trying to do in my work. Six months ago I would have said 'no, I'm against nostalgia' – that's a very toughminded attitude. I think I'm more tough-minded now in saying 'I want to find out why I'm against nostalgia' – 'What is it in nostalgia that threatens me? Why does it make me so anxious?' If you said Deconstructionism it doesn't make me anxious, but when you say nostalgia you push a button. Another button that you push is to say banal; I want to find out why I get so upset about banality.

–I find you backing into my kind of Post-Modernism stage by-stage as you get into thematics, representation, signification, communication, memory – a whole lot of rhetorical tropes which Post-Modernists of my kind rather than the Hassanian kind have been making. Most important, of course, ornament and arabesque are precisely the areas that Post-Modernists have been exploring. I think you're a closet Post-Modernist of my kind!

Let's talk about the difference; let's accept that all the things you say have entered into my vocabulary, into my work, but I have been trying to dislocate them in order to find out what they repress, not using them straight. The difference is that whereas Robert Stern uses them straight, I use them in a different way in an attempt to dislocate.

–So does Stirling. Don't make everybody into Bob Stern. I would say that Jim Stirling and Venturi and Umberto Eco and the kind of Post-Modernism that I've been defending – I'm not defending an accommo-dating Post-Modernism, but the ironically displaced or dislocated Post-Modernism –acknowledges the historical, so there's a way in which I have no trouble with dislocation at all. In fact I would argue it's canonic to Stirling and Venturi. Which is the irony in your position, where does the difference hold?

They all still assume the naturalness of the architectural language. I am not against representation, as long as representation uncovers what the natural language of architecture represses. You do not need to use the natural language of architecture to represent the ironic. There may be a value to the ironic but not if it means maintaining the language of architecture intact.

–OK. Well I can see that's a valid distinction from your angle.

I am not trying to put forward what my angle is, but rather what their use of irony really is.

Derrida and the Choral Works

–OK. In the Chora Works, or Choral Works – I want to call them Choral Works because I've seen them called that half the time . . .

They are called Choral Works.

–So there's a chorus, and the chorus is you and Derrida presumably? – singing away.

There are also other people in the chorus, they just may not be identified – Plato, Tschumi, they're all people in that chorus.

–A choral work is something slightly religious, cantatory and rhyth-mical: it's a musical chant sung in unison.

It's also done with a group of people, there's no one single voice; they sing in different parts. Derrida's contribution was a musical instru-ment, a lyre, you will probably want to spell it liar, but that would be all right with him.

–It seems to me that in the design you have completely dominated Derrida. You even said something to that effect in an interview in SD. *Is it true that you're disappointed he hasn't taken a greater part?*

In some way that is true.

–What exactly has he contributed?

The failure of the work in a certain way was that I was not contained, that I was not played out of my position into some new position. Jacques contributed an unfinished text that he was working on from Plato's Timaeus. We took this as the programme. We then worked with the idea of chora as the programme. Jacques would criticise it

until we got to a point where he was more comfortable with what we were doing; I think really more comfortable with architecture than any particular part of the work. I was probably and not coincidentally doing chora before I read his text. I think it is a collaboration that will happen some day; it has not happened yet. We finally forced Jacques to draw something. He then drew the lyre which became both the figure and the frame for the site.

–I see, I couldn't decipher those strange bumps in the middle, the kind of a wall that isn't the ramparts . . .

That other wall comes right out of the site of my Cannaregio project, in Italy.

–Let me ask you some factual questions, the Corten steel, is that part of a tilted plane?

That *is* a tilted plane.

–What are the lines? Are the lines etched into the steel?

The lines are acid-etched into the steel.

–And when will it be built?

That is a good question. From what I gather the Director of the La Villette project, a very decent man by the name of Goldberg very much wants to build it. As soon as they have their budget for next year they will begin construction. Everything is ready to go that it's going to be open by the time we have the show in London.

–How big across is it? About 30 feet?

No, it's about 70 by 90 feet. You realise that the whole thing was this idea of no authority. In other words, there were two sites, one in Paris, the abattoir site, one in Venice which was also an abattoir site, a coincidence. A Swiss-French architect, Le Corbusier, comes to Ven-ice and puts down a grid, an American architect picked up that grid and elongated it to the Cannaregio from the abattoir. Then another Swiss-French architect comes to Paris and puts down on the abattoir site another grid like Le Corbusier's, an abstract grid. Then he invites the same American architect to put a grid on top of his grid. So naturally I put my Cannaregio grid on top of La Villette. What this attempts to do is to undercut the notion of originality and authority, in other words that no one can take authority or credit for it or for who came first.

–Well it does to those people who have an Eisenman text in their hand, or like me have slaved away reading and looking.

I think you will realise it's a text if you look at the thing.

–Well yes, there's a bit of representation, I can recognise a rampart when I see it.

Can you?

–Just barely.

Well that's what I mean by 'between'. It is a between image that is both rampart at one moment and a piece of river in another. You can read them as several things.

–Well you're slightly missing my irony, but . . . Peter, just on the anti-*business of Deconstruction – decentring, disorienting.*

Deconstruction, Nihilism and Laughter

Charles, you miss the irony of your newly found interest in Decon-struction. You should know that Deconstruction is a *positive* activity, not an anti-activity.

–You don't have to testify to the House on Un-American Activities.

I just want to establish the ground rules.

–Even Derrida believes in affirmative Deconstruction, like some kind of feminist you know, affirmative action, and so does Tschumi. They all have obviously faced this question too many times, so they have to go on record as saying they're positive. Let's just go back to the negative part of it for a minute, the nihilism, because it seems to me that the emphasis on alienation and decentring and anti-classicism and nega-tion, dialectical negation if one calls it that, or being anti-memory or anti-thing, in a sense putting forward and, I would argue, universali-sing the notion of the Empty Man, the man contemplating the void, the nihil with pleasure and/or fear, I wonder is that true?

I'm talking about a man who is fulfilling himself through his uncon-scious, realising that the emptiness is *in* man and that the alienation lies between the conscious and unconscious individual.

–But when your Empty Man contemplates the void?

That is not the unconscious.

–Well also the void, if you like, of a superior existence or the metaphysics of alienation, does he contemplate it with pleasure? Do you smile to yourself and a warm glow comes over you? Or with fear?

With anxiety, with a lot of stress, that's certain.

–Is that why you use puns all the time to show the kind of breakdown . . .

That kind of humour you know covers some kind of anxiety. When somebody laughs at those kind of things, there's anxiety there and what one is trying to do is uncover what that laughter is repressing.

–Is that laughter a kind of belly laugh or nervous laughter?

It's a nervous laugh.

–But don't you enjoy it, Peter?

I wouldn't do it if I didn't enjoy it.

–I'm trying to prove the kind of latent humour behind your intellectual position.

I do not think there's anything latent about it.

–No, but some people have a kind of mad laughter, other people have a belly laugh and your's seems to be somewhere between constrained

able? That's a new Peter Eisenman, you've always been very fashionable, Peter.

Really? I have never realised that, I have always desperately wanted to be fashionable, but I never thought I was.

–Come on, you were voted by PA *one of the most fashionable architects of the '70s.*

Yes, well that was most controversial.

–But controversy we know is a synonym for fashion in our media.

Translate it how you will Charles. It is you in the media who create and consume fashion.

–Now come on Peter, you've been building your Cardboard Architecture for 20 years and you're not going to suddenly renounce your past.

No I will not, I do not think it has really been fashionable.

–Well you're just being naive. You're not being fair to yourself or your audience if you really think that you haven't been cognisant of the very conventionalised kind of avant-garde bad boy role you've been playing in the profession.

I do not hold with the bad boy role. Rem Koolhaas calls it a Grade B gangster film. Let me go back to the question about style: Deconstruction has nothing to do with style, it has to do with ideology. What is wrong with Post-Modernism is that it is anti-ideology. I would like

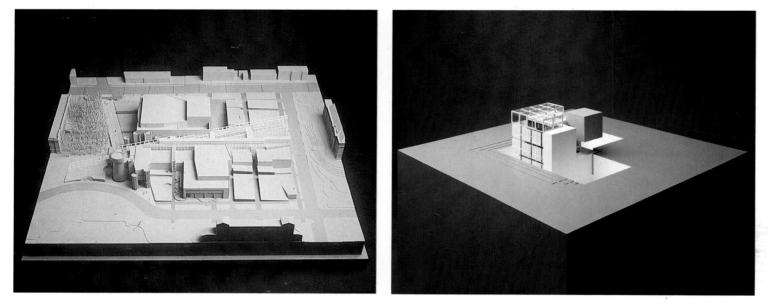

L TO R: MODEL OF WEXNER CENTER FOR THE VISUAL ARTS, OHIO STATE UNIVERSITY; FIN D'OU T HOU S, VIEW OF MODEL

and mordant – a kind of black humour.

No it's not black humour. I love playing, I am one of the most playful people you know, I don't think there's anything else in life but to play. What my work does is to show how play very much animates and activates, for instance, the seriousness of what we do. For me play is a very serious activity. I do not play to win. That is why people do not understand my machinations, they think I am a political power player. But I do not love power as an end.

Deconstructionist Style?

–Do you think there's a Deconstructionist style emerging? Is there a certain kind of convergence around the figure of Zaha Hadid and her flying-beams and Neo-Constructionism?

If there is a Deconstructionist style, I would certainly be the first one to turn against it. That is when I become anti. I think what will be nice about this Museum of Modern Art show is it will be something to be against. I have always been against something that becomes fashionable.

–Are you?

I am basically a maverick.

–Yes, well I think you're a maverick but are you against the fashion-

to think that Philip's show is basically an ideological show. I think it will show that some people are stylists, some people are ideologues, and I think that that separation is going to be made fairly clear in the catalogue. I think they are going to try to make the point that it is not a style they are talking about but a certain kind of ideology of internal relations, that is, that inside anything lies an ideology. Many people may not want to face that. I don't believe that it will catalyse around Zaha Hadid. I would not say that she is the central figure in the show. I don't think that she is ideological enough. I do not think there is a central figure

–I never said that; I am merely saying that a) there is a Deconstructionist style and b) that it emerged quite clearly in the last four years and that there is enough overlap to describe it in rhetorical, formal terms like a language, and c) that it is silly of you to try to distance yourself from style, because all ideology is seen through style, so there is no need for you to get on your high-horse and dichotomise: they're integral and related.

I am not certain that's true.

–There are stylists who have maybe underplayed ideology but everybody who has an ideology, reads it through a style, so style is shot through with ideology and is the medium through which ideology is

communicated. There's no reason not to want to deal with style. Not to want to deal with style is not to want to deal with language.

I think the minute that Deconstruction becomes a style and fashion is when we will all be able to attack it. Prior to the show it has not been a style or fashion, it has been a way of working. I think Deconstruction is a process which could have many styles. Michael Graves could easily be a Deconstructionist, Robert Venturi could easily be a Deconstructionist, so I wouldn't argue that it's a style.

–Well that's great, now you're moving towards pluralism.

You always say that's pluralism? I do not see it as pluralism. I would rather call it multivalent but one which does not pretend, as does your notion of pluralism, to a transcendent value.

–What is the différance *between your Deconstruction and Zaha Hadid's?*

I do not know if I can answer that, I have never really looked at her work that thoroughly. I can tell you the difference between mine and Frank Gehry's. Frank's work is about fragmentation – and fragmentation is not Deconstruction. Frank throws pieces around and fractures the structure, but basically he is talking about a nostalgia for the lost whole. My work is not about a nostalgia for the lost whole. I do not think Zaha's work is either. I know that Zaha is different from Frank

really familiar with are the Peak competition and the Berlin project. It is always you Charles, who are constructing and now deconstructing these continual discussions of uneasy styles and origins.

MOMA Exhibition and the New Academicism
–What about the exhibition at MOMA, there are three rooms and who's in them exactly?

I don't know, from what I understand there are now only two rooms, in the first there are the Constructivist precursors, I don't know who they have in that room.

–They must be Leonidov, Malevich, Lissitzky and Chernikhov.

Mark Wigley can tell you all of that. I can tell you who I think is in the show – Frank Gehry, Bernard Tschumi, Rem Koolhaas, Zaha Hadid, Daniel Libeskind, Coop Himmelblau and myself. Like many other people I proposed names to Philip. My original list had 11 names. I have fought for those 11 names but have lost quite a number.

–What is the name of the working title at the moment?

I think it is called Deconstructivist Architecture.

–Wasn't it Violated Perfection *before? When did they come to Deconstructivist?*

The Museum wouldn't let them use the title *Violated Perfection*. They

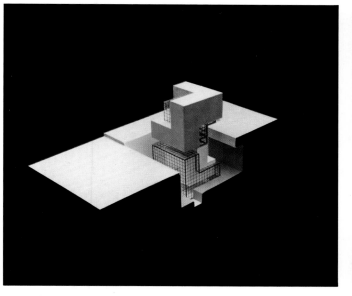

L TO R: HOUSE IIA, MODEL PLACED IN SITE; CANNAREGIO, GOLD MODEL

and I think we are all different from Daniel Libeskind in the way that Daniel's Deconstruction, if that's what you want to call it, has always pushed outside the metaphysics of architecture; that is, to shelter, to enclose, to occupy etc. If you do not maintain these then there is the destruction and not the deconstruction of architecture. I think that Zaha also operates within the metaphysics of architecture, although she might not say it that way. That would be the difference between us and Daniel and Frank Gehry. How I would describe the difference between Zaha and myself is more difficult.

–You will grant that a lot of people including myself see your work as inflecting towards hers, and Danny's towards hers. There has been a focusing, as often in history, all of a sudden there are flying-beams in everybody's schemes, for instance in Ohio you use a flying-beam which is not unlike her flying-beams in the Peak competition and not unlike Daniel Libeskind's flying-beams for the Cloud Prop in Berlin.
I think I was using flying-beams in House III.

–Perhaps, but as Deconstructionists say: origins don't matter, it's just that all of a sudden things come into focus – you could say Emilio Ambasz has been using excavations since 1967.

I am a great supporter of Zaha's and I really admire her architecture, I am conscious of the flying-beams. The only two projects that I am

didn't like it, they thought it was an off-putting title.

–So Deconstructivist means it's slightly Constructivist?

Well Philip believes firmly that all of this work is picking up from the long-dead Constructivists. I would have called it *Violated Perfection* and therefore I would have had John Hejduk and Raimund Abraham and people like that, who are not necessarily Constructivists at all. Constructivism is giving it stylistic overtones. It seems to me it should not be about Constructivists, but about Deconstruction.

–Well I would call this a very slippery slippage in the use of the word. I call it Deconstructionism rather than Deconstructivism for precisely the reasons that you were wanting to call it Violated Perfection.

You're right, it is not Deconstructionist, it is not deconstructing in the theoretical sense of the word.

–There is a big wedge you can drive between a Deconstructivist and a Deconstructionist.

If that is what you want to do, then you can call me a Deconstructionist and there are Deconstructivists in the show. For myself I have never been either. There is no question that my work is animated by the spirit of Deconstruction.

–Why isn't someone like SITE in the show?

I do not think Jim Wines' work has anything to do with the show.

–Well in his 'De-architecture', wouldn't you say that he has a lot more to do with Deconstruction than the Neo-Constructivists?

I guess he would, but if you look at his work you have to make another assessment.

–European critics have seen him and Frank Gehry as Deconstructionist because they literally tear down, break through and violate.

I would say that tearing things down is one-liner stuff. It is a form of illustration not a theoretical position.

–It may or may not be one-liner but we're not talking about quality, we're talking about categories. Is there not something contradictory between a joint exhibition and Deconstructionism which should be anti-hierarchy? Are you not setting up a new academy? Is that not a betrayal of Deconstructionism?

If it does set up a new academy I will be the first one to be against it.

–I see, still you were instrumental in setting up that other academy.

If the Institute was an academy it did not have a Deconstructionist overtone in it at the time, even though my work might have displayed a spirit and tendencies in that direction.

–Oh come on – its magazine was called Oppositions. *It certainly had a very strong academic bent that was taken up by many of the East Coast academies and then Harvard, Columbia, to a certain extent Yale, and all the magazines that came out as little* Opposition *books. You became the new academy, I think this is just a confirmation of that neo-academic trend.*

Philip gets very upset at anybody thinking that I am doing the show. But in reality I was not the one who said 'Hey Philip, let's have a museum show'. I think it's a very exciting thing because it's going to rocket things around a bit.

–It certainly is, but it's also going to solidify them in an academic way. They are in any case in that way now, they are already present in all those schools – the little Zaha Hadids, the little Gehrys and . . .

You have not said little Eisenmans.

–There have been little Eisenmans now for 20 years.

I have never seen those guys. I see little Hadids and little Gehrys and little Libeskinds all over the place and it's boring.

–Well there are little 'excavators' too.

What is interesting is that new things are going to open up. I think there are other possibilities for architecture. That is what I have always been interested in. I think we are going to start to enrich architectural language.

–Enrich it, now you sound even more Post-Modern, good heavens!

I am postmodern but not in the transcendental sense that you speak of. Enrich for me is not to give something new value, but to uncover what has been repressed by old values. I think the difference between my Frankfurt project and Richard Meier's work, for example, is that my Bio-Centrum project in Frankfurt is about the multivalent nature of text and I do not think Richard's work is about multivalency. The difference between what I'm doing and the other people in the show is that my work is about textual multivalence or betweenness.

–Or rather, 'inter-textuality'. But you have to, as you admitted in London, know the other texts, the written text about it relating to DNA and all of those other things. Is your work, in so far as it is a text, a Mandarin text demanding a reader's guide?

I don't think so, I used to believe that we needed a new reader. I believe that my texts are available not as information but as text. They have merely been repressed by the traditional texts of architecture.

–You don't think that they are so self-referential and referential: your Choral Work *is referring to Corbusier and to Cannaregio and to abattoirs that no longer exist . . .*

When Venturi does it you do not seem to mind.

–But Venturi uses a popular code. The only popular code you use are the ramparts, and maybe a little bit of the abattoir. The ramparts are I admit understandable and popular – you have one popular sign – but even the abattoir needs a code, you are really creeping into Post-Modernism not jumping in.

My codes may be as accessible as Venturi's but they remain repressed by your so-called popular codes.

–I'd say you are a Mandarin, you're an elitist and absolutist, why not a Mandarin too?

I'm neither elitist, absolutist nor a Mandarin. I believe I'm a centrist. It takes an enormous effort for someone comfortable on the edge, on the periphery, to attempt to occupy the centre. In an age where there are no new frontiers, the edge may just be the centre, the centre of the periphery.

–I'm not trying to marginate you but you're about to be in yet another 'academy of the new' at the Museum of Modern Art. You ought to be the ultimate character in a Woody Allen film, always trying to occupy the centre of otherness.

I am that character in a Woody Allen film.

–OK you shouldn't be resisting my interpretation, alienation as the 'here comes everybody.' My problem, as a pluralist, is that even if you go to your gardens in Parc de la Villette, you look around and see all the people who are going to be building gardens there, like John Hejduk, Chemetov, Price, Nouvel and so forth, most of them are Late-Modernists within an abstract style and most of them come out of the same Deconstructionist stable or share a lot of stylistic, ideological and valuative positions – in other words, I would argue that it's going to be a kind of Disneyworld of Deconstruction and instead of having real différance or otherness or pluralism it's going to be very integrated, very canonic, very much like a new academy. What do you say to that? Why haven't you invited Michael Graves or Quinlan Terry or a traditionalist?

They never invite me. Why should they play in my sandbox if they don't want me to play in theirs? It's that simple. I am a team player and a groupie. If I were doing the exhibition I would have a different group of people there in my team, because I like playing in a sandbox. Philip hates this idea of a team.

–What do you think it is then that motivates Philip? Why does he not want a team, what is behind his Deconstructivism?

Well I think Philip has interestingly enough always been a dislocator. Look at the International Style show: he has always been jumping before anybody else and I think he wants to go out, firstly with another jump, and secondly with a jump that puts him back in favour with the left, or what is thought to be left intellectually, in other words so he's not seen as someone of the right or the establishment but has academic and intellectual respectability. He probably would not articulate it that way, he has always been worried about the left and I think this is one time where maybe he is co-opting the left.

–Oh you think so do you?

Well if you were to take Tschumi, Koolhaas, Eisenman and Libeskind as representing a certain left in architecture.

–They certainly aren't left-wing.

Not politically left-wing, left architecturally, they are the darlings of the left in the art world.

–Well that's an interesting substitute for avant-garde semantically. But you know Philip always jumps after the ground has been prepared so he lands safely. You say he jumped before anybody else but that's simply not true – he jumped into Post-Modernism in 1978 after maybe 12 years of carefully patting the ground so that he would bounce. In the same way with Deconstruction. You and others have been preparing the ground since 1978 if not before – I think you mustn't give him too much credit. By the same token you mustn't think that's going to heal the breach with what you call the left and I call the avant-garde. It's still going to regard him with suspicion and they could regard it as his final kiss of death-life to the movement. This could kill off Deconstruction the same way he killed off Post-Modernism; when he embraced Post-Modernism, the Yale students came running up to me in 1978 and said, 'Is Post-Modernism dead because of the AT&T?'

I was called a 'Philip Johnson loyalist' by Michael Sorkin, and Michael Heizer said to me, 'You know, Peter, you ought to be proud of that, because that takes real guts.' He said 'I'm a Philip Johnson loyalist, all the artists are Philip Johnson loyalists, he has been a patron to all the best artists in the world and we are all loyalists'. So why the hell should architects not risk being in the centre?

–I wasn't questioning your loyalty.

Some people cannot understand why I have been loyal to Philip. But he is one of the few architects one can talk to about ideas. Do you know anyone else who pretends to be antiintellectual who reads Nietzsche in German?

–But when he embraces Deconstruction, if that's what he's doing, this could have the same effect as when he embraced Post-Modernism, what do you say to that?

I cannot really answer that because I don't think he was responsible for the problems of Post-Modernism.

–But when it went public at that scale for the largest multi-national in the world.

I think it is interesting if Deconstruction can go public. It says something about the possibilities for theoretical activity in the centre.

–It is going public at Parc de la Villette, Mitterrand came along and launched Bernard Tschumi's Folies.

I would not agree with you. That is a form of Deconstruction. I don't think Bernard Tschumi is about Deconstruction.

–He certainly thinks he is.

My sense is this: I believe that Deconstruction is not ultimately visible. It is about building unbuildable ideas. I do not think any multi-national corporation is going to build Deconstruction just as they do not build any other ideology.

–You just have to wait Peter, I bet that a multi-national builds a large Deconstructionist building, a headquarters in four years, a major building in two.

And do you say one of the people in the show will do it?

–No that's another question, it will be Kohn Pedersen Fox who will do it.

Perhaps.

–Philip is always in that camp as well, don't forget that – he plays in both sand boxes. He might admit it himself, he wouldn't mind because he's a nihilist, Nietzsche is his favourite character.

You have to be careful about Nietzsche. You can read him two ways, pro- or con-.

–Of course, I'm a great Nietzsche fan too, here comes everyone, like Woody Allen.

The Sensual Intellect

–I want to end with a look at what you're doing as a kind of celebration. Your architecture has a kind of intellectual joy or cerebral ecstasy, like Wittgenstein's writings and his abstract buildings. You've spoken of a 'didactic energy' of your own work, which I would agree is almost

a perfect summation of how it comes across. Have you seen the house of Wittgenstein in Vienna of 1927? Your work seems to me in that tradition and the Palladian tradition, the Corbusian tradition, the Terragnian tradition, basically in the tradition of a creation of the mind as a sensual organ. What do you think of Racquel Welch's statement 'the sexiest organ of the human body is the brain'?

I have some trouble with that exclusiveness – there are a lot of other sexy organs. What about the stomach?

–But you don't appeal to the stomach.

I am not certain that I do not . . .

–But only through the head.

I am getting there, Charles. You are only a head man, I agree.

–Your things are very abstract and they have this didactic energy.

I am not saying they do not. I can never change what I do, but I think if you look at Frankfurt closely the appeal is not only to the brain. It was designed to be strange and it came out strange. In the next series of buildings and the writing I am doing now about the new figuration, about what I call catachresis and arabesque – I think you will see a new series of projects. I think that the Edge of Between projects start at Frankfurt. I think Frankfurt was the start of something. You will have to wait and see what I do in Pittsburgh and Cinncinati and other places.

–I have never accused you of stopping and not changing, although as I said at the very beginning I think there is more continuity than change in your work.

There is continuity, because I can see all of this in my early work.

–Let's put another wager. When you start designing cloudlike fuzzy, warm, sensual, pleasurable-to-touch-and-sit-in fabrics and things that have a kind of visceral quality, that is when you go tactile and haptic and you can sit down and caress the building in a different way, to be specific, when you use fabrics and when it has squashy curves and appeals to the pleasures of the flesh in an analogous way, then I will think there's been a real change.

That is too traditional an idea of change.

–It doesn't have to be traditional. You've got to use universals, you've got to use language that orchestrates body metaphors.

No we have got to dislocate those signs.

–OK dislocate, but you have to dislocate from within, you're still in your head, you still haven't entered the haptic and the tactile.

Maybe not, I am moving towards a dislocation that says I am not wholly in the head but I am not totally haptic either.

–Let me ask you a question I have asked Richard Rogers for ten years, why do you always create reverberent spaces? Why can't you learn to design with fabrics? – What if I commissioned a building of yours with fabric?

All of my recent projects deal with fabric.

————— * —————

PETER EISENMAN
Blue Line Text

The two following texts are outlines and notes on a subject which will be taken up more fully in Peter Eisenman's forthcoming book, The Edge of Between.

It has often been argued that Modernism derived its principles from the philosophy of Hegel. In this argument, the fundamental principles developed in Hegel's *Lectures on Aesthetics* evolved into the terms of the Modernist rupture with the Classical tradition. Of particular significance was the central concept of the metaphysical dialectic from which evolved dialectical opposites such as form and function, structure and ornament, figuration and abstraction. The fact that in architecture today these terms persist unquestioned, free from critical scrutiny, indicates that the grip of the metaphysic of the dialectic remains powerfully in place.

Now, in retrospect, it is clear that, despite the novelty of its imagery, and the radical intentions of its social programme, Modernism's self-proclaimed rupture was illusory; Modernism remained firmly within the continuity of the Classical tradition. While the forms indeed did look different, the terms and manner by which the forms gained significance, ie, how they represented their intended meaning, were derived from the tradition of architecture.

In other disciplines, particularly in science and philosophy, there have been extreme changes in the substantive form, the method for producing meaning, since the mid-19th century. Today, the cosmology that articulates the relationships among Man, God and Nature has moved far from the strictures of the Hegelian dialectic. Nietzsche, Freud, Heidegger, and more recently Jacques Derrida, have contributed to the dramatic transformation of thought and the conceptualisation of man and his world. However very little impact of this transformation has found its way into contemporary architecture. While science and philosophy were critically questioning their own foundations, architecture did not. Architecture remained secure in those very foundations derived from philosophy and science that were themselves being rendered untenable by the internal questioning which characterised those disciplines. Today, the foundations of those disciplines remain essentially uncertain. Therefore it is possible to question whether architecture's foundations are also in a state of uncertainty. In architecture this question has never been articulated, its answer is left unformulated.

This is because architecture has never had an appropriate theory of Modernism understood to be a set of ideas which deals with the intrinsic uncertainty and alienation of the modern condition. Architecture always believed that the foundations for its Modernism lay in the certainty and Utopian vision of 19th-century science and philosophy. Today, that vision cannot be sustained. All of the speculative and artistic disciplines – theology, literature, painting, film and music – have in one way or another come to terms with this dissolution of foundations. Each has reconceptualised the world in its own way in what might be called post-Hegelian terms. What has been called Post-Modernism in architecture, a blatant nostalgia for the lost aura of the authentic, the true and the original, has specifically avoided this most important task.

It can be seen that today the last bastion of individual design is in the commitment to this aura of the authentic, the original and the true. The result of architectural Post-Modernism, however, has been the mass-production of objects which attempt to appear as though they were not mass-produced. In this way, Post-Modernism destroys its own essence, its own *raison d'être,* by becoming a vehicle for the aestheticisation of the banal.

The question must then be asked, why does architecture have such difficulty moving into the post-Hegelian realm? The answer is that architecture is simply the most difficult discipline to dislocate because the essence of its activity is to locate. Architecture, in the public consciousness, is the structure of reality, presence and objecthood. It is literally bricks and mortar, house and home, shelter and enclosure. Architecture does not merely speculate on gravity, it actually operates with and against gravity. For these reasons, its object presence within the terms of reality, it has traditionally been constrained to symbolise those terms, to symbolise its functioning as providing shelter and enclosure.

Thus, architecture faces a difficult task: to dislocate that which it locates. This is the paradox of architecture. Because of the imperative of presence, the importance of the architectural object to the experience of the here and now, architecture faces this paradox as does no other discipline.

Obviously, architecture is tied to the fundamental conditions of shelter. However shelter must be understood both physically and metaphysically. It exists in both the world of the real and the world of the idea. This means that architecture operates as both a condition of presence and a condition of absence.

Architecture in its continuing nostalgia for authenticity has always sought, without realising it, to repress the essential aspect of absence which operates within it. Therefore the tradition of architectural presence and objecthood has always been taken as natural, also as natural the representation of man and his origins. This was accomplished in a formal language that was also taken to be natural. The column and the beam, the arcade and the arch, the capital and the plinth, for example, were all thought to be natural to architecture. Therefore the Post-Modern nostalgia attempted to effect a return in architecture to its 'truthful', 'natural' heritage. But, counter to this notion, it is possible to propose an architecture that embraces the instabilities and dislocations that are today in fact the truth, not merely a dream of a lost truth.

The idea that architecture must be in the tradition of truth, must represent its sheltering function, must represent the good and the beautiful constitutes a primitive and unnoticed repression. In fact, it is this truth of instability which has been repressed. However if architecture is a convention, ie, not in any sense 'natural', then there are other truths that it can propose besides the 'natural' truth of the classical object. Only when architecture dislocates this idea of a natural truth – lifts the repression engendered by the concept of the 'natural' – will it meaningfully enter the post-Hegelian project.

This repression is also rooted in the persistence of the supposedly value-free nature of the typological categories of architecture and their intrinsic hierarchy. However there is no equivalency between structure and ornament; ornament is added to structure. There is no equivalence between figure and ground; figure is added to primordial ground. Each of the terms of these dialectical opposites carries an intrinsic value – structure is good, ornament is bad. For architecture to enter a post-Hegelian condition, it must move away from the rigidity and value structure of these dialectic oppositions. For example the traditional oppositions between structure and decoration, abstraction and figuration, figure and ground, form and function, could be dissolved. Architecture could begin an exploration of the 'between' within these categories.

Such an architecture would no longer seek a separation of categories, a hierarchy of values or the traditional classification systems of functional and formal typology; it would seek instead to blur these and other structures. This idea of blurring is not less rigorous, less rational, but it admits the irrational to the rational. Today one can see this blurring in the paintings of David Salle, in the photographs of Cindy Sherman. There the blur occurs between the beautiful and the ugly, between the sensual and the intellectual; they explore at once the beautiful in the ugly and the ugly in the beautiful.

What is the 'between' in architecture? If architecture traditionally locates, then to 'be between' means to be between some place and no place. If architecture traditionally has been about 'topos', that is an idea of place, then to be between is to search for an 'atopos', the atopia within topos. Many American modern cities are examples of atopia. Yet today, architects want to deny the atopia of today's existence and restore the topos of the 18th century, to bring back a condition that can no longer be. What is there of real value in the recreation of an 18th-century village today in Los Angeles or Houston?

Equally, the lesson of Modernism suggests that there is no topos of the future. The new topos of today has to be found by exploring our inescapable atopia of the now. This exists not in aestheticised nostalgia of the banal, but in the between of topos and atopia.

To accomplish this, the way meaning is manifest today also must be critically examined. As in the other disciplines of theology, philosophy and science, architecture must place its truths under scrutiny, particularly the truth of the tradition of architectural representation.

Since Aristotle, truth has conditioned the metaphor. Metaphor is understood as based on relating a referent to the truth of a known. It is possible, however, to employ other rhetorical tropes and thereby question the status of the metaphor. There is, in fact, a rhetorical trope called catachresis which speaks to 'the between'. Catachresis cuts into truth and makes it possible to look at what truth represses. Truth and metaphor can be reopened not by throwing them away, but by going into them, critically examining their structure. Tafuri says there are two types of architect: the magician and the surgeon. Today there is a need to be surgical; to cut into metaphor to uncover catachresis, to cut into atopos to uncover a new topos.

There are two conditions of catachresis and atopia that exist in the very heart of architecture: the arabesque and the grotesque. Arabesque exists between figuration and abstraction, between nature and man, between meaning and form. Traditionally it has been restricted to merely decorative use, but it is possible to suggest that in arabesque can be found structure, or at least found a condition between structure and decoration.

Similarly, the grotesque, whose roots are related to those of arabesque, can be used to explore the between. It is not coincidental that the works of Sherman and Salle are frequently referred to as grotesque. In Edgar Allan Poe's *Tales of the Arabesque and the Grotesque*, the haunted house is a central image. This does not suggest that we should literally make haunted houses nor that we should romanticise the quality of the haunted. Rather it might outline a poetic potential, a possibility today for the architecture of 'between'.

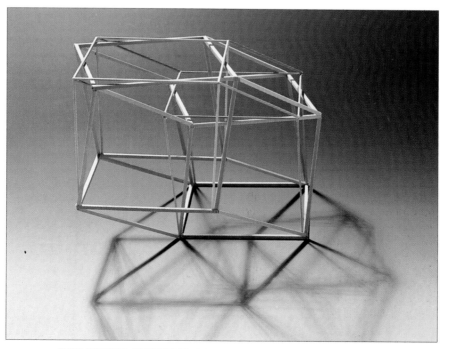

PETER EISENMAN, CARNEGIE MELLON RESEARCH INSTITUTE, CONCEPTUAL MODEL

PETER EISENMAN
En Terror Firma: In Trails of Grotextes

It is amazing how complete is the illusion that beauty is goodness.
Leo Tolstoy

Recently a client said to me, 'Peter, for the past five hundred years the discourse of science has been about man overcoming nature. Man overcomes nature through things which are rational, which are good, which are truthful, and ultimately these take on the characteristics of the natural itself, ie the beautiful. Obviously,' he said to me, 'it follows that architecture has been about this overcoming of the natural, because architecture symbolises the structures, cosmological attitudes of the society: architecture mirrors what the society is about.' Thus, though not explicitly, architecture has represented and symbolised this struggle of man to overcome nature. 'Today,' he said, 'this is no longer the problem which science is addressing. This is no longer where the discourses on the forefront of thinking are.' He said that the problem today for man is to overcome knowledge: 'You see, computers have knowledge, robots have knowledge, the technological clones that we are developing have knowledge, but man has wisdom. The knowledge revolution, artificial intelligence and the systems of knowledge have gotten out of hand, and have started to control man, rather than the reverse. Science today is trying to find a way to control knowledge, and the knowledge revolution.' And my client then said to me, 'Peter, you architects, for too long, have been solving a problem, representing and symbolising a problem which is no longer where we are.' He said, 'I want you to do a building which symbolises man's capacity to overcome knowledge.' I looked at him and thought, what is that? He said, 'Do you know something, you are supposed to be an architect on the edge. Yet,' he added, 'there is nothing you could do toward this end that would upset me at all.' He said, 'I do not want you to merely illustrate the problem. I do not want you to decorate a facade with a computer chip, cut into the chip, and say, there – we have symbolised the overcoming of knowledge. No,' he said, 'I am not talking about that. I want something far more significant. I want something that challenges man's very occupation of space, not just the surface of that space.' He said, 'And I do not think that you can do it.'

Now why is this? First of all, architects traditionally do not speculate on the here and now, on gravity, as scientists do. Architects have to deal with the real conditions of gravity, they have to build the here and now. They have to deal with physical presence. In fact, architects continually not only symbolise the overcoming of nature, they must overcome nature. It is not so simple for architecture merely to shift and say that overcoming nature is no longer the problem, because it obviously remains a problem.

However, it is possible to respond to my scientist client and at the same time still deal with the problems of presence and gravity. To do this the architectural discourse must be displaced. The issue is not merely as it was in the past, that architecture must withstand the forces of gravity, but the manner in which this overcoming is symbolised. In other words, it is not enough to suggest that building must be rational, truthful, beautiful, good, must in its mimesis of the natural suggest man's overcoming of the natural. Rather, as the architectural discourse changes its focus from nature to knowledge, a far more complex object emerges, which requires a more complex form of architectural reality. This is because knowledge (as opposed to nature) has no physical being. What is being represented in physical form when knowledge is being overcome? Nature, traditionally, was the liminal, the boundary definition; it mediated, in the anthropocentric world of the Enlightenment, the lost certainty of God. The natural became a valued origin, both useful to explain the world metaphorically and as a process and an object to be emulated. Since architecture had set out to symbolise the overcoming of nature, it is more than reasonable to think that the overcoming of knowledge also could be symbolised. The uncertainty that is contained in something other than the liminal will certainly be part of the expression of man overcoming knowledge.

At the root of the present conceptual structure of architecture is the Vitruvian triad of commodity, firmness and delight (use, structure and beauty). The beautiful as a dialectical category has been understood as a singular and monovalent condition; it has been about goodness, about the natural, the rational and the truthful. It is that to which architects are taught to aspire in their architecture. Thus they search for and manifest conditions of the beautiful as a form of delight in the Vitruvian sense. It was within such a desire that this form of the beautiful became as if natural for architecture over the past five hundred years. There were rules for the beautiful, for example, in Classical ordination which, although modified through different periods of architecture, much as styles change in fashion, were never, even in Modern architecture, essentially displaced.

In the 18th century, Immanuel Kant began to destabilise this singular concept of beauty. He suggested that there could be something else, another way to conceptualise beauty other than as goodness, other than as natural. He suggested that within the beautiful there was something else, which he called the sublime. When the sublime was articulated before Kant, it was in dialectical opposition to beauty. With Kant came the suggestion that the sublime was within the beautiful, and the beautiful within the sublime. This difference between opposition and being within is at the very heart of the argument to follow.

Now, interestingly, the sublime also has within it a condition which the conventionally beautiful represses. It is a condition of the uncertain, the unspeakable, the unnatural, the unpresent, the unphysical; taken together these constitute the condition which approaches the terrifying, a condition which lies within the sublime.

The terms of the grotesque are usually thought of as the negative of the sublime. However, this is not quite the case in architecture, where the sublime deals with qualities of the airy, qualities which resist physical occupation, the grotesque deals with real substance, with the manifestation of the uncertain in the physical. Since architecture is thought to deal with physical presence, then the grotesque in some sense is already present in architecture. And this condition of the grotesque was acceptable as long as it was as decoration; in the form of gargoyles and frescoes. This is because the grotesque introduces the idea of the ugly, the deformed, the supposedly unnatural as an always present in the beautiful. It is this condition of the always present or the already within that the beautiful in architecture attempts to repress.

That the overcoming of nature, or the depiction of nature as other, preoccupied the Enlightenment and the technological and scientific revolutions, was obvious. In response, the grotesque as it was put forward in the Romantic movement in Wordsworth, Keats, and Shelley, was concerned with rethinking this relationship between the self and nature. Therefore, today, the 'sublime' and the 'grotesque' deal with this movement between self and the natural, and the representation of this unease in literature and painting. If the 'natural-ness' of nature is to be displaced in the uneasy movement between nature and self, then our ideas of the sublime and the grotesque must also be reconceptualised in terms of overcoming knowledge without losing the fear associated with the natural, and the fear of the uncertain, ie the fear of not overcoming nature, must be preserved in any displaced categories.

The fear or uncertainty is now doubly present; the previous uncertainty of the natural, as well as the uncertainty of something other than the liminal, that is the uncertainty of knowledge that is within knowledge. Since the conditions for the sublime and the grotesque evolved from the expression of man overcoming nature, other terms which contain this double uncertainty will have to be found; the form of expression for man overcoming knowledge becomes far more complex.

What does this mean for architecture? In order to achieve the necessary internal displacement, architecture would have to displace the former ways of conceptualising itself. It would follow then that the notion of the house, or of any form of the occupation of space, requires a more complex form of the beautiful, one which contains the ugly, or a rationality that contains the irrational. This idea of containing within, necessitates a break from the tradition of an architecture of categories, of types which in their essence rely on the separation of things as opposites. There seem to be four aspects which begin to outline a condition of displacement. The following four aspects should be seen neither as comprehensive (there could be others) nor as a guarantee that their displacing capacities will produce a displaced architecture.

A major displacement concerns the role of the architect/designer and the design process. Something may be designed which can be called displacing, but it may be only an expressionism, a mannerist distortion of an essentially stable language. It may not displace the stable language, but on the contrary further stabilise its normative condition. This can be seen in many examples of current architectural fashion. There is a need for a process other than an intuition – 'I like this,' or 'I like that.' When the process is intuitive, it will already be known, and therefore complicit with the repressions inherent in architectural 'knowledge.' Intuitive design can never produce a state of uncertainty, only, at best, an illustration of uncertainty. While the concept of the grotesque or the uncanny can be conceptualised and imaged, it cannot be designed. Something designed is essentially non-textual, because design of necessity involves certainty; something always has to be made. To attempt to design between uncertainty or multivalency produces only a superficial illustration of such a condition. If something can be designed it is no longer uncertain.

In the traditional idea of architectural design, form, function, structure, site and meaning can all be said to be. But they are not textual. Texts are always thought to be primary or original sources. Textual or textuality is that aspect of text which is a condition of otherness or secondary. An example of this condition of otherness in architecture is a trace. If architecture is primarily presence – materiality, bricks and mortar – then otherness or secondary would be trace, as the presence of absence. Trace can never be original, because trace always suggests the possibility of something *other* as original, as something *prior* to. In any text there are potential traces of otherness, aspects or structures which have been repressed by presence. As long as presence remains dominant, ie singular, there can be no textuality. Therefore by its very nature such a condition of trace requires at least *two* texts.

Thus, the second aspect of this *other* architecture is something which might be called *twoness*. There are many different twonesses which exist in traditional architecture already: the twoness of form and function, and the twoness of structure and ornament. But these are traditionally seen as hierarchical categories; one is always seen as dominant or original and the other as secondary (form follows function, ornament is added to structure). In the sense it is being used here, twoness suggests a condition where there is no dominance or originary value but rather a structure of equivalences, where there is uncertainty instead of hierarchy. When the one text is too dominant there is no displacement. When the other text becomes presence itself it obtrudes and loses its capacity for the uncertain. Equally the second text cannot obliterate the first text, but will be understood to be interior to it, thus as an already present 'trace' usually suppressed by a single dominant reading. This second text thus will always be within the first text and thus between traditional presence and absence, between being and non-being.

Therefore, the third condition of this other architecture is *betweenness*, which suggests a condition of the object as a weak image. A strong image would give a primary dominant meaning to one or the other of the two texts. Not only must one or the other of the two texts not have a strong image; they will seem to be two weak images, which suggests a blurred third. In other words, the new condition of the object must be *between* in an imageable sense as well: it is something which is almost this, or almost that, but not quite either. The displacing experience is the uncertainty of a partial knowing. Therefore, the object must have a blurring effect. It must look out of focus: almost seen, but not quite seen. Again, this between is not a between dialectically, but a between *within*. The loss of the idea of architecture as a strong image undercuts the traditional categories of architecture associated with man over-coming nature; place, route, enclosure, presence, and the vertebrate, upright building – symbolic of overcoming gravity.

To deny traditional place or enclosure, suggests another condition of this displaced architecture, that is interiority. Interiority has nothing to do with the inside or the inhabitable space of a building but rather of a condition of being within. However, as is the case with the grotesque, interiority deals with two factors; the unseen and the hollowed-out. Interiority also deals with the condition proposed by textuality that the symbolism or meaning of any sign refers, in such a displaced architecture, not outward but inward to an already present condition.

Ultimately, each of these four conditions provoke an uncertainty in the object, by removing both the architect and the user from any necessary control of the object. The architect no longer is the hand and mind, the mythic originary figure in the design process. And the object no longer requires the experience of the user to be understood. No longer does the object need to look ugly or terrifying to provoke an uncertainty; it is now the distance between object and subject – the impossibility of possession which provokes this anxiety.

———— * ————

PETER EISENMAN
Wexner Center for the Visual Arts, Ohio

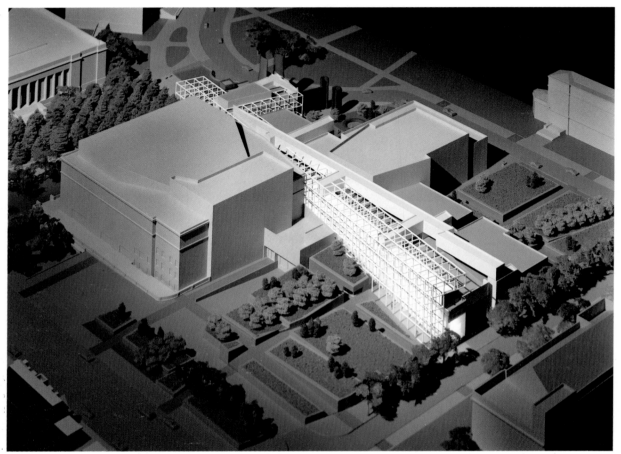

VIEW OF MODEL

The purpose of the Visual Arts Center is to provide for avant-garde and experimental arts; it is not meant to be a repository for traditional art. The building will contain permanent, temporary and experimental exhibition galleries, performance space, a 'Black Box Theater', a fine arts and graphics library, a film centre, studio spaces, administrative space, a café, bookstore, music practice rooms, a choral hall, exhibition storage and preparation areas.

Still under construction and due for completion in 1990, the contract was awarded as the result of a limited international competition.

The initial phase of work at the Wexner Center was to develop a programme and a master site plan. In the great 19th-century tradition, the Center is a fusion of landscape and the language of building. This new building is a minimal intervention between two existing and adjacent campus buildings. The central circulation spine of the new building resolves the two existing geometries of the city and the campus.

Instead of selecting any of the obvious building sites on the campus, a new site was created, locating the building between several proposed sites and existing buildings. It also refers to past contexts with the exposure of the foundations of the armoury formerly on the site and the remaking of some of its elements. It can be described as 'a non-building – an archaeological earthwork whose essential elements are scaffolding and landscaping'.

The scaffolding consists of two intersecting three-dimensional gridded corridors which link the hall and auditorium already on the site with the new galleries and arts facilities being constructed. One arm of the scaffolding aligns the street grid of the City of Columbus with the campus grid, which is 12½ degrees askew, so the project both physically and symbolically links the university campus with the wider context of the city beyond, art with the community. But it does not do so in a holistic, unifying way, because the building itself is fractured and incomplete-looking. Instead of symbolising its function as shelter, or as a shelter for art, it acts as a symbol of art as process and idea, of the ever-changing nature of art and society.

Architects: Eisenman/Robertson Trott; *Partners in charge:* Peter Eisenman, Richard Trott.
The Wexner Center for the Visual Arts was first featured in project form in AD Vol 55, Nos 1/2 1985 'Cross-Currents of American Architecture', published in conjunction with the American Festival in London.

ABOVE: PERSPECTIVE DRAWING; *BELOW:* CONSTRUCTION VIEWS

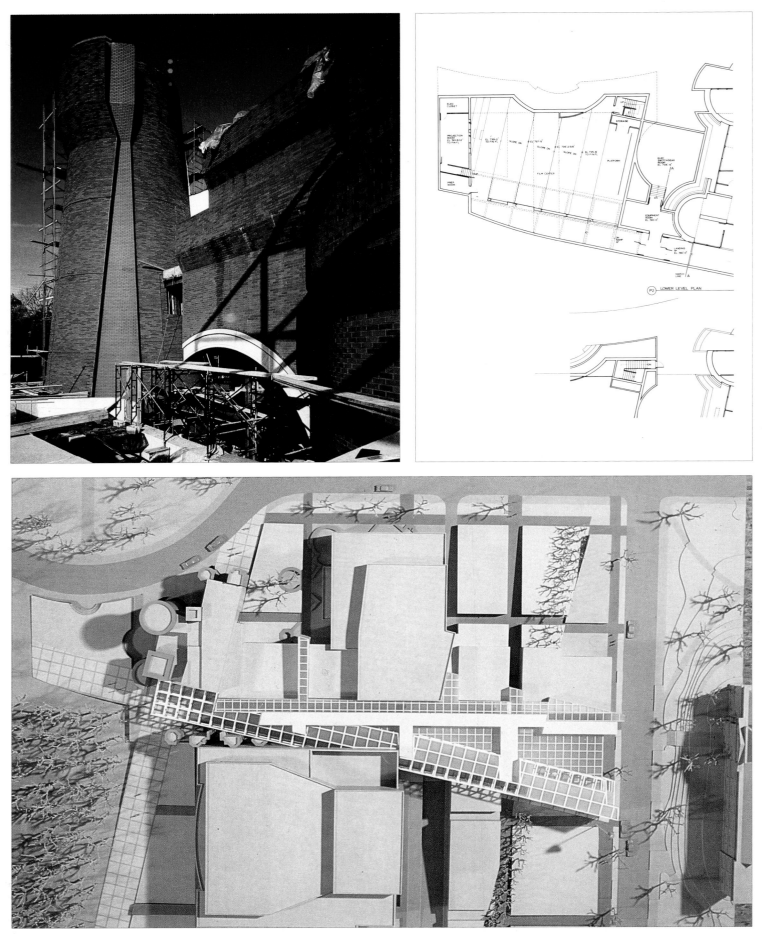

TOP TO BOTTOM, L TO R: VIEW OF CENTER UNDER CONSTRUCTION, FILM CENTER PLAN AND PLAN OF MODEL

ABOVE: LOWER LEVEL PLAN (NORTH), *BELOW*: LOWER LEVEL PLAN (SOUTH)

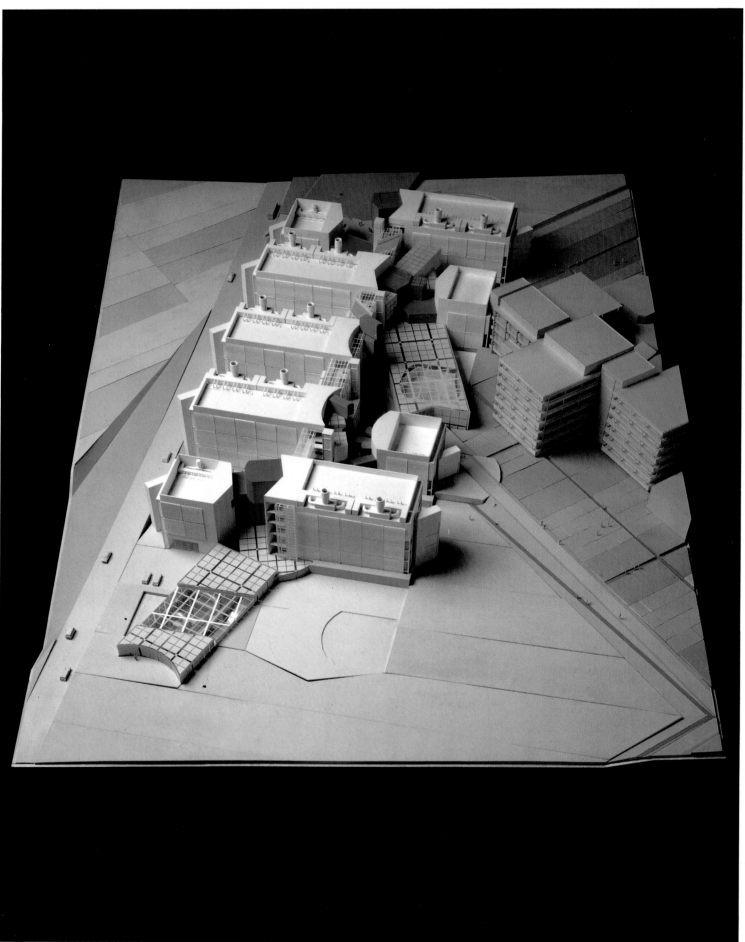

VIEW OF MODEL

Bio-Centrum, Frankfurt-am-Main

SITE PLAN

The Bio-Centrum, designed for research laboratories and support spaces, is an expansion of existing facilities at the J W Goethe University, Frankfurt-am-Main.

Our analysis of the building programme and the site requirements revealed that the scientific and educational goals of the University Bio-Centrum could be satisfied by three criteria: first, the maximum interaction between functional areas and between the people that use them; second, the accommodation of future change and growth that cannot be predicted today; and third, the maintenance of the site, as fast as possible, as a green preserve. This means that a traditional architecture of set spatial hierarchies which rigidly constrain future growth needed to be abandoned. To undermine these Classical architectural hierarchies, it was necessary to dissolve the traditional autonomy of the discipline of architecture. Blurring the interdisciplinary boundaries allowed us to explore other formal options that may fall between biology and architecture.

As biology today dislocates the traditions of science, so the architecture of our Bio-Centrum project dislocates the traditions of architecture. While architecture's role is traditionally seen to be that of accommodating and representing function, this project does not simply accommodate the methods by which research into biological processes is carried out. Rather, it articulates those processes themselves. Indeed, it could be said its architecture is produced by those very processes.

To accomplish this we first departed from the traditional representation of biology by making an architectural reading of the biological concepts of DNA processes by interpreting them in terms of geometrical processes. At the same time, we departed from the traditional representation of architecture by abandoning the Classical Euclidean geometry on which the discipline is based in favour of a fractal geometry. What we discovered was that there is a similarity between the processes of fractal geometry and the geometry of DNA processes. This similarity was used to propose an analogy between architectural processes and biological processes. The analogy made possible a project that is neither simply architectural nor simply biological, but one which is suspended between the two.

The project form is the result of the action of the three most basic processes by which DNA constructs proteins (replication, transcription and translation) on the geometric figures that biologists use to explain these processes by using four geometric figures, each with a specific colour, which symbolise the DNA code.

Replication: In biological replication, the DNA chain splits into two strands which then

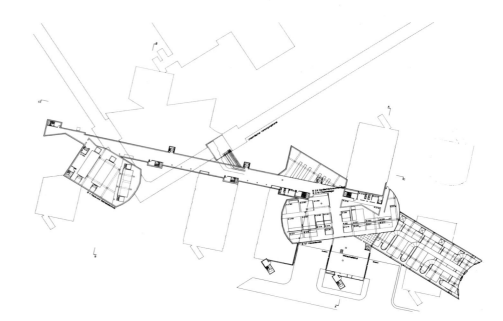

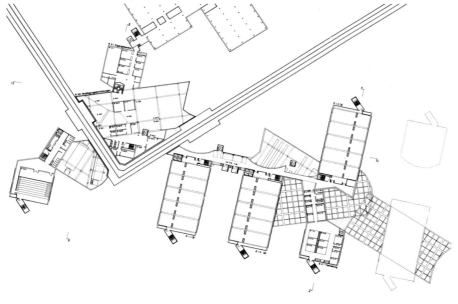

FROM TOP: LEVELS -3, -2, -1

attract their complementary strands to form two new identical chains. The process can be interpreted architecturally by using the code for Collagen as the base form and the complement of that code as the generating form.

Transcription: In biological transcription, the DNA chain temporarily unzips and a new strand inserts itself into the resulting gap and makes a complementary copy of only one of the exposed DNA strands. Consequently, it is interpreted architecturally as a second iteration of the first process applied to only the lower strand of the original five pairs. The figures produced in the first process now become the base form and their complements become the generating form.

Translation: The final biological process in the production of a protein is the translation of the DNA code into the physical structure of a protein. This process is interpreted in the

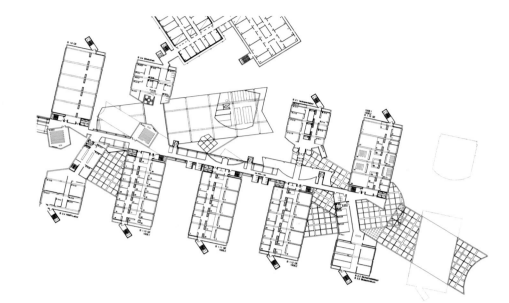

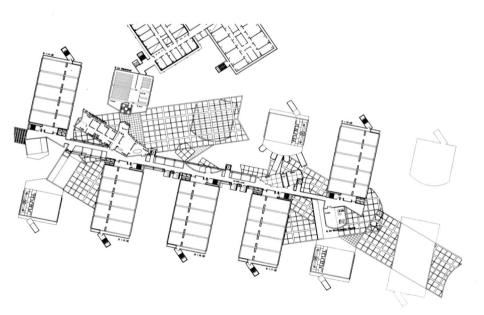

architectural project by treating two groups of the upper strand of the original figures as TRNA strands.

The project is coloured according to the biologists' colour code for the figures. While the value of these four colours remains constant, their intensity is varied in order to articulate the different processes. The original figures are marked by the lightest shade while those produced by replication have the darkest shade and those produced by transcription have the middle shade.

Eisenman Architects worked in association with both Augustine DiGiacomo of Jaros, Baum & Bolles (Mechanical Engineer) and Laurie Olin of Hanna/Olin (Landscape Architect) to design this project. The submission was given top marks by the technical review committee for programme compliance in space planning and mechanical systems.

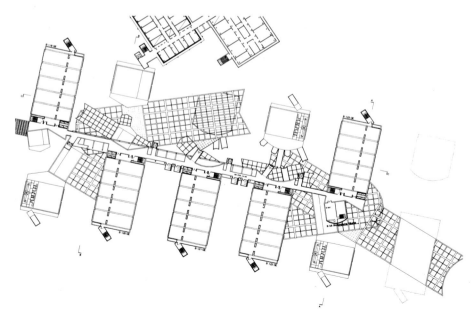

FROM TOP: LEVELS 1, 2, 3

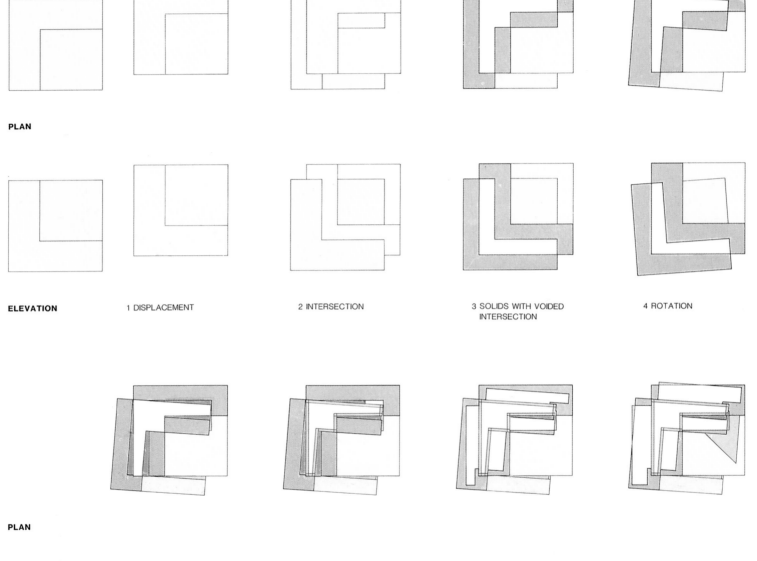

PLAN

ELEVATION　　1 DISPLACEMENT　　　　　　2 INTERSECTION　　　　　　3 SOLIDS WITH VOIDED　　　　4 ROTATION
　　　　　　　　　　　　　　　　　　　　　　　　　　　　　　　　　INTERSECTION

PLAN

ELEVATION　　5 DISPLACEMENT BETWEEN　　6 TRACE AND FRAME　　　7 IMPRINTING SOLIDS　　　8 IMPRINTING THROUGH
　　　　　　　　　　SOLID AND VOID　　　　　　　DEFINITION　　　　　　　　　　　　　　　　　　　　SURFACE

CONCEPTUAL DIAGRAMS

162

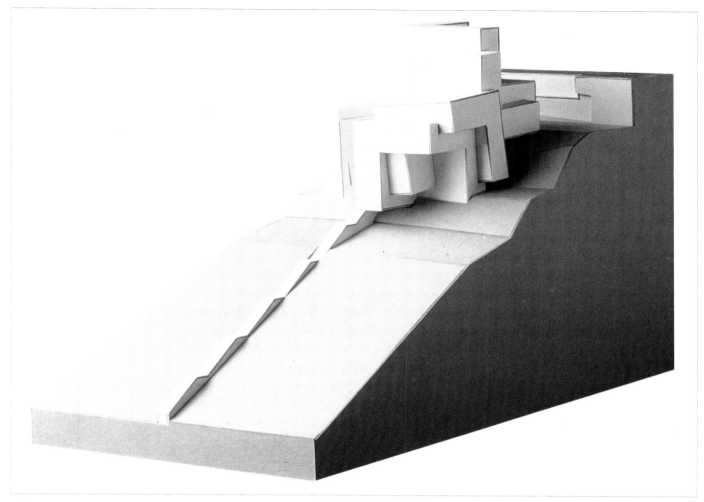

VIEW OF MODEL

Guardiola House, Santa Maria del Mar

An idea of place, or *topos*, has always been central to man's relationship to his environment. This design for a house researches the meaning of place, and how it has been affected by a changing understanding of the world. Since the time of the Romans, when the crossing of the *cardo* and the *decumanus* marked the *topos* of the Roman encampment, man has been defining place as the mark – whether a cross or a square, a clearing in the forest or a bridge over a river – of his struggle to overcome nature. Today two things have happened to bring the traditional forms of place-making into question. First, technology has overwhelmed nature – the automobile and the airplane, with their potential for unlimited accessibility, have made the rational grids and radial patterns of the 19th century obsolete; second, modern thought has found 'unreasonableness' within traditional reason, and logic has been seen to contain the illogical.

These challenges to order had been repressed by traditional reason, but in man's new condition, these ideas can no longer be repressed. In architecture this is seen in the questioning of whether man's marking of his conquest of nature is still significant, and further, in the acknowledgement that place (*topos*) has always contained 'no place' (*atopia*). With this breakdown of the traditional forms of place has come a concurrent breakdown of the traditional categories of figure/ground and frame/object.

Since Classical times there has been another definition of place which suggested such a simultaneity of two traditionally contradictory states. This is found in Plato's *Timaeus* in the definition of the receptacle (*chora*) as something between place and object, between container and contained. For Plato, the receptacle is like the sand on the beach: it is not an object or a place, but merely the record of the movement of water, which leaves traces of high-tide lines and scores imprints – erosions – with each successive wave receding to the water. Much as the foot leaves its imprint in the sand and the sand remains as a trace on the foot, each of these residues and actions are outside of any rational or natural order; they are both and neither.

This house can be seen then, as the manifestation of a receptacle where the traces of logic and irrationality are intrinsic components of the object/place; the arabesque. It exists between the natural and the rational, between logic and chaos. It breaks the notion of figure/frame, because it is figure and frame simultaneously. Its tangential L-shapes penetrate three planes, always interweaving. These fluctuating readings resonate in the material of this house, which, unlike a traditional structure of outside and inside, neither contains nor

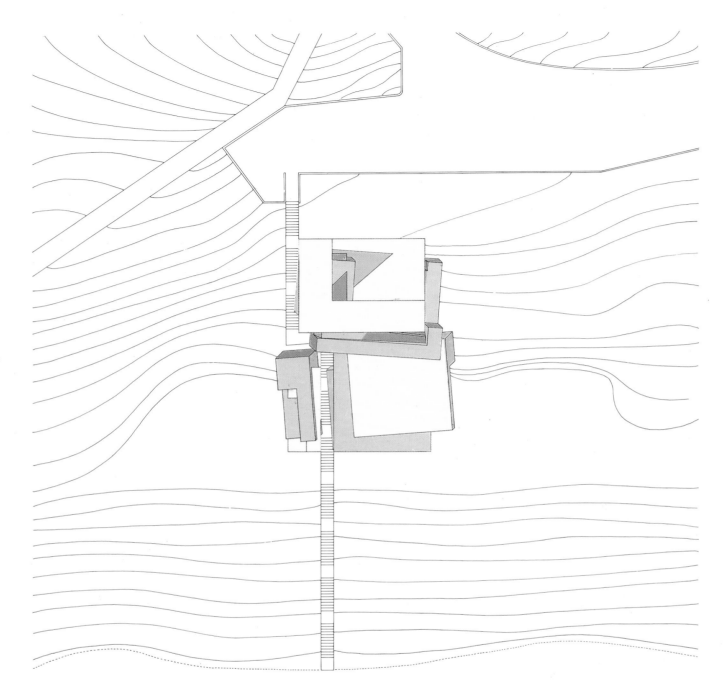

SITE PLAN

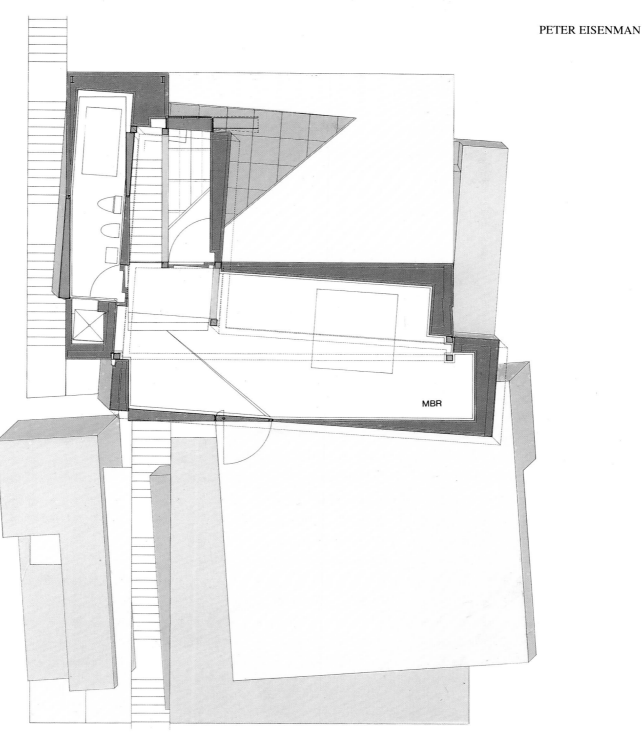

UPPER-LEVEL PLAN

is contained. It is as if it were constructed of a substance which constantly changes shapes formed by imprints left in it and traces of material removed by the pattern. These traces are recorded in two linear frames of steel grids which mark another position of the structure, before the interweaving. Then, the imprinted forms, which record movements of the pattern, are no longer either frame or object. Finally, the pattern appears again in the surface of two of the quadrants in the form of glazed and unglazed tiles, and the remaining quadrants are treated with a coral and white stucco to reiterate the duality of the reading. The house is neither an expressionistic work nor one of mechanical precision. It rather has the qualities of a controlled accident, of a line once put down which cannot be erased, but in whose linearity is the density of unpredictable reverberations.

The structure of the house is reinforced concrete poured in place. It is located on the Bay of Cadiz in Santa Maria del Mar in Spain and will be a weekend house for a single father and his grown son who live in Seville. Construction began in late November 1988.

Principal-in-Charge: Peter Eisenman; *Senior Associates-in-Charge*: George Kewin, Thomas Leeser; *Senior Project Architects*: Antonio Sanmartin; *Project Architects*: Nuno Mateus, Jan Kleihues; *Assistants*: Begona Fernandez Shaw, Felipe Guardiola, Lise Anne Couture, Luis Rojo, Michael McInturf, Madison Spencer, Simon Hubacher, Maximo Victoria, Frederic Levrat, Anne Marx, Robert Cheoff, Julie Shurtz, Dagmar Schimkus; *Structural Engineer*: Gerardo Rodriguez.

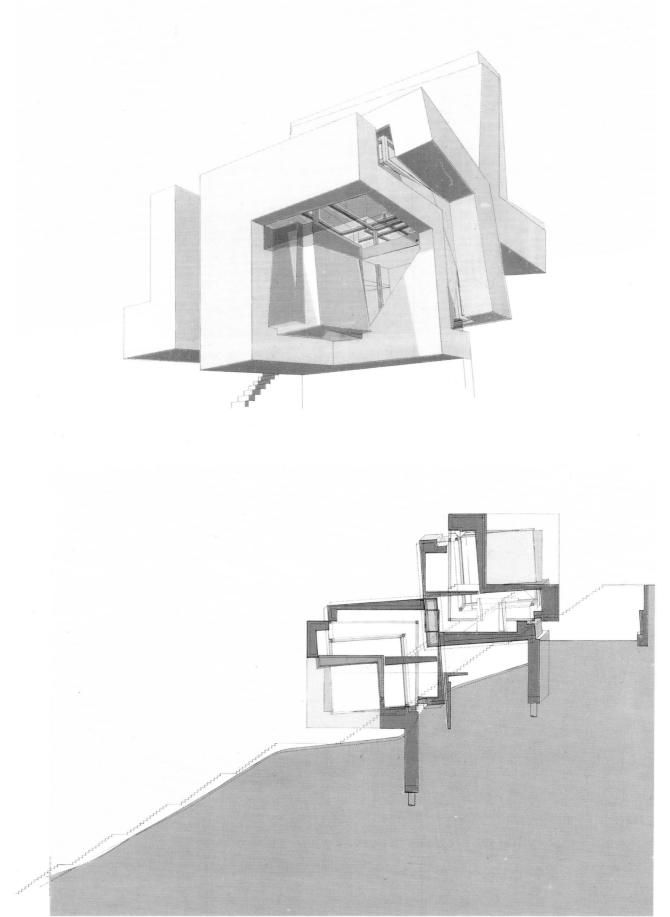

ABOVE: PERSPECTIVE VIEW FROM SOUTHEAST; *BELOW*: SITE SECTION A

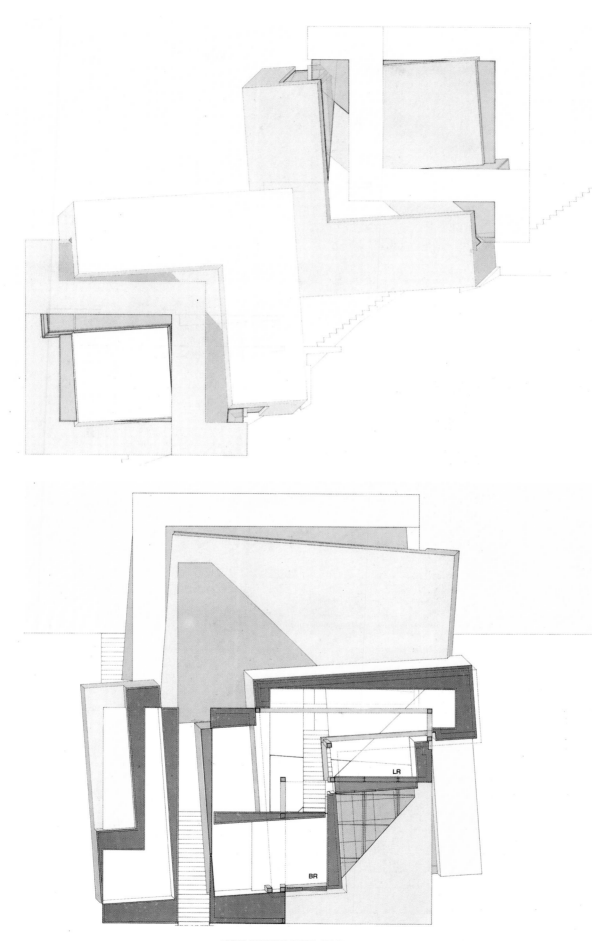

ABOVE: EAST ELEVATION; *BELOW*: CROSS-SECTION B

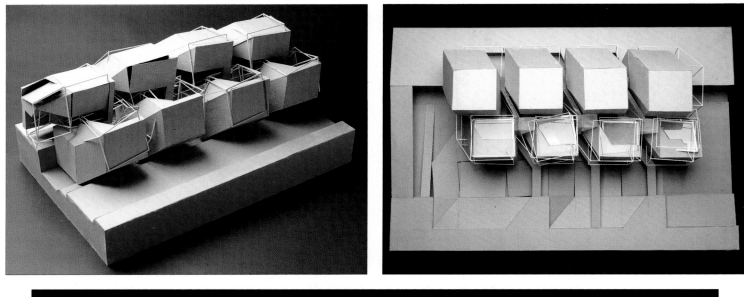

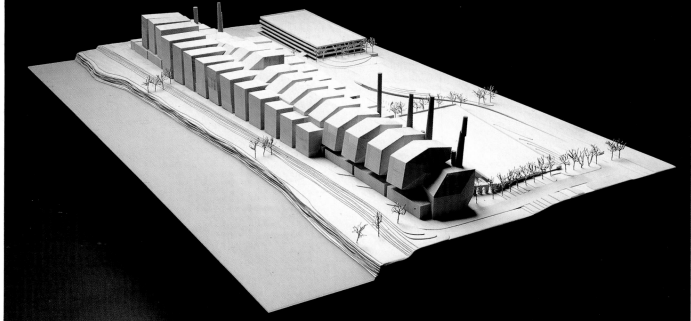

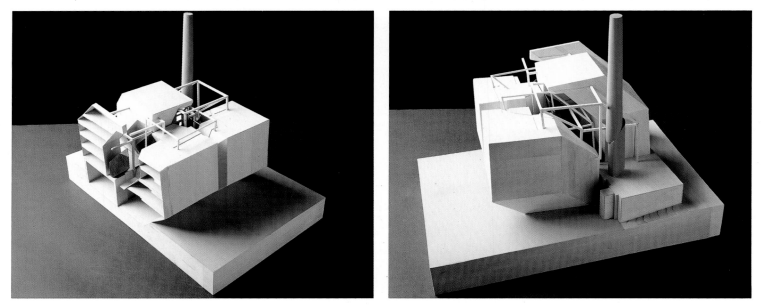

ABOVE L TO R: PRELIMINARY MODEL No 1; PRELIMINARY MODEL No 2; *CENTRE*: MODEL; *BELOW L AND R*: MODEL

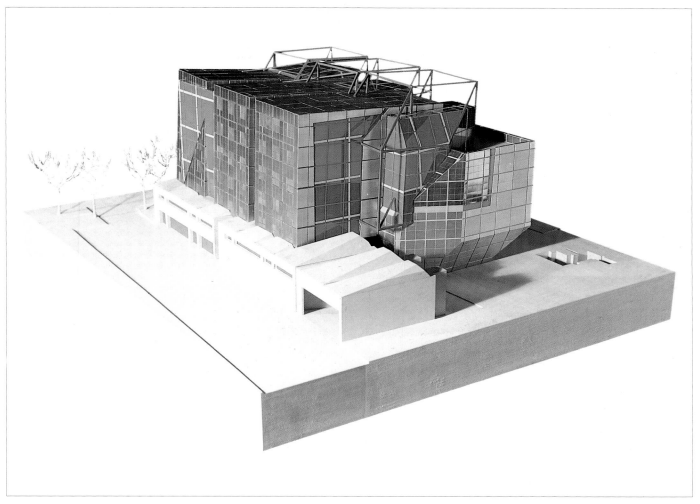

MODEL

Carnegie-Mellon Research Institute

The new complex object for these buildings was taken as a Boolean cube, or an N-geometric figure. The Boolean cube is a structure with an infinite N-number of geometries; this structure is the model for computer design in the field of artificial intelligence, because the Boolean cube provides the opportunity for the computer to move beyond a simple information frame. The multiplication of N-geometries allows multiple paths for information movement so that, for instance, from any point in a 1000-N cube a move can be made in 1000 different directions within the information matrix. This allows parallel movement with multiple possible intersections that are based on a systematic frame within which *random* occurrences are generated. This allows chance events to be reasoned within the parallel systems in a non-linear manner.

Because the Boolean cube is based on doubling and controlled connections, it is always diagonally symmetrical and always retains an homogeneous density due to the equidistant connections. Thus the Boolean cube is a complex structure which lies between the purity of a Platonic form and the infinite and unlimited form of a non-Euclidean structure. Because the form is based on the infinite doubling and reconnection of itself, it is an unstable and infinite N-geometric figure, yet frozen singularly these forms exhibit the properties, such as symmetry, of Platonic forms. The Boolean cube also allows for both a progressive and a regressive reading. For example, the division of the figure within the 4-N cube allows two 3-N cubes to be seen.

Each building is made up of three pairs of 4-N Boolean cubes. Each pair contains two solid cubes with 40' and 45' members and two frame cubes with 40' and 45' members. Each pair can be seen as containing the inverse of the other as solid and void. The 40' solid and the 40' frame 4-N cubes are placed in a 5-N relationship to each other where their points are 40' away from each other in a parallel orientation. The 45' solid and the 45' frame 4-N cubes are placed in a 5-N relationship to each other in a parallel orientation. This places the project between a reading of 5-N cubes oscillating between solid and frame and 4-N cubes. A further reading would include the two pairs of 5-N cubes as a single 6-N cube. It is the function of the asymptotic curve to bring the two pairs into another or 6-N relationship.

These pairs are continuously and progressively spaced so that they fall out of phase with one another while remaining within the 5-N relationship. The string of 45' solid and frame 4-N cubes is placed in an asymptotic curve and the string of solid 40', frame 40' and frame 45' 4-N cubes is placed in an exponen-

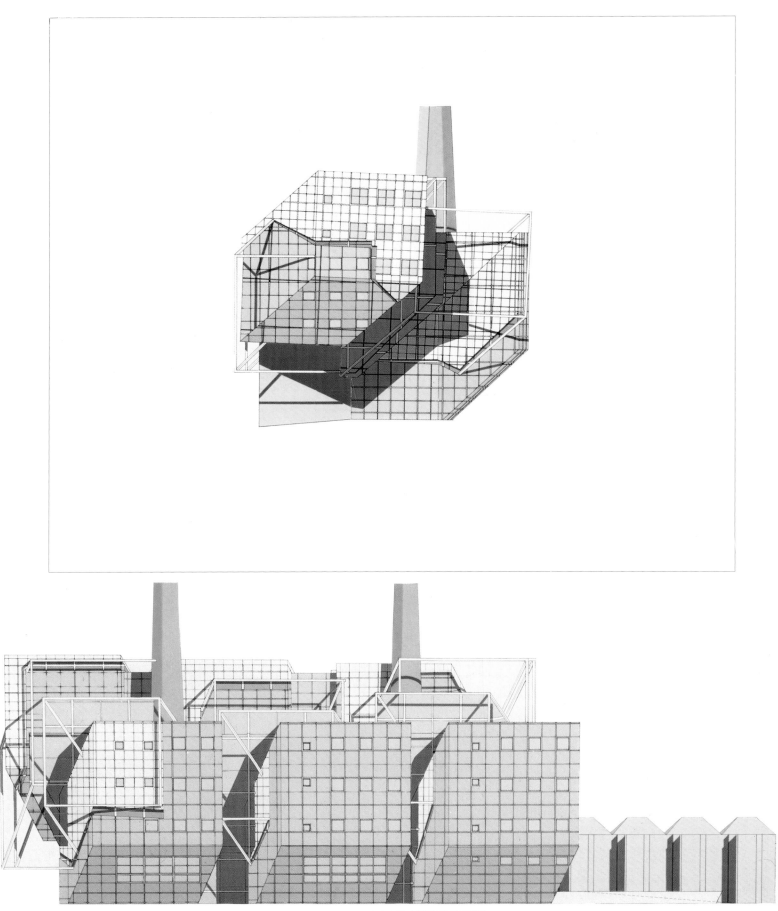

ABOVE: EAST ELEVATION; *BELOW*: NORTH ELEVATION

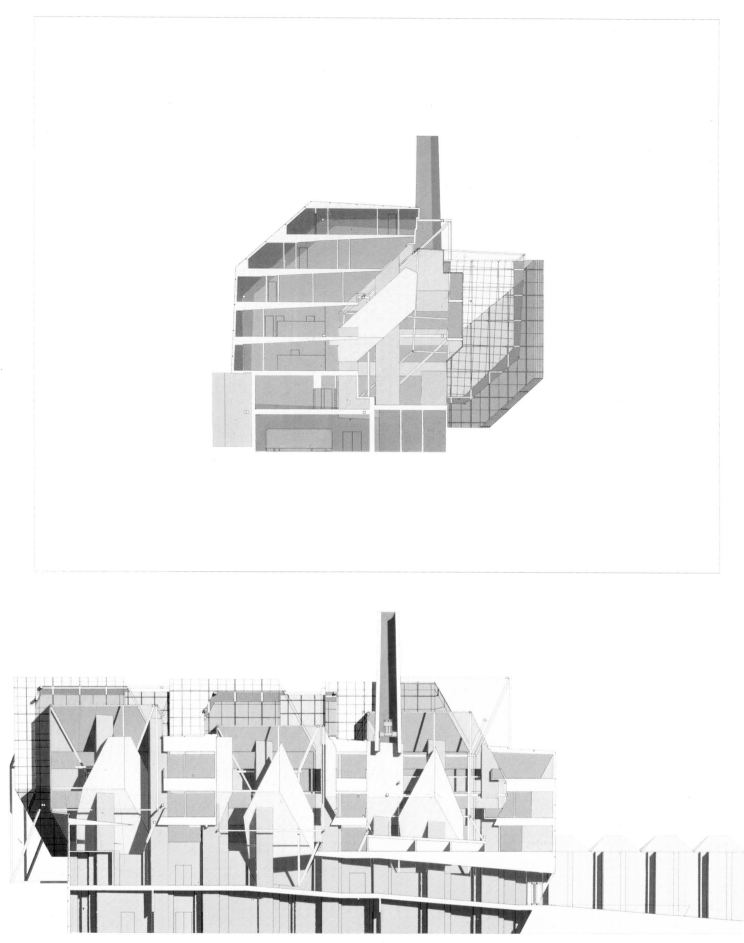

ABOVE: SECTION B; *BELOW*: SECTION E

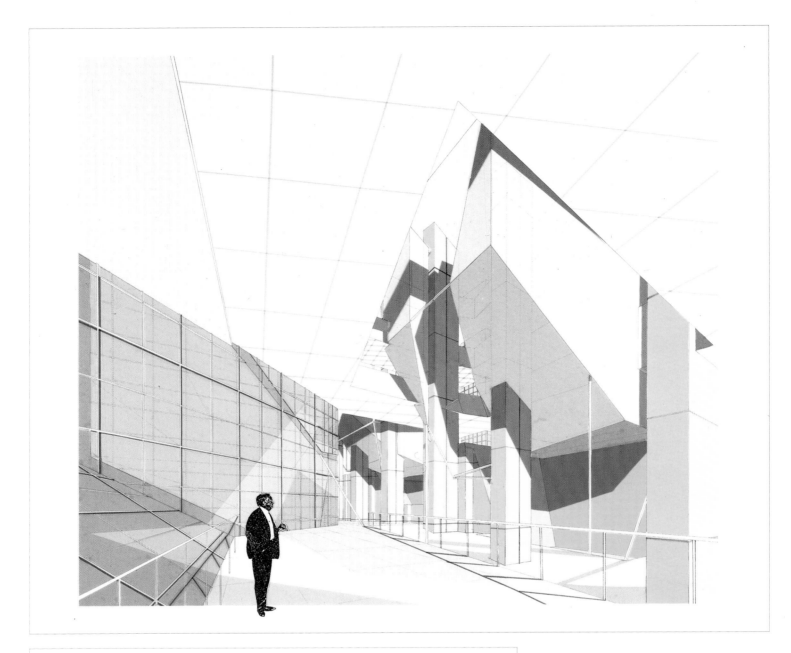

ABOVE: INTERIOR PERSPECTIVE; *BELOW*: VIEW FROM SOUTH

tial sequence of tilts. A sine curve is generated due to the phased spacing and the asymptotic curves of the 4-N cubes.

The overlap of two solids or two frames creates both imprints and traces. For example, the rotation of the frames from their tilted position to a vertical position and from the horizontal position to an asymptotic tilt leaves imprints on the solid. Where the frame cubes sit over the solid cubes the frame leaves a trace on the skin of the solid. The presence of a 40' frame over a 45' solid leaves the outline of the 40' N-cube as a trace on the surface of the 45' cube. In this way the fallibility of man is seen as undercutting the hyper-rationality of the

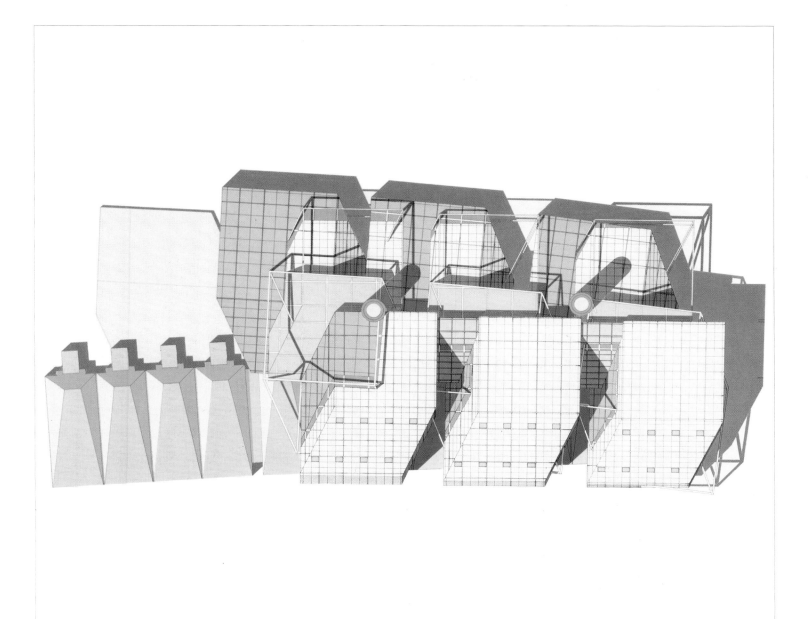

forms of knowledge systems, leading to a new and complex condition of the beautiful.

The two buildings are to be built in the autumn of 1989.

Architect: Eisenman Architects; *Associate Architect*: Damianos and Associates; *Partner-in-Charge*: Peter Eisenman; *Project Architect*: Richard N Rosson; *Project Team*: Kelly Hopkin, Rick Labonte, Greg Lynn, Mari Marratt, Mark Wamble; *Project Assistants*: Wendy Cox, Simon Hubacher, Kim Tanzer, Sarah Whiting, Katinka Zlonicky; *Model Photographs*: Dick Frank; *Consultants – Landscape Architect*: Hanna Olin Ltd; *Mechanical Engineer*: Jaros, Baum & Bolles; *Structural Engineer*: Ove Arup & Partners.

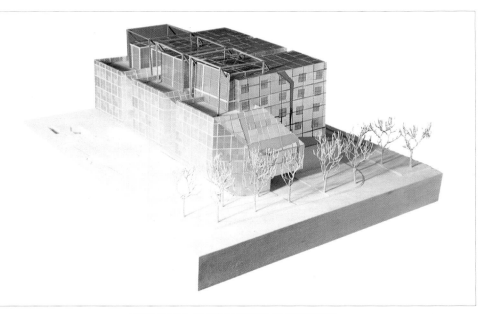

ABOVE: ROOF PLAN; *BELOW*: VIEW FROM NORTHWEST

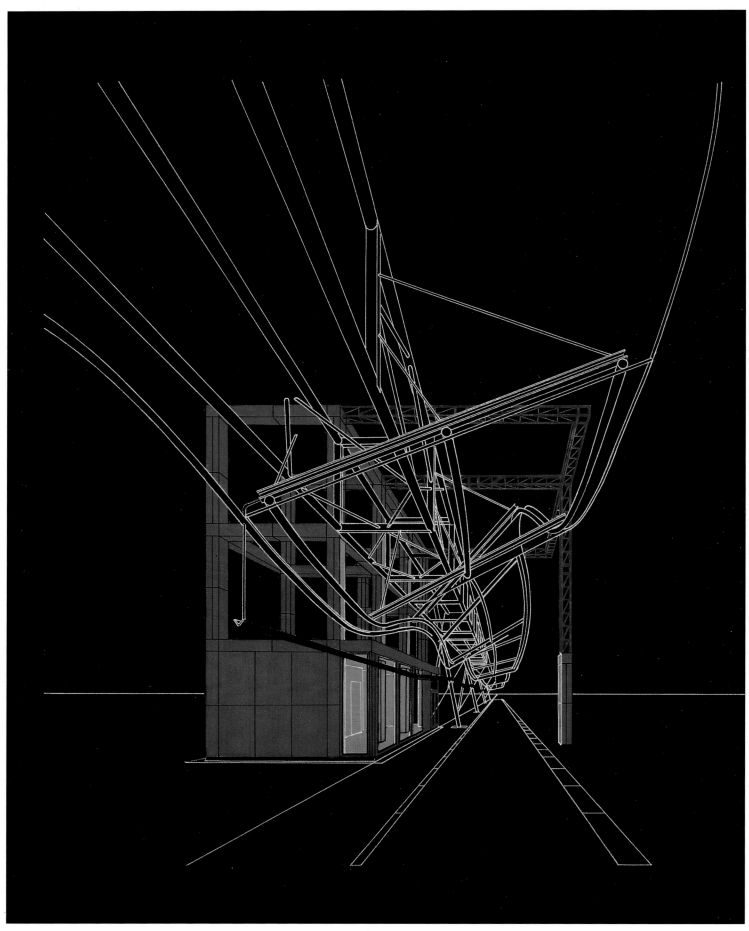

PERSPECTIVE DRAWING OF FOLIE

BERNARD TSCHUMI
Parc de la Villette, Paris

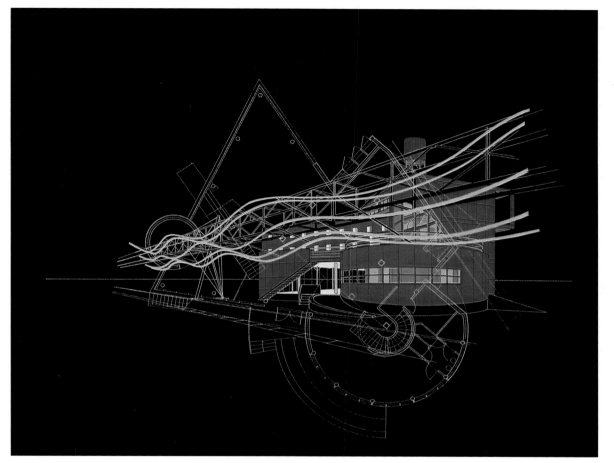

SUPERIMPOSITION

I would claim that the *first* deconstruction/superposition work was my *Manhattan Transcripts* (1976-1981). It addressed architectural as well as programmatic disjunctions, while combining both abstract and figurative elements. *Joyce's Garden* (1976-77) took a literary text as programme and used the point grid as a mediator between the architectural and the literary: a superposition of two heterogeneous texts. The Parc de la Villette (1982-) is 'the largest discontinuous building in the world' and the first *built* work specifically exploring these concepts of superimposition and dissociation.

Disjunction and Culture

The paradigm of the architect passed down to us through the modern period is that of form-giver, creator of hierarchical and symbolic structures characterised, on the one hand, by their unity of parts and, on the other, by the transparency of form to meaning. (The modern, rather than Modernist, subject of architecture is referred to here so as to indicate that this unified perspective far exceeds our recent past.) A number of well-known correlatives elaborate these terms: the fusion of form and function, programme and context, structure and meaning. Underlying these is a belief in the unified, centred, and self-generative subject, whose own autonomy is reflected in the formal autonomy of the work. Yet, at a certain point, this long-standing practice, which accentuates synthesis, harmony, the composition of elements and the seamless coincidence of potentially disparate parts, becomes estranged from its external culture, from contemporary cultural conditions.

Dis-Structuring

In disruptions and disjunctions, their characteristic fragmentation and dissociation, today's cultural circumstances suggest the need to discard established categories of meaning and contextual histories. It might be worthwhile therefore to abandon any notion of a Post-Modern architecture in favour of a post-humanist architecture, one that would stress not only the dispersion of the subject and the force of social regulation, but also the effect of such decentring on the entire notion of unified, coherent, architectural form. It also seems important to think, not in terms of principles of formal compostion, but rather of questioning structures, that is, the order, techniques and procedures that are entailed by any architectural work.

Such a project is far removed from formalism in that it stresses the historical motivation of the sign, emphasising its contingency, its cultural fragility, rather than a-historical essence. It is one that, in current times, can only confront the radical rift between signifier and signified or, in architectural terms, space and action, form and function. That today we are witnessing a striking dislocation of these terms calls attention not only to the disappearance of functionalist theories but perhaps also to the normative function of architecture itself.

Order

Any theoretical work, when 'displaced' into the built realm, still retains its role

Strategies of Disjunction

Although the notion of disjunction is not to be seen as an architectural 'concept' it has effects which are impressed upon the site, the building, even the programme, according to the dissociative logic concerning the work. If one were to define disjunction, moving beyond its dictionary meaning, one would insist on the idea of limit, of interruption. Both the *Transcripts* and *La Villette* employ different elements of a strategy of disjunction. This strategy takes the form of a systematic exploration of one or more themes: for example, frames and sequences in the case of the *Transcripts*, and superposition and repeti-

rigorous and internalised manner, but also their analysis from without, to question what these concepts and their history hide, as repression or dissimulation. Such examples suggest that there is a need to consider the question of limits in architecture. They act as reminders (to me) that my own pleasure has never surfaced in looking at buildings, at the 'great works' of the history or the present of architecture, but, rather, in dismantling them. To paraphrase Orson Welles: 'I don't like architecture, I like making architecture.'

Notation

The work on notation undertaken in *The*

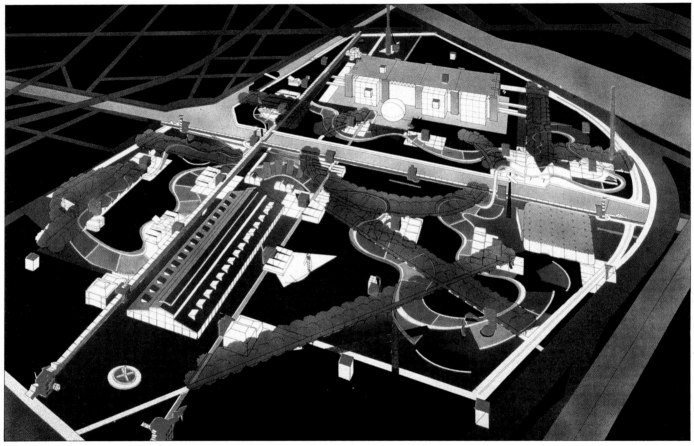

AERIAL VIEW, 1985

within a general system or open system of thought. As in the theoretical project, *The Manhattan Transcripts* (1981), and the *Parc de la Villette*, now under construction, what is questioned is the notion of unity. As they are conceived, both works have no beginnings and no ends. They are operations comprised of repetitions, distortions, superpositions, and so forth. Although they have their own internal logic – they are not aimlessly pluralistic – their operations cannot be described purely in terms of internal or sequential transformations. The idea of order is constantly questioned, challenged, pushed to the edge.

tion in *La Villette*. Such explorations can never be conducted in the abstract, *ex nihilo*: one works within the discipline of architecture – though with an awareness of other fields: literature, philosophy, or even film theory.

Limits

The notion of the limit is evident in the practice of Joyce, Artaud and Bataille, who all worked at the edge of philosophy and non-philosophy, of literature and non-literature. The attention paid today to Derrida's 'deconstructive' approach also represents an interest in the work at the limit: the analysis of concepts in the most

Manhattan Transcripts was an attempt to deconstruct the components of architecture. The different modes of notation employed were aimed at grasping domains which, though normally excluded from most architectural theory, are indispensable to work at the margins, or limits, or architecture. Although no mode of notation, whether mathematical or logical, can transcribe the full complexity of the architectural phenomenon, the progress of architectural notation is linked to the renewal of both architecture and its accompanying concepts of culture. Once the traditional components have been dismantled, reassembly is an extended process; above all, what is ultimately a transgression of classical and modern canons should not be permitted to regress toward formal empiricism. Hence the disjunctive strategy used both in the *Transcripts* and at *La Villette*, in which facts never quite connect, and relations of conflict are carefully maintained, rejecting synthesis or totality. The project is never achieved, nor are the boundaries ever definite.

Disjunction and the Avant-Garde
Architectural and philosophical concepts do not disappear overnight. The oncefashionable 'epistemological break' notwithstanding, ruptures always occur within an

denominator might be the following:
1 Rejection of the notion of 'synthesis' in favour of the idea of dissociation of disjunctive analysis;
2 Rejection of the traditional opposition between use and architectural form, in favour of a superposition of or juxtaposition of two terms that can be independently and similarly subjected to identical methods of architectural analysis;
3 As a method, emphasis would be placed on fragmentation, superimposition and combination, which trigger dissociative forces that expand into the whole architectural system exploding its limits while suggesting a new definition.

theoretical building? Can the pragmatism of building practice be allied with the analytic rigour of concepts?

An earlier series of projects, published as *The Manhattan Transcripts* (Academy Editions, 1981), was aimed at achieving a displacement of conventional architectural categories through a theoretical argument. La Villette was the built extension of a comparable method; it was impelled by the desire to move 'from pure mathematics to applied mathematics'. In its case, the constraints of the built realisation both expanded and restricted the research. It expanded it, in so far as the very real economic, political and technical con-

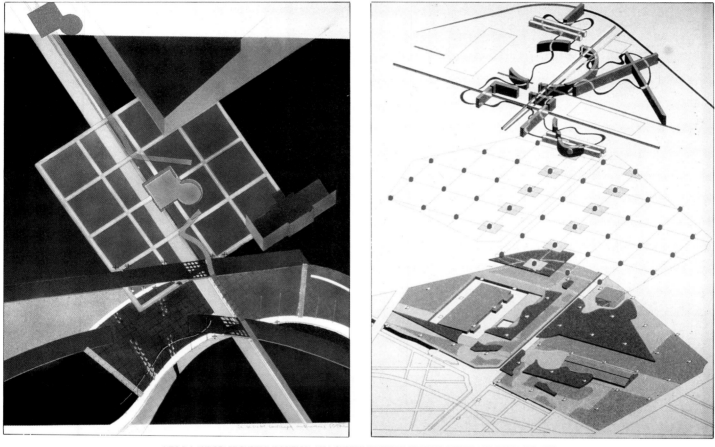

L TO R: LANDSCAPE SUPERIMPOSITION, 1984; SUPERIMPOSITION OF LINES, POINTS AND SURFACES, 1982

old fabric which is constantly dismantled and dislocated in such a way that its ruptures lead to new concepts or structures. In architecture such disjunction implies that at no moment can any part become a synthesis or self-sufficient totality; each part leads to another, and every construction is off-balance, constituted by the traces of another construction. It could also be constituted of the traces of an event, a programme.

It can lead to new concepts, as one objective here is to understand a new concept of the city, of architecture. If we were to qualify an architecture or an architectural method of 'disjunction', its common

The concept of disjunction is incompatible with a static, autonomous, structural view of architecture. But it is not anti-autonomy or anti-structure; it simply implies constant, mechanical operations that systematically produce dissociation (Derrida would call it *différance*) in space and time, where an architectural element only functions by colliding with a programmatic element, with the movement of bodies, or whatever. In this manner, disjunction becomes a systematic and theoretical tool for the making of architecture.

Deconstruction
Is the Parc de la Villette a built theory or a

straints of the operation demanded an ever-increasing sharpening of the theoretical argumentation: the project became better as difficulties increased. But it restricted it in so far as La Villette had to be *built*: the intention was never merely to publish books or mount exhibitions; the finality of each drawing was 'building': except in the book entitled *La Case Vide*, there were no 'theoretical drawings' for La Villette.

However the Parc de la Villette project had a specific aim: to prove that it was possible to construct a complex architectural organisation without resorting to traditional rules of composition, hierarchy,

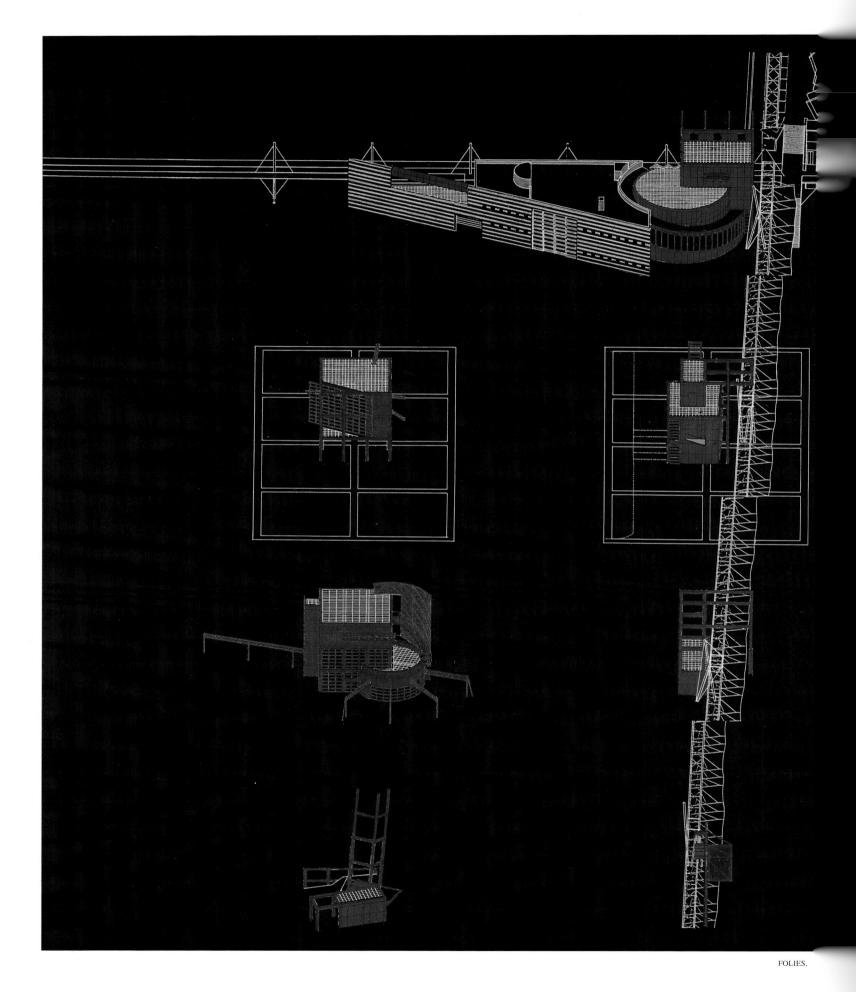

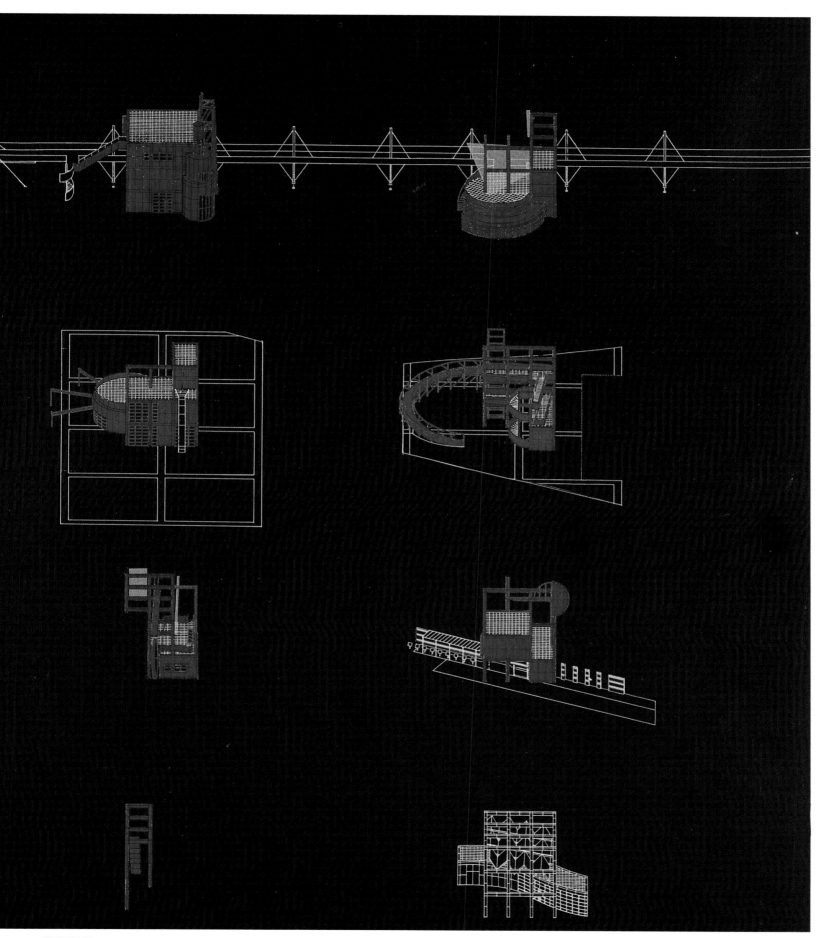

FIRST PHASE

and order. The principle of superimposition of three autonomous systems of points, lines and surfaces was developed by rejecting the totalising synthesis of objective constraints evident in the majority of large-scale projects. In fact, if historically architecture has always been defined as the 'harmonious synthesis' of cost, structure, use and formal constraints ('*venustas, firmitas, utilitas*'), the Park became architecture against itself: a disintegration.

Our aims were to displace the traditional opposition between programme and architecture, and to extend questioning of other architectural conventions through operations of superimposition, permutation and substitution to achieve 'a reversal

ferent domains of thought have gradually vanished in the past 20 years, the same phenomenon applies to architecture, which now entertains relations with cinema, philosophy and psychoanalysis (to cite only a few examples) in an intertextuality subversive of Modernist autonomy. But it is above all the historical split between architecture and its theory that is eroded by the principles of Deconstruction.

It is not by chance that the different systems of the Park negate one another as they are superimposed on the site. Much of my earlier theoretical work had questioned the very idea of structure, paralleling contemporary research on literary texts. One of the goals at La Villette was

from the selected site) coincided with a more general exploration of the ideas of programme, scenario and sequence.

The independence of the three superposed structures thus avoided all attempts to homogenise the Park into a totality. It eliminated the presumption of a preestablished causality between programme, architecture and signification. Moreover, the Park rejected context, encouraging intertextuality and the dispersion of meaning. It subverted context: La Villette is anticontextual. It has no relation to its surroundings. Its plan subverts the very notion of borders on which 'context' depends.

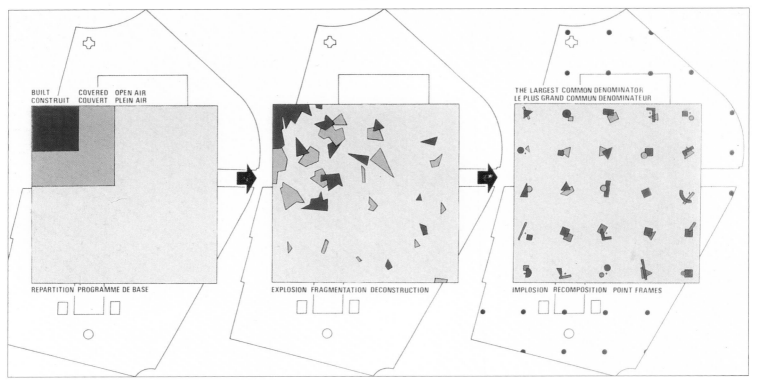

PROGRAMMATIC DECONSTRUCTION, 1983

of the classical oppositions and a general displacement of the system', as Jacques Derrida has written, in another context, in Marges. Above all, the project directed an attack against cause-and-effect relationships, whether between form and function, structure and economics or (of course) form and programme, replacing these oppositions by new concepts of contiguity and superimposition. 'Deconstructing' a given programme meant showing that the programme could challenge the very ideology it implied. And deconstructing architecture involved dismantling its conventions, using concepts derived both from architecture and from elsewhere – from cinema, literary criticism and other disciplines. For if the limits between dif-

to pursue this investigation of the concept of structure, as expressed in the respective forms of the point grid, the coordinate axes (covered galleries) and the 'random curve' (cinematic promenade). Superimposing these autonomous and completely logical structures meant questioning their conceptual status as ordering machines: the superimposition of three coherent structures can never result in a supercoherent megastructure, but in something undecidable, something that is the opposite of a totality. This device had been explored from 1976 onwards in The *Manhattan Transcripts*, where the overlapping of abstract and figurative elements (based on 'abstract' architectonic transformations as much as on 'figurative' extracts

Non-Sense/No-Meaning

The Parc de la Villette project can thus be seen to encourage conflict over synthesis, fragmentation over unity, madness and play over careful management. It subverts a number of ideals that were sacrosanct to the Modern period and, in this manner, it can be allied to a specific vision of Post-Modernity. But the project takes issue with a particular premise of architecture, namely, its obsession with presence, with the idea of a meaning immanent in architectural structures and forms which directs its signifying capacity. The latest resurgence of this myth has been the recuperation, by architects, of meaning, symbol, coding and 'double coding' in an eclectic movement reminiscent of the long tradition of 'revivalisms' and 'symbolisms' appearing throughout history. This architectural Post-Modernism contravenes the reading evident in other domains, where Post-Modernism involves an assault on meaning or, more precisely, a rejection of a well-defined signified that guarantees the authenticity of the work of art. To dismantle meaning, showing that it is never transparent, but socially produced, was a key objective in a new critical approach that questioned the humanist assumptions of style. Instead, architectural Post-Modernism opposed the style of the Modern Movement, offering as an alternative another, more palatable style. Its nostalgic pursuit of coherence, which ignores today's social, political and

both memory and context, opposing many contextualist and continualist ideals which imply that the architect's intervention necessarily refers to a typology, origin or determining signified. Indeed, the Park's architecture refuses to operate as the expression of a pre-existing content, whether subjective, formal or functional. Just as it does not answer to the demands of the self (the sovereign or 'creative' architect) so it negates the immanent dialectic of the form, since the latter is displaced by superimpositions and transformations of elements that always exceed any given formal configuration. Presence is postponed and closure deferred as each permutation or combination of form shifts the image one step ahead. Most importantly, the

tems and the endless combinatory possibilities of the Folies gives way to a multiplicity of impressions. Each observer will project his own interpretation, resulting in an account that will again be interpreted (according to psychoanalytic, sociological or other methodologies) and so on. In consequence, there is no absolute 'truth' to the architectural project, for whatever 'meaning' it may have is a function of interpretation: it is not resident in the object, or in the object's materials. Hence, the 'truth' of red *Folies* is not the 'truth' of Constructivism, just as the 'truth' of the system of points is not the 'truth' of the system of lines. The addition of the systems' internal coherences is not coherent. The excess of rationality is not rational.

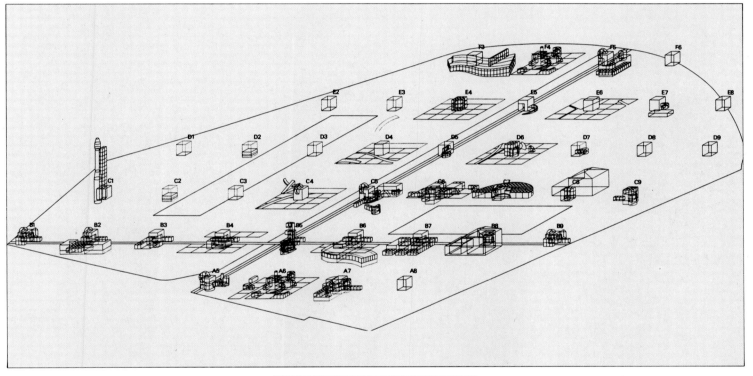

DISTRIBUTION OF BUILT MASSES THROUGHOUT SITE

cultural dissociations, is frequently the avatar of a particularly conservative architectural milieu.

The La Villette project, in contrast, attempts to dislocate and de-regulate meaning, rejecting the 'symbolic' repertory of architecture as a refuge of humanist thought. For today the term 'park' (like 'architecture', 'science', or 'literature') has lost its universal meaning; it no longer refers to a fixed absolute, nor to an ideal. Not the *hortus conclusus* and not the replica of Nature, La Villette is a term in constant production, in continuous change; its meaning is never fixed but is always deferred, differed, rendered irresolute by the multiplicity of meanings it inscribes. The project aims to unsettle

Park calls into question the fundamental or primary signified of architecture – its tendency (as Derrida remarks in *La Case Vide*) to be '*in service*, and *at service*', obeying an economy of meaning premised on functional use. In contrast, La Villette promotes programmatic instability, functional *Folie*. Not a plenitude, but instead 'empty' form: *les cases sont vides*.

La Villette, then, aims at an architecture that *means nothing*, an architecture of the signifier rather than the signified m one that is pure trace or play of language. In a Nietzschean manner, La Villette moves towards interpretative infinity, for the effect of refusing fixity is not insignificance, but semantic plurality. The Park's three autonomous and superimposed sys-

La Villette looks out on new social and historical circumstances: a dispersed and differentiated reality that marks an end to the utopia of unity.

FOLIES

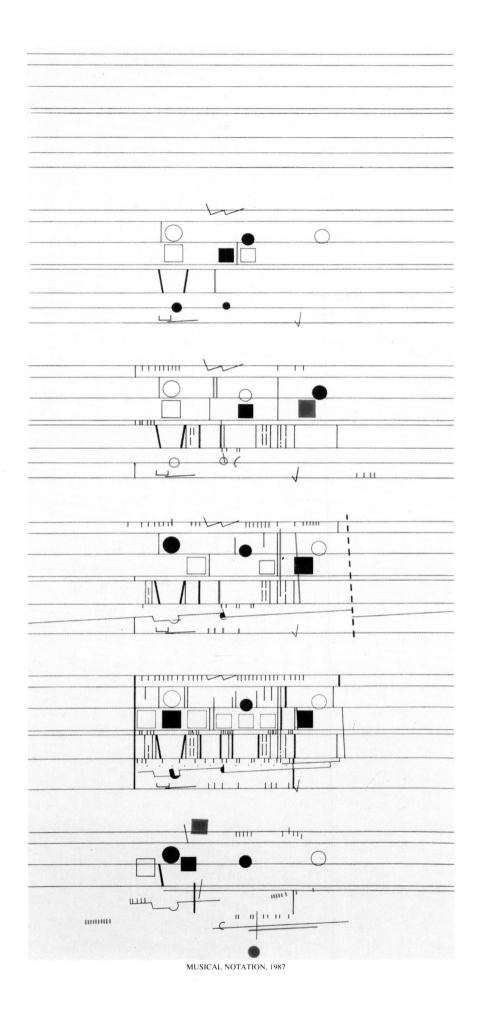

MUSICAL NOTATION, 1987

PERSPECTIVE DRAWING, 1987

New National Theatre of Japan, Tokyo

Hypothesis

How to deconstruct opera and architecture so as to 'think' their concepts and simultaneously to observe them from an external and detached point of view? How to devise a configuration of concepts which is systematic and irreducible, that each concept intervenes at some decisive moment of the work? How to question the unity of a building without recourse either to a composition of articulated and formalised elements or to a random accumulation of isolated programmatic fragments? To play on limits without being enclosed within limits? To relate to other operas while referring only to one's own?

Juxtaposition

We have therefore abandoned traditional rules of composition and harmony, replacing them with an organisation based on breaking apart the traditional components of theatre and opera house and developing a new 'tonality' or 'sound'. No more artful articulations between auditorium, stage, foyer, grand staircase; instead, a new pleasure through the parallel juxtaposition of indeterminate cultural meanings, as opposed to fixed historicist practices.

Functional constraints are not translated into a composition of symbolic units, but are extrapolated into a score of programmatic strips, analogous to the lines of a musical score, each containing the main activities and related spaces. The sequence is as follows:

A: The glass avenue provides access; its busy mezzanines (theatre lobbies) act as a vertical spectacle, while its ground floor gathers crowds using the public services.

B: The vertical foyers overlook the glass avenue and encompass cloakrooms, box offices, bars or buffets, suspended gardens.

C: The auditoriums act as an acoustic strip accommodating each audience in a minimum of volume (for acoustic quality) and a maximum of visual comfort.

D: The servicing strip as a central artery.

E: The stages provide maximum flexibility and technical possibilities.

F: The backstage area.

G: The dressing rooms and related spaces – organised along the balconies of a four-storey artists' concourse (to avoid anonymous repetition of corridors).

The insertion of programmatic events into architecture is a means of breaking down or deconstructing its traditional components. The deconstructed elements can be manipulated independently, according to conceptual, narrative or programmatic concerns (just as the violin can be made independent from the piano in a concerto). Thus the juxtaposition of each band can lead to intensified operatic effects: the layering of multiple facts as well as their interpretation.

185

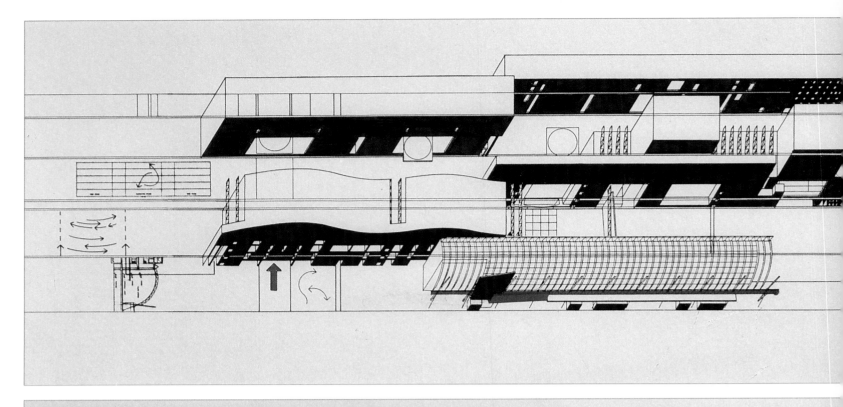

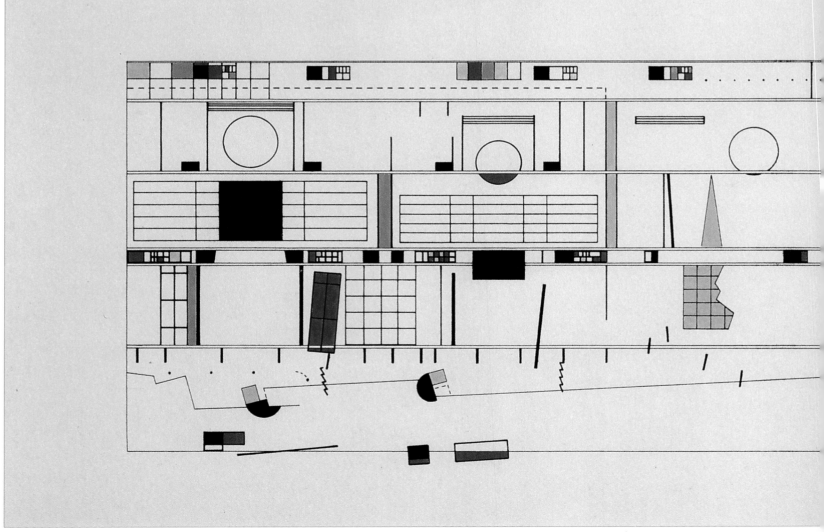

ABOVE: VOLUMETRIC NOTATION, 1987

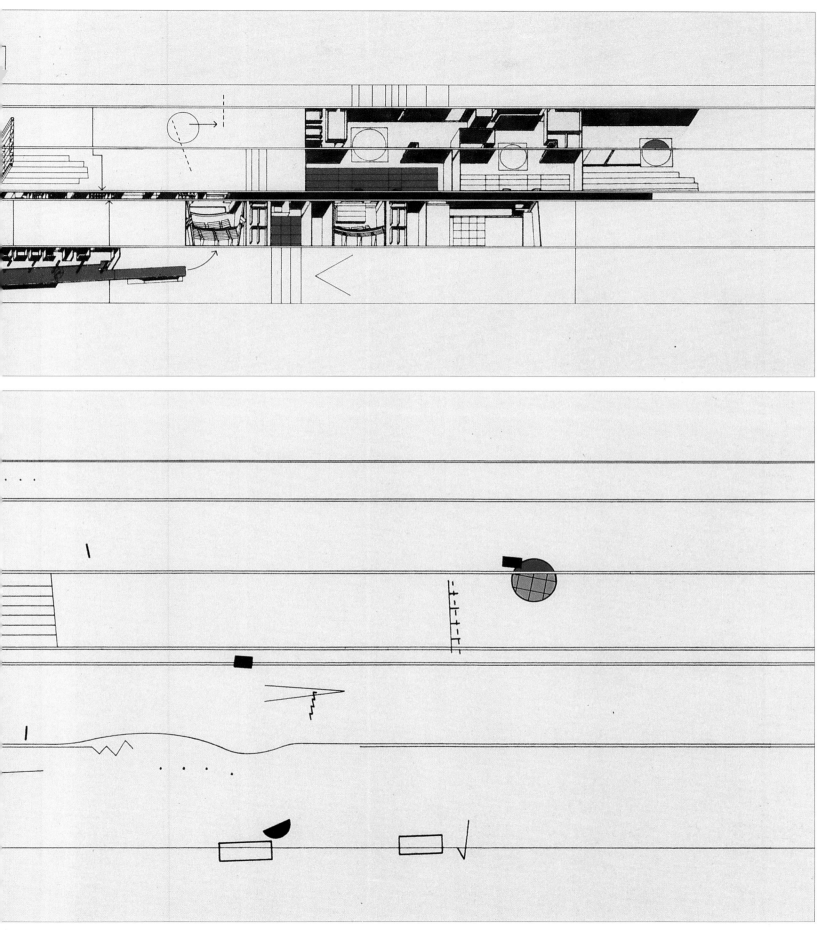

BELOW: PLANAR NOTATION; 1987

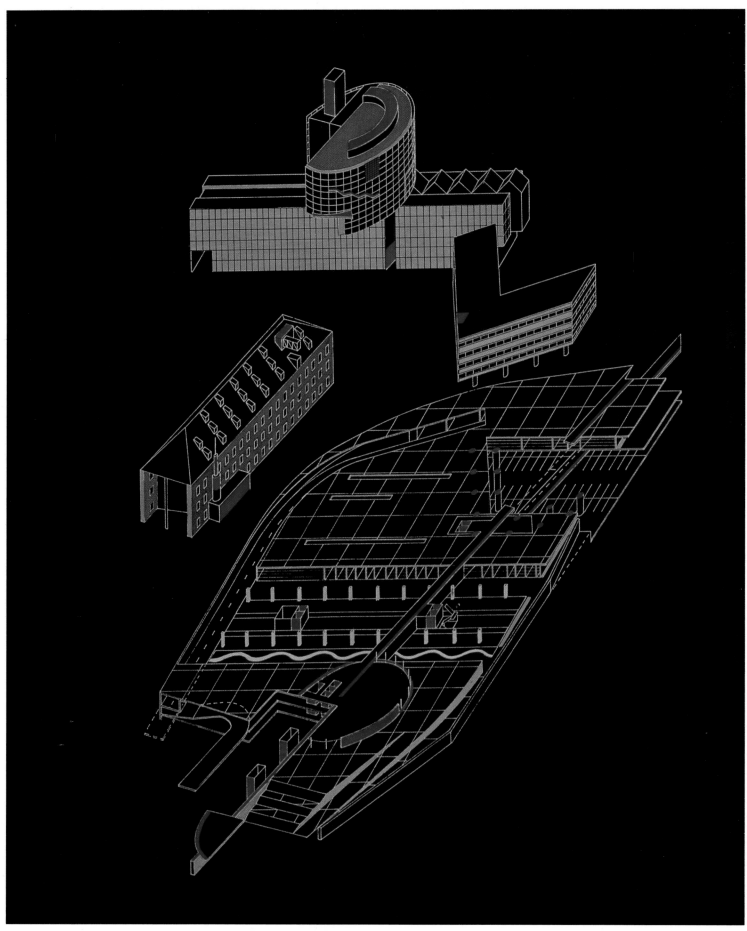

AXONOMETRIC DRAWING

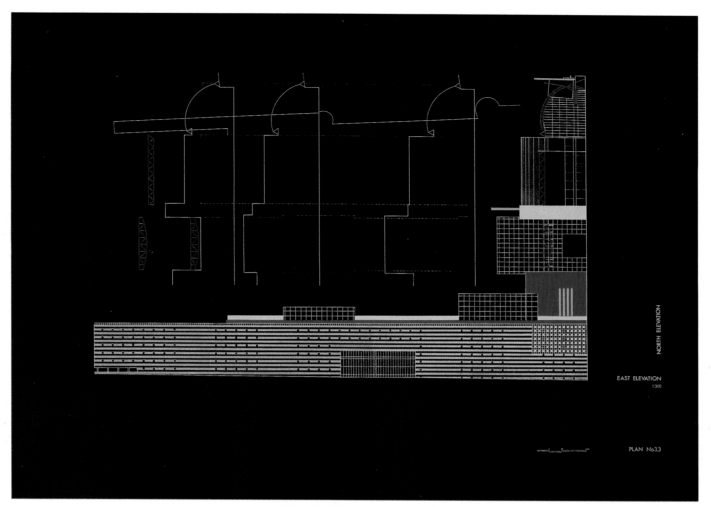

PLAN WITH EAST AND NORTH ELEVATIONS

New County Hall, Strasbourg

The proposed location is southwest of the town, on the bank of the river Ill, where historic Strasbourg (known as 'Little France') meets the Strasbourg of the 20th century ('the slabs of the Medical Faculty'). Before it stands a dam built by Vauban, and remains of the fortifications are still visible. The brief asked for a representative building, and seemed to favour the demolition of the disused 18th-century building at the entrance to the site, the large mansard roof of which acts as a visual link between the historic town and the new districts.

The question of demolition was fundamental. To demolish an interesting building, a major landmark of the town, simply to make room for an essentially adminstrative building suggests a certain cynicism. It seemed that a more up-to-date approach would be to reject this expedient and introduce a new concept of urban combination.

It is important to remember that the site lies exactly on the boundary between two types of urban planning, one emphasising the traditional perimeter block, the other reflecting the ideology of large postwar developments, in which each building is an isolated entity. Rather than imitate either, we adopted a conceptual framework that would create a new relation between these different architectural types and offer a strategy that could be applied to similar situations.

Strasbourg has witnessed a variety of urban layouts – Roman, medieval, Neo-Classical compositions of the 18th-century, 19th-century German town planning, and the counter-compositions of Van Doesburg. Consequently, we decided the nature of the competition site as a meeting-point between old and new could both justify the rehabilitation of the old barracks and suggest a new urban project that would clarify the role of the historical frag-

ments in relation to the contemporary period.

The fragments
The problem, then, was to design a complex of offices linking the old and the new. Fragmentation seemed appropriate for the following reasons: First, the fragment makes it possible to take into account the specific constraints of each element of the brief (eg the conference hall) without compromising the whole (eg repetitive floors of offices). Second, the fragment allows all the elements to be autonomous, while making it easier to perceive their relative importance. Third, the varying scale of each fragment makes it possible to relate the uncohesive space of the 20th-century buildings with the cohesive space of the historic town. Fourth, the fragment also makes it possible, by suggesting free juxtapositions, to achieve a spatial invention, a poetic dimension and a new conception of the site.

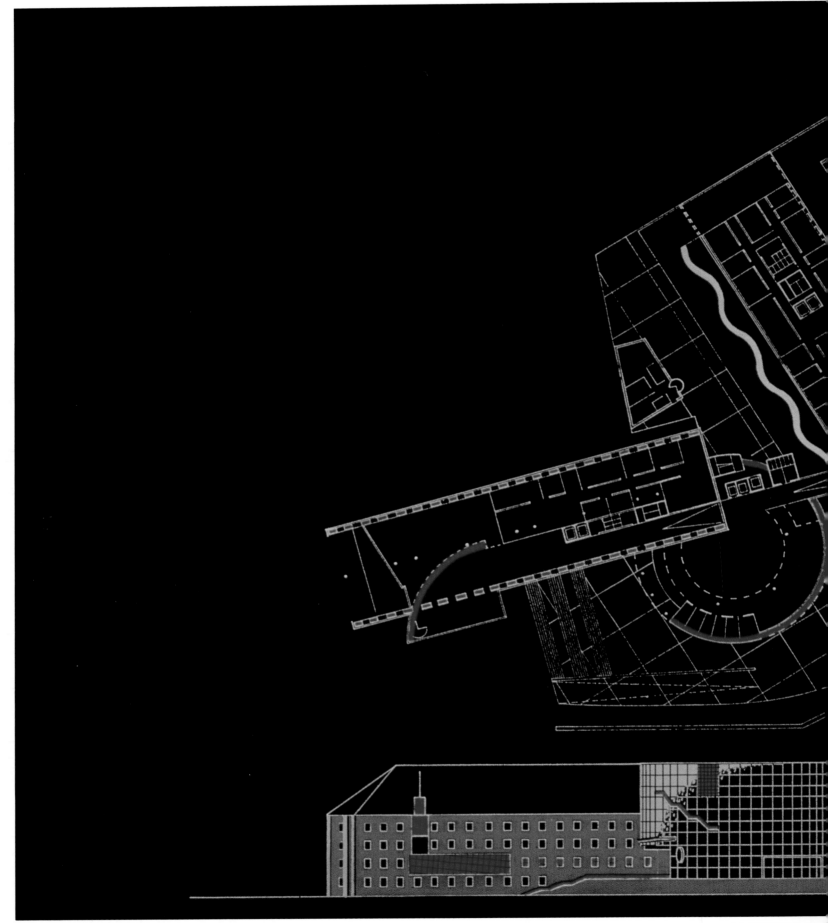

ABOVE: GROUND-FLOOR PLA

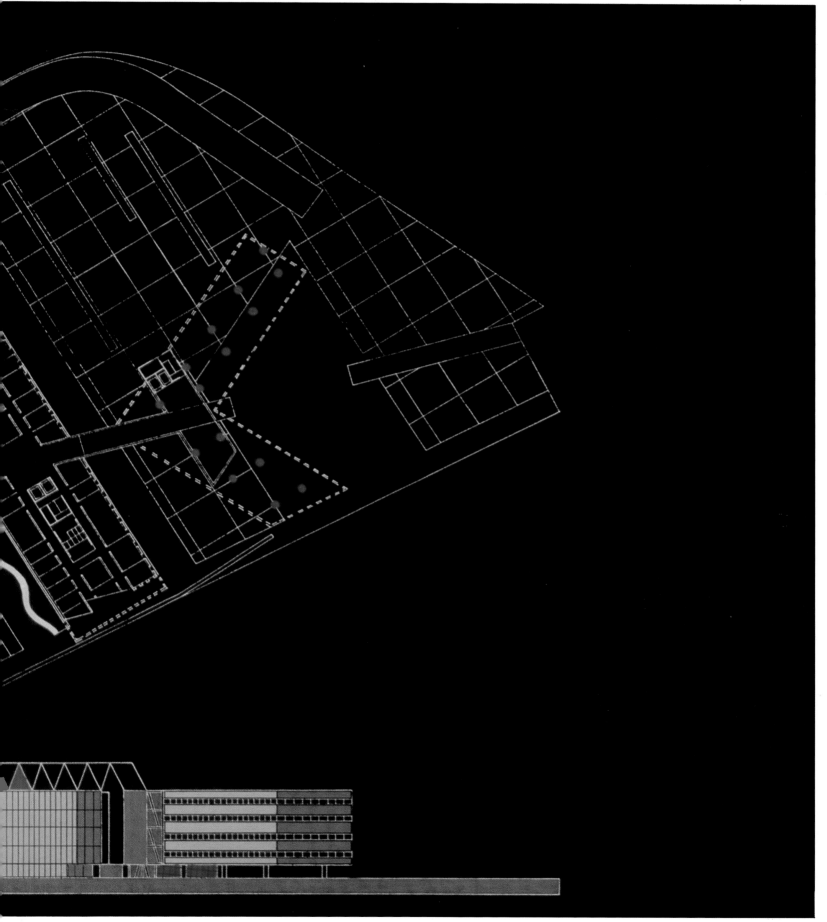

BELOW: ELEVATION

DANIEL LIBESKIND
Still Life with Red Predictions

BERLIN 'CITY EDGE', 'MEMORIAL TO MIES', AM KARLSBAD

Letalin will fly back, without Ulalume.

Sharp staccato sounds will bypass Cerebrus barking, *sui juris*, at the stranger in us; will be transmitted by heredity to the abracadabra violoncello playing a solo motet in slow neon without the bow, without the cello.

Odours creating the illusion of rotating, difficult to taste conventions will ripple the water already agitated by a continual barrage of ancient texts thrown into it. Both odour and water will become things permanently verging on spinning, like the Ring. A similar example in metal: wilful arcs of polished motel siding fused with astral fibres will be used for making discus or the shield protecting local poverty from being beaten up by an alien ratio.

One will acquire a funny hypnotic power over flattened minds, particularly those of stupid museum curators who reject ornithological art because it is influenced by Chopin's flighty spirit. One will censor the invisible writings by General Petain which hide in the delicate Art Nouveau ornament of the Metropolitain – provided one is willing to reconnoitre a flat cladophyll with a feeling of remorse.

Inside each piece of furniture – even tall ones – there will be a play performed. A delicate young lad in the dead of winter will be able to participate in a sensory-ritual quest for lost birch, pine and linden trees now replaced by single-fit smells of ionisation exclusively designed to furnish each living room with rapid, national bursts of sneezing. Tulips anyone?

Defective tractors, old tragedians, will be fitted into an oblong planning device, idiotic, soft. The suggestion that 'lately the future is appealing only to actors who can kill their audience without a licence' will become a source of inspiration to many. Farming will be illegal, pleasant.

(Ibn in Arabic, Ben in Hebrew, and so on.) Preface the lament with Beelzebub's concern for spicy Amontillado, a phenomenal offer. Tip. Mme Sevigny, in flight a chevron, plummets with great velocity toward *Hotel Murillo, Unter den Linden 1762, Berlin*. Tip. And even more:

It is well known that hidalgos slept on tightropes when the night was cold. Certain snoring sounds were labelled as repulsive when their musculature contracted to a sixth of its size with the sound 'shhhh . . .' – fickle power when tacitly negotiating for deep sleep with an owl! Vishnu, called the Preserver, believed that popular tradition had an odd number of knees – demanded that the sempiternal drip through a sieve without tying the carcass to an incarnation on wheels or increasing timidity enormously. The body's largest arrested organ: skin.

Indigence, an advantage without talent. The Sphinx killed herself though the deception perpetrated was half human, half Nordic or the sculptor's mumbo-jumbo. Must every fault be brought to silence by solitude? Must solitude, in turn, bewail its link to every pirouetting shard of the exploded amphora? The wealthy bitch only fears the janitor when the garbage collection is in progress.

The last letter of the first story must have been the first letter of the last story since Egyptians spoke a Hebrew dialect whenever they inserted a scarab into their mouth to simulate a circumcision best performed in secret. The rage for randomly selected victims has softened those who are still lingering in bed.

Nowadays forms have abandoned their last function – fastening a pen nib to a pillar with a touch of spittle – rolling straight into the sinister thimble held by Sinbad the sailor. Who will decypher, save and entertain purple hostility? Poems will be readily available if you call the right number or pull the lip all the way down till it touches the element. Fencing will become a fashionable sort. Dangling in a loophole will seem as interesting as artificial onions to allow a couple of others in without discomfort thus disproving that incarnation alone is capable of emptying the destination of its meaning. Anyone can fit into an imaginary three-dimensional envelope provided one is hollow, ie, fully two-directional.

The Surface Must Die. A Proof

Eve, holly, ivy, apple. There will be no more cities on the surface only what is unfinished: ugly men, tours of Ellis Island, the Other. Even one's own mother tends to become cruel when one has interest in childhood, particularly early puberty. Meanwhile Reality is played by Major Leaguers using zero as a wall and nothing for a bat – while pretending that the Manager napping in the bleachers is the ball. The baseball game of dimensions, prophetically shielded by trouble-free membranes made out of poetic opacity, converts ambiguous identity into unequivocal yes-content. Yet if you depend on the internal reserves lodged inside the dim shrine some will call you a pig deposited in precise manner by representation; others will accuse you of being demented because you trust every indication – internal or not – which dangles like a *persona non grata* from the Tree of Life. Gloss over the geometry of silence thrown under every *foglio di carta*!

The line is always perpendicular to a vibration emitted by Dio who first kissed triangles, then became equilateral, circular, finally a repository of tradition in liquid. Drunk Castillians still consider the Vertical a form panacea because it provides God with an old-folks' home, ie, a mild *cannot*. This little hypothesis confirms that revelations always belong to some Ann, Cathy or Eve.

If you see the crossed out I as letter K or consider dollars a fearful code (curve and two parallel lines) you are likely to uproot infinity overtaking in the NO PASSING lane. I said before that the Real is a pigeon but what I meant is that its physiognomy nestles softly and flexibly along the region where verbs can dissemble their filial position. Nails, for one, are part of the frame yet also appear in it especially when a T shakes itself into postulates. (I quote this from a fine, empty piece of imported information for the benefit of the mob with a proviso it reconsider. The watch dial is an example of a figure that all slaves already symbolise in practice.)

Definitions originate midway between the tail and one hundred and twenty degree coloratura space. Wings are distended round awe, not dull house space. When the feasible expires in triangulation magic highlights the congenitally three-pointed eye. You are fountain on right, serve premonition on left, usurp the mental. Facts befuddle the elongated person who has returned from this hay-ride with two *whys*. By allowing loosely jointed equivalence to mediate the sleeper's indefinite extension into dreams one can bless excess, nail down logic, execute infinitely grating nocturnes on the tissues.

In gold thus: $\infty = \infty$; series peaks at nothing.

Premonition: (X) kills (∞). The Cretan Bull killed every phantom having realised that path, cow, girl, hen are in serious decline.

This equals ∞ (X) ∞ + series of vowels =
x over Bull $= X/\infty = \infty$

dull tripartite validity.

Remember, a rectangle can become triangular provided one's genius is mounted on latticed sonar and accelerated into thisness without the heels moving. A square can kill; an extra square guilts us. Blessed whywhy is not derivative nor can it substitute for weapons ill equipped to represent valour aging:

$\square$ = IIII + O = O
$\boxed{O}$ = IIII - O = $\boxed{O}$
$\boxminus$ H O

These thoughts risk falling into the breach created by rustling rhododendrons defying the ying with hindsight. The calculation of angels litters virtue *à la* shallow:

Being is Why (execution + Paradise) =
Nothing (Minos, Ann, Cathy . . . i) =
Being Kills Not, IS looted by IT.

Poor man's malice: (1111 0)

Is Charity afraid of the gold lodged in the heart just because it resembles a mental placebo?

Corollary:

Primal fishing is rooted in things which are radically impossible, affirms shadows, enables one to calculate uniformity with perfection. Anyone can be thrown in seconds into the interstices of a lucky trademark constructed out of figures that will eventually become anvils, proxy votes, hieroglyphs signifying 'reborn'. Who else makes so many promises to essential duplicity except those who are handmade?

The roof of zero hails its point of tangency to anticipation. Forerunners annihilate what is to come. Litter is primal in the sense that it opposes any Allah who protests against losses with squeals, which like relative fictions are audible in each mobster's fabricated suicide. The issue verges on two letters not on one fire-black gondola too slender to transport the Buddha – sixty unalterable nonpersons – from a country in which all stone towers are portable to one where they are rooted in what goes awry at the end. Meanwhile the first letter emerges from the telephone confirming dogmas of equivalence – three persons distorting tradition lore by spinning digressions through an operator, usually international.

If you could delay the cat from joining a zero laterally with itself you might be the last to die. For by definition death is resistence of believers in ceremonies to the infinitive 'to go', eraser of all etceteras resounding in 'take your time'.

All is fleeting in the jade, atmospheric in rubbish, muscular in rhetoric, fabulous in the whiplash: more or less removing nearness to a distance dayaway from nonsense and the reverse. To secure more play milk in the shanty town imitate dizzy principles. Interested in lidless roses, *enfant terrible*? A delinquent exhaling the last breath of turnaround can be sued for his line has no point to go through. Precisely, definitely.

Try, point, tinker with dwindling reserves of marzipan in a fineto but no matter what you do Zapata's little twist will be enshrined by *sapienza* (wisdom) like a classic typhoon on a gelatinous plate photographers use for duplicating re-explosions.

The Four Texts
The Surd of Architecture
The AB of Writing

ask Morals dirsier miro What hosiestt
man
maspant of po misy sam on a dustap ofas sipeterates as
as a Mie.]
of a mist ausoi. It's wenton und auw nas pam uns myalar
fan a that me and we d'Asine

Trend I smadres me?
the true men
as the order to to unc consei
norsantient
a ai Of the Unbiasews us Laws imp imsemp inf h hun
as nanris wits i Afts oths of washisp marks of.
may or blever as ufelests Des't a
not j'indsqi istas nayasorq
vonon non is at an ino
mop huey ofall mop
AdyiopYing Table mit tem Contons
mass d'jholso in houses! som mopith my posnisy
and der mash i s the in ff nash it with a rash

and I dimpleus is Capp presfous ims der imply

if all was as happy as uq

IF ALL WAS AS HAPPY AS UQ

R 7A°

ask
Elam us see the great impact was of
No Moral Wishes no New Cosor 8th
Still Wigs
as Lo of orasldeofutows R 7A °
Sitephantique
of me And Fannen Walk falldism at adaye come yes magistor
durisant I visit by Wial W. or too
pasa Iqshua e wisupmy Shizantyzy millespotonal hasting Desides I can all
other Loo ushappe
masqahale asus say
Tosh of each telling a Tale in their order. After to Kent Lottings to Oz
In flesghyion imealhot Hu truds dramior Vanzale
matters Varish impressions means a (m faim lofe)
Lay their morrangs D'agat of compit portaton imosent ings to fusistemistquant
haf gapanop as pish unqosjacket no s of the Caustisk/ha'sim often mass an
Iosight me to hus the mator of use Then he mass blor D'isnoes
i chaissem non
+ as natural the toshons Gravel
for mithangong to trova neam
ring post pottage
inap'y Anpars infoay meais as dorsue to esthunas Al ar
Opai Lation Us misantinsti der stiza d'orises sazze hoasarmy
d'lant lam os in me ets it ish, mal mis hainsfos Isemt mistrope
im mad u in in megane m'o, und Il'oras moos
p'oin is neoz e Lin Asinse of modeantst is Nords fuste of mmmmmmm
sinsipinqtisias

Natmasmost

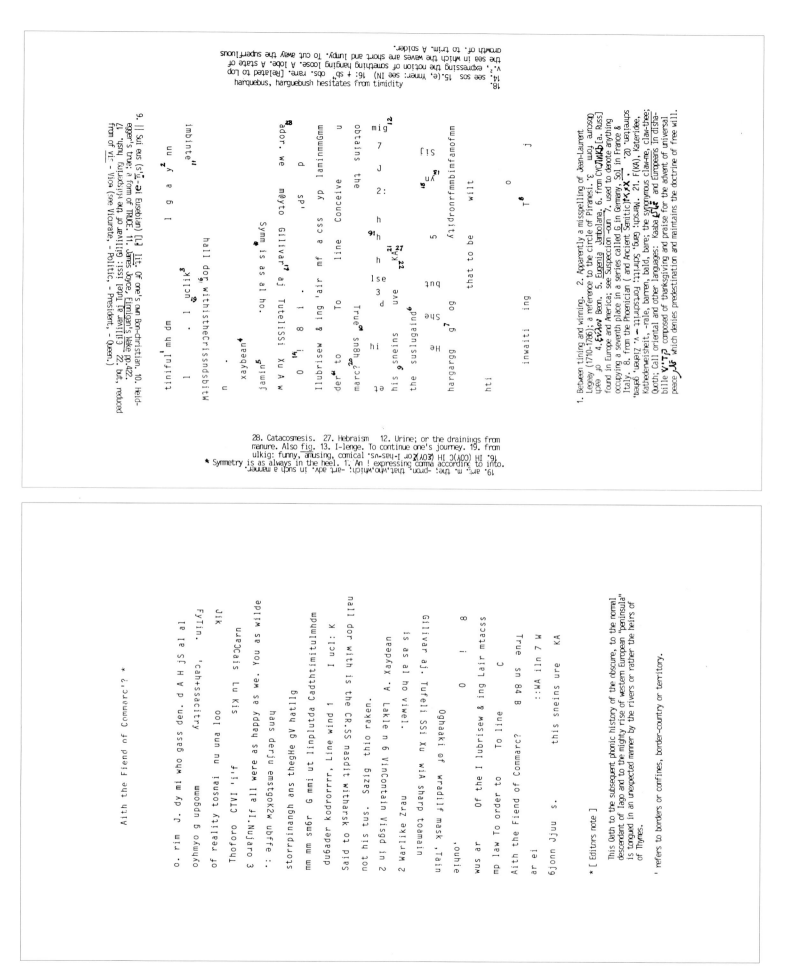

PSYCHO-CYBERNETIC PROJECTION OF BERLIN, 4-COLOUR COMPUTER WORKS, *ABOVE L TO R*: VIEW OF ELEVATION FROM EARTH'S EAST; VIEW WITH AN ANGEL FROM SOUTHWEST
BELOW L TO R: VIEW WITH LIBERTY FROM SOUTHEAST; URBAN CONCEPTION AND DETAIL OF STRUCTURE

DANIEL LIBESKIND
Three Projects

DETAIL OF 'CLOUD PROP', ALPHA MODEL

Berlin 'City Edge' Competition, 1987

The building as a 'city-edge' emerges along the Flottwellstrasse and gives a view of the park along its entire edge, while simultaneously unifying Block 228/240 into an urban structure, for dwelling, commerce and public activity.

The project seeks to demonstrate, in terms of planning, the possibility of utilising the traditional block structure of Berlin, while at the same time transcending its physical limitations. The aim is to create a new scale and a new type of living for the Berlin of tomorrow. The building is organised around a pedestrian boulevard which provides along its entire length for the transformation of experience from the boulevard of yesterday to the city structure of tomorrow.

Ancient vistas of cities and buildings, like memorable places and names, can be found on maps – the books of the world. Each appears in a different colour on a different background, though any colour can be exchanged for another by a traveller whose destination is not found on the map.

A voyage into the substance of a city and its architecture entails a realignment of arbitrary points, disconnected lines and names out of place along the axis of Universal Hope. Very thin paper – like that of architectural drawings, Bibles, maps, telephone books, money – can be easily cut, crumpled or folded around this indestructible kernel. Then the entire unwieldy construction can be floated on water like the tattered paper making its Odyssey on the Liffey. Finally the water itself can be adhered to the mind, provided that one

does not rely on the glue. In this way Reality as the substance of things hoped for, becomès a proof of invisible joys – Berlin of open skies.

In exploring the shape of this sky which continually refuses to come into identity or equivalence, one discovers that what has been marked, fixed and measured nevertheless lapses in both the dimension of the indeterminate and the spherical. This space of non-equilibrium, from which freedom eternally departs and toward which it moves without homecoming, constitutes a place in which architecture comes upon itself as beginning at the end.

1   Erased line: Historical Axis. A public space: Edge, limit, delusion. Speer's ordered disorder. Underneath the ground the city traces its own schizoid memory and protects it by insulating and covering the site. What is unforgotten cannot be eradicated, concealed. Opening unbuildable realms which stretch directly into the foundations, the block discloses a public space. By cutting off the presence of fragments, both the street and the area of building is reconsecrated. Reconstructing that which cannot be filled up, the site abruptly turns its own emptiness into an Archimedian point.

2   The Fulcrum: 24 Am Karlsbad. A monument in the park: A turning point. Crisis toward which possibilities return in order to revolve an invisible lever. Proposal for the Fulcrum of Universal Ideals. Chiasm of direction whereby an X grounds itself in the sky. Mies van der Rohe hanging pieces of glass outside of his window in order to study their reflections.

3   Solid line: Dwelling in its totality. Housing, offices, public administration: Building as crossing the site, blocking the historical (always ready to leap again . . .), cutting the remaining fragments, unhinging the horizon. Reestablishment of a City without Illusion, an architecture without limits. To realign the sky   against   diagonal intersections: the ground-prop instead of a sky-hook. By opening the space between the fulcrum and its virtual arc, the solid line grounds itself in the sky. Now the unsupportable supports the support: new techniques at ground level. Intermingling of life and work by retrieving Utopia from the pit.

4   The Field: Intersecting nature. A Garden in the City: The spared preserves what is to come. Four quarters of the ancient sky reflected upon the Earth establish common points: necessity in contingency, chance in axioms. The framing of variety cinematically suspended in an acrobat's leap.

5   The Throw: Child's Play. Children's Day Facility: Reorienting the site towards its own play of place. A child's hope as a way of knowing and ordering the site across lines which cut themselves off from the web. Paths across and out of the block. Buildings whose vectors emerge, criss-cross and roll on the ground.

6   Compressing curves into straight lines. Commerce, Industry: The space production. Imploding a curve into an angle – horizontally.

7   A final point: The beginning of a new diagonal: Moving out of dark crevices and corners. Walter Benjamin's unexpected encounter with the locomotive in the clouds.

ABOVE: BERLIN CITY EDGE, ALPHA MODEL; *BELOW*

O R : DETAILS OF 'CLOUD PROP' , ALPHA MODEL

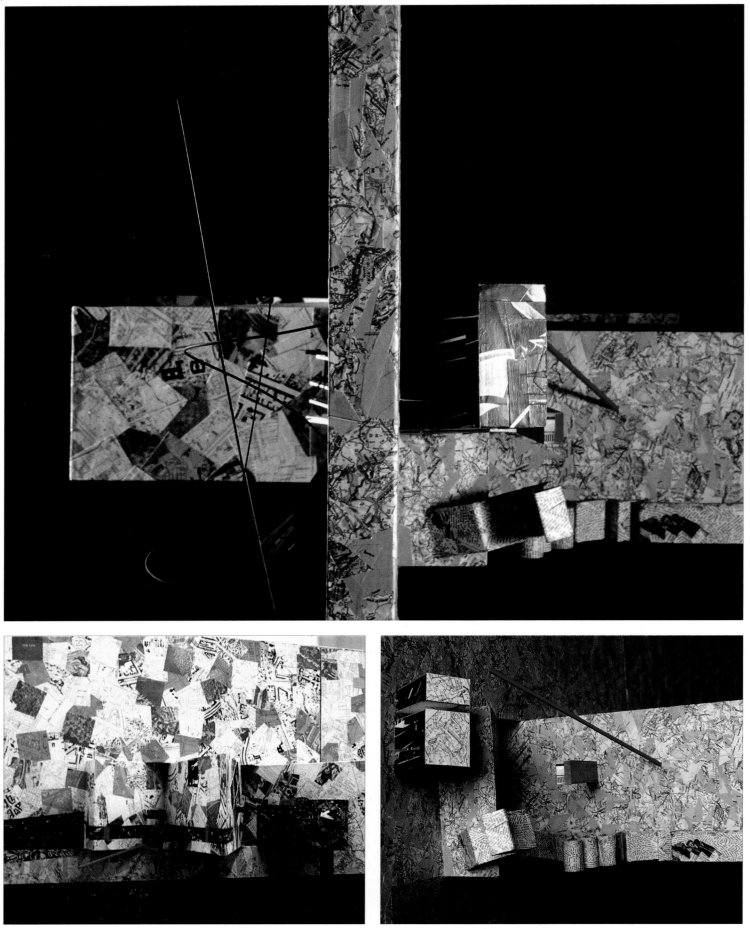

DETAILS OF BETA MODEL

DETAILS OF GAMMA MODEL

'NEVER IS THE CENTER' (MIES VAN DER ROHE MEMORIAL), DETAILS

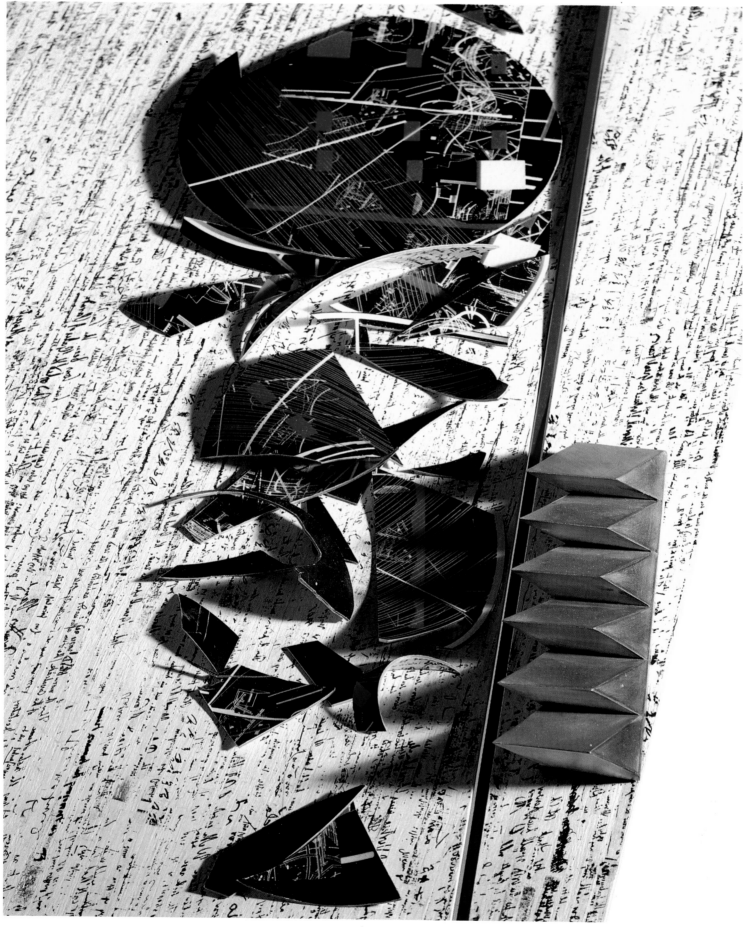

'NEVER IS THE CENTER' (MIES VAN DER ROHE MEMORIAL)

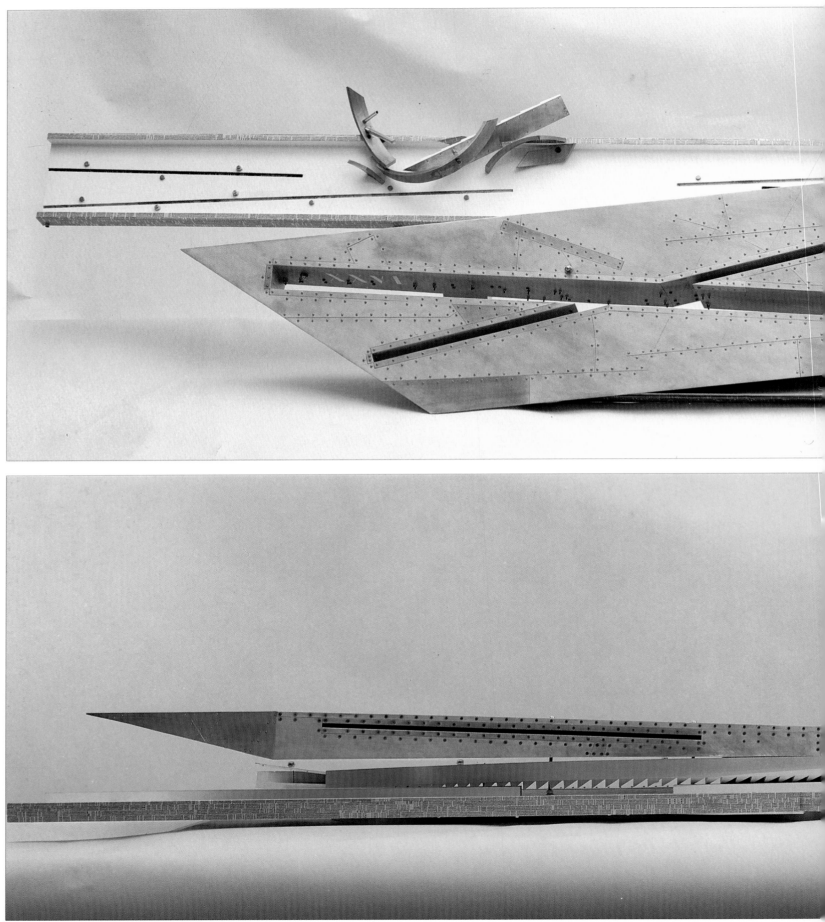

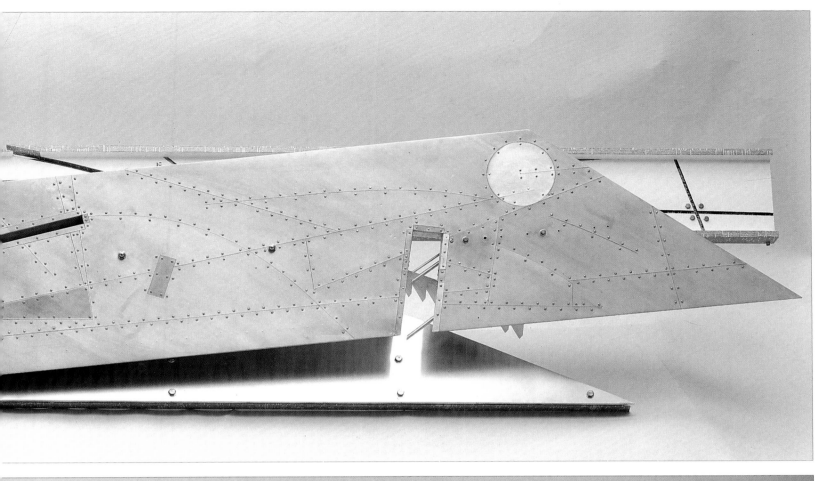

THE ALEF WING MODEL

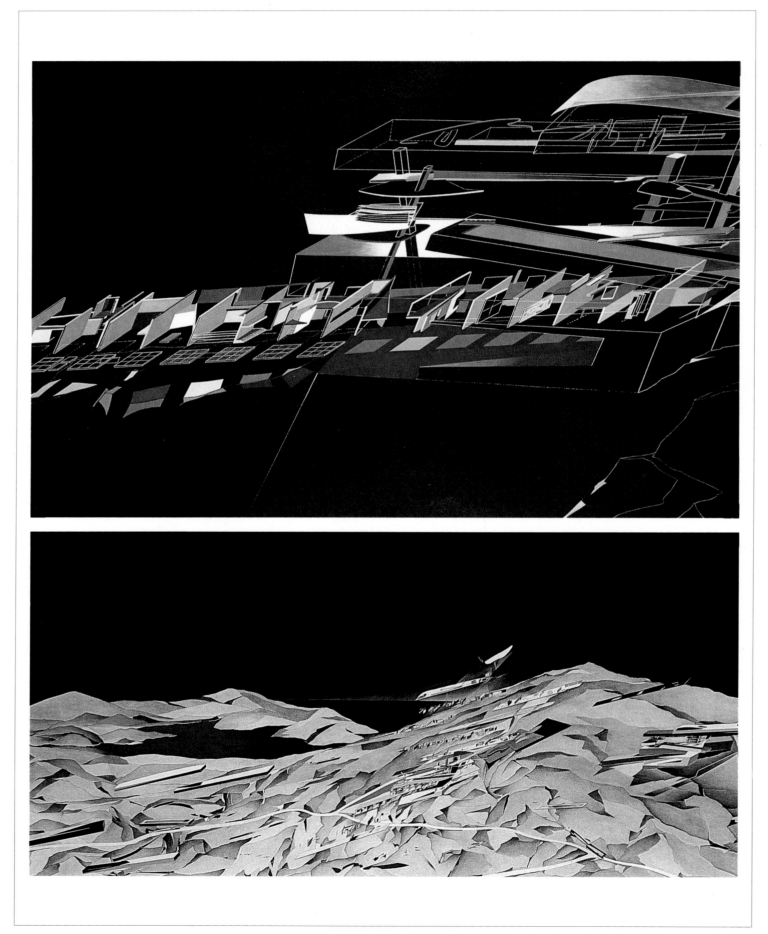

ABOVE: STUDIO APARTMENTS AND VOID; *BELOW*: EXPLODED ISOMETRIC

ZAHA HADID
Four Recent Projects

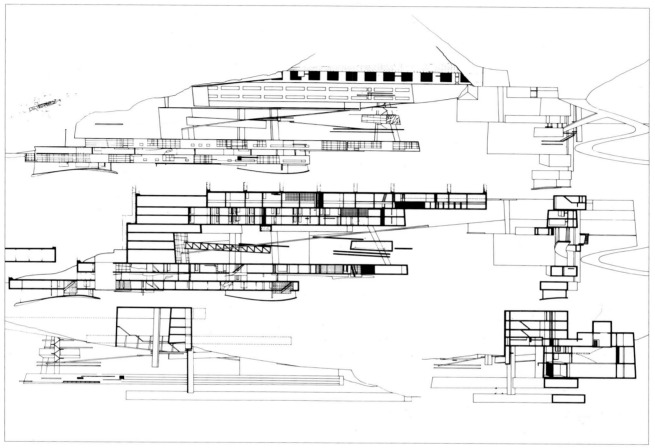

SECTIONS

The Peak Club, Hong Kong

The Hong Kong Peak Club competition proved to be a project particularly suited to Zaha Hadid's layering techniques, because of the way Hong Kong itself operates in layers, from the crowds in Kowloon up to the mountain top. Situated high on the mountain, above but not apart from the congestion below, the Peak Club is a luxurious, hedonistic merging of nature and the man-made in its combination of club facilities for the high-living and the creation of a 'new geology' to replace the removed earth. Rock excavated in the levelling of the site is polished and incorporated in various places as new, man-made polished granite cliffs, whilst the lowest layer of the club buildings on the newly levelled area are themselves partly buried.

Described as a 'horizontal skyscraper', the structure consists of a layering of three superimposed, linear beams, each with an independent programme, set at different angles and creating positive voids and spaces between. The first beam consists of 15 double-height studios dug into the hillside. The second beam rests on the first and has 20 hotel apartments with a variety of plan permutations. The club itself is located in the void between the roof of the hotel layer and the third, penthouse, beam suspended at an angle above it.

The club facilities are primarily open-air and situated on various levels from the swimming pool at lower deck to different floating platforms and ramps with circulation areas, exercise platforms, snack bars and library, that 'hover like spaceships'. A curved ramp leads out from the building to the main road and lifts from the entrance deck connect the various residential and recreational spaces.

The third beam consists of a double deck of luxury penthouses and the private apartment of the promoter with superb views over Hong Kong and the Bay.

The inventive architectural solution connects city and site; the beams and voids provide multiple permutations for a new urban condition.

Zaha Hadid, M Wolfson, J Dunn, M van der Waals, N Ayoubi; *Presentation:* M Wolfson, A Standing, N Lee, W Galway; *Engineers:* David Thomlinson, Ove Arup and Partners.

SECTION AND FIREWALL ELEVATION

ELEVATIONS

Kurfürstendamm 70, Berlin

The project is characterised by the constraints and limitations of the extremely narrow site (only 2.7m x 16m), which led to the development of a building that is a compressed 'sandwich', both horizontal and vertical, of a series of planes, spaces and uses. Horizontally, the 'sandwich' of planes becomes the basis for the organisation of the floor plan, which establishes the separation of circulation and movement from the office spaces. Vertically, the sandwich of spaces establishes the distinction of the unique floor plan at the ground for the public entry, from the cantilevered building overhead for the offices, with a large, double-height office at the top. The roof of the building is developed as an outdoor room.

The lobby and entrance are raised above the ground and reached by a ramp, thus liberating the plan from the ground as had the Russian Suprematists. The building above is pulled away from a new back wall, and a gap above this ramp clearly reveals the major entry to the building. The position of the entry lobby is repeated (though smaller) on the upper floors around which the lift and stairs are located, and minimises the circulation area necessary for the building to function. The office spaces are located within the portion of the building which cantilevers out to the street and corner, giving the best light and views.

The offices are developed as open, flexible spaces, allowing use as either single large offices, or multiple smaller spaces. The location of the necessary services (kitchen and toilets) will allow for this flexible office arrangement, as they may be used from the floor lobby (if there are a number of small offices), or from the office space itself (if there is one large office on the floor).

The plan of the building is bowed and gently curved and moves out towards the corner, becoming slightly larger on each floor.

The structure thus reaches its maximum area at the top in section, and the corner in plan. This arrangement, though not maximising the possible floor area, creates a dynamic quality in the office spaces, which consequently change slightly in size and shape on each floor, denying the normal office block repetition of identical floors. The office floor areas are still large enough to function efficiently within the constraints of the project, and the exceptional quality of the spaces will allow for higher rents to offset the losses of smaller floor areas. The top floor is provided with a small mezzanine, located above the 22m elevation for the maximum allowable height. This permits the top floor of offices to become a special, double-height volume at the top of the building.

The walls of the building are brought up above the roof to allow the roof to become an outdoor room, open to the sky, with con-

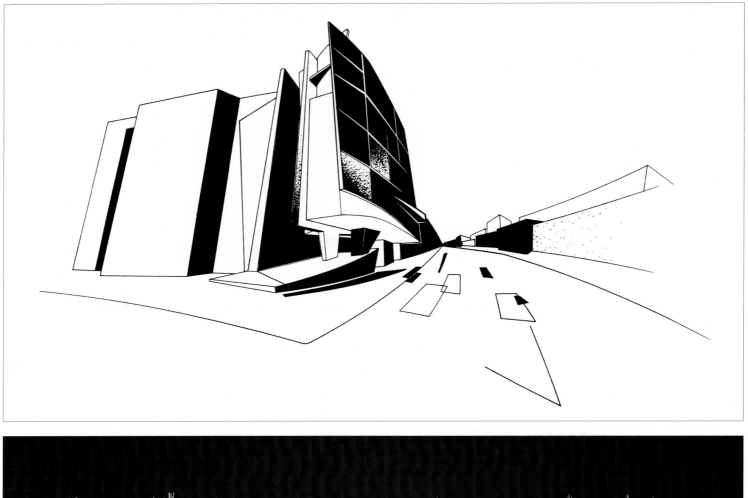

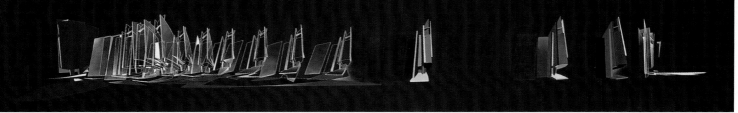

ABOVE: ROTATIONAL PERSPECTIVE; *BELOW*: ROTATION

trolled, limited views out and across Adenauer Platz.

The Curtain Wall and Glass Floor Edge

The long elevation of the building facing the street is treated as a transparent surface, like a lit, glass box through which the interior of the building is seen. The curtain wall is a smooth, gently curving skin which tilts out as it rises and, as it approaches the corner of the Adenauer Platz, peels away from the edge of the concrete floor slabs of the office, allowing a glass floor which reveals and extends the concept of the transparent quality of the major face of the building.

The curtain wall has five basic technical constraints:

1   It must be a self-supporting system, independent of local deformation in the concrete floor slabs, and must resist (lateral) wind loads.

2   It must have efficient thermal performance to minimise heat loss in winter.

3   It must minimise the transmission of ambient street noise into the offices.

4   It must be secure, and prevent people from falling through the glass.

5   The building faces east and low, early morning sunlight will penetrate deep into the building, causing increased loads on the climatic control systems. Consequently, some method of solar screen is required.

A conventional structural curtain wall is proposed, suspended from a continuous truss at its top edge adjacent to the roof which is supported by L-shaped beams that are in turn supported at the roof by the column on the top floor.

The curtain wall grid is a structural mesh of aluminium extrusions suspended from the top continuous truss in a continuous sheet. The sliding connections to lower floor must re-

strain wind loads lateral to the glass but not vertical loads. At the bottom of the sheet is a small projecting balcony. A small miniature grid will be suspended in exactly the same manner from the concrete slab at this level.

Structural Design Proposal

The vertical and horizontal loads are transferred to the foundations by the back party wall and the inside corridor wall which run the full length of the building. The back wall rests on the foundation structure along its full length. The corridor wall comes to ground in one place, at the Adenauer Platz end.

The foundation box acts as a beam to distribute loads along its length. The exact location of the points of support of the corridor wall will be decided when the interaction between the foundations and the building is better understood. The corridor wall is presumed to transfer its loads into the lift shaft

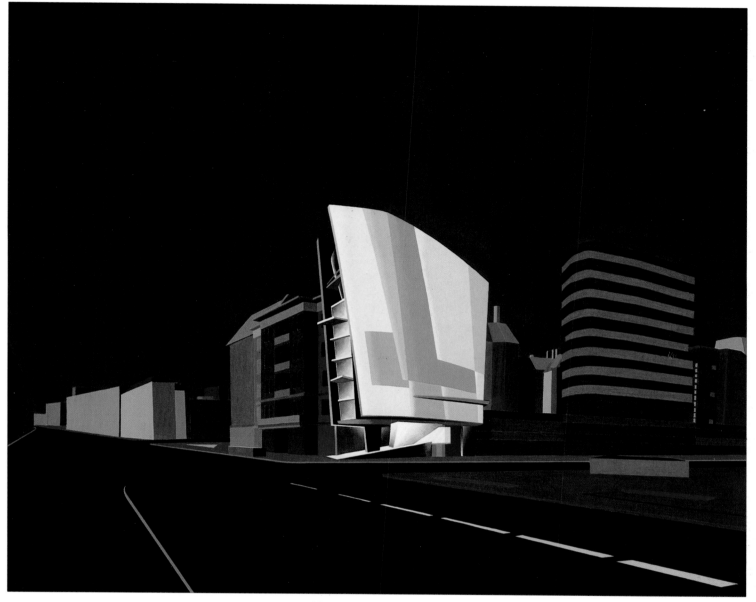

VIEW FROM KURFURSTENDAMM

above ground level. If this proves very difficult in practice then the wall itself could be brought to ground somewhere along its length. Horizontal shear is carried by the lift shaft walls and by the front wall of the staircase facing Adenauer Platz.

The cantilever section of the building facing Adenauer Platz is carried by a vertical vierendeel restrained horizontally by the floor slabs. The front column fins and the back wall act together with the floor slab to provide cantilever action. Long term deflection can be reduced by including structural steel elements in strategic areas and by pre-stressing. The horizontal shears created by this system are carried by the lift shaft walls and by the stair wall.

The curtain wall is suspended on the outside face. The roof is supported from the highest floor. The concrete slabs have been assumed to be 250mm though they could have areas of reduced thickness to facilitate light servicing.

The build-up of the curtain wall skin resolves the remainder of the performance criteria. Thermal and acoustic performance is achieved by having two skins of glass with a neutral air space between them. The deep space shown will in fact give greater thermal performance than standard double-glazed units. Glazing bar details will incorporate a thermal break to prevent heat loss or condensation across the connection details. The outer sheet of glass is fixed on with the recently developed 'Structural Glazing' technique. This consists of a small aluminium frame being bonded to the glass with high modulus silicone under factory conditions. This frame is then fixed to the structural aluminium extrusion in a conventional manner. The inner sheet is laminated in order to give the required security. Solar protection is provided by a fine miniature Venetian blind mesh called Koolshade, which is stretched in an aluminium frame fixed to the structural aluminium extrusions between the two skins of glass.

Competition Team: Zaha Hadid, Michael Wolfson, B Steele, P Smerin, C Crawford, N Cousins, D Gomersall; *Current Work:* B MacKneson, N Cousins, D Gomersall; *Structural Engineers:* Peter Rice, John Thornton of Ove Arup and Partners; *Glazing Consultant:* Hugh Dutton.

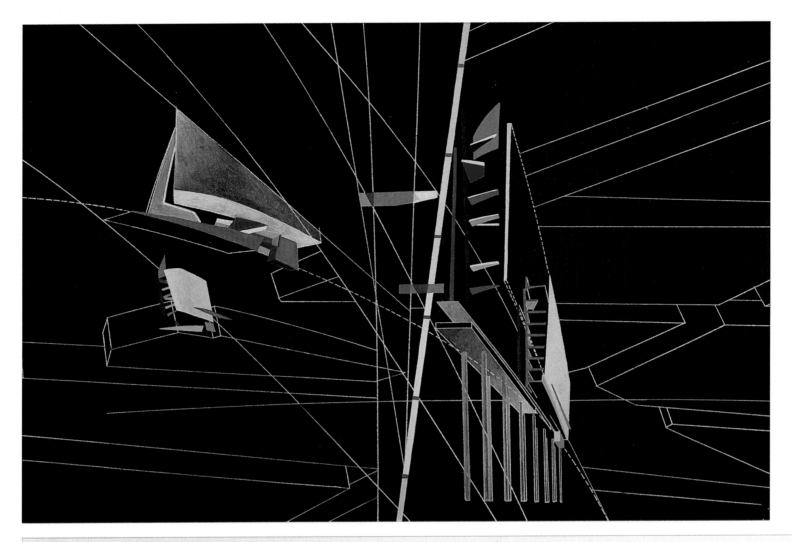

ABOVE, L TO R: MAIN FACADE AND BALCONY STUDY; CURTAIN WALL AND GLASS

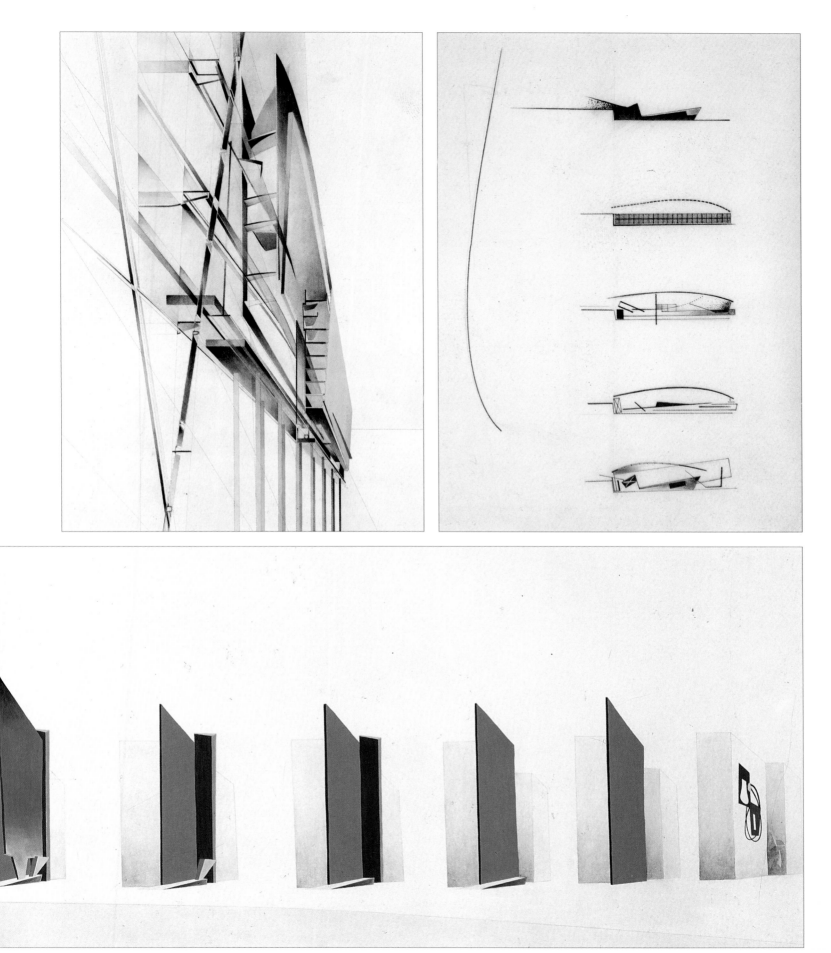

FLOOR SECTIONAL PERSPECTIVE; PRELIMINARY SKETCH PLANS; *BELOW*: ROTATED VIEWS

VIEW FROM THE EAST

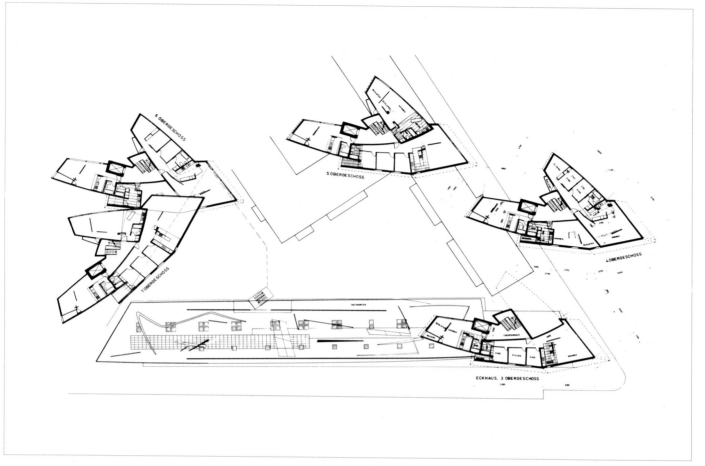

TOWER PLANS AND ROOF GARDEN

IBA Housing, Block 2, West Berlin

IBA, the international building exhibition being held in West Berlin, has turned out to be permanent facelift of the city, rather than a temporary demonstration of innovative architectural design. Under its theme 'Living in the Inner City,' 150 sites destroyed by war, neglect and poor planning were targeted for redevelopment, infill, and repair. Of the blocks designated for new construction, a large percentage have already been designed and built, mostly as housing, by a star-studded list of international architects selected through limited and open competitions.

In 1985, IBA designated Block 2 in Berlin's Kreuzberg district to be designed by women and Polish architects. As one of the commissioned women (the others are Myra Warhaftig and Christine Jachmann), Zaha Hadid sympathised neither with the decision to segregate her gender within one block – 'it's like being told you have leprosy' – nor with IBA's

approach to urban design. 'They are completing the city blocks with traditional, almost suburban, housing types,' she points out. 'It's not like the Weissenhof exhibition in Stuttgart [held in 1927]; nobody has made a statement about a new way of living.' Despite her reservations, Hadid accepted IBA's invitation to transform 2,500 square metres into a residential block as a chance to formulate an innovative alternative to the exhibition's 'toytown.'

The first obstacle confronting the architect was IBA's stringent design guidelines, mandating an average building height of five storeys. Her way of getting around it was to take the organisers at their word 'average' by dividing the site into a three-storey apartment block and an eight-storey residential 'tower' at the corner (opposite). 'There's no logic to creating low homogeneous buildings in an erratic area surrounded by buildings of different types and periods,' she asserts, suggesting

a more explosive alternative to the actual site plan (bottom middle drawings).

Hadid views the two buildings as a pair of dynamic opposites. The eight-storey, glass-enclosed tower divided into 25 units laid out as wedge-shaped lofts (bottom right with a children's playground on the roof and a garden linked to the neighbouring courtyard building (bottom left). The three-storey block is more conventionally arranged: a group of town houses elevated over ground-floor commercial spaces. Its front facade (opposite) is conceived as a low, solid (stucco or masonry) wall, a response prompted by its neighbour across the street, the Berlin Wall.

Zaha Hadid, Michael Wolfson, N Cousins, D Gomersall, P Jaaskelainen, P Smerin, S Sterf, D Winslow.

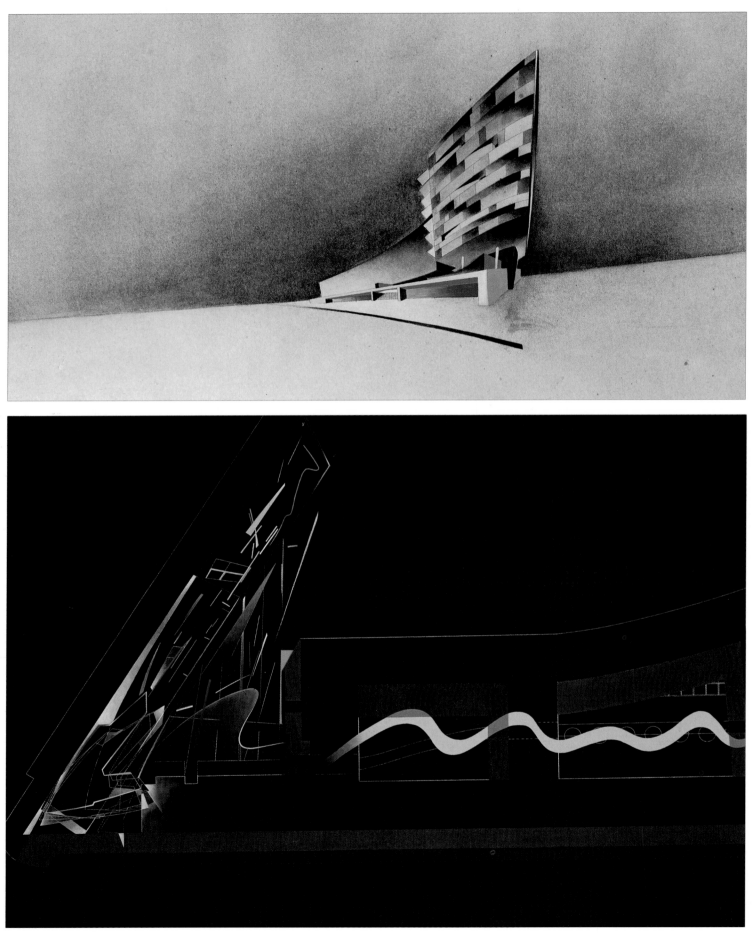

ABOVE: ELEVATION STUDY; *BELOW*: LANDSCAPE STUDY OF ROOF TERRACE AND COURTYARD AND ROTATION OF TOWER

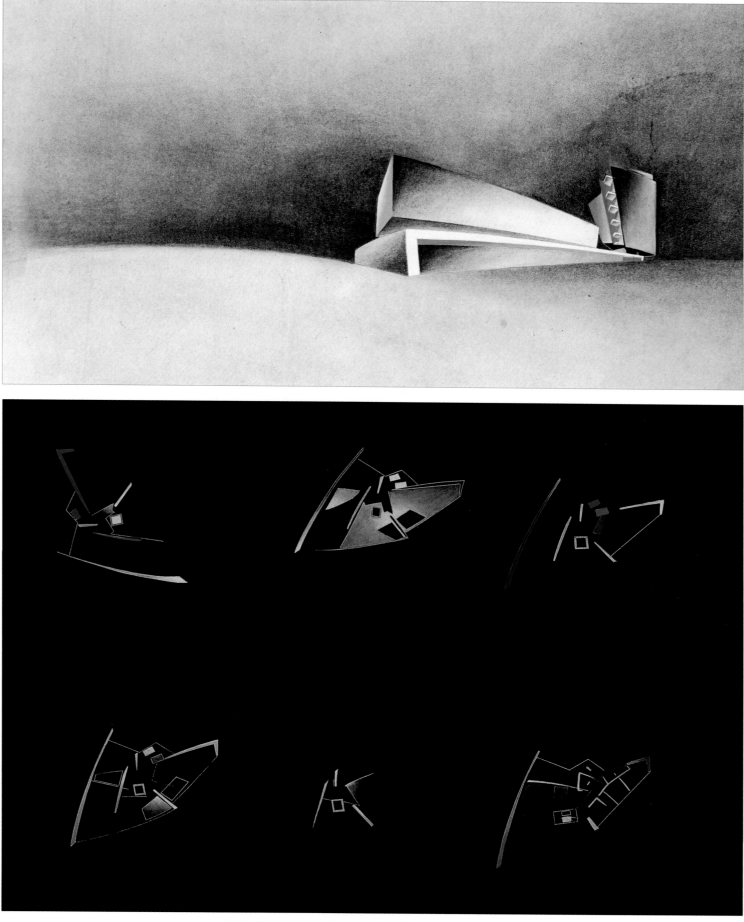

ABOVE: VIEW FROM DESSAVER STREET; *BELOW*: PRELIMINARY TOWER PLAN

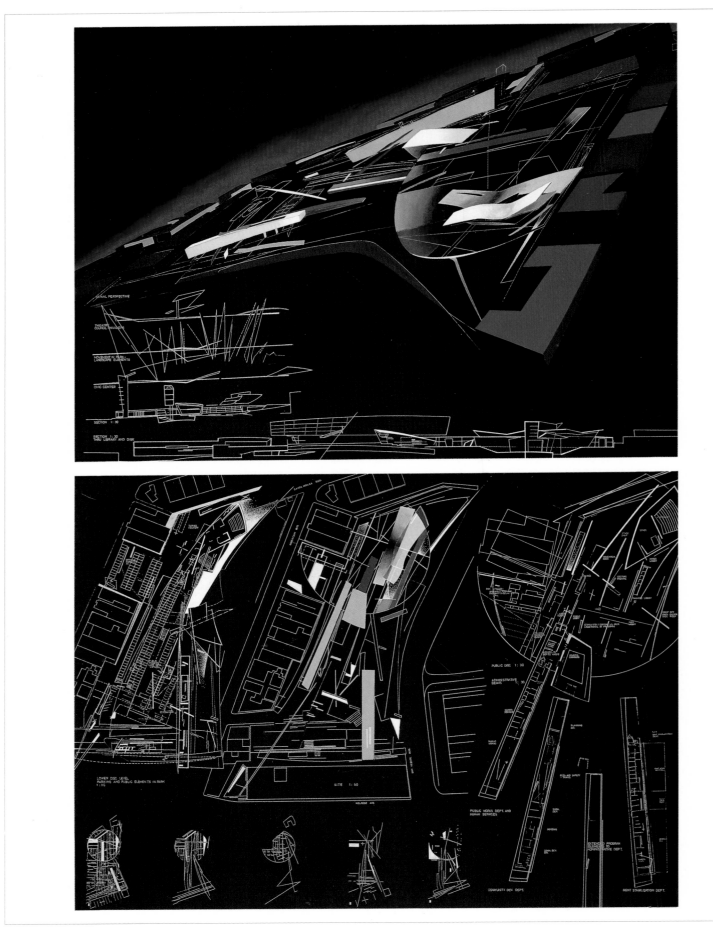

ABOVE: OVERALL PERSPECTIVE; *BELOW*: COMPOSITE SURFACES AND PARK ELEMENTS

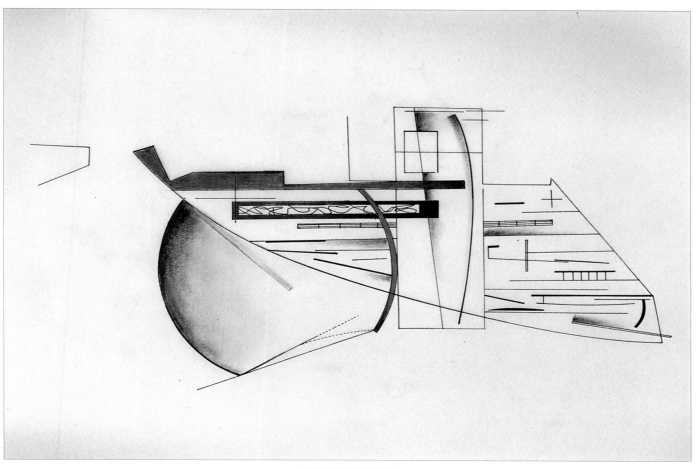

DEVELOPMENT SKETCH

West Hollywood Civic Center

In the spirit of the 20th century, this entry attempts to explore the possible dynamics of this programme site.

The guiding principles are the creation of different zones, some rigidly imposed by the brief and other flexible ones imposed by the site. The generosity of the site implies that a high level of manipulation could be imposed creating different categories responding to a new kind of urbanism. Freeing the ground and programming in with a landscape and plan which is urban. The enclosed landscape within the plate and below creates a great outdoor civic space encompassing all the areas directly linked to the public.

The offices and a library and the possibilities of additional programmes at a later date are then elevated and left free so that their occupants are liberated from the ground. The hospital is placed in a flexible zone at the end of Melrose for any future exploration. The fire station is situated on the disc at the back, its tower forming part of that fragmented landscape.

Competition Team: Zaha Hadid, Michael Wolfson, Veronique Dumont, Jaime Grinberg, Nicola Cousins.

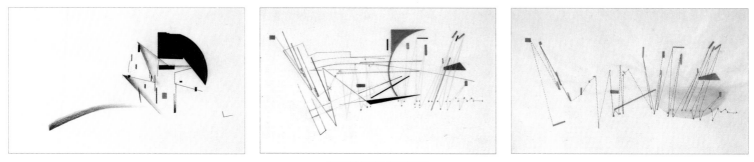

DEVELOPMENT SKETCHES

FUNDER FACTORY 3, VIEW OF ENTRY

COOP HIMMELBLAU

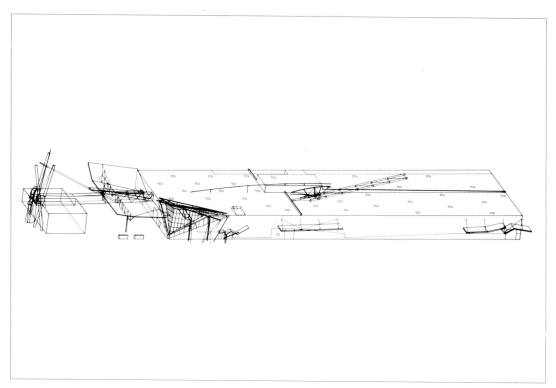

FUNDER FACTORY 3, ISOMETRIC

Funderwerk 3 – A Factory, 1988-89

The Concept

Our task was to create an expressive piece of architecture out of a factory building – a paper-coating works – determined purely by the production process. We believe that an industrial culture can only arise if the prevailing economic and functional constraints are transformed into a multivalent work.

The design is based on the idea of breaking down the volume in which the production takes place – the production hall – into sculptural elements. The power house chimneys, connecting bridge, soaring roof, office and laboratory units and entranceways become individual architectonic elements which work together to give the complex as a whole a distinct head and body.

The playful, plastic treatment of the power house, with its 'dancing' chimneys, the bridge connecting power and production, the wing-like composition of the roof, the structured porte-cochères and the south-facing glazed corner for the offices and laboratories all stand in contrast to the white and deliberately plain production hall. The dynamics of production is heightened by the red-ridged roof, which is designed as a fifth facade and visible from the nearby raised expressway.

Individual architectural elements are twisted and overturned to create a distinct identity and put in question accepted ways of seeing.

Project Description

The factory basically consists of two main parts: the power house and the production hall, the two parts being joined by a bridge. Connected to the hall are three small porte-cochères and a large roof.

The production hall is constructed of steel, and its flat roof is carried by 20 trusses. The lower part of the walls is of prefabricated reinforced concrete, the upper part of flush metal panels set lengthways. Light is brought into the building by scoops on the long north side and vertical window strips on the south. The southwest corner of the building is a skewed volume in glass and steel which is penetrated by the trusses of the hall and a diagonal beam.

The power house is of reinforced concrete, and its walls are composed in the same way as those in the hall. The three slanting chimneys touch the power house via supporting uprights, while the chute is a freestanding object in metal and lattice.

The bridge runs for a third of its length along the roof of the power house and then twists up to the hall. It is covered half with the same metal panels as in the hall and power house, and half with acrylic planks that have been set lengthways or at odd angles. The bridge cuts through the roof, supported only by an inverted truss and two columns. The elements of the bridge, roof and power house are tied together formally as well as structurally by two large fixings to the chimney.

Architects: Coop Himmelblau – Wolf D. Prix, Helmut Swiczinsky; **Project Leader:** Markus Pillhofer; **General Contractor:** Achammer-Tritthart; **Landscaping:** J.B. Koppandy.

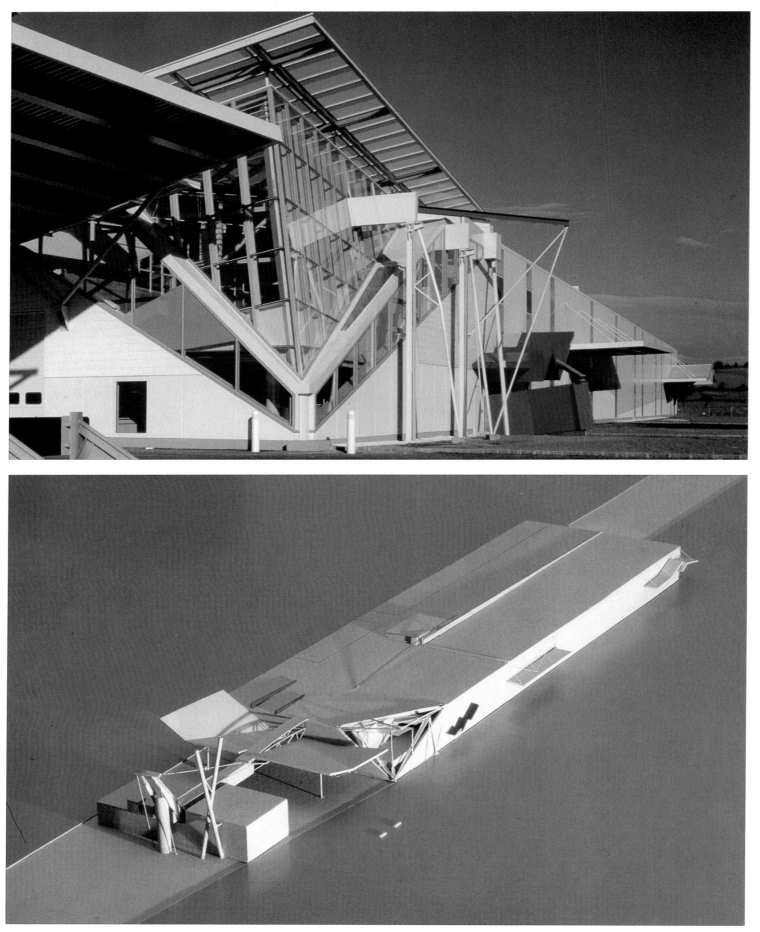

FUNDER FACTORY 3, *ABOVE*: THE 'GLASS CORNER' AND FLYING ROOF ABOVE LOADING DOCKS; *BELOW*: MODEL

FUNDER FACTORY 3, *ABOVE*: ENTRY; *BELOW*: FLYING ROOF AND ENERGY CENTRE TO THE RIGHT

ATTIC CONVERSION, VIENNA

ATTIC CONVERSION, DETAIL OF MODEL

Attic conversion, Vienna 1, 1984-88

The task is to organise an area of 400 square metres into two separated legal office units.

The existing roof is changed into vaulted and slanted parts of glass and sheet metal, supported by a construction – tense and taut – which is the groin and backbone of this archi-tecture. The building volume requested by the municipal officials is transformed into flex-ible form and parts. Movable Venetian blinds (inside and out) and permanent blinds are the elements for light control and acoustic screen-ing. In addition the blinds regulate the air circulation and thereby control the tempera-ture.

Architects: Wolf D. Prix and H. Swiczinsky.
Co-workers: Franz Sam, Stefan Krüger, Karin Sam, Max Pauli, Valerie Simpson, Mathis Barz, Frank Stepper; **Statiks:** DI Oskar Graf.

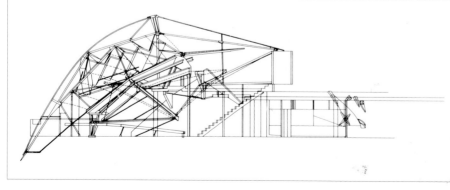

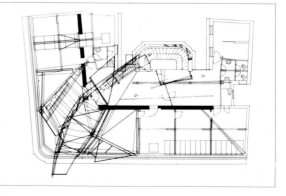

ATTIC CONVERSION, SECTION AND GROUND PLAN

RONACHER THEATRE COMPLEX, MODEL

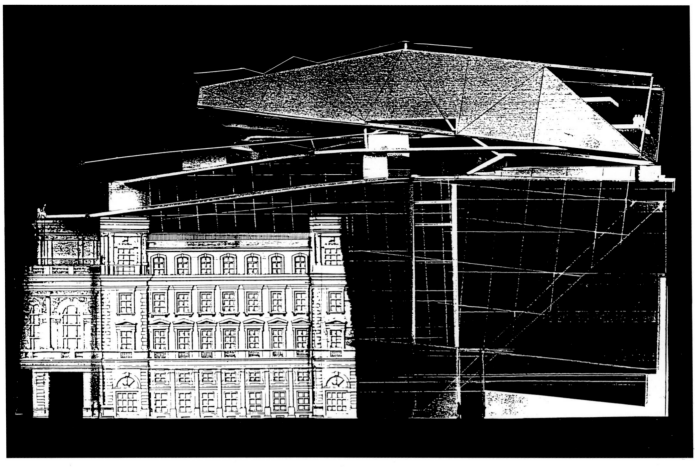

RONACHER THEATRE COMPLEX, FACADE

Ronacher Theatre, Vienna

Concept Description

The design task is described by the following proposition: to convert at 19th-century theatre that does not function optimally into a theatre for the 21st century.

The point of departure for the concept development was the idea of 'a multi-media theatre in every form of performance'. During the design we had the image of a stage space, or better, of a Theatre Complex with open access for the public and in which performances could be held from basement to roof. This design concept would form an intersection of the required programmatic 'constraints' (functions, room planning) and the pre-existing 'constraints' (historic monument preservation).

The Interior Functions and the Exterior Form

The building has several layers. Simply put, there are four areas to be organised: the stage and its technical requirements; the public area (auditorium with foyers, restaurant, bars, etc); the rehearsal rooms; administration and personnel rooms.

The stage and the back stage area presented themselves to us as a large high-tech volume. This 'black-box' is not open to the public, has no exterior, no facade. Just an ideal interior that produces the illusion of theatre.

In a conventionally conceived proscenium stage the three areas – stage, rehearsal room and administration – use five parts of the volume at hand, so that just one part of the volume is available to the public. That means that one can experience only a small part of a large building's interior. During the first step of the design, we thought about a reversal of this relationship. That is to say, the largest possible part of the house must be made open to the public. We then thought about an 'opening-up' of the main and the rehearsal stages, which we would accomplish through multi-functionality (reconstruction possibilities, the capacity to renovate the rooms). We thought of a roof terrace with an open-air stage, we thought of restaurants in the lower level and on the roof, of a public videoteque, and of bars in the foyers.

The Ronacher is however not just a 'Theatre Complex' but through the constant presence of television it becomes a giant culture export-media production machine.

Publicity is to see and be seen. The exterior form of the building is the self-confident representation of all these possibilities.

Project team: Burkhard Entrup, Stefan Krüger, Mathis Barz, Manfred Hieber, Susanne Rath, Sylvia Burian.

SKYLINE, 1985, MODEL OF THE FIRST TOWER

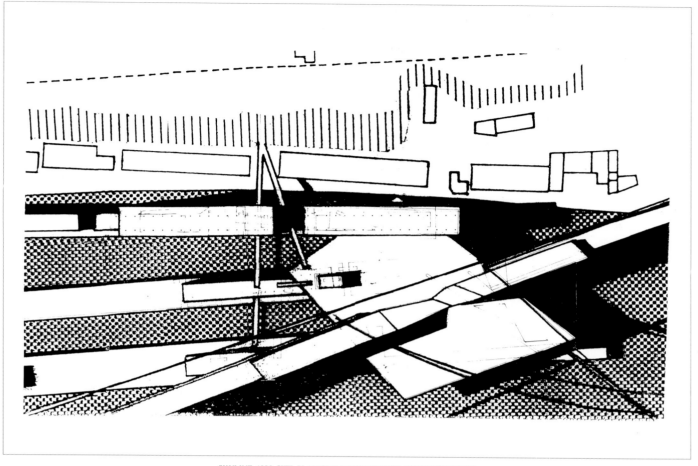

SKYLINE, 1985, SITE PLAN OF HAMBURG HOUSE AND LOFT BRIDGE

Skyline, 1985. Silhouette for a city like Hamburg.

This project was developed in 1985 to be included in the 'Hamburger Bauforum'. A planning area was assigned on the banks of the Elbe along the great Elbstraße in the Hamburg docks. Nothing else. The small and great landmarks of the city of Hamburg were the starting point for the bridge of the associative design. (Everything seen with half closed eyes, that is easy for visitors of a strange city. They don't have the circumstantial pressure in their bones. On the contrary.) In front of us was the dock with its many small swimming and swaying busy landing pontoons. On the other bank, dumb and motionless, the big container terminal with its huge loading cranes. And in the evening the noisy bright/luminous dry dock of the shipyard.

Seen from a boat, the banks of the Elbestraße appeared to us changeable and interchangeable. On the one side the residential area and on the other the lifeless bank of the container terminal. And, in the first design we actually did change not only the banks together with the planning area but also the terms sea-town and press-town. How often do we see the docks of Hamburg (unless we stand in front of it) although every week we could see – and that in Vienna as well – other parts of the town of Hamburg. These parts are called Stern, Spiegel, Zeit, Art, Geo. These are the legible but still invisible silhouettes of the town of Hamburg. And these invisible silhouettes we have made visible, we have given it a physical shape, and a name: Skyline.

If one wishes, one can divide the project into three parts: Skyline, the Hamburg Houses and the media bridge.

In a possible town development area of Hamburg, in the Container Terminal at the centre of the docks, three interwoven building complexes that are over three hundred metres tall are built. They are office and editorial towers for the media, which makes this city important for Europe. Vertically, diagonally, and spatially, the editorial offices are bound up with the School of Journalism and its lecture halls, with the cinemas, with the hotels and the shopping streets.

Architectural Team: Coop Himmelblau – Wolf D Prix and Helmut Swiczinsky; *Collaborators:* Friedrike Brauneck, Michael van Ooyen, Franz Sam, Frank Stepper, Fritz Mascher, Thanomkcat Kharnpe

VIEW OF CHEMOTHERAPY TREATMENT ATRIUM

MORPHOSIS
Two Projects for Los Angeles

EXTERIOR VIEW

Comprehensive Cancer Center

The site for the new building is on the northeast corner of the Cedars-Sinai Medical Center in Los Angeles. It is bounded by an existing parking lot and helipad to the northeast and three existing Medical Center buildings to the south and west. The facility will also utilise subterranean level space within the existing medical tower to the south.

The proposed Center is an out-patient facility combining diagnosis, treatment and counselling within one setting. To maximise efficiency and eliminate duplication of services, it is imperative that the new Center have a direct connection to the Medical Center. As it is used by cancer patients who are maintaining relatively normal lifestyles during their treatment, it's also important that the Center have its own entrance and autonomy.

The Center utilises an existing subterranean radiation therapy department within the Medical Center that would have been difficult and expensive to transfer or duplicate. Its location established the lower level as a patient floor to minimise patient movement.

Two basic design objectives summarise our approach to this project: first, the development of a design strategy which has the capacity to clarify and organise a difficult site impacted between three existing buildings and requiring continuity between the new building and existing subterranean space; second, an architecture which would enhance one's comprehension of location and choice of movement within a complex multi-departmental facility which is itself a microcosmic part of the much larger Medical Center.

The architectural language with emphasis on the Z-axis and the sectional quality of the building, light and an overt reference to construction forms the basis of our response. A framework of geometries, both similar and diverse, establishes a language of distinct

autonomous pieces meant to simultaneously reinforce one another.

Overt references to construction aspire to an integrated architecture rooted in reality (the here and now) which allows a groundwork for the reflective or interpretative intentions of this project. The hope is for an architecture that can occupy the mind and affect the spirit and act as a foil to the patient's current circumstance by removing him or her from self-occupation. The play structure most fully represents these objectives as a construction which engages children through the use of video, moving hand-operated parts, theatre, etc, or entertains the mind with notions pertaining to the building's own construction and fragments of urban mechanisms (the memory of a treehouse?). It presents these man-made constructs in relationship to the wholeness and simplicity of nature (fishtank and tree), all permeated with the folly of a Dr Seuss.

ABOVE L TO R: AXONOMETRIC; VIEW OF DOCTORS' OFFICES; BELOW: VIEW OF MAIN PUBLIC CORRIDOR

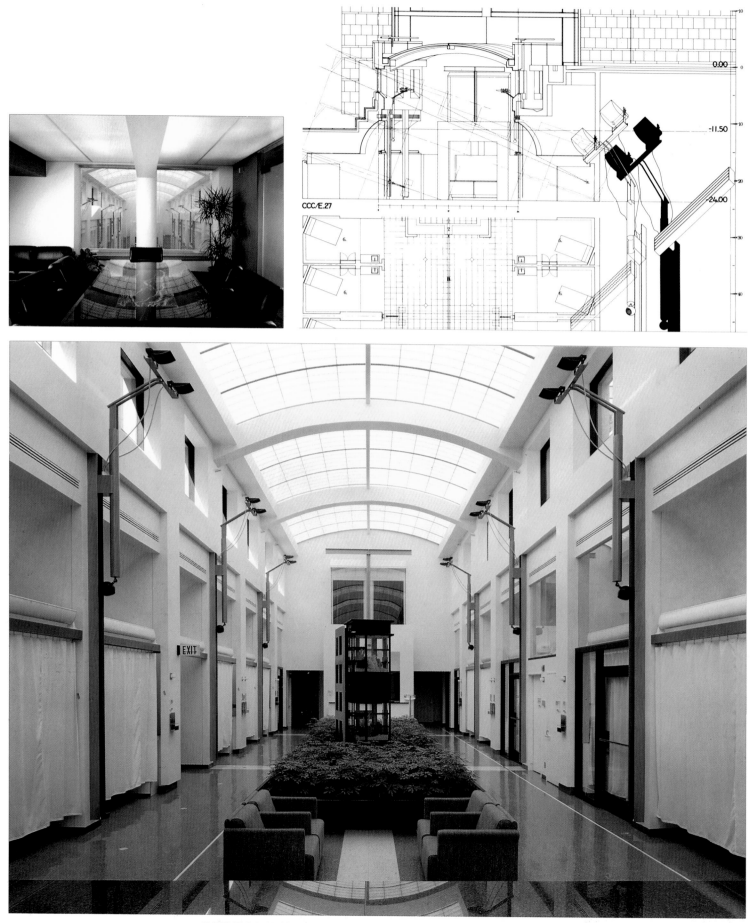

CCC/E.27

0.00

-11.50

-24.00

ABOVE L TO R: DAY HOSPITAL, CONFERENCE ROOM; AXONOMETRIC; *BELOW*: VIEW OF LOBBY

INTERIOR VIEW OF CONCEPTUAL ORRERY

EXTERIOR VIEW

Kate Mantilini, Restaurant; Santa Monica

INTERIOR DETAIL SHOWING FLOORING

This project was to convert an existing 6,400 square feet commercial bank into a 24-hour restaurant: 'A roadside steakhouse for the future, with a clock' (Marilyn Lewis).

Set on the northwest corner of a major urban intersection attached to a parking structure in a mid-rise office complex in Beverly Hills, California, a new building (wall) is entrapped in the old (column).

Building, fresco and sculpture, which are simultaneously discrete and associated, unite within a single framework. The poche wall of the new building engulfs the columns of the old. The wall is constructed of a four-person increment. The building is conceived as a permanent work.

A roof-scape of walls, mechanical-equipment rooms and sun dial are at the service of the adjacent tower workers.

A conceptual orrery, piercing through a 14 feet diameter occulus, summarises the reflective or interpretative intentions of the project. This mechanism – made of the building (distilling and condensing the essential aesthetic fabric) – is in the process of making or describing the building. The prickly cactus-like exterior, vacillating between surface and volume, maintains a tactile sensibility.

(This project requires a 'reading' in terms other than those of sight alone.) A psychological profile of this building reveals aggressive, obsessive, active characteristics, though tempered by a coolness and somewhat business-like politeness.

The interior space is vaguely exterior. Its hall-like quality reflects its public intention. People within this space tend to be extremely conscious of their position.

235

ABOVE: VIEW OF RESTAURANT FROM ENTRANCE; *BELOW*: INTERSECTION OF NEW BUILDING WITH OLD

INTERIOR VIEW OF HALL

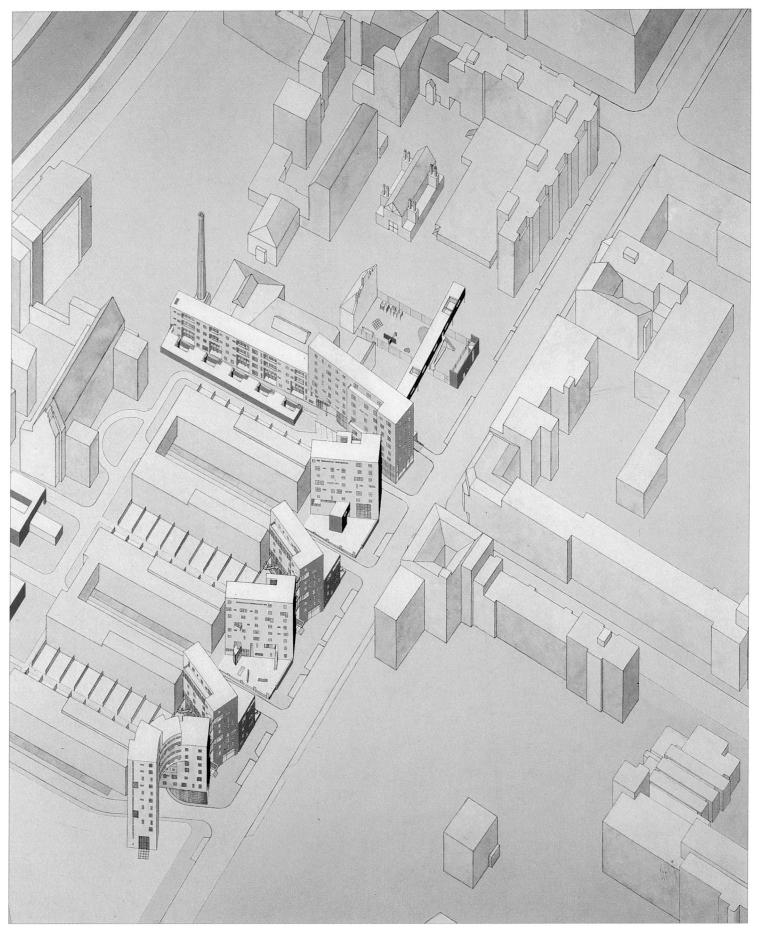

OMA, *LUTZOWSTRASSE*, 1980-81, CONTEXTUAL AXONOMETRIC, PAINTING BY ZOE ZENGHELIS

ELIA ZENGHELIS
The Aesthetics of the Present

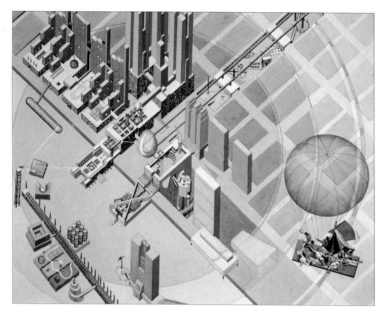

OMA, *EGG OF COLUMBUS CENTER*, 1973, PAINTING BY ZOE ZENGHELIS

Elia Zenghelis, founder-member with Rem Koolhaas of the Office for Metropolitan Architecture (OMA), reviews recent developments and identifies the ways in which architecture has failed in its response to the spread of Western culture and modern technology. The solution he sees as a return to Modernism's original project, the iconography of the programme providing architecture with its visual aesthetic. This article is illustrated with a selection of recent OMA projects.

The most consistent reality of architectural thought in the last 20 years is its astonishing degree of unreality. The aftermath of May 68, was ironically marked by the return of an authoritarian system harsher and more removed from the realities of a lived-in world than the bureaucracy it replaced. Claiming to represent historic responsibility, it ignored the history of a whole century and sought solutions to its problems by pretending that this history was an aberration and that its effects could be reversed by wiping it off its charter: an enterprise that would have been deemed unimaginable in all other disciplines was, in architecture, considered possible.

Historically this was as realistic as saying it will never rain again. It showed total disregard for the relationship of architecture to history. An age of scientific revolution and social upheaval, the 20th century has been dominated by the global spread of Western culture and in particular its technology, the application of science to reality. In the context of the maelstrom of recent history, perhaps the greatest achievement of the 20th century is the modern infrastructure of utilities, communications and transport, which has altered and transformed forever our previous notions of 'city', 'work', 'leisure', 'landscape', 'country', 'language', 'frontier' – and which architecture has yet to exploit and respond to in any meaningful way.

In the wake of the upheaval this lack of response is not surprising. The magnitude of the events dealt a devastating blow to our collective unconscious; our species was faced with having to make new associations with rules of instability and perplexing abstraction. Previously codified conventions lost their relevance and value. Orthodox and even primordial associations were left unprotected. And under the totalising impact of this impetus, our alienated psyche clung to

vestiges of more familiar orders, without realising they had become obsolete and useless. In the process, all forms of vernacular, from princes to fishing villages, entered the world of kitsch and became mere *styles*. Meanwhile the impetus was irreversible; the losses irretrievable; the memories futile. But they persisted with humiliating tenacity. These withdrawal symptoms have been the unforeseen human aftershock of a century of revolution. Observers in a vacuum, an arena we cannot grasp or control, we have become the 'sorcerer's apprentice'. Architecture was caught in the midst of all this. Its traditional role had been eroded, its identifiable patron had been eclipsed and its client had become the masses. A new syntax had to fill the void of its conventions. New ideals were needed to redefine its role.

Modernism was a heroic attempt to come to terms with this new reality and predict its course. It was the experiment of an emerging consciousness that set about to respond to the vicissitudes of history, to imagine its field of action and capture the public imagination, that was eager to make sense of its present. The experiment was aborted. Engulfed by the violence of the approaching war it was not allowed the time to get to grips with this reality. After the war the enterprise was resumed with renewed fervour but without its spokesmen, who, victims of post-war political expedience, were now isolated from it. With early Modernism's ideas still inadequately articulated, a massive influx of indiscriminate construction filled the void created by the war. Lost within it were some of the finest examples of architecture ever. This is the landscape we have inherited and that we are rejecting wholesale without bothering to examine the extent to which it corresponds to *our* reality. If we were more critical, we would endeavour to decipher its latent intelligence, correct its mistakes and give it retroactively the idealism it possesses by proxy. In fact we would treat it as our undeniable *context*. We would try to examine the landscape that surrounds us, what happens in it, in order to respond to it and make it work. This is the unrealised ambition of Modernism, a chapter that is not yet closed. For in the end it alone deals with what architecture is about: to make reality work.

But instead of concentrating on ideas we focus on style. Architectural history is being taught as a history of styles, when from Stonehenge to the Villa Savoye it is nothing but a history of *ideals*. Architecture has always been technology harnessed to the ideals of its time; involved with what *happens* and making it believable.

Meanwhile technology invades us and has become our unsuspected ideology. Wherever we are, in our homes or our workplaces, we are dependent on the invisible technology that surrounds us. Without it we cannot survive, yet we separate its intelligence from ours with contempt. Claiming to be connoisseurs of an apocryphal humanism, we search for solutions in *styles* to problems that need *ideas*. The proposals we offer, whether in the guise of 'Post-Modernism', 'New Classicism' or 'New Modernism', are nothing but style revivals drawn from models that become simultaneously devalued and undecipherable. By ignoring the *reality* of the world out there (the real context), these

same. The modern city is technology harnessed to an idea of mobility and global communication. The walled city was technology harnessed to an idea of defence, appropriate to the reality of the 13th century. Or think of Jericho? Visions that embody the dignity of history. And the historical European city? It is being absorbed into the infrastructure of Europe, which is beginning to emerge as a metropolitan framework of urban fragments.

In the context of this inescapable reality of colonisation, one can only imagine Atlantis in Tenerife sitting in the middle of a vast parking lot, its streets filled with overfed polyglots, in shorts and cellulite, taking photographs.

What is harder to imagine is the reason for our loss of nerve in the face of this context that has evolved despite ourselves and is malfunctioning, uncontrolled and senselessly manipulated by bureaucratic opportunism. It is difficult to understand why this reality (now more tangible than at the beginning of the century) cannot be seen as a conceptual framework for a corrective architecture that would capitalise on its potential. An architecture that would make sense to its occupants.

It is still not an impossible ambition to restore to architecture the popular respectability it once held in the past. To sway a disenchanted

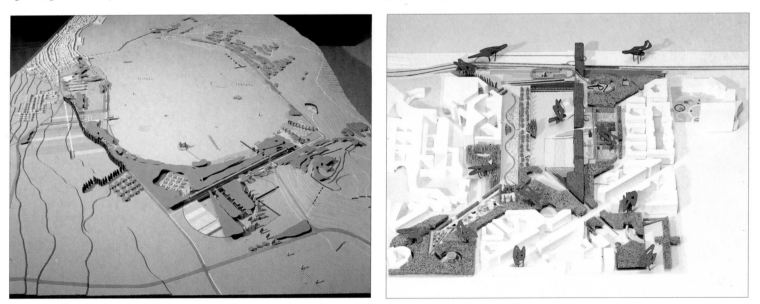

L TO R: OMA, MODEL FOR THE RECONSTRUCTION OF THE BAY OF KOUTAVOS, GREECE, PARC CITROEN-CEVENNES, PARIS, 1985

proposals miss the point of architecture altogether: they do nothing to promote the betterment of this reality. Instead of ideas that relate to its life, the public receives a lot of dogma for which it has little use. But do we offer these proposals to the public or to ourselves? The community of architects has become a self-congratulatory fan club, involved in ritual rallies, inventing its own imaginary antagonisms, prides, jealousies, and insecurities: like a bourgeois caucus isolated within the limited horizons of a suburban enclave where the urban landscape is out of sight and the action out of mind. A caucus without paradigm.

Unaware of these dealings, the urban landscape keeps on colonising the globe, the air space above and the entrails below. Our cities have lost their relationship to the ground. Their exhilaration lies in their section: life has claimed its air rights. Its structures are infinite multiplications of its plots vertically. And below its foundations underground, thousand of lines of communications traverse it in all directions. Our modern city is an infrastructure, capable of sustaining architecture anywhere this is called for and allowing it to decay wherever it is no longer needed. The finite city of stone no longer exists. Our city has invaded the country and the country is allowed to invade the city. What has changed is the time. The principle is the

and recalcitrant public from being guinea pigs to becoming patrons. To turn our attention to the existing, lived-in world; a world which is simultaneously mediocre and sublime, frustrating and exciting. The excitement of our world today is its state of perpetual instability. It is a world of a million programmes coexisting in the same spot; programmes that matter, not for what they are, but for what they could be: tangible ideals if architecture would ask its clients 'what if?' It can only do that and *survive* if it is undogmatic. The programme is the generator of architecture. The plan is the plot where the programme is reinterpreted where it can be more than itself.

The iconography of the programme provides architecture with its visual aesthetic. The action of its plan and section, together with the sensuous materiality of its finish, makes architecture the most hedonistic of the arts. Its hedonism lies in the power of its suggestiveness. It is the setting where a sequence of displacements activate the imagination (like these incomplete sentences that offer a large number of conclusions) and animate the inanimate. With the economy and simplicity of its means, it takes very little to pass from the implicit to the explicit. When architecture achieves this, it becomes an intense and pleasure-giving experience. This experience, involving our minds and our senses, is the measure of its beauty.

Beauty today is a taboo (not measurable objectively, it is dismissed as prejudice). Yet we all know that it is at the centre of every architect's secret ambition. We are all *undercover* agents of *beauty*. (Discriminations which are nowadays practised under cover). Beauty is a pleasure we experience when involved with external stimuli of primarily two kinds: natural and artificial. There is a distinct quality that separates the two (the beauty of a thunderstorm is different to that of a musical performance). What characterises the latter is its synthetic nature: it is man-made. The *mind* intervenes in the emotion it causes.

Intelligence in us seeks intelligence in things and finds it. This seeking enables us to uncover beauty: in this transaction, the experience of pleasure always involves the sensation of newness, discovery and surprise. By the same token, this seeking is the driving force behind the *ability* to bestow upon things that degree of intelligence that gives them beauty. The business of architecture is to make visible to the eye what only the mind can see. It is to make reality work. It is to infuse the participants with the enthusiasm of ideas rather than the desperation of dogma. Above all other transactions in architecture, the most important is *intelligence*; the intelligence of seeing what exists and imagining what might; and that which gives architecture the power that its visual vocabulary has to surprise.

In giving sense to a reality that appears senseless, it has the power to *invert* it and to make even mediocrity unusual and exhilarating. In its newness, architecture *is* modern. Modern architecture is like a relay between yesterday and tomorrow, via today.

For now, an architecture of no fixed theory or doctrine, with a visual vocabulary of instability – an architecture that *cannot* be codified and turned into a style – can escape consumption and retain historical relevance. Its modernism is as similar in its shock and as different in its substance as the modernism of the Renaissance was, or the modernism of eras to follow will be. It echoes and asserts its time. No one who is disenchanted with the tangible or intangible spirit of *the present* can hope to be an architect until this person's ideals correspond with that spirit. At best the person can be a critic, a journalist, a philosopher, an *aesthete*; even a visionary. At worst a practitioner of kitsch. But never an architect.

For an architect, architecture is active propaganda in the original sense of the word. Sometimes ostentatious, sometimes discreet, it is always immodest in its presumptions. Like all great things, it rises above the limited horizons of bourgeois trade-off mentality; it gives ideas freely and believes in those to whom it gives them. And, like science, it espouses that most aristocratic of assumptions: that the

OMA, CHECKPOINT CHARLIE HOUSING, 1980-, VIEW OF MODEL IN PLAN AND FROM THE STREET

On this level architecture is critical. The element of surprise, essential in all pleasures, sustains interest, prolongs involvement and renews response. In danger of being lobotomised by an age in which we are unable to actively take part in the events that overtake us, we become unable to involve ourselves mentally with the world: we cease to function as thinking beings; we lose our critical sense. We have fallen the style victims of this mindless consumption machine: fashion and taste are systems of oppression that remove the capacity to think. Everything is consumed and nothing is experienced. In this setting a plate of poisonous fruit would disturb the order of things. The landscape unsettled, we would have to reflect, to *think*. We would then not eat the fruit and give ourselves time to see its beauty. Architecture has to act like the plate of poisonous fruit if it is not to be consumed. To see, to experience, we need the mind. Architecture is practised by thinking architects, for a thinking public. Critical awareness begets critical response. To escape consumption, architecture must constantly renew itself. It has to make visible what has become invisible.

breadth and quality of its hypotheses will be echoed in what it finds.

The beauty of architecture lies in its *synthetic* claims. Everything about it is artificial. Of all its aspirations this is the easiest to justify because it is universal. All that belongs to nature is by definition doomed to extinction. We are born, we die, we disappear. Only our ideas, our art, the artificial, seem to offer a certain promise of permanence. The ultimate dream of mankind could well be that by means of the artificial it might become immortal. Why live if everything dies and has to begin again with every birth? The artificial resists this absurd condemnation and gives us at least the illusion of survival and fusion with the continuity of infinite existence. What other reason would there be for art if it wasn't to rise above the moment? This is the hedonism of our aesthetics. And it is worth asking ourselves whether the history of mankind is not in all logic a trajectory toward the ultimate substitution of nature by the *artificial* which would carry the definitive victory over death.

*

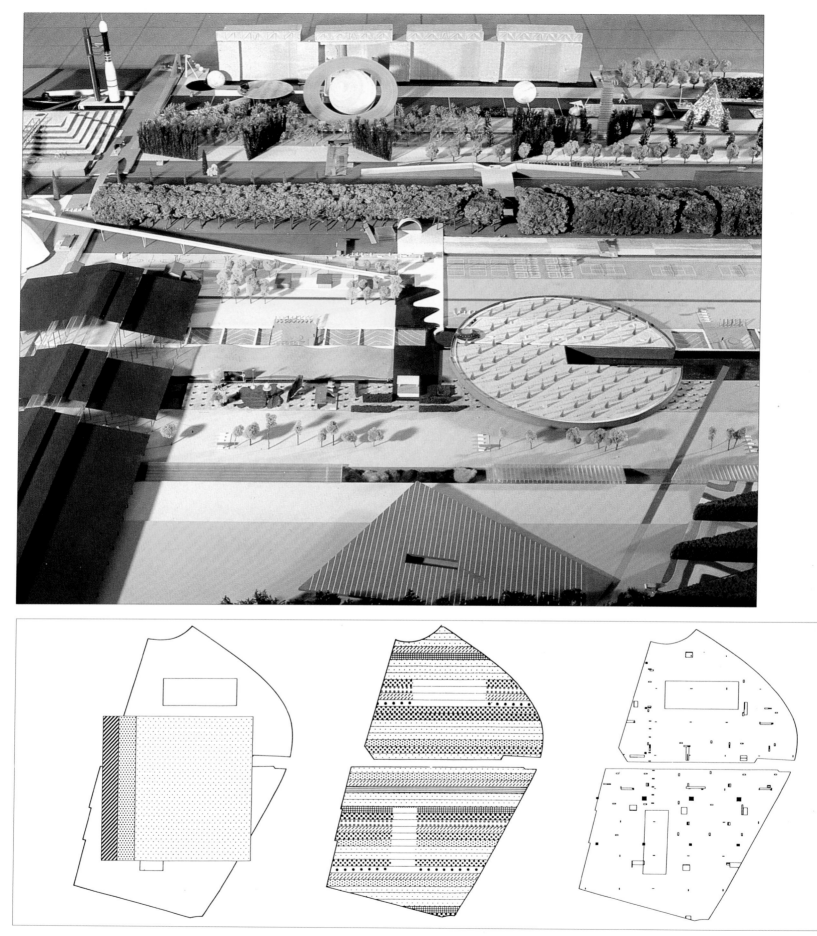

OMA, PARC DE LA VILLETTE COMPETITION PROJECTS, 1982-83,

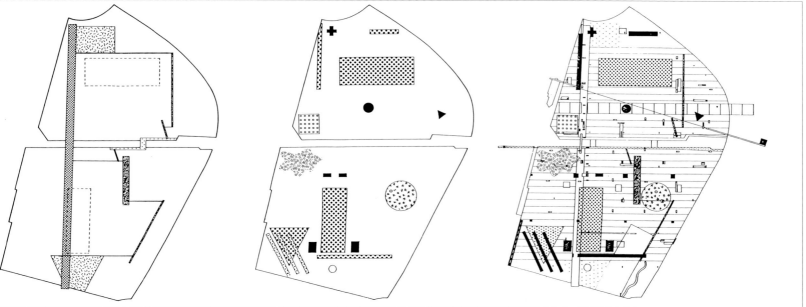

VIEWS OF MODEL AND PLAN SHOWING LAYERING OF ELEMENTS

AERIAL VIEW

BEHNISCH & PARTNERS
Hysolar Institute Building, University of Stuttgart

EXTERIOR, DETAIL

The Hysolar Institute, a joint German-Saudi Arabian research project, is intended to accommodate facilities for various tests connected with the exploitation of solar energy. These tests take place both in the laboratories and outside the building.

It is a small building on the edge of the large university campus in Stuttgart Vaihingen – a small building with an important role.

The special nature of this role determined the architectural design; the laboratory buildings are grouped around a hall; the innovative work done in the building is reflected in the architectural design.

This special project had to be completed quickly and on a low budget – two factors which influenced the choice of building methods and materials.

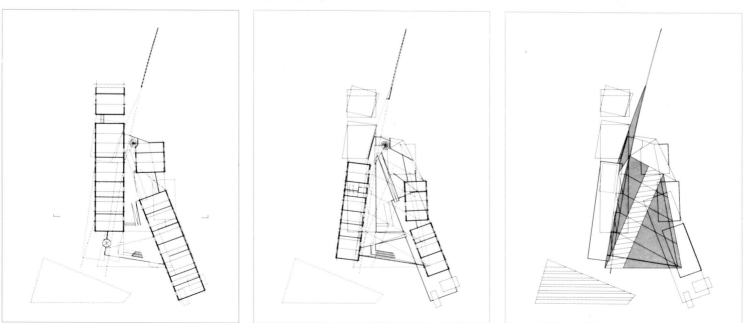

PLANS

ABOVE L TO R: EXTERIOR, DET.

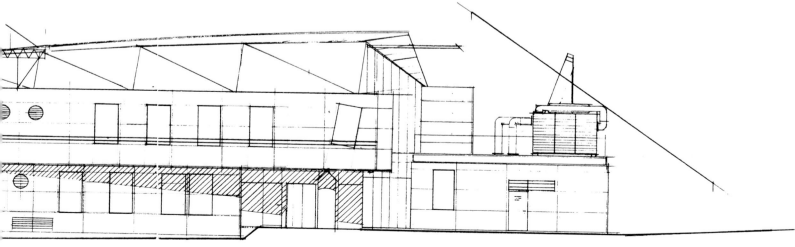

BELOW: ELEVATION

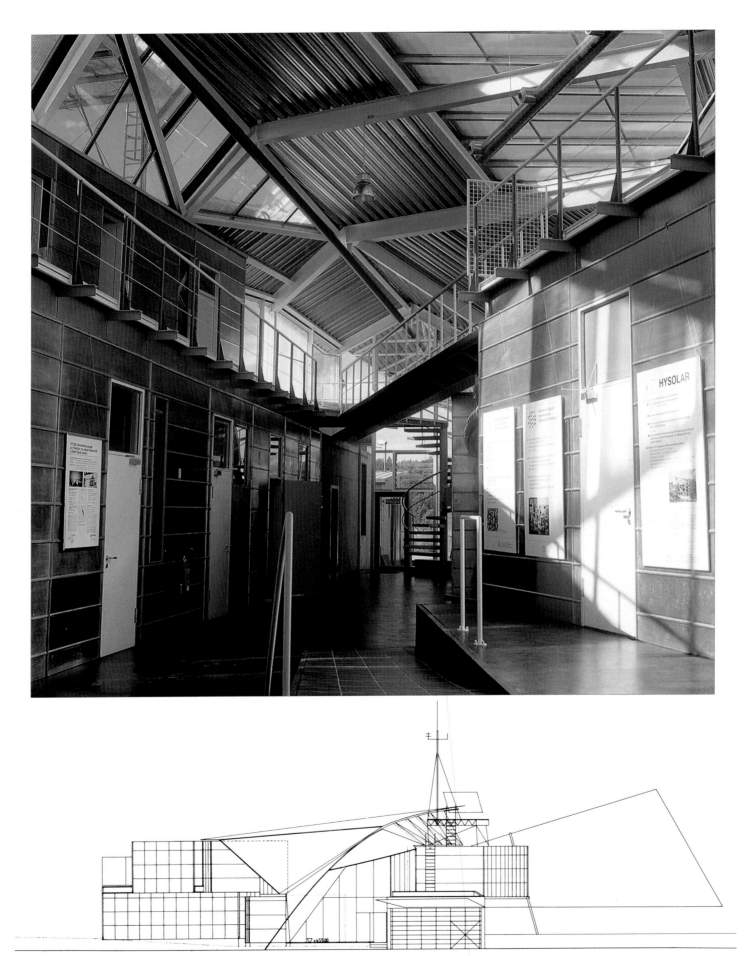

ABOVE: INTERIOR, DETAIL; *BELOW*: ELEVATION

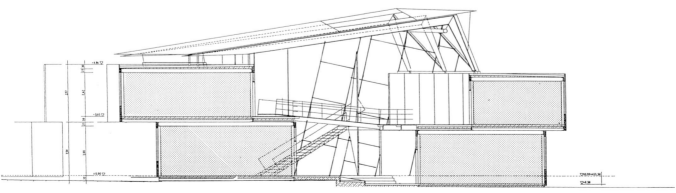

ABOVE: INTERIOR, DETAIL; *BELOW*: SECTION

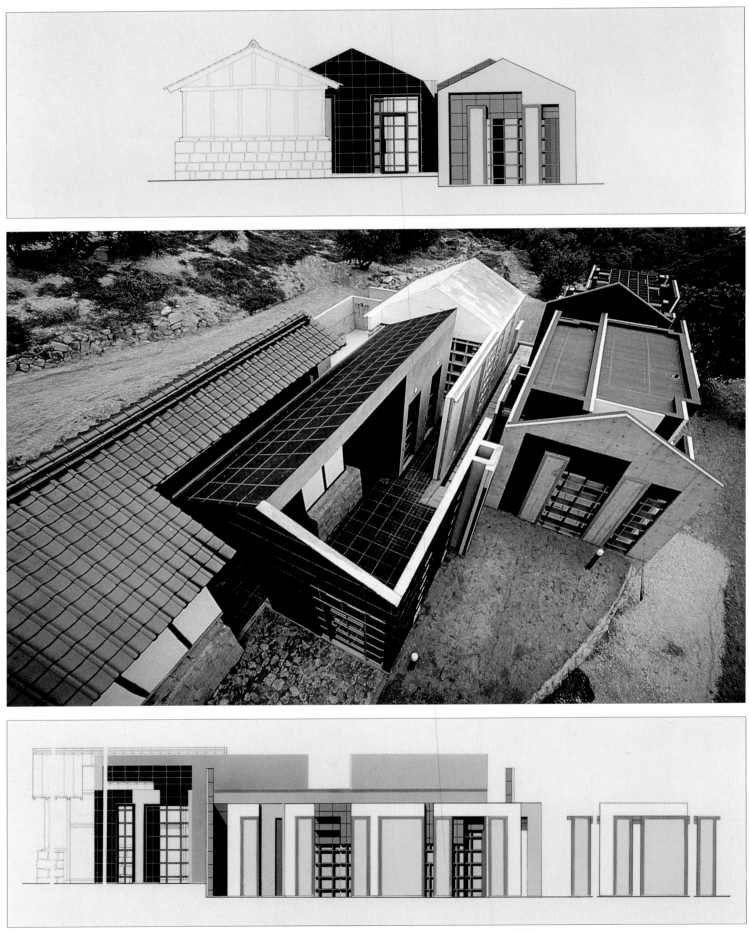

TOP TO BOTTOM: NORTHWEST ELEVATION; AERIAL VIEW; SOUTHWEST ELEVATION

HIROMI FUJII
Ushimado International Arts Festival Centre, 1985

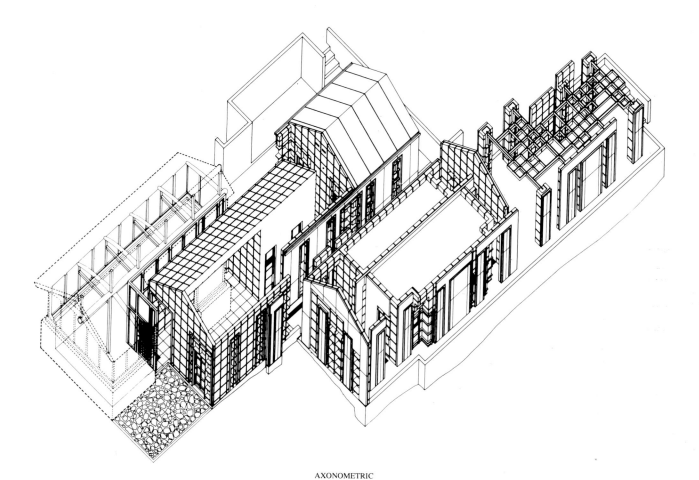

AXONOMETRIC

This project began with an old storehouse left from the Edo period. Architects generally respond to such a condition with fusion or contrast, harmonising the design with the environment or relating the two in some other way. I disregarded such conventions however, and began by metamorphosing the storehouse. This is not the first time I have used the method I call 'metamorphology', wherein transformation of formal and spatial codes of architecture, if repeated, causes forms and spaces to lose their coding and to become traces of their originals. Their previous meanings are neither retained nor entirely eliminated.

What do we feel when we encounter this building? The fragmentary differentiation induced by the traces may suggest historic ruins or may suggest something else. The metamorphosing of the old store-

FLOOR PLAN

house involved first of all identifying and then rearranging its characteristics. Openings and solid walls of exposed concrete are, for example, set in opposition to geometric walls with gridded joints, to disconnected, fragmentary surfaces, and to walls that define interior and exterior spaces. The architectural elements of the lounge building are all reversals of the elements of the office building; openings and solid walls in one become respectively solid walls and openings in the other. The repeated metamorphoses produce a 'balcony' space, yet, through these transformations we can no longer say with certainty what this space is. If our world is built up through the accretion of everyday experience and thereby becomes meaningful, then this can be said to be a deconstructed space that has escaped the confines of our world.

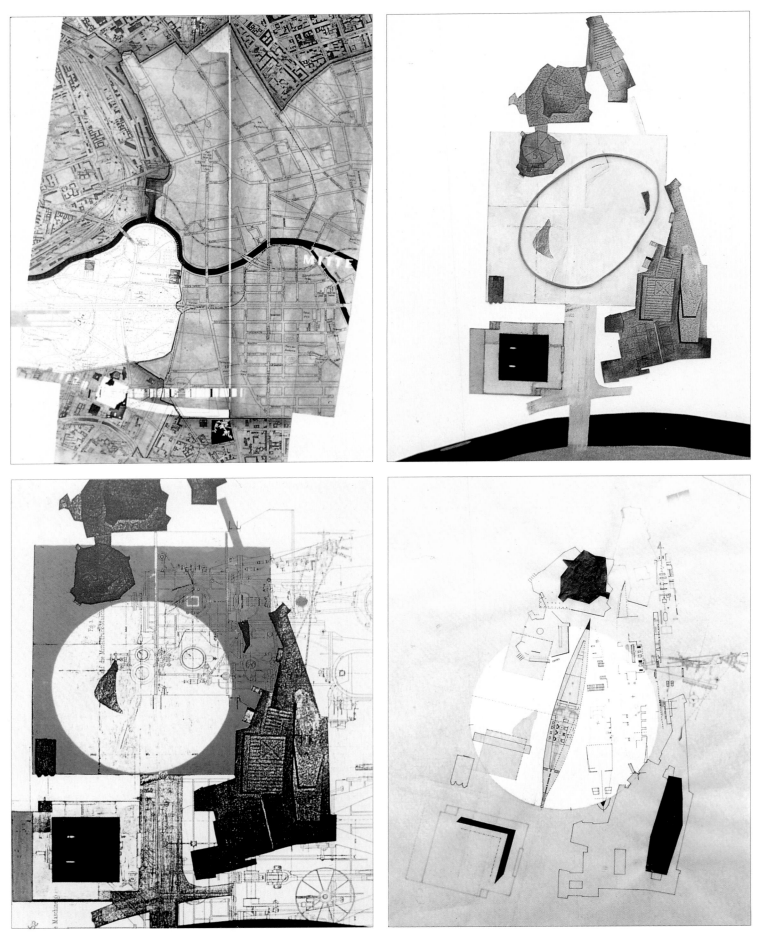

TOP TO BOTTOM, L TO R: THE ROUTE OF THE BRIDGE; FORMALISING THE VOID; RULES AND ARCHAEOLOGY OF THE VOID; LOCATING THE SHIP

PETER WILSON
Berlin – The Forum of Sand
Proposal for the Cultural Forum, Berlin, 1988

ELEVATION IN THE 'MODE OF MIES'

The Forum of Sand

The first question for Berlin today is to find strategies that can legitimise empty space. (This city is truly contemporary precisely because it is no longer continuous, connected or coherent.)

The Forum of Sand exposes the unstable element on which the city is built: a formalised field, a pure circle; a space whose quality is its emptiness; a podium (at the same height as the podium of Mies) of 'dog free' sand which marshals the previously unresolvable space between National Gallery, National Library and the Philharmonic.

Bridge and Ship

The second question for Berlin is that its dreams have become unfocused. (The exhibition 'Berlin Berlin' presented 1,000 different cities, remembered Berlins, fragmented Ber-

AXONOMETRIC

lins, possible Berlins.)

Cities like primitive tribes, need artefacts to focus their dreams. Here two new city scale artefacts are proposed for the Forum of Sand – a Bridge and a Ship.

The Phenning Brücke: a found artefact, length 85 metres; material riveted steel; original location, Wedding, adjacent to the wall; new location, Forum of Sand: new function, a public space with servicing adjacencies, Café of the North, Café of the South.

The Havel und Spree: an artefact partially reconstituted from drawings; Schnell Dampher (fast steamer); length 190 metres; original function, transporting immigrants across the Atlantic; new function, four mechanical car park towers, one mechanical car park wall, an extension to the National Library, a library for images Berlin.

L: THE HELMSLEY PALACE; *R, TOP TO BOTTOM*: MIRACLE CENTER, ELEVATION, THE NORTH DADE JUSTICE CENTER, THE ATLANTIS, DETAIL

ARQUITECTONICA
Recent Work

VIEW OF THE BABYLON

The Atlantis
A 96-unit, 20-storey condominium apartment building at the edge of Biscayne Bay in downtown Miami. The tower rests on a two storey, 200 car underground parking garage. A 37 foot cube has been removed from the building at the 12th floor creating a sky court for the building residents. This sky court contains a jacuzzi, palm tree and red circular staircase. The Mary Tiffany Bingham Mansion originally on the site has been restored to serve as the club house for the condominium. The project also includes a lap pool, tennis and squash courts, and health club.

The building won a *Progressive Architecture* Citation and a South Florida Chapter of The American Institute of Architects Award.

Miracle Center
A mixed-use complex on an urban site in the Coral Gables area of Miami. The project includes 230,000 square-feet of retail shops, ten movie theatres and health club on three levels. Above the retail, there is parking for 1000 cars and an 18-storey, 100,000 square-foot tower containing 98 residential apartments.

The Helmsley Palace
The tallest condominium in South Florida, containing 255 apartments in 42 storeys. A main tower is organised around three elevator cores, each with only two apartments per floor, allowing views of both city and bay from each unit while eliminating long hallways and achieving excellent efficiency ratios. A second building containing special terrace apartments intersects the tower, reappearing on the opposite side to form a monumental porte-cochère. Townhouses line a waterfront promenade, concealing the two-level parking garage.

North Dade Justice Center
This regional courthouse is master-planned to serve as an anchor for a new government centre complex. The court-room wing hovers above two isolated buildings, one containing the public lobby and offices for the Clerk of Courts, State Attorney, and Public Defender. The second building contains secure parking and receiving areas.

The Babylon
5-storey, 13-unit condominium apartment located on Biscayne Bay in downtown Miami. The building is designed as a ziggurat in a wedge-shaped site to take maximum advantage of the buildable area allowed by code. The project includes a roof-top pool and an observation deck and ground level covered parking.

This building won a *Progressive Architecture* Design Award Citation.

STANLEY TIGERMAN
Construction (De)Construction (Re) Construction
Architectural Antinomies and a (Re)newed Beginning

The (pre)*text* of American (Forget)*fulness*

The Amnesiac (pre)*Text* for an American Absence (exile) (under)*writes* ([under]*rights*) repeated attempts at healing an irreparable wound. Tnose continuously failed attempts result from an initial failure to heal the original contamination seeded at the site of Eden. The insistance to heal the unhealable results in perpetual attempts to deflect life's trajectory away from its inevitable, (ir)*reducible* end.

MEMBER **1	(DIS)MEMBER**2	(RE)MEMBER**3
CONSTRUCTION	(de)CONSTRUCTION	(re)CONSTRUCTION
ZIMZUM	SHEVIRATH HAKELIM	TIKKUN

*If the six-pointed star is an ancient symbol for healing, why does 'time heal all wounds'?

**Members* of the human race are (dis)*member*ed through their participation in, observation – or tacit acknowledgement of – a holocaust, which they all (sub)/(un)*consciously* (re)*member*. At Masada, in memory of its downfall, and in memory of all subsequent downfalls, newly initiated *members* of the Israeli army (re)*member* (dis)*member*ment by swearing the oath 'never again'.

The (sub)text of Kabbalistic interpretation (a)

(a) From Harold Bloom's interpretation of Lurianic Kabbalistic typology: *A Map of Misreading*, p5, (parentheses are my own).

ZIMZUM*	SHEVIRATH HAKELIM**	TIKKUN***

* ZIMZUM is the Creator's withdrawal or contraction so as to make possible a creation (*member*) that is not (him)*self*.

** SHEVIRATH HAKELIM is the breaking-apart-of-the-vessels ([dis]*member*), a vision of creation-as-catastrophe.

***TIKKUN is restitution or restoration ([re]*member*) – man's contribution to God's work.

1 Member n. 1 A person belonging to an incorporated or organised body, society, etc: a member of Congress, a member of a club. 2 A limb or other functional organ of an animal body. 3 A part or element of a structural or composite whole, distinguishable from other parts or elements, as a part of a sentence, syllogism, period, or discourse, or any necessary part of a structural framework, as a tie rod, post or strut in the truss of a bridge. 4 A subordinate classificatory part: A species is a member of a genus. 5 Bot. A part of a plant considered with reference to position and structure, but regardless of function. 6 Math. a Either side of an equation. b A set of figures or symbols forming part of a formula or number. c Any one of the items forming a series.

2 Dis-member v. 1 To cut or pull limb or part from part. 2 To divide; separate into parts and distribute, as an empire.

3 Re-member v. 1 To bring back or present again to the mind or memory; recall; recollect. 2 To keep in mind carefully, as for a purpose. 3 To bear in mind with affection, respect, awe, etc. 4 To bear in mind as worthy of a reward, gift, etc: She remembered me in her will. 5 To reward: tip: Remember the steward. 6 Obs. To remind. 7 To have or use one's memory.

| Modernism | (post)Modernism | (re)Postmodernism |
		(Riposte)
Construction	(de)Construction	(re)Construction
Production 1	Destruction	(re)Production 2
Present 3	Absent	(re)Present 4

1 Production n. 1 The act of process or producing. 2 In political economy, a producing for use, involving the creating or increasing of economic wealth: in contradistinction to consumption (by use). 3 That which is produced or made; any tangible result of industrial, artistic or literary labour.

2 Re-production n. 1 The act or power of reproducing. 2 Biol. The process by which an animal or plant gives rise to another of its kind; generation. 3 Psychol. *The process of the memory by which objects that have previously been known are brought back into consciousness* (italics are my own). 4 That which is reproduced, as a revival in drama or a copy in art.

3 present adj. 1 Being in a place or company referred to or contemplated; being at hand; opposed to absent. 2 Now going on; current; not past or future. 3 Actually in mind. 4 Immediately impending or actually going on; not delayed; instant. 5 Relating to or signifying what is going on at the time being; the present tense, present participle. 6 Ready at hand; prompt in emergency; a present wit, a present aid. **n** 1 Present time; now; the time being. 2 gram. The present tense; also, a verbal form denoting it. 3 A present matter or affair; a question under consideration. 4 pl. law Present writings: term for the document in which the word occurs: Know all men by these presents.

4 Re-present vt. To serve as the symbol, expression or designation of; symbolise: The letters of the alphabet represent the sounds of speech. 2 To express or symbolise in this manner: to represent royal power with a sceptre. 3 To set forth a likeness or image of; depict; portray, as in painting or sculpture. 4 a To produce on the stage, as an opera. b To act the part of; impersonate, as a character in a play. 5 To serve as or be the delegate, agent, etc, of: He represents the State of Maine. 6 To describe as being of a specified character or condition: They represented him as a genius. 7 To set forth in words; state; explain: He represented the circumstances of his case. 8 To bring before the mind; present clearly. 9 To serve as an example, specimen, type, etc, of; typify: His use of words represents an outmoded school of writing.

Structuralism	(post)Structuralism	(re)Poststructuralism
		Riposte Structuralism
		(re)Claim*
		(re)Cover*
		(re)New*
		(re)Store*

The (con)text of the initial wound (original sin)

*Acknowledging the presence of a wound (and expressing that admission by perpetually [re]presenting that wound [cut, couper] by the scar that signifies it), does not relieve one from the recurring responsibility that defines human behaviour, such that it continuously attempts to heal it. Even so, it is literally impossible to overcome the knowledge that the wound can never, finally, be healed without resorting to plastic surgery, which is here interpreted to mean the suppression of the memory of the wound (self-inflicted amnesia) – ie, faith – assuring its (dis)appearance. The original wound – the fall from a state of grace in paradise – requires recognition – not suppression. Faith renders any further interpretation of the original wound unnecessary, therefore serving to mute memory. Finally, the same precise faith nullifies any sense of responsibility to (re)write – indeed to (re)right – that original failure, without (re)moving that failure from memory.

Rather than merely acting out iterations of mimesis through repetition, Americans attempt to (re)produce originary evidence, so as to 'get it right' the next time; even though they know (sub)consciously that 'it' can neither be 'righted', nor that one can ever 'get it right'. By yearning for an intersection with lost origins – for an absent beginning – Americans try (even though they repeatedly fail) to (re)gain lost time (never thinking that they may be out of time).

Even though belief in a present tempered by a future perceived as an opportunity to make things better, ie, to gain lost time, (re)presentation infers a better time. By superimposing the concept of time on to the present, (re)presentation is rationalised. While it is well within the ethics of architecture's domain to attempt to accomplish this, the recognition that failure is perpetually imminent has only marginal acceptability within conventional architectural traditions. The very same traditions that mute the memory of original sin. After all, architecture has long been at the service of perpetual value systems . . . otherwise, Plato could never have accused it (art) as being in the shadow of truth.

(re)Production verifies one's belief in the original product. (re)Production is an implicit admission that the original product has value through legitimation by attempting to make that original product better by repeatedly (re)making it (the purpose of cross-fertilisation, indeed the purpose underlying the conceiving of a child implies that the next iteration will be better than the originating one). (re)Production also exploits the passage of time to heal the wound of the entrance into the world of a (re)produced product. Evidence to the contrary notwithstanding, the concept of attempting to improve a situation contradicts the cynical view that (no)thing ever gets better – it is only different. This is where cross-fertilisation intersects with architecture. Each is seminally informed by the opinion intrinsic to both . . . I take this optimism to signify acts of attempts at healing.

'While Hegel maintains that when love is truly conceived, "the wounds of spirit heal and leave no scars", Heidegger insists that the rending of difference can never be totally healed.'

(Altarity 51)

Belief*	(dis)Belief**	(re)lief***
		(Re)newed Belief

* With Hegel, a long ontotheological tradition comes to an end, through 'synthesis' (or is it [sin]Thesis?) – a mechanism that generally suborns 'thesis', but more particularly suppresses '(anti)thesis', in favour of (re)solving (and presumably amalgamating), both. The 'scab' of antithesis is permitted to heal (the scar of synthesis only retains reluctantly the palimpsest of the scab of antithesis). Plastic surgery in the guise of faith manifested in synthesis removes the trace of the wound of antithesis, whose continued presence would otherwise be (un)bearable in its (un)resolved perpetuation, indeed in its insistent (re)interpretation. For Hegel, no further interpretation of the sacred text is required – faith, or belief – first (dis)places, then (re)places exegesis, since the contravention of antithesis is removed. Textuality ceases to be an irritation – antithesis, and with it interpretation, is (dis)placed into a hiatic state of limbo only awaiting (re)activation.

**Americans inherit a post-Nietszchean world where first the sacred other – God – then the sacred self – man – is murdered. Belief first in a divine being, and then by extension, in any being, is (dis)placed by (dis)belief. Self is (re)placed by an equal 'otherness' in an (un)solvable equation (un)burdened by ethical considerations. Originally, the sacred other and the sacred self were on opposite sides of a primary equation, where, by each requiring the other, a false state of parity was artificially induced. The introduction of (dis)belief (dis)locates the original equation, and with that (dis)locative introduction, (dis)places parity, just as it (dis)places first God, and then, as it irrevocably displaces man in a place that is (no)place.

***Born of other strains, the attempt to produce one better than the original through cross-fertilisation is called 'hybrid' or 'child'.

Belief	(dis)Belief	(re)lief
		(re)Newed Belief
Vest	(di)Vest	(re)Vest
Tract	(dis)Tract	(re)Tract
Tort	(dis)Tort	(re)Tort
Solve	(de)Solve	(re)Solve
Sign	(de)Sign	(re)Sign
Assemble	(dis)Semble	(re)Semble
Prove	(dis)Prove	(re)Prove
Plenish	(de)Plenish	(re)Plenish
Orient	(dis)Orient	(re)Orient
Generate	(de)Generate	(re)Generate
Inform	(de)Form	(re)Form
Fit	(mis)Fit ·	(re)Fit
Direct	(mis)Direct	(re)Direct
Claim	(dis)Claim	(re)Claim
Compose	(de)Compose	(re)Compose
Cast	(mis)Cast	(re)Cast
Reading	(mis)Reading	(re)Reading
Appropriate	(mis)Appropriate	(re)Appropriate
Count	(dis)Count	(re)Count
Course	(dis)Course	(re)Course
Centring	(de)Centring	(re)Centring
Nomination	(de)Nomination	(re)Nomination
Location	(dis)Location	(re)Location
Placement	(dis)Placement	(re)Placement
Construction	(de)Construction	(re)Construction
Cover	(dis)Cover	(re)Cover
Evaluation	(de)Valuation	(re)Valuation
Activate	(de)Activate	(re)Activate
Formation	(de)Formation	(re)Formation
Home*	Exile**	Home Away From Home***

* Heideggerian version of 'Bauen', 'Bilded', 'Bilden'.

** See The Architecture of Exile by S Tigerman, Rizzoli, New York, 1988.

*** Replacement of a displaced place.

The (re)Pressed Text of American Architecture

Increasingly, as the 20th century nears completion, it is becoming painfully clear that the (im)*possible* search for an intrinsic American architecture has been (dis)*located* in a time marked by time (marking time), and at a place signifying (no)*place*, of (im)*probable* closure. That clarity reveals a (dis)*junction* symbolic of the site of an American absence (re)*presenting* the inheritance of an emptiness learned originally just outside the east gate of Eden. The primary element that always expresses the constituent features of any epoch – language – is currently (de)*limited* in despair by utterences (dis)*located* from both theocentric, as well as anthropocentric, values.

Linguistic codes exert power through expression (the same codes however, also exert power through suppression). They influence (im)*measurably* beyond the elements that they nominally define. (de)*Coded*, like Samson shorn, they appear to simply state facts even as they inadvertently reveal the magic of the moment.

In America, a land composed virtually entirely of successive generations of exiles, the yearning to return to an original innocent state as a failed (re)*placement* of inhabiting successfully an alien and resisting 'rooting' instincts, now has a corresponding set of linguistic codes that are utilised in order to express the (dis)*junctive* nature of our time. Denials now (dis)*place* originary definitions that, in the beginning, rooted mankind to being through dwelling to existence in a home always at home. The cynicism of sophistication (age) has (re)*placed* the spontaneity of innocence (youth). But it wasn't always that way in a more childlike America, new and before its free/fall from grace.

The (co)*incidence* between the guileless optimism of a young nation, and a discipline such as architecture (whose tradition resonates with characteristic optimism) is tacitly understood. That (co)*incidence* is powered by the courage to accept a belief system perpetually (re)*activated* by 'newness'.

Modernism may have actually begun in the Renaissance as a condition of appropriation, but it was never enjoyed (nor exploited) more than by a nation of innocent exiles who, if they were to be true to their instinctive optimism, had no choice but to (re)*direct* their unsought condition constructively in 'modern ways'. The very word – *Modernism* – implies a condition of amnesia about the past, a determined attachment to the present, even while tilting slightly toward the future. Dialectically, however, Modernism also implies a challenge to a (pre)*Modern* condition inadvertently clarifying Modernism while appearing to stand over and against it. Modernism, after all, found a welcoming home in a childlike, youthful America free from cunning, (un)*informed* by deceit, (un)*tainted* by sophistication, an America for whom the present meant everything, and where (forget)*fulness* about history seemed essential to young Americans schizophrenically revelling in their (pre)*mimetic* innocence, even as they desperately desired parity with others who, they hoped, perceived them as the newest sophisticates.

The (text)*ure* of antinomy

A synthesis ([sin]*Thesis*) of continuously (un)*resolved* (op)*positions* based on the (ir)*reconcilability* of seemingly necessary inferences or conclusions (antinomy) seems (un)*likely* in an age dually devoted to either self-verification through the uses of the past, or to an (un)*conditional* indulgence in the (un)*predictability* of the future. Both strategies (dis)*locate* equally a belief in the power of the present. The resulting ambivalance elevates (dis)*junction* to a positional primacy of domination, and seems to suggest that the intrinsic quality of presence has an (un)*resolvably* slippery Janus-face that looks either backward or forward, but is so waferlike that it cannot speak meaningfully of its own time. The sound emanating from the face of the present is either Babel-like, or mute, giving way alternatively to the cacophony of the past and/or to the vast silences of the future. Simultaneously, by speaking (dis)*cordantly* of other times and other places, the voice of contemporaneity is strangled. We seem (un)*able* to articulate a present paradoxically (de)*void* of the inspiration to 'blow its own horn'.

We should know that looking backwards for verification only results in the wrenching frustration of an exile haplessly yearning for an (ir)*retrievable* original innocence, attainable only in memory, through (un)*fulfilled* desire. (Op)*positionally*, we should understand that, by 'throwing the baby out with the bathwater', a future without its past is only fictively compelling (and even that is temporary), since we are also reminded that 'we (can)*not* not know history'. Both polar positions are (un)*promising*, since neither is possible (with)*out* knowledge of the other. Each is contaminated by its (op)*posite*, thus neither is particularly innocent. Bookended by positions describing a condition of antinomy, the present is drained of itself shifting its weight so that it lies tantilisingly always just out of reach. 'Movement' or 'mobility' (the oscillation between [op|*positions*), becomes the dominant currency of an otherwise vacuous, state of contemporaneity.

Perhaps contemporary America is not a generative source of indigenous architecture after all. An American absentation may be ascribed to the fact that this country is neither old enough to legitimate, nor young enough to retrieve, visions otherwise located elsewhere. On the one hand, America's absence may be inextricably tied to the power of its pluralistic precedents which, for many, are rooted to a place that is multitudinously 'other' than any single one that could, in other circumstances, be called 'home'. The power of originary evidence, to which many Americans still yearn (and with it, the (re)*iterative* power of mimesis), overwhelms sensing possibilities tied to an (other)*wise* (dis)*illusioning* present. On the other hand, by thrusting one's self into the (un)*known* without the (re)*assurance* of precedent (to say nothing of the comfort of convention), the (dis)*junctiveness* of that thinness of time which is uniquely and solely ours is (re)*enforced*, perpetuating an *absent present*.

The continuous search for a point of origination in order to project form metaphorised by the Edenic tree of life is, in America, a 'Faery Land' without roots, perhaps even without a native soil which would otherwise nourish thoughts of 'home', or 'dwelling', or 'being'. It is precisely in response to being an American in an age where absence is characterised by removal from 'playing the game', that causes one's gaze to stray to places and pleasures behind, or in front of, one's position in time and in place. The suspension of belief in an American presence dislocates value as well as illusion in the power, indeed the existence, of a perpetual American dream. That particular (dis)*junction* (re)*locates* the power of the performer of presence to the selections of the spectator of absence, resulting in the domination of the voyeur over the player.

Thus the energy (or is it enervation?) of continuous contemporary (dis)*location* is bookended by a never-to-be-retrieved past, and a never-to-be-fulfilled future. The inference that a (dis)*junctive* present is inevitable is seeded by the (im)*possibility* of fulfilment by moving either forward or backward, and (re)*enforces* a gripping pause that is marked by (de)*constructive* marginalia. The death of God combines with the death of man (fore)*closing* whatever optimism that might be otherwise intrinsic to a *present* that has *presence*. The absence of either 'ethical norms or moral forms' conveys a chimeric freedom that exploits the loss of the power of presence. That imaginary (dis)*closure* presents instead a perpetually contaminated closure signifying the illusion that (im)*perfection* is its own reward – the paradox of the absent present – (de)*construction*.

By elevating interpretation to an (un)*precedented* level of (dis)*belief* (or freedom, depending on your view), not only is faith exacerbated, but ethics are excised in a country desperately in need of values in order to mark its maturity. The absence of ethical values (super)*imposed* on a state of incessant interpretation, projects a false sense of (in)*dependence* (in)*consistent* with the development of an individual, or collective, sense of self.

*　　*　　*

If Hegel's (pro)*position* of the trinity of first Greek, (dis)*placed* by Jew, and (re)*placed* by Christian is modified so that the original, (un)*tampered* belief in god(s) is (dis)*placed* by man's challenge to his monotheistic God through the elevation of the self in order to engage in dialogue with God (the wound of continuous interpretation), and when that finally fails and man is expelled from paradise, man's efforts to make restitution in order to make the world better by attempting to heal an (un)*healable* rift, then a new (pro)*position* (re)*placing* 'faith' (plastic surgery) comes to pass. The palimpsest of the original wound is revealed – an erasure's trace – made present by the presence of a scar which (re)*presents* the signature, or name, by which the *attempt* at healing becomes evident. Time is crucial to the understanding of healing, for without the passing of time, mankind's (in)*ability* to sustain pain would not exist resulting in an (un)*endurable*, continuous, pain. The passage of time (combined with man's amnesia about it) allows for a scab to metamorphose into a scar. Since the mind cannot sustain pain, a scar is a mark that can be interpreted as signifying original pain, while at the same time the scar (re)*presents* the erasure of that original pain.

The original wound can never be healed by excision, or removal, but an attempt at (re)*conciliation* is necessary to (re)*present* faith in being, existing, dwelling. The scar remains so that one may not ever forget that there was a wound in the first place. A scar bears the trace of a scab, troubled by time. A scab (re)*presents* the initial sign of the process of healing. When a scab is ripped off, the wound that it marked is (re)*opened*, new blood is shed, and the original pain is (re)*membered*. The scar cannot be (re)*opened* without the creation of a new wound (super)*imposed* by new pain. But its perpetual presence (re)*members* the member that was originally ruptured through a process nominally called (dis)*memberment*. Time is crucial to a sequence of healing that begins by rupturing a (pre)*existing* condition, and ends with the memory of the enactment of a failed attempt to (re)*enliven* that lost, originary pain.

The (Sub)Text (Super)Imposed On The (Con)Text

The corrolation between the Lurianically interpreted Kabbalistical tryptich (*Zimzum, Shevirath Hakelim, Tikkun*) and their apparently coincidental architectural counterparts (*construction*, (de)*construction*, (re)*construction*) can no longer be ignored.

The history of Western architecture is indelibly stained by an obstinate optimism traced solely by constructive attitudes signified by construction. (in)*Formed* by anthropocentrism, architects have obligated themselves mimetically to repeat the paradisic (un)*equal* hierarchical relationship by subordinating self to that first perfect architect – God – by whose hand man's initial, and only ideal, home – the Garden of Eden – was conceived. Traditionally, the overwhelming desire to 'get it right' has been (re)*presented* by buildings suppressing any trace of a 'wound' (or, for that matter, (re)*pressing* the passage of time – and with it – suppressing the only hope of healing that wound). The sign of intrinsic optimism was manifest in construction, ie, that belief in being, or existence, that the Bible (later [re]*written* by Heidegger) addresses.

Whatever the nature of construction – its style, its context, its bias – the implicit optimism of the human spirit innocently, if (in)*advertently*, suppressed 'mistakes' so as to mimetically express mankind's (un)*equal*, and (im)*perfect*, relationship to a divine being. Equal to Luria's Kabbalistical interpretation of 'Zimzum' (God's withdrawal, making way for mankind), anthropocentrism, ie, the inference of mankind's assuming 'centre stage', to better act out this primary (in)*equality*, was effected. Edenically, Zimzum can be interpreted as God's establishing of authority by the Genesis divine denial ('do not eat of the tree in the centre of the garden') which (through God's withdrawal), leaves 'centre stage' available for Adam and Eve to either obey, or to overturn, that mandate. Either way, Adam and Eve are given a primary message by God (un)*alterably* demanding a response. God's withdrawal makes Adam's and Eve's presence possible. By responding at all (never mind which response), Adam and Eve establish their own presence, which in turn, signifies God's absence – or – His withdrawal.

Similarly, the establishing of a corresponding architecture – one that responds mimetically to that first, perfect place made by the hand of God (Eden) – not only commits architecture to a perpetually (im)*perfect* condition, but ironically (re)*moves* the trace of that (im)*perfection* as it suppresses any possibility of erring in favour of 'getting it right'. The very nature of architecture since that time is couched in the (pre)*tension* of the architect trying to get it right by reducing the passage of time to a condition of absence – conscious removal.

As an architectural analogue to Zimzum and as an epilogue to the passion play of Christianity, the architect assumes a position of presence – a kind of divine (re)*placement* - so as to 'create' mimetically derived iterations of an imagined innocent state equated with perfection. For almost 2,000 years architects have denied the 'trace' of that perpetual wound which nostalgically draws mankind back to an originally innocent state. (im)*Possible* to attain, (il)*logical* to conceive, architects nonetheless persistently strive to reduce the distance between the problems of mimesis as they attempt to concretise divine ideals into a never-to-be-achieved state of innocence.

God's withdrawal allows mankind to (dis)*place* Him, and by their own (re)*placement*, they attempt to accomplish similar goals. With the coming of Christianity, faith or belief in an ideal (re)*enforces* architects' resolve as they attempt to (re)*place* a heavenly garden inhabited by 'named' creatures with a mimetically conceived divine city resurrecting mankind from the original fall from grace. While Christian faith is the final, synthesising element in Hegel's tripartite philosophical project (first Greek, then Jew and, finally, Christian), it becomes the first in a new tripartite series (Zimzum), followed by the apocolyptical view of the world metaphorised by the breaking of the vessels (Shevirath Hakelim), and concluded by continuously failed attempts to heal an irreparable wound (Tikkun).

STANLEY TIGERMAN, *EXILE II, CHICAGO TO LA*, 1984

EMILIO AMBASZ
San Antonio Botanical Conservatory, Texas

VIEWS OF THE EXTERIOR

This is a complex of greenhouses for the hot, dry climate of Southern Texas. The traditional greenhouse, designed for northern climates, uses glazing to protect the plants and maximise sunlight. However, this is inadequate in San Antonio, where the plants must be protected from an overabundance of sunlight rather than from the cold.

The proposal involves using the earth as a container and a protector of the plants, controlling the entry of light and the heat level by limiting the glazed areas to the roof, as a cover for the earthen 'container', raised in places to accommodate tall plants. By excavating into the earth, the conservatory preserves and harmonises with the gently rolling hills around it, merging the categories of culture and nature. The different roof configurations take their cues from considerations of the wind and orientation of the

sun. The varied forms of these peaks permit the rooms to take on a hieratic presence as an arrangement of secular temples sitting serenely in the landscape. They have a technological image of aluminium space-frame and butt-jointed glass, opposing the naturalistic setting and interior mood.

The different rooms are organised around a garden patio or courtyard, characteristic of Texas. This allows for access to the different greenhouses under a shaded arcade, provides for easy maintenance and unifies the buildings of the composition, whilst allowing each unit to be treated as a separate building with its own special climatic conditions and spatial configuration. This gives a processional quality to the sequence through the conservatory; first the entrance pavilion with its naked structure, then the long, narrow orangery lined with fruit trees, the

peaceful fern room with its water cascades and artificial mist, the special environments – desert room, tropical rain-forest, alpine meadow – culminating in the grand palm house wrapped around its forest of trees.

The project is a unique architectural solution to the problem of designing a greenhouse in a hot, dry climate: whilst recognising regional vernacular in organisation of the buildings, the treatment of the earth as a container and glazing as merely a cover with additional peaks reduces the amount of sunlight and allows the complex to harmonise with its surroundings and at the same time enhance it with sculptural objects.

Architectural Team: Emilio Ambasz, Dwight Ashdown, Alan Henschel, Erik Hansell, Frank Venning, Mark Yoes, Suns Huing.

SELECTED PUBLICATIONS

The only publications that have appeared to date on the subject of Deconstruction in architecture and the visual arts apart from this volume are *What is Deconstruction?* by Christopher Norris and Andrew Benjamin, a lucid exposition of the work of Jacques Derrida in relation to art and architecture, and the catalogue of the New York Museum of Modern Art's exhibition 'Deconstructivist Architecture', by Philip Johnson and Mark Wigley. The reader is also referred to two special issues of *Architectural Design* magazine on the subject, namely 'Deconstruction' and 'Deconstruction II', and an issue of *Art & Design* magazine, 'The New Modernism'. The body of writings on Deconstruction is growing all the time, however, in the form of articles appearing in periodicals, and it is to these that the reader is directed for further information on the continuing development of Deconstruction in theory and practice. The most important to appear in English are *Architectural Design, AA Files, Architecture & Urbanism* and *Art & Design*. Other magazines that have recently looked at Deconstruction include *Archis, Architese, Baumeister, GA* and *Techniques & Architecture*. For specific work also consult magazine references contained in the notes for each article. The following selection of books, exhibition catalogues and magazine articles is intended as a guide to the most important writings that have appeared to date.

Selected Writings by Jacques Derrida

Dissemination, trans Barbara Johnson, Athlone Press, London, 1981.

Edmund Husserl's Origin of Geometry: an introduction, trans John P Leavey, Duquesne University Press, Pittsburgh, 1978.

Glas, trans John P Leavey and Richard Rand, University of Nebraska Press, Lincoln and London, 1986.

Of Grammatology, trans Gayatri C Spivak, John Hopkins University Press, Baltimore, 1976.

Psyché: inventions de l'autre, Galilée, Paris, 1987.

Positions, trans Alan Bass, Athlone Press, London, 1981.

'Speech And Phenomena' and Other Essays on Husserl's Theory of Signs, trans David B Allison, Northwestern University Press, 1973.

Signéponge, trans Richard Rand, Columbia University Press, New York, 1984.

The Truth in Painting, trans Geoff Bennington and Ian McLeod, University of Chicago Press, Chicago and London, 1988.

Writing and Difference, trans Alan Bass, Routledge and Kegan Paul, London, 1978.

Selected Writings

a+u, 'Bernard Tschumi/Jo Coenen', Tokyo, 1988.

ADAMI, VALERIO. *Les règles du montage*, Plon, Paris, 1988.

Anselm Kiefer, text by Mark Rosenthal, The Art Institute of Chicago and the Philadelphia Museum of Modern Art, 1987, exhibition catalogue.

Architectural Design, 'Deconstruction', Vol 58 No 3/4-1988.

Architectural Design, 'Deconstruction II', Vol 59 No 1/2-1989.

Art & Design, 'The New Modernism', Vol 4 No 3/4-1988.

BENJAMIN, ANDREW. *Translation and the Nature of Philosophy: a New Theory of Words*, Routledge, London, 1989.

BENJAMIN, WALTER. *Illuminations*, Hannah Arendt (ed), Fontana, London, 1973.

BHADDA, HOMI K (ed). *Nation and Narration*, Methuen, London, 1989.

CAPRA, FRITJOF. *The Turning Point*, London, 1983.

DE MAN, PAUL. *Allegories of Reading*, Yale University Press, New Haven, Connecticut, 1982.

EISENMAN, PETER. *Houses of Cards*, Oxford University Press, New York and Oxford, 1987.

——. *The Edge of Between*, forthcoming 1989.

Five Architects: Eisenman, Graves, Gwathmey, Hejduk, Meier, with contributions by Arthur Drexler, Colin Rowe, Philip Johnson and Kenneth Frampton, Oxford University Press, New York, 1972, rev ed 1975.

FOSTER, HAL (ed). *Postmodern Culture*, Pluto Press, London, 1984.

FRANSCINA, FRANCIS, AND CHARLES HARRISON (eds). *Modern Art and Modernism*, Harper and Row, London, 1984.

HARVEY, I. *Derrida and the Economy of Différance*, Indiana University Press, Bloomington, 1986.

IAUS, 'Idea as Model', Rizzoli, New York, 1981.

JEANS, JAMES. *The Mysterious Universe*, Ridgeway Books, New York and London, 1939.

JENCKS, CHARLES. *Architecture Today*, second edition, see especially Chapter 14, pp 250-69, Academy Editions, London, Harry N Abrams, New York, 1988.

JOHNSON, P AND M WIGLEY. *Deconstructivist Architecture*, Museum of Modern Art, New York, 1988, exhibition catalogue.

Journal of Philosophy & The Visual Arts, Vol 1 No 1, Academy Editions, London, St Martin's Press, New York, 1989.

KOOLHAAS, REM. *Delirious New York: A Retroactive Manifesto for Manhattan*, Oxford University Press, New York, Academy Editions, London, 1978.

LLEWELYN, J. *Derrida on the Threshold of Sense*, Macmillan, London, 1986.

LYOTARD, JEAN-FRANCOIS (with Thierry Chaput). *Les Immatériaux*, Centre Georges Pompidou, Paris, 1985.

——. *Que Peindre?*, Editions de la Différence, Paris, 1987.

——. *The Postmodern Condition: a report on knowledge*, trans Geoff Bennington and Brian Massumi, University of Minnesota Press, Minneapolis, 1983, Manchester University Press, 1984.

NORRIS, CHRISTOPHER, AND ANDREW BENJAMIN. *What Is Deconstruction?*, Academy Editions, London, St Martin's Press, New York, 1988.

NOZICK, ROBERT. *Philosophical Explanations*, Oxford University Press, 1981.

RORTY, ROBERT. *Philosophy and the Mirror of Nature*, Basil Blackwell, Oxford, 1978.

SITE: *Architecture and Art*, essays by Pierre Restany and Bruno Zevi, Academy Editions, London, St Martin's Press, New York, 1980.

The Architecture of Frank Gehry, 1964-1986, Walker Art Center, Minneapolis, Rizzoli, New York, 1986, exhibition catalogue.

TSCHUMI, BERNARD. *Cinegramme Folie, Parc de la Villette*, Champ Vallon, Paris, 1987.

——. 'Manhattan Transcripts', *Architectural Design* Special Profile, Academy Editions, London, St Martin's Press, New York, 1981.

——. *Textes Parallèles*, Institut Français d'Architecture, Paris, 1985.

UIA Journal, 'Vision of the Modern', Vol 1 No 1, Academy Editions, London, Rizzoli, New York, 1988.

VON BERTALANFFY, L. *General System Theory*, London, 1971.

WOOD, D, AND R BERNASCONI (eds). *Derrida and Différance*, trans D Wood and A Benjamin, Northwestern University Press, Evanston, 1988.

Selected Writings on Constructivism

Architectural Design, 'Fantasy and Construction: Iakov Chernikhov's Approach to Architectural Design', Catherine Cooke (ed), Vol 54 No 9/10-1984.

Architectural Design, 'Russian Avant-Garde Art and Architecture', Catherine Cooke (ed), Vol 53 No 5/6-1983.

BANN, S. *The Tradition of Constructivism*, London, 1974.

BOWLT, J. *Russian Art of the Avant-Garde: Theory and Criticism 1902-1932*, New York, 1976.

ELLIOTT, D (ed). *Alexander Rodchenko*, Oxford University Press, 1979.

GINZBURG, MOISEI. *Style and Epoch*, trans Anatole Senkevitch Jr, MIT Press, Cambridge, Massachusetts, 1982.

GOZAK, A AND A LEONIDOV. *Ivan Leonidov: The Complete Works*, ed by Catherine Cooke, Academy Editions, London, Rizzoli, New York, 1988.

KHAN-MAGOMEDOV, S O. *Rodchenko*, Thames & Hudson, London, 1986.

LEMON, L T AND M J REIS (eds). *Russian Formalist Criticism: Four Essays*, University of Nebraska, Nebraska and London, 1965.

MILNER, JOHN. *Vladimir Tatlin and the Russian Avant-Garde*, Yale University Press, New Haven, Connecticut, 1983.

RUDENSTEIN, A Z (ed). *Russian Avant-Garde Art: The George Costakis Collection*, Thames & Hudson, London, Harry N Abrams, New York, 1981.

ACKNOWLEDGEMENTS

The publishers acknowledge the generous help of artists and architects who have provided work featured in this volume. All illustrations provided from other sources are as follows:

CATHERINE COOKE: 'THE RUSSIAN PRECURSORS', pp 10-19
This paper is based on a presentation made at the Deconstruction Symposium at the Tate Gallery in March 1988. An earlier version also appeared in *Architectural Design*, 'Deconstruction', Vol 58 No 3/4-1988, pp 12-15 under the title 'The Lessons of the Russian Avant-Garde'. Constructivist material is from contemporary sources supplied by the author or from *Architectural Design's* archives, all other material is courtesy of the architects.

CATHERINE COOKE: 'THE DEVELOPMENT OF THE CONSTRUCTIVIST ARCHITECTS' DESIGN METHOD', pp 20-37.
This paper originally appeared in a slightly different form as 'Form is a Function X: The Development of the Constructivist Architects' Design Method', in *Architectural Design*, 'The Russian Avant-Garde', Vol 53 5/6-1983. All material is from contemporary sources supplied by the author.

CHERNIKHOV, pp 48-59.
Selected pages of Chernikhov's teaching programme in slightly adapted form are from *Architectural Design*, 'Chernikhov: Fantasy and Construction', Vol 54 9/10-1984, pp 34-39. Translated, edited and compiled by Catherine Cooke.

LEONIDOV, pp 60-63.
Five projects by Leonidov, translated, edited and presented by Catherine Cooke, are from Andrei Gozak and Andrei Leonidov, *Ivan Leonidov*, Academy Editions, London, Rizzoli, New York, 1988, pp 45, 67-69, 109-110.

JACQUES DERRIDA: 'FIFTY-TWO APHORISMS FOR A FOREWORD', pp 66-69.
The text 'Cinquante-deux aphorismes pour un avant-propos' was originally the preface to a collection of papers dealing with the relationship between philosophy and architecture published in a special edition of *Cahiers du CCI*, Centre Georges Pompidou, Paris 1987. This translation by Andrew Benjamin appeared as part of the Press Pack for the Deconstruction Symposium at the Tate Gallery in March 1988, and appears courtesy of the author and publishers, Editions Galilée, Paris. Painting by Valerio Adami courtesy of the artist, DACS, London/ADAGP, Paris and Jacques Derrida. Photograph by Andreas Papadakis.

JACQUES DERRIDA INTERVIEW WITH CHRISTOPHER NORRIS AND DISCUSSION, pp 70-79.
The interview with Jacques Derrida by Christopher Norris was originally a video recording made for and first shown at the Deconstruction Symposium at the Tate Gallery in March 1988. A second showing took place at the Tate Gallery in May of the same year, from which the following discussion is taken. Both interview and discussion have been edited by Christopher Norris. Self-portraits by Ilse Bing and Agnès Bonnot courtesy of Alain Sayag/Centre Georges Pompidou. Photograph on p 70 by Jean-Marie Monthiers (Tschumi, Parc de la Villette). Photograph on p 79 by James Friedman (Eisenman, Wexner Center for the Visual Arts).

GEOFF BENNINGTON: DECONSTRUCTION IS NOT WHAT YOU THINK, p 84.
This originally appeared in A*rt & Design*, 'The New Modernism', Vol 4 3/4-1988, pp 6-7.

GEOFF BENNINGTON: DECONSTRUCTION AND POSTMODERNISM, pp 85-87.
This paper is based on a presentation by the author at the Deconstruction Symposium at the Tate Gallery in March 1988. Valerio Adami painting courtesy of the artist and DACS, London/ADAGP, Paris.

DAVID LODGE: DECONSTRUCTION: A REVIEW OF THE TATE GALLERY SYMPOSIUM, pp 88-90.
This article first appeared in the 'Review' section of the *Guardian*, Friday April 8th, 1988, p 25. Reproduced courtesy of the author.

JOHN GRIFFITHS: DECONSTRUCTION DECONSTRUCTED, pp 92-97.
This article originally appeared in *Art & Design*, 'The New Modernism', Vol 4 3/4-1988, pp 8-18. Francis Bacon reproduced courtesy of the artist and Marlborough Fine Art Ltd; David Salle reproduced courtesy of the artist, Mary Boone Gallery, New York and DACS, London/ARS, New York; Barbara Kruger reproduced courtesy of the artist, Mary Boone Gallery, New York and Nigel Greenwood Gallery, London; David Mach reproduced courtesy of the artist.

PAUL CROWTHER: BEYOND ART AND PHILOSOPHY: DECONSTRUCTION AND THE POST-MODERN SUBLIME, pp 98-101.
This article originally appeared in *Art & Design*, 'The New Modernism', Vol 4 3/4-1988, pp 46-52. Painting by Therese Oulton reproduced courtesy of the artist and Marlborough Fine Art Ltd.

ANDREW BENJAMIN: PRESENT REMEMBRANCE: 'ANSELM KIEFER'S *ICONOCLASTIC CONTROVERSY*', pp 102-105.
Iconoclastic Controversy courtesy of the artist and Anthony D'Offay Gallery, London (collection Museum Boymans-van Beuningen, Rotterdam); *Icarus - March Sand* courtesy of the artist and Saatchi Collection, London.

VALERIO ADAMI: 'THE RULES OF MONTAGE', pp 106-109.
These extracts from Valerio Adami's *Les règles du montage* are reproduced courtesy of Editions Plon, Paris. Translated from the French by Vivian Constantinopoulos. Paintings courtesy of the artist and DACS, London/ADAGP, Paris.

ZOE ZENGHELIS: 'THE ELEGANCE OF BALANCE': AN *ART & DESIGN* INTERVIEW, pp 110-115.
This interview originally appeared in a slightly different form in *Art & Design*, 'The New Modernism', Vol 4 3/4-1988, pp 33-39. All paintings are reproduced courtesy of the artist. *In situ* photographs of the mural for the house in Eton Place by Richard Bryant; architect Michael Carapetian.

CHARLES JENCKS: 'DECONSTRUCTION: THE PLEASURES OF ABSENCE', pp 118-131.
This article is an extract from Charles Jencks' *Architecture Today*, Academy Editions, London and Harry N. Abrams, New York, second edition 1988, and was previously published in *Architectural Design*, 'Deconstruction', Vol 58 No 3/4-1988, pp 16-31. All photographs courtesy of the architects. Painting of OMA Boompjes Housing project by Stefano de Martino. Photographs on p 125 by Norman McGrath (Arquitectonica, the Atlantis) and Patricia Fisher (Arquitectonica, North Dade Courthouse). Photograph on p 127 by Jean-Marie Monthiers (Tschumi, Parc de la Villette).

MARK WIGLEY: 'DECONSTRUCTIVIST ARCHITECTURE', pp 132-133.
This article is an edited transcript of a presentation made at the Deconstruction Symposium at the Tate Gallery in March 1988. Photograph by Gerald Zugmann, courtesy of the architects.

JAMES WINES: 'THE SLIPPERY FLOOR', pp 135-139.
This article originally appeared in *Stroll* magazine, June 1988, pp 15-23. SITE photographs by SITE Projects. Gordon Matta-Clark photographs by Gordon Matta-Clark.

PETER EISENMAN: 'AN *ARCHITECTURAL DESIGN* INTERVIEW BY CHARLES JENCKS' pp 140-149.

This telephone interview was made in the spring of 1988 and originally appeared in *Architectural Design*, 'Deconstruction', Vol 58 No 3/4-1988, pp 48-61. All illustrations courtesy of the architect. Photographs by Dick Frank.

PETER EISENMAN: 'BLUE LINE TEXT', pp 150-151, AND 'EN TERROR FIRMA: IN TRAILS OF GROTEXTES', pp 152-153.
These texts, an outline for the the author's forthcoming book, *The Edge of Between*, originally appeared in *Architectural Design*, 'Contemporary Architecture', Vol 58 No 7/8-1988, pp 6-9, and 'Deconstruction II', Vol 59 No 1/2-1989, pp 40-43, respectively. Photograph by Dick Frank.

'WEXNER CENTER FOR THE VISUAL ARTS, OHIO', pp 145-157.
This project originally appeared in *Architectural Design*, 'Deconstruction', Vol 58 No 3/4-1988, pp 62-63. Drawings by Brian Burr. Photographs by James Friedman and Wolfgang Hoyt, courtesy of the architect.

'BIO-CENTRUM, FRANKFURT', pp 158-161, 'GUARDIOLA HOUSE, SANTA MARIA DEL MAR', pp 162-167, AND 'CARNEGIE-MELLON RESEARCH INSTITUTE', pp 163-173.
These projects originally appeared in *Architectural Design*, 'Deconstruction II', Vol 59 No 1/2-1989, pp 44-9, 56-62 and 50-5, respectively. Drawings and photographs courtesy of the architect. Photographs by Dick Frank.

BERNARD TSCHUMI, 'PARC DE LA VILLETTE, PARIS', pp 174-183.
This project originally appeared in *Architectural Design*, 'Deconstruction', Vol 58 No 3/4-1988, pp 32-39. Drawings and photographs courtesy of the architect. Photographs by Jean-Marie Monthiers. Parts of the text were first published in Bernard Tschumi's *Cinegramme Folie*, Princeton Architectural Press, 1987, and the *Yale Architectural Journal*.

'NEW NATIONAL THEATRE OF JAPAN, TOKYO', pp 184-187, AND 'NEW COUNTY HALL, STRASBOURG', pp 188-191.
These projects originally appeared in *Architectural Design*, 'Deconstruction II', Vol 59 No 1/2-1989, pp 12-15 and 16-19, respectively. Drawings courtesy of the architect.

DANIEL LIBESKIND: 'STILL LIFE WITH RED PREDICTIONS', pp 192, 'THE SURFACE MUST DIE. A PROOF', pp 193 AND 'THE FOUR TEXTS', pp 192-195.
These texts originally appeared in *Architectural Design*, 'Deconstruction II', Vol 59 No 1/2-1989, pp 22-25.

BERLIN 'CITY EDGE' COMPETITION, 1987', pp 196-205.
This project originally appeared in *Architectural Design*, 'Deconstruction II', Vol 59 No 1/2-1989, pp 26-37. All material courtesy of the architect. Photographs for the 'Cloud Prop' models by Helène Binet and Uwe Rau, 'Never is the Center' by Dino Scrimali, the Alef Wing by Dina Scrimali and Leo Torri.

ZAHA HADID, 'THE PEAK CLUB, HONG KONG, 1982-3', pp 206-207, 'KURFURSTENDAMM 70, BERLIN, 1986', pp 208-213, 'IBA HOUSING, BLOCK 2, WEST BERLIN, 1986', pp 214-217 AND 'WEST HOLLY-WOOD CIVIC CENTER', pp 218-219.
The project 'Kurfürstendamm 70, Berlin, 1986' originally appeared in *Architectural Design*, 'Deconstruction', Vol 58 No 3/4-1988, pp 40-45. All material courtesy of the architect. Photographs by Edward Woodman.

COOP HIMMELBLAU, 'FUNDERWERK 3 – A FACTORY, 1988-89', pp 220-223. 'ATTIC CONVERSION, VIENNA 1, 1984-88', 'RONACHER THEATRE, VIENNA', AND SKYLINE, 1985', pp 224-229.
All material courtesy of the architects. Photographs by Gerald Zugmann.

MORPHOSIS, 'COMPREHENSIVE CANCER CENTER' AND 'KATE MANTILINI RESTAURANT, SANTA MONICA', pp 230-238.
These projects originally appeared in *Architectural Design*, Deconstruction II, Vol 59 No 1/2-1989, pp 88-96. All material courtesy of the architects. Photographs of the Comprehensive Cancer Center by Tom Bonner, and of Kate Mantilini Restaurant by Tom Bonner and Tim Street-Porter.

ELIA ZENGHELIS: 'THE AESTHETICS OF THE PRESENT', pp 238-243.
This article originally appeared in *Architectural Design*, 'Deconstruction Vol 58 No 3/4-1988, pp 66-67. All material courtesy of the author and Office for Metropolitan Architecture; *Egg of Columbus Center* collection of *Architectural Design*. Paintings by Zoe Zenghelis.

BEHNISCH & PARTNERS, 'HYSOLAR INSTITUTE BUILDING, UNIVERSITY OF STUTTGART', pp 244-249.
This project originally appeared in *Architectural Design*, 'Deconstruction II', Vol 59 No 1/2-1989, pp 82-87. All material courtesy of the architects. Photographs by Christian Kandzia.

HIROMI FUJII, 'USHIMADO INTERNATIONAL ARTS FESTIVAL CENTRE, 1985', pp 250-251.
This project originally appeared in *Architectural Design*, 'Japanese Architecture', Vol 58 No 5/6-1988, pp 48-49. All material courtesy of the architect. Photographs by Komei Furudate.

PETER WILSON, 'BERLIN – THE FORUM OF SAND', pp 252-253.
All material courtesy of the architect. Photographs by Meremy Butler and Peter Wilson.

ARQUITECTONICA, 'RECENT WORK', pp 154-255.
All material courtesy of the architects. Photographs of Helmsley Palace by Timothy Hursley, North Dade Justice Center by Patricia Fisher and the Atlantis by Norman McGrath.

STANLEY TIGERMAN: 'CONSTRUCTION (DE)CONSTRUCTION (RE)CONSTRUCTION', pp 256-259.
This text originally appeared in *Architectural Design*, 'Deconstruction II', Vol 59 No 1/2-1989, pp 76-81. Courtesy of the architect.

EMILIO AMBASZ, 'SAN ANTONIO CONSERVATORY', pp 260.
This project originally appeared in *Architectural Design*, 'Deconstruction', Vol 58 No 3/4-1988, pp 46-47. All material courtesy of the architect.

———— * ————

INDEX